Learning a New Land

This book has been awarded Harvard University Press's annual prize for an outstanding publication about education and society, established in 1995 by the Virginia and Warren Stone Fund.

LEARNING A NEW LAND

IMMIGRANT STUDENTS IN AMERICAN SOCIETY

Carola Suárez-Orozco

Marcelo M. Suárez-Orozco

Irina Todorova

The Belknap Press of Harvard University Press

Cambridge, Massachusetts, and London, England

First Harvard University Press paperback edition, 2010

Library of Congress Cataloging-in-Publication Data

Suárez-Orozco, Carola, 1957–
    Learning a new land : immigrant students in American society /
Carola Suárez-Orozco, Marcelo M. Suárez-Orozco, Irina Todorova.—1st ed.
    p.   cm.
Includes bibliographical references and index.
ISBN 978-0-674-02675-9 (hardcover)
ISBN 978-0-674-04580-4 (pbk.)
1. Children of immigrants—Education—United States.
2. Academic achievement—United States.
I. Suárez-Orozco, Marcelo M., 1956–
II. Todorova, Irina.   III. Title.
LC3746.S83 2008
371.826'9120973—dc22   2007026034

Contents

Tables

Figures

Learning a New Land

■ ■

The Long View on Immigrant Students

THE AMERICAN STORY is one of immigration and accommodation, in which groups of people from diverse backgrounds arrive and seek to forge a common destiny. After the peoples we now call Native Americans made their way to these lands, three major human flows—the settlement of the original colonists, the involuntary transfer of African slaves until the Civil War, and the great trans-Atlantic diaspora that began at the end of the Napoleonic Wars and endured until the Great Depression—set the stage for the current realities of immigration to the United States.

Today, immigration is once again a momentous social force, compelling Americans to face the challenge and opportunity of integrating and harnessing the energy of the greatest number of immigrants in the nation's history. By 2005 there were well over 35 million immigrants in the United States—some 12.4 percent of the U.S. population.[1]

Many facets of the story of immigration to the United States are well known, captured in endless iterations in family narratives, legends, poems, folk songs, novels, memoirs, films, history and civic textbooks, academic monographs, and research reports. Yet our understanding of the experiences of immigrant children and youth remains limited. This gap in our knowledge is troubling because immigrant-origin children are entering the United States in unprecedented numbers, making them the fastest-growing segment of the youth population.[2] Today, 20 percent of young people growing up in the United States have immigrant parents, and it is projected that by 2040, one in three children will be growing up in an immigrant household.[3]

How does immigration shape the changing realities and experiences of recently arrived youth? What ambitions do these newest and youngest Americans bring with them, and how effectively are we as a society harnessing their energies? Do boys and girls experience the migration journey differently? These and other questions motivated us to organize a large-scale research project to assess how young newcomers manage their journey to the United States, how the process of immigration changes them and their families, and what obstacles and opportunities they encounter.

Immigration is a complex, multifaceted phenomenon involving many factors and variables that may be viewed through a variety of lenses. We chose to focus on the role of formal education in easing or complicating the transition of immigrant youth for several reasons. Worldwide, schooling has emerged in the last half-century as the surest path to well-being and status mobility. Schooling is now powerfully associated with such beneficial developments as better health, smaller families, and greater economic security. Solving the big problems of the day, whether deep poverty, infectious disease, environmental degradation, global warming, or terrorism, will require the active engagement of well-educated, cognitively flexible, and culturally sophisticated individuals able to work in groups. Schools, then, will need to nurture young minds to be able to synthesize knowledge derived from various academic disciplines, wrestle with social and ethical dilemmas, and work across cultural boundaries with individuals of different races, religions, and cultures. In order to foster higher-order cognitive skills, competencies, and interpersonal sensibilities, schools will have to accomplish more than ever before. If schooling is to be relevant and in synchronicity with the problems and opportunities of the day, it will need to prepare youngsters to deal with the increasing complexity and diversity that characterize their lives.

Schooling is particularly important for immigrant youth. For them, it is the first sustained, meaningful, and enduring participation in an institution of the new society. Today, more immigrant children spend more time in schools than ever before in the history of the United States. It is in schools where, day in and day out, immigrant youth come to know teachers and peers from the majority culture as well as newcomers from other parts of the world. It is in schools that immigrant youth develop academic knowledge and, just as important, form perceptions of where they fit in the social reality and cultural imagination of their new nation. Moreover, they learn about their new society not only from official lessons, tests, and field trips, but also from the "hidden curriculum" related to cultural idioms and codes—lessons often learned with and from peers and friends.

Relationships are critical to the process, and it is in schools that immigrant youth forge new friendships, create and solidify social networks, and begin to acquire the academic, linguistic, and cultural knowledge that will sustain them throughout their journey. It is not only in the classroom but also in the schoolyard, on field trips, and on the bus ride to and from home that they will struggle to learn the English language that is so necessary for their success in the United States. Immigrant students, new to the American system, will be heavily reliant on school personnel—teachers, counselors, coaches, and others—to guide them in the steps necessary to successfully complete their schooling and, perhaps, go on to college. It is in their interactions with peers, teachers, and school staff that newly arrived immigrant youth will experiment with new identities and learn to calibrate their ambitions. Some will find nourishment for their dreams, while others will have their hopes crushed. The relationships they establish with peers, teachers, coaches, and others will help shape their characters, open new opportunities, and set constraints to future pathways. It is in their engagement with schooling most broadly defined that immigrant youth will profoundly transform themselves.

LISA: The Longitudinal Immigrant Student Adaptation Study

Our study of the pathways that immigrant youngsters trace in their American journey began as a series of conversations and exchanges involving a cultural psychologist with strong developmental interests (Carola Suárez-Orozco) and a psychological anthropologist with a long history of involvement in the field of immigration and refugee studies (Marcelo Suárez-Orozco). During the project, we were joined by cultural health psychologist Irina Todorova, a senior research fellow who came to play an important role in the analysis and interpretation of the vast amounts of data collected for this project.

Previous research had made important inroads in understanding the dynamics characterizing the most recent wave of immigration within the available data sets and conceptual and analytical frameworks. These studies, however, have not, by and large, addressed the realities of immigrant children and youth, leaving one with the impression that the U.S. economy attracts a huge number of socially disembodied immigrant workers who have no children and families. A close examination of immigration patterns in most contexts suggests that where immigrant workers are drawn, families sooner or later follow.

Those few systematic studies that have examined immigrant children and families often reported variability in the immigrants' experiences with education, finding jobs, and family income, but generally failed to make sense of these differences. Many such studies relied heavily on self-reported data or used protocols of dubious cultural relevance to the new immigrant groups under consideration. Other studies seemed to repeatedly confound the experiences of immigrant youth (that is, the foreign-born who come to the United States) with the fortunes of those of immigrant origins (children whose families have been in the United States for two, and in some cases three, generations). While there are similarities between the experiences of immigrants and those of the second generation, their realities are distinct and must be separately understood.

What do immigrants (those born abroad) have in common with the second generation (those whose parents were born abroad)? Principally, the first and second generation share foreign-born parents. Therefore, they are likely to grow up in households where cultural, linguistic, and social traditions, while in flux, retain some of the distinct flavors that immigrants bring with them to the new country. Both the first and second generations may share challenges and stressors typically associated with lower status, including high levels of poverty, persistent experiences of ethnic and racial discrimination, segregation, community violence, and poor schools.[4]

Second-generation immigrants, however, have certain obvious and consequential advantages over their foreign-born peers. Youth of the second generation will not have to contend with the intense disorientation of arriving in a new country. They do not have to learn from scratch the cultural nuances and social etiquette that make life predictable and easier to manage. Learning the new cultural code is stressful and exhausting, as anyone living in a foreign land for a few weeks can attest. Typically, second-generation youth do not have to struggle with the challenge of learning a new language, which is a reality for the vast majority of immigrants arriving from non-English-speaking countries. Further, all second-generation children are U.S. citizens, whereas many first-generation children must contend with the realities of undocumented status. There are well over 11 million unauthorized immigrants in the United States—and nearly 60 percent of the nation's largest immigrant group—Mexicans—reside in the United States on an unauthorized basis. According to some recent estimates, approximately 1.8 million children are in the United States without legal papers, and an additional 3.1 million children are born in the United States to undocumented alien parents.[5]

It is not surprising, then, that the second generation tends to have higher academic achievement, better experiences in the labor market, and higher income levels than the newcomers. Yet the foreign-born generation has some advantages over the second generation. For example, there is evidence to suggest that in several areas of well-being and health, immigrants are better off than the second generation. Indeed, babies born to immigrant mothers tend to be healthier than second-generation babies, and immigrant children are less likely to be obese, to experiment with drugs and alcohol, or to engage in a host of other risky behaviors. This is paradoxical because immigrants tend to have higher levels of poverty and less education than their U.S.-born peers. Yet the data suggest that while the second generation has an educational and economic edge over the first generation, such advantages may not spill over to broader considerations of health and well-being.[6]

A number of observers have noted the importance of understanding the long-term adaptations of immigrants, in the second generation and beyond. They point out that in the next dozen or so years, the size of the second-generation cohort will grow. For example, according to one study "almost all (93 percent) children of immigrants under 6 are [U.S.] citizens."[7] Among Hispanics, the largest immigrant group, one estimate claims that the "population will grow by 25 million people between 2000 and 2020. During that time the second generation will account for 47 percent of the increase compared to 25 percent for the first. Moreover, the second generation will more than double in size, increasing from 9.8 million in 2000 to 21.7 million in 2020. At that point the second generation will outnumber the first generation, which will total 20.6 million."[8]

We applaud the efforts to focus on the second generation, but as scholars of immigration we chose to focus on the experiences of newly arrived first-generation immigrant youngsters. The first generation already in the United States will continue to cause profound changes to our society. The most unsettling debates in the area of immigration today—such as undocumented immigration and the issue of English-language learning—have nothing to do with the second generation. Furthermore, schools all over the country are wrestling with how best to educate newly arrived immigrant children. In 2005, half of the students in New York City public schools came from immigrant homes; 9.5 percent had arrived in the United States within the past three years.[9] In Los Angeles, the nation's second-largest city, half of the population is foreign-born and more than 73 percent of the students in public schools originate in Hispanic homes—most of them immigrants and children of immigrants.[10] How the first generation adapts will clearly set the stage for how their children—the second generation—will do.

To gain a more complete understanding of the experience of immigration, we designed a study that is unlike any other in the field today. Our study focuses exclusively on the experiences of recently arrived foreign-born youth and their families. It does not confound that experience with the realities of the second generation or of those who arrive as babies or as very young children (the so-called 1.5 generation). All of the participants in our study were born abroad, had parents who were born in the same country, and had developed a clear sense of identity rooted in their national origin prior to migration to the United States. When our study began, our participants had spent at least two-thirds of their lives in their country of origin and spoke a native language other than English upon arrival. This study captures the realities of those youth who are contending with the profound changes of moving to a new country, with all that implies: culture shock, linguistic disorientation, the loss of old relationships, as well as the excitement of blazing a path to a new horizon.

Recently arrived immigrant youth from Central America, China, the Dominican Republic, Haiti, and Mexico were recruited for the study. These five regions of the world were selected for a variety of reasons. They represent migration from Latin America, the Caribbean, and Asia—the source of nearly 80 percent of all new arrivals to the United States today. Given the high proportion of Mexicans among immigrants to the United States, no study of recently arrived immigrant youth would be complete without including them. Families from Mexico tend to come for economic reasons as well as to reunite with relatives who had migrated ahead. We included Central Americans from Nicaragua, El Salvador, Honduras, and Guatemala, because many of these families felt compelled to come to the United States in large numbers in the aftermath of the various sporadic Central American civil wars, which intensified in the 1980s and concluded with the end of the Cold War. We included Dominicans and Haitians, because these are two groups of Caribbean origin that are coming at brisk rates into the United States, particularly the East Coast, but have been the focus of relatively little scholarship. We included Chinese immigrants not only because they represent the new Asian migration to the United States, but also because of their sheer numbers: they are the second-largest newcomer group after Mexicans and are currently the fastest-growing group from Asia.[11]

We recruited approximately eighty participants from each of these regions of the world. In the fall of 1995, we negotiated entrance into seven school districts in areas of Boston (where we recruited Chinese, Dominican, and Haitian participants) and San Francisco (where we recruited Mexican and Central American participants) that have high densities of recently arrived immigrant students. We recruited from fifty-one schools in all (by the end of the study, our participants were spread across over a hundred schools). Participating schools agreed to provide access to students, teachers, staff, and school records. With the help of teachers and staff, we identified recently arrived immigrant students whose parents were both from the same country of origin. Our research assistants were bilingual and bicultural and, in most cases, from the same immigrant origin as our participants—for example, Mexican-origin research assistants worked with Mexican-origin students. The research assistants described the project to potential participants when requesting their involvement. The prospective participants were told that their participation would last for five years, until the summer of 2002, and that we were interested in investigating the experience of immigration for newly arrived immigrant youth.[12]

We began the study with 407 recently arrived immigrant students.[13] Attrition is always a concern in conducting a longitudinal study; it is all the more so in this case, given the high mobility rates of immigrants. Nonetheless, five years later, in 2002, our sample size was a respectable 309—representing an attrition rate of 5 percent annually.[14] We compared the participants the first year of the study to those remaining in the study at the end in order to determine if we had a selective attrition rate that might bias our sample. We compared the sample on forty characteristics (such as grades the first year of the study, parental education, intact families, mental health, various dimensions of engagement, and the like). We found the first year and last year samples to be nearly identical according to these measures.[15]

To date, few studies of immigration have taken a developmental perspective. To understand the experiences of immigration over time, we chose to work with youngsters old enough to have developed, prior to migration, a firm sense of belonging to their country of origin. They were also old enough to articulate and reflect on their changing experiences of immigration. Our participants were between the ages of nine and fourteen during the first year of the study, with a mean recruitment age of 11.8. The groups were nearly comparable in age, with the exception of the Haitians, who were, on average, nearly one year younger than the other participants. During the recruitment process, we attempted to include an equal number of boys and girls. As is often the case in developmental research, we were somewhat more successful in recruiting girls than boys (53 percent versus 47 percent of the sample, respectively).[16]

Immigrants to the United States are more diverse now than ever before. They range from highly educated and skilled individuals to those of humble backgrounds with very low levels of educational attainment. Currently we are experiencing a bimodal migration wave, in which a larger proportion of less-skilled, less-educated new arrivals are accompanied by a smaller but nonetheless substantial group of very highly educated immigrants.[17] On average, our informants' mothers (or maternal figures) had received 9.2 years of schooling, with a range from no formal schooling to twenty-one years of formal education, and a third of the mothers had completed high school. The mean maternal years of education were fairly comparable among groups, although there were some significant differences.[18] Dominican mothers reported the highest levels of educational attainment with a mean of 11 years of schooling, while Central American mothers reported the least, with a mean of 7.3. On average, our informants' fathers (or father figures) reported having received 8.8 years of education, with a significant range from no formal schooling to twenty-six years of schooling; only a quarter of the fathers had completed high school.[19] Chinese fathers had completed the most education (10.9 years on average), while Mexican fathers had received the least (a mean of 6.2).[20] These large ranges in years of education are consistent with national data showing that immigrants are over-represented at both the high and low ends of the educational spectrum, with a larger proportion at the lower end.[21]

While some immigrants arrive in the United States with considerable resources, most arrive with relatively little. The poverty rate for children growing up in immigrant homes is double that of native-born families in the United States.[22] In our sample, there were some group differences in total yearly household income, though the difference was not statistically significant.[23] Twenty-six percent of our immigrant families across all groups subsisted on household incomes of less than $20,000 a year. Nearly half had household incomes in the range of $20,000 to $40,000 a year. A small number of Chinese and Mexican households reported incomes greater than $80,000, while only two Dominican families, one Central American family, and no Haitian families did so.[24]

Many of the immigrant families in our sample were among the working poor. They worked in a wide variety of occupations, but especially those related to restaurant, janitorial, medical service, production, and construction work.[25] In their countries of origin, many had worked in similar occupations as well as in agricultural work. Few of our participants' parents were unemployed. During the first year of the study (1997), fully 96 percent of the total sample of immigrant fathers were working. By the last year of this study (2002), however, only 64 percent of the fathers were employed. This change may well be due to the economic downturn following the attacks of September 11th. Central American fathers were the most likely to be unemployed in the first year of the study (11 percent), but by the last year, Dominican fathers had become the most likely to be unemployed (58 percent).[26] Mothers were less likely to be employed outside the home than fathers. Twenty percent of the total population of mothers reported staying at home, with significant differences among the groups. Central American mothers were most likely to work outside the home (91 percent the first year and 86.8 the last). While many of the mothers reported that they had not worked outside the home when living in their homelands, mothers in all the groups were more likely to be working outside the home after immigrating. In their countries of origin, mothers had been more likely to stay home with their children (32 percent) with significant differences among the groups (43 percent of Mexican mothers stayed home, whereas only 21 percent of Chinese mothers did so).[27]

The recently arrived immigrant students in our sample lived in a wide variety of family constellations. Some lived alone with one parent while others shared space with several families and boarders. Our participants lived in households ranging in size from two to seventeen people. Central American and Mexican participants lived in the largest households (with a mean of 6.40 and 6.38 family members, respectively) while the Chinese lived in the smallest (with a mean of 4.38). Immigrant youth often do not live in traditional family constellations composed of two married parents and children—rather they often live in extended family systems composed of, say, an uncle and mother or a father and stepmother. Sixty-eight percent of our total sample lived in families with two parental figures.[28] Twenty-six percent lived in households that included extended family members such as grandparents, aunts, uncles, and cousins in addition to the parents and children. In our analyses, rather than using "intact" or "two-parent family" as a criterion, we distinguish families with two or more adults or parental figures from those headed by only one adult. Families with more than one adult are generally able to provide closer supervision, greater earnings, and more guidance to children. By the last year of the study, there was a considerable range of familial arrangements among the groups in our study (Table I.1). While 82.1 percent of Chinese participants lived in families with at least two parental figures in the home, only 39.6 percent of Dominicans did so.[29]

The families in our study arrived in the United States after leaving cities in their homelands. But there were significant differences among groups in this regard; Haitians, for example, reported having arrived from more urban and less rural origins than did all the other groups.[30] Migration often occurs in stages: immigrants may first migrate internally within their own country from a rural setting to a city before going on to immigrate to a new country. This phenomenon may explain why many families in our sample reported that they had migrated from urban centers.[31]

We recruited our study participants through public schools that served a high percentage of immigrant students. In order to place their experiences—our sample—in context, we compared it to the general population living in the same region. According to the Census for 2000 (a year we were in the field collecting data), 37 percent of the population living in the San Francisco metropolitan area and just over a quarter of the population living in the Boston metropolitan area were foreign born. Forty-six percent of the population in San Francisco reported speaking a language other

Table I.1 Characteristics of students, by country of origin (Part A, in percent)

Characteristic	Total sample N = 309	China N = 72	Haiti N = 50	Dominican Republic N = 60	Central America N = 57	Mexico N = 70
Gender—males [N=134] n.s.	43.4	36.8	46.8	37	41.2	53.1
Gender—females [N=175] n.s.	56.5	63.2	53.2	63	58.8	46.9
Two-parent home ***	67.6	82.1	57.8	39.6	74	76.6
Problematic family separation*	14.2	11.4	18.9	17.5	18.2	4.9
Extended family in the home	26	7.3	35.15	22.2	49.1	20.6
High-school graduate mother***	33.3	51.6	7.3	48.1	20	28.1
High-school graduate father*	23.6	39.3	17.1	17.7	26.5	15.3
Working father***	64.4	84.4	66.7	39.6	72	64.1
Working mother*	72.9	69.8	60.5	69.4	89.8	72.4
Household income						
< $20,000	26.7	17.7	25	35.4	22.9	31.6
$20,001–$49,999	44.9	47.1	53.1	33.3	52.1	42.1
> $50,000+	28.4	35.3	21.9	31.3	25	26.3
Low-income students in school (50% +)***	59.2	41.2	40.4	98.1	43.1	75

Note: Year 5 of the study. For categorical variables we report percentage and establish significance with Chi-square.
Significance levels: n.s. = not significant, *<.05, **<.01, ***<.001.

Table I.1 Characteristics of students, by country of origin (Part B)

Characteristic	Total sample Mean	(SD)	China	Haiti	Dominican Republic	Central America	Mexico
School segregation rate***	77.9	(23.61)	57.9	73.53	90.96	83.01	87.49
Percent of schools' students passing state high stakes English test***	31.98	(25.68)	60.97	37.62	19.66	21.41	15.38
Reported school problems, Yr3***	24.05	(5.69)	20.83	23.99	26.1	24.25	25.80
Reported school problems, Yr5***	20.21	(5.62)	17.45	21.99	20.39	20.01	21.83
Age upon arrival*	9.92	(1.96)	10.29	9.57	10.15	10.18	9.39
Psychological symptoms, Yr1***	19.28	(9.09)	14.81	22.07	19.39	19.78	21.53
Psychological symptoms, Yr5 (n.s.)	18.61	(9.76)	16.66	21.89	19.09	19.02	17.53
Family problems scale***	10.83	(2.95)	9.44	12.13	10.69	11.94	10.58
Relational engagement, Yr3*	26.2	(2.24)	26.43	26.43	25.38	26.04	26.54
Relational engagement, Yr5 (n.s.)	36.2	(5.02)	35.44	37.23	36.23	36.18	36.25
Behavioral engagement, Yr3 (n.s.)	21.76	(3.29)	22.28	21.74	22.44	21.43	20.95
Behavioral engagement, Yr5*	20.84	(4.37)	22.06	20.49	20.58	21.11	19.82
Cognitive engagement, Yr3***	11.88	(1.99)	10.96	12.3	12.59	11.86	12.02
Cognitive engagement, Yr5***	11.6	(1.97)	10.53	11.6	12.36	12.27	11.59
Schooling attitudes, Yr5 (n.s.)	5.97	(1.37)	5.81	6.09	6.04	6.06	5.94
Motivation, Yr5 ***	12.20	(3.55)	14.87	11.21	12.16	10.80	11.27
Reported peer support **	33.83	(5.22)	34.07	35.59	34.88	33.74	31.56
English-Language Proficiency SS, Yr3***	66.79	(19.64)	75.94	72.09	65.47	59.54	60.03
English-Language Proficiency SS, Yr5***	74.68	(19.32)	83.94	74.77	71.04	69.69	71.83
Bilingual Verbal Ability Test SS, Yr3***	88.57	(17.96)	104.68	86.57	84.1	78.54	84.68
Bilingual Verbal Ability Test SS, Yr5***	91.98	(19.75)	112.61	86.37	84.31	83.22	88.19
Woodcock-Johnson Test of Achievement (combined score)***	90.46	(16.6)	104.02	89.02	83.29	83.72	89.02

Note: For continuous data we report least square means and establish significance with analysis of variance. Significance levels: * <.05, ** <.01, *** <.001.

than English at home, while 34 percent in Boston did so. By definition, participants in our study were newcomers; thus, all of the parents in our sample reported speaking a language other than English at home. Our participants had mothers who were less educated than the metropolitan average in both San Francisco and Boston, but they were more likely to have working fathers (Table I.2).

Our participants were also less likely to be found in the lowest and highest categories of household incomes when compared to the greater population in the same metropolitan areas; they tended to be concentrated in the middle categories at approximately the same percentage rates as the general local population (Table I.3).

We also compared our sample to the general U.S. foreign-born population from the same countries of origin at the time we were in the field. These data include foreign-born individuals counted by the 2000 Census and included the range of immigrants that encompassed newcomers to those who had lived many decades in the United States. We specifically examined the level of educational attainment as another gauge of socioeconomic status—one particularly pertinent to the educational attainment of children. For Mexicans and Dominicans, we found that the percentage of

Table I.2 Our sample in context

	Mexican and Central American participants: San Francisco area		Chinese, Dominican, and Haitian participants: Boston area	
Population	Our sample	Metro area	Our sample	Metro area
N	125	776,733	185	589,141
Percent foreign born	100.0	36.8	100.0	25.8
Percent who speak a language other than English (parents / pop. 5 yrs or older)	100.0	45.7	100.0	33.4
Percent high school graduate or higher (mothers / pop. 25 yrs or older)	24.4	81.2	39.4	78.9
Percent employed (fathers / pop. 16 yrs or older)	77.6	63.3	67.1	58.9

Note: Where data in our sample differ from U.S. Census categories, both categories are shown in parentheses, with our sample category preceding the U.S. Census category.
Source: U.S. Census Bureau, Census 2000.

Table I.3   Household income

Population	San Francisco		Boston	
	Our sample	Metro area	Our sample	Metro area
N	125	776,733	185	589,141
Average household income, in dollars	—	55,221	—	39,629
Percent earning:				
< $10,000	4.4	9.8	5.0	15.5
$10,000–19,999	22.1	—	20.6	—
$10,000–24,999	—	13.5	—	18
$20,000–29,999	20.4	—	26.2	—
$25,000–49,999	—	22.3	—	26.5
$30,000–49,999	42.5	—	31.2	—
$50,000 +	10.6	54.4	17.0	40.0

Note: Where our categories differed slightly from those used by the U.S. Census, both categories are shown.

Source: U.S. Census Bureau, Census 2000.

mothers in our sample who had graduated from high school was comparable to the general U.S. foreign-born sample from the same countries. Our sample from Hong Kong had a slightly lower rate of high school graduation, while our mainland Chinese mothers were significantly less likely to have graduated from high school than the national average; this seems to be a reflection of the realities in the Boston metropolitan area. Our Central American population (recruited in the San Francisco area) was less educated than the national foreign-born population from the same countries, as was our Haitian sample (recruited in the Boston area). It is important to note that the participants in our sample were all recent arrivals. Immigrants from these same countries of origin who arrived thirty years ago tended to be significantly more educated than the most recent newcomers from these same lands (Table I.4).

While we do not claim that our sample is representative of all immigrants from these countries now living in the United States, we are confident that our participants are representative of newcomer children who left these countries during the late 1990s to live and attend public schools in the Boston and San Francisco metropolitan areas. While every destination city is different and every country of origin shapes the decision to immigrate in unique ways, there are many common denominators of experience on which our study seeks to shed light.

Table I.4 Educational attainment, by country of origin (participants in Year 5)

	Percent high school graduates or higher	
Country of origin	Mothers of our sample	Total U.S. foreign-born population[a]
China		
Mainland China [N = 52]	31.4	68.4
Hong Kong [N = 15]	73.3	84.4
Central America		
El Salvador [N = 27]	7.4	34.7
Guatemala [N = 15]	13.3	36.9
Nicaragua [N = 10]	60.0	60.9
Honduras [N = 2]	0	43.7
Dominican Republic [N = 58]	48.3	48.1
Haiti [N = 50]	9.3	62.3
Mexico [N = 69]	29.0	29.7

Source: U.S. Census Bureau, Census 2000, 5 percent Public Use Microdata Sample.
[a]Persons age 25 years or older.

Working with youth from diverse linguistic and cultural backgrounds is challenging. Interviews and test items that are developed for one group are often linguistically or culturally insensitive to the realities of another. For example, the word igloo may be common knowledge to a young child raised in a middle-class Western setting with regular access to images of igloos on cartoons but will be meaningless to a child growing up on a Caribbean island with no television. Thus in recent years there has been a growing consensus that research must be grounded in the communities in which the research emerges. Sound cross-cultural research requires time to get to know the realities of the community. It requires the development of research protocols with the participation of community members in order to validate assumptions about what is and is not relevant or meaningful. Community members' participation is also needed to make sure that interpretations of emerging findings are accurate.[32]

The Longitudinal Immigrant Student Adaptation Study used an interdisciplinary and comparative approach. Ethnographic participant observations were essential for elucidating participants' point of view. Our ethnographic work identified themes relevant to each of our groups and described the various contexts in which our participants lived and attended school. When we began to detect patterns, we developed interviews to quantify and capture these observations so that comparisons could be made.

Throughout, we used triangulated data as a means to counteract the challenges to validity commonly found in studies of individuals from highly diverse backgrounds.[33] Participants in research often seek to be well regarded by those who are capturing their experience and thus may change their behaviors simply because they are being studied.[34] Over the years, we have found that immigrant youth are particularly likely to put themselves forward in the best possible light. Hence, triangulated data serve to counteract the inherent limitations of self-reported data. By sifting through self reports, parent reports, teacher reports, and our own observations, we were able to establish both concurrence and disconnection in what youth say they do, what others say they do, and what we saw them do.

We asked a number of the same questions annually but also nested a number of studies within the larger project. In the first year of the study, we concentrated on learning about the incoming realities of the immigrant youth and their families. In interviews with both the students and their parents during the first year of the study, we asked a series of questions: What were their origins in their native country? What were their motivations for coming to the United States? Who in the family had come first and what were the patterns of arrival? In what kinds of living situations were the children in our study residing? What were their educational experiences in their country of origin? What were their initial impressions and challenges in their schools, neighborhoods, and new homeland?

In the second year of the study, our structured interview focused on the reunited family from the student's point of view. We followed up on several emerging findings from the first year. For example, we had found that the majority of the students in this study had been separated from their parents for extensive periods before coming to the United States, so we asked about that experience. Our research team also conducted extensive focused ethnographic observations in our participants' schools and neighborhoods.

During the first two years of the study, we were struck by the variation in patterns of academic engagement and disengagement among groups and individuals and between genders. By the third year, we had developed strategies to differentiate among these academic trajectories. We developed measures of academic engagement and disengagement and then asked the same questions about these processes in each of the remaining years of the study.

In addition, during the fourth year we developed a protocol to examine the networks of relationships of our participants. Our ethnographic observations and the emerging data from the interviews made it clear to us that the kinds of relationships our participants were in played a significant role in their well-being and in their academic trajectories. For example, we found that having a school or neighborhood mentor such as a coach, involved teacher, church member, or community advocate helped keep students engaged in school. Likewise, having an older sibling or cousin who had successfully gone on to college eased the college admissions process.

In the last year of our study, in addition to repeating questions about academic engagement and achievement, we asked our students a series of questions related to identity development and inquired about their experience of discrimination. We also explored differences between the experiences of immigrant girls and boys in their families, neighborhoods, and schools. We re-interviewed parents with questions that we had asked their children, and we followed up by asking the parents a series of detailed demographic questions.

A Community of Scholars: Our Bilingual/Bicultural Research Team. A project of this kind required the assistance of many insiders from the communities under consideration.[35] Given the number of countries from which our immigrant sample was drawn, a team of bilingual/bicultural research assistants was crucial to the success of this project. By training, supervising, and retaining bicultural and bilingual research assistants, we were able to establish rapport and trust within the communities, and we gained entry into immigrant populations that might otherwise have been difficult to access. The research assistants were crucial for minimizing the attrition rate. They served as cultural advisers by providing feedback on the validity of interview questions for students of their country of origin, helping to assure the validity of translations, and putting the emerging findings in context. The majority of our research assistants were master's or doctoral students from universities such as Harvard; Tufts; University of Massachusetts Boston; University of California, Berkeley; and University of California,

Davis who were enrolled in a range of social science programs, including human development and psychology, sociology, psychology, teaching and learning, social work, and journalism.[36]

Research assistants were largely responsible for recruiting students; conducting student, parent, and selected teacher interviews; making focused ethnographic observations across school contexts; taking notes and administrating interviews, as well as translating the completed interviews. They were required to maintain detailed research notes and to develop theoretical memos that they submitted to the principal investigators (PIs) on a monthly basis. Research assistants attended training lectures conducted by the project co-directors and by eminent educational anthropologists, sociologists, and cultural experts. Boston-area research assistants met weekly with the co-directors in sessions that functioned as "ethnographic supervision"—a model we borrowed from clinical practice. As a result, research assistants were guided in the kinds of observations they should be making. They also returned from the field with narratives of what they had observed and encountered. These discussions shed light on emerging patterns and helped maintain the quality of the data collection. The San Francisco research assistants met weekly with our West Coast project coordinator and approximately monthly with one of the co-directors to discuss emerging issues. This steady stream of communication provided research assistants with intensive supervision and guidance and kept the principal investigators apprised of developments in the research.

Because this project involved a diverse population, we recruited cultural advisers to provide us with guidance on the groups under consideration that we ourselves had not studied before (specifically, the Asian and Caribbean immigrants).[37] The cultural advisers were academics who had extensive experience working in the field with each of the populations under consideration. Acting as a critical resource for the research teams, these cultural advisers had a dual role: they worked with us to train the research assistants and they helped us to interpret emerging findings.

Ethnographic Participant Observations. Ethnography allowed us to develop rapport and trust with our participants, to identify what was most relevant in their daily lives, and to recognize the various interpersonal concerns present in each immigrant community. Further, it served to guide us in the development of systematic strategies of assessment. The ethnographic process was also important when it came to interpreting findings in locally relevant contexts. The current design and purposes of this study, however, required us to develop a strategic adaptation of this research tradition. We conducted "focused" and "selective" ethnographic observations in several key school sites.[38] Based on systematic observations of interactions among students and staff in classrooms, hallways, school libraries, cafeterias, assemblies, on field trips, and in various informal conversations with school personnel, we crafted profiles of the school contexts and how they shape the perceptions and opportunities of immigrant youth. Repeated home and neighborhood visits supplemented the ethnographic data.

Our participants were distributed initially among more than fifty schools and by the fifth year of the study among more than one hundred schools. For the school profiles, we selected a subsample of twenty school sites with a high density of participants for each one of the immigrant groups (five or more participants). We selected sites that were representative of schools that immigrant students typically attend. We worked in a number of highly segregated schools with deep poverty that were plagued with weak leadership, "burned-out" staff, chronic turnover problems, low expectations, and generally violent, hostile atmospheres. We also worked in some schools with a more positive ethos, strong leadership, and innovative staff and curriculum with a climate of safety and mutual respect. For the duration of the project, three to four research assistants working with each immigrant group spent a minimum of one day a week in schools, conducting fieldwork and taking copious field notes.

Structured Interviews. Over the course of the study, we developed and deployed techniques to follow up on the tentative theoretical constructions emerging from the ethnographic process.[39] Structured interviews enabled us to consider continuities and changes in immigrant students' motivations, aspirations, frustrations, and everyday realities and how these interacted to influence individual agency. We strove to establish how these dynamics are related to academic engagement, schooling processes, and outcomes. Through the longitudinal design, we were able to explore the nature of changes over time—changes in attitudes toward school and the future, as well as changes in school behavior—with interview questions and procedures that were culturally sensitive. The triangulated data fed our theoretical formulations as well as the interpretation of our data.

Our study involved students from distinct language and cultural backgrounds, and conducting research on such a diverse population forced us to reexamine the traditional social science assumptions of validity and reliability.[40] In short, questions and prompts that were valid for one group were not necessarily valid for another. In addition, there were few existing measures for learning about the experiences of any immigrant group, and we were not confident that those that were available were reliable. The insider research assistants played an essential role in this regard, guiding us as we developed protocols that would be both relevant and equivalent across groups.

The scales that we developed over the years had several unusual features. First, they were developed to be administered entirely on a verbal basis; students were not asked to read items, because we did not want to jeopardize the validity of responses provided by students with limited literacy skills. Given the volume of data we were gathering, the length of each scale was also a consideration.

To make the interviews as engaging as possible, given their length, we used a variety of question formats. Generally, we began each section with an open-response question, for three important reasons: first, to introduce a new topic in a smooth transition; second, to allow the elicitation of unanticipated responses; and third, to capture children's experiences in their own words. We included some Likert scale questions (with response formats such as "very true" to "very false" and "always" to "never") as well as questions that asked students to align themselves with statements that "Some students are like X BUT others are like Y."

Structured interviews were translated into Spanish, Haitian Creole, Mandarin, and Cantonese (and then back-translated) by our bilingual research teams. Interviews were piloted to establish age, cultural, and linguistic appropriateness before data collection began each year.

We developed scales on topics including behavioral engagement, cognitive engagement, relational engagement, academic self-efficacy, optimism, psychosomatic symptoms, and school attitudes, among others.[41] For these items, the agreement among raters was very high; the margin of error was a result of coder oversight rather than variance in rater assessment of an open-ended question.[42] For open-ended questions, several coders (the principal investigators along with post-doctorate fellows or senior graduate students) read the data to compile a tentative list of categories and emerging themes. The list was further refined to reflect both theory-driven and data-driven categories. Each category was defined in a first draft of the coding procedures. The coding team then coded 20 percent of the data together, discussing the rationale for why each item was to be coded in a particular manner. When there was disagreement, the item was further discussed until a consensus was obtained. This discussion led to revisions of the coding protocols. Inter-rater reliability was established by selecting ten interviews, to be coded independently by a team of five to eight coders, depending on the year. Cohen's kappa statistic of agreement was calculated for each item.[43]

Each student's network of social relations was measured via a carefully constructed instrument devised for this project. The instrument identifies the members of the participant's network and what roles they play in the child's life—family, peers, adults in school, adults in community, and family in country of origin. It also measures the density of the network, the various functions of the relations, and their convergence or divergence in supporting academic engagement. This is very important because data suggest that when peers, parents, teachers, counselors, and natural mentors converge in sending and acting on the same message that school is important, students are more likely to remain engaged.

Narrative Tasks. The Thematic Apperception Test (TAT) is a projective narrative instrument developed in the 1930s by psychologists Henry Murray, Christina Morgan, and their associates.[44] This narrative technique was designed to elicit the interpersonal concerns of respondents. The TAT rests on the logic that participants, when presented with ambiguous stimuli such as a series of vague drawings, will reveal much about their interpersonal relations, aspirations, and ongoing concerns.[45] The TAT was originally designed for individual psychological assessment but has also been used by research anthropologists doing cross-cultural work to reveal normative interpersonal concerns in specific cultural groups. In working with immigrant populations, we have found that the TAT can be a powerful tool for systematically eliciting key, normative patterns of interpersonal relations, attitudes, and preoccupations.[46]

While the TAT has been misused in some cross-cultural research, we have found in our own work that it can be a useful way to learn about shared emotionally charged concerns, which typically are difficult to ascertain by direct questioning or interviews.[47] For example, in previous research we explored how the TAT poignantly illuminated preoccupations with survivor guilt among Central American refugees, loss among Mexican-origin immigrants, sense of inadequacy among second-generation Mexican-Americans, and boredom among American mainstream youth.[48] In the current study, we carefully standardized the test's administration, modified the stimuli to be culturally relevant, obtained adequate sample sizes, took advantage of the longitudinal design (administering the TAT during year one and again during year five of the study), and delineated a strict scoring method.[49]

As part of both the Year 1 and Year 5 interviews, we administered modified versions of TAT Card 1 (an ambiguous drawing of a youth pensively looking at a violin in front of him) and Card 2 (a drawing of a young woman with books overlooking a farm scene with various folk in the nearby field) to all the immigrant youngsters in our study. The original cards were scanned by computer and modified to depict phenotypically ambiguous figures. Participants were asked to make up a story, giving a narrative with a past, a present, and a future based on what he or she saw in the pictures. Each informant was asked: What are the characters in the pictures doing? What are they thinking and feeling? What has led up to the situation? How does the story end? The research assistants wrote down the story that the participants narrated in response to each card. During Year 1 of the study, the stories were usually told in the participants' native language and later translated by the research assistants. By the fifth year, many participants chose to narrate their responses to the TAT in English. Two raters (Carola Suárez-Orozco and Irina Todorova) read through approximately fifty stories, compiling lists of themes that emerged from the data and establishing inter-rater reliability.[50]

We also employed a series of sentence-completion tasks because we had found them to be particularly useful for assessing academic attitudes. To this end, in each year of the study we used a number of sentence-completion tasks eliciting concerns related to schooling, such as: "Schools are . . .," "Teachers are . . .," "In five years from now I will . . .," and others. We also asked a series of questions designed to detect intergroup attitudes, including: "Most [people from participants' country of origin, for example, Mexicans, Haitian, and so on] are . . . "; Most Americans are . . ."; Most Americans think that [people from participants' country of origin, for example, Mexicans, Haitians, and so on] are . . ."[51] These projective techniques provide rich results that are especially useful when supplemented by ethnographic data and in the context of the ongoing rapport between the informant and her or his research assistant.[52]

Teacher Perspectives. To get a more grounded perspective on the changing realities of immigrant youth today, we gathered two Teacher Behavior Ratings, one from a language arts or social studies teacher and another from a math or science teacher. These data yielded the teachers' perspectives on the academic engagement, classroom participation, and behaviors for each youth in our study. These data were essential for comparing how teachers view the academic engagement of immigrant youth with how the youngsters view their own engagement. These data were collected in the third through fifth years of the study.[53]

In addition, during the third year of the study, we interviewed seventy-five teachers from twenty schools in our study that had high densities of immigrant-origin students. We asked them a series of questions about their experiences working with immigrant students. Our questions covered a range of topics. What were teachers' perceptions about the challenges that immigrant students face in school? What challenges did they face as teachers in teaching recently arrived immigrant students? What were their impressions about their immigrant students' academic performance? What gendered patterns of performance, if any, did they perceive? How likely did they think immigrant students were to go on to college? How much interaction took place between immigrant and nonimmigrant students? What were their perceptions about immigrant parents' involvement in their children's education?[54] These interviews served to complement and triangulate data derived from parent interviews, student interviews, and ethnographic observations.

Educational Outcome Data. Grades were a primary outcome measure used in this study. Report cards were gathered for each participant during each year of the study. An academic grade-point average was calculated averaging the grades for math, science, language arts, and social studies courses.

When we began this study, we intended to complement the grades with the standardized achievement data collected by each school district. These tests are administered in groups with little or no accommodation to English-language skills and they tend to be culturally biased. Further, nearly every school district used a different achievement test, which rendered it impossible to make valid comparisons across sites. Hence, this data was deeply problematic. Our self-report language skill data (that is, the answers we received to questions such as, How well do you understand English? How well do you read in English? How well do you speak in English? How well do you write in English?) also were highly subjective: some students have far more exacting and self-critical standards than others. As a result, we decided to administer measures individually to shed light on English language and native language proficiency as well as on academic achievement (using national norms). We administered the Bilingual Verbal Abilities Test (BVAT) during the early part of the academic year in both the third and fifth years of the study, during a session separate from the annual structured interview.[55]

Administration. Our bilingual research assistants individually administered the structured interviews and other measures during all five years of the study. They usually met participants at the schools and conducted interviews at lunch, after school, or during class time, depending on the participant's availability and the activities occurring at school on the day of the interview.[56]

Each interview was a one-on-one conversation conducted in the language of the student's preference; some were entirely conducted in their native language, others, especially by the end of the study, largely in English. Many involved code-switching—such as from Spanish to English. For this reason, items were available in the student's native language and in English on the same protocol. The interviews took an average of one and a half to two hours to administer. For those youth who had difficulty staying focused that long, research assistants broke the interview into two sessions. Because the research assistants also conducted ethnographic fieldwork in the schools (where they also interviewed teachers), as well as visited the participants' homes to interview parents, the students came to know the research assistants well. Four years after the empirical, field-based part of the study was complete, the research assistants were still hearing from project participants who wanted to update them on changes in their lives. In one case, a young man from Mexico located an research assistant years after she had moved from Berkeley to New York to share with her the latest news in his life.

The parent interviews were conducted during the first and last years of the study. The first year, the information gathered in the parent interviews centered primarily on issues related to the decision to migrate, the parent and student educational histories, household composition, parental employment histories, and other demographic data. The last year of the study, the parent interview was developed to elucidate detailed demographic data (household composition, educational and employment histories, and the like). We also asked a series of questions that paralleled questions we had posed to the students, which touched on topics such as experiences of discrimination, plans for their children's educational future, and changing family relations. As with the student interviews, bilingual and bicultural research assistants conducted the interviews in the parents' language of choice. The parents always chose to speak in their language of origin, whether Spanish, Haitian Creole, Cantonese, or Mandarin. As in the case of the student interview protocols, a mixture of question formats was used with parents both to sustain attention and to allow responses that would provide context-rich, "in their own words" information, as well as easily quantifiable data. The interviews were most often conducted in the parents' home, but at the parents' request, occasionally they were held elsewhere. Sometimes the parents preferred to meet at the local library or in a nearby restaurant. Interviews with parents typically took two hours, though they ranged from an hour and a half to four hours.[57] We asked that the person who had the most contact with the youth in our study participate in the interview. Most often the mother (or a maternal figure such as an aunt or grandmother) chose to be involved, but in some cases (usually in Haitian families), the father chose to give the interview.[58] The interviews sometimes turned into festive events after the research assistant had completed the protocol. In one case, the family had prepared a feast, complete with favorite Mexican dishes, to honor the research assistant's visit. In another case, the mother was waiting for the research assistant at the bus stop to welcome her with a dozen roses and escort her to her home.

In a separate encounter, our research assistants administered the Bilingual Verbal Abilities Test and the Woodcock-Johnson Test of Achievement subtests to each participating student in our sample. They chose as quiet and private a space as possible in the public-school setting, or in some cases, went to a local public library to conduct the tests. The tests were individually administered in both native language and English in a session that tended to take between an hour and an hour and a half to complete.

First, the research assistants administered items from the three Bilingual Verbal Abilities Test subtests (picture vocabulary, oral vocabulary, and verbal analogies) in English beginning at a basal point we set for the study.[59] Once the student had reached the established ceiling on each of the subtests in English, the students were shown items they had missed and asked whether they knew the correct answer in their first language. Research assistants continued administering test questions in the youth's native language until the ceiling had been established.[60] The four subtests from the Woodcock-Johnson Test of Achievement-Revised (reading skills and reading comprehension, which make up the Broad Reading scale, and math skills and math reasoning, which make up the Broad Math scale) were then administered according to the recommendations made by the publisher.

Not surprisingly given all of these contacts with the participants, their teachers, and their families, we collected a vast array of data over the five years of the study. These data included:

Student interviews	Years 1, 2, 3, 4, and 5
Parent interviews	Years 1 and 5
Bilingual Verbal Abilities Tests	Years 3 and 5
Woodcock Johnson Test of Achievement	Years 3 and 5
Report cards	Years 1, 2, 3, 4, and 5
Teacher behavioral checklists	Years 3, 4, and 5
Student network-of-relationships interviews	Year 4
Narrative tasks (TAT)	Years 1 and 5
Sentence completions	Years 1, 2, 3, 4, and 5
School-focused ethnography	Year 2
Teacher interviews	Year 3
Focus participant ethnography	Years 3, 4, and 5
75 case-study portraitures	Developed Year 3 and expanded Years 4 and 5

Details about these data can be found in the online supplement to this book.

Immigrant Youth Portraits. The portraits included in this book bring to life the trends and patterns that emerged from the extraordinary data set we

assembled. They are based on years of ethnographic rapport, technical language and achievement tests, structured interviews, narrative tasks, and repeated parent and teacher interviews. We integrated these materials during
yearly case-study development work, thus developing detailed holistic portraits of immigrant students. These portraits give voice to the uniqueness
and complexity of each evolving immigrant story, aspects that tend to become muted in the more typical aggregated quantitative analyses.[61] The
case studies are particularly important for placing the process of youth development and change in context and for elucidating the diversity of social
interactions and experiences that shape these immigrant students' social
and academic adaptation.[62] The case studies illustrate how the multiple
influences from each student's academic, family, and peer worlds inter-
sect and combine in unique ways with their personal characteristics to
shape each migrant journey. They include detailed descriptions of the
complexities of each youth's situation before embarking on the journey
to the United States, their circumstances of moving, their points of entry
into U.S. communities and schools, and the multiple events, barriers, opportunities, and resources that have shaped their experiences during the
five years of the study. Mainly, however, they aim to present the youth's
and family's perspectives and interpretations related to these phenomena.
The case studies provide unique insights into the phenomenon of immigrant youth adaptation and contribute to ongoing theoretical debates in
the field.[63]

During the third year of the study, we selected seventy-five youth, fifteen
from each of the five immigrant groups, and developed case studies for
each that was updated annually until the study was complete. These portraits represented a range of academic profiles, including some who were
highly engaged in school, those who were half-heartedly engaged, as well
as students who seemed completely disengaged. Research assistants were
trained in our case-study procedures and wrote detailed case-study drafts
according to the guidelines we had given them.[64] When we began developing these case studies, of course, we had no way of predicting the particular
twists and turns each child's journey would take.

Once we had established five trajectories of academic performance (using statistical procedures described in Chapter 2), we classified each of the
seventy-five case studies according to the particular performance trajectory they fell into. We then read through the seventy-five case studies and
selected a group of twenty-one that both represented a range of students

and provided the richest data. The portraits were then further developed to include the vivid and illustrative quotes and vignettes documented in the original data files.

Each of the included portraits illustrate characteristics and experiences that we found through our overall study to be somewhat typical of other students in the same achievement trajectory. Of course, each immigrant life is unique and irreducible. Nonetheless, each portrait demonstrates the many ways that immigrant youth are propelled to become high achievers or conversely to become disengaged low-achievers. The subjects of these portraits represent the experiences of students from various immigrant groups as well as of both boys and girls.[65]

The portraits bring to life and give color to the sometimes abstract statistical findings we present elsewhere in the book. They include information from a range of sources, including parent interviews, student interviews, teacher interviews and behavior checklists, grades, standardized tests, structured narrative techniques, and ethnographic observations. We hope that in addition to giving voice to the complex realities of immigrant youth, the portraits will serve as a model for those struggling to integrate complex mixed-method studies that are both longitudinal and comparative.

Through the portraits, we hope to share the triumphs and frustrations, dreams and disillusionments of newly arrived immigrant youth. Too often, scholarly depictions of immigrant adaptation are frozen, one-frame pictures—sometimes repeated one-frame pictures—that fail to capture the complex, dynamic process of adapting to life in the United States. As readers accompany the youth through their adaptation journeys, we hope they will be moved by these dramatic narratives of adversity, determination, and accomplishment, as well as—all too often—defeat.

CLYDE Kluckhohn wisely noted that a human being is in some ways like *all* other human beings, like *some* other human beings, and like *no* other human being.[66] This is also true, of course, of immigrants. While each individual immigrant journey is distinctive, over the years we have found that immigrants share experiences that link them one to another. In this book, we provide insights into these shared experiences of immigration by highlighting the triumphs and frustrations of newly arrived people from Asia, the Caribbean, and Latin America.

We believe that to understand fully the reality of another, we must first examine the interplay of that individual's disposition, social worlds, and economic contexts. With children, some contexts are of particular significance, so we pay special attention to families, peers, and school. We look at how hard it can be to master academic English, a task that presents a significant challenge to all of the newly arrived immigrant youngsters we met. And we highlight both how daunting—or encouraging—the student's reception in the new country can be. Children who are marked as immigrant outsiders soon begin to discern the attitudes, moods, and ambivalences of the host society. The meaning they make of anti-immigrant hostilities as well as their perception of their opportunities will influence their integration. The experience of immigration is also highly gendered in ways that are complex and sometimes paradoxical. Hence we examine carefully the ways in which immigrant girls and boys respond academically to their new environment.

Rather than relying on country-of-origin comparisons, we wanted to emphasize the patterns of achievement that unfolded over the course of our longitudinal study. In this book, then, we specifically compare and contrast the experiences of immigrant youth who sustain over five years impressively high grades with the lives of immigrant students whose academic engagement and performance decline precipitously over time. This approach provides a unique insight into why many recently arrived students struggle academically, whereas some others do remarkably well.

As in earlier generations, the United States is being challenged and enriched by waves of immigrants eager to make a better life for themselves and especially, their children. Their experiences, positive and negative, in our schools and communities can teach us a great deal about our national priorities, values, and goals. Will we continue to stifle the energy of those who arrive ready to succeed at all costs, or will we match this enthusiasm with resources to help them excel? Will we allow fear and hostility toward immigrants to infect the culture of our neighborhoods and schools, or will we truly welcome these newcomer families, recognizing in them elements of our own histories and aspirations? Will we dampen the prospects of those students who are emerging multilinguals by imposing high-stakes English-language testing and other obstacles, even as we seek to enhance our native students' fluency in world languages? The choices are ours, and the consequences are great—for newly arrived immigrant students, their school and neighborhood communities, and our nation as a whole.

■ ■

CHAPTER 1

Academic Engagement and Performance

THE IMMIGRANT JOURNEY is driven by dreams for a better life. Immigrant parents almost always frame their decision to move as a chance to provide better opportunities for their children. Most see education as essential for their children's success in the new culture.

Extreme circumstances in a family's homeland may also compel the migration of one or more family members. At age twelve, Rosette migrated with her father to the United States.[1] Though this meant leaving her mother behind, she explained that her father had "decided to come to the U.S., because you never know when school is in session in Haiti. You always have to ask when there is school. They are always doing something strange in the street—killing. You can't get an education. My father wanted me to come so that he can give me an opportunity for tomorrow."

Migration is not for the faint of heart. It almost inevitably involves feelings of dislocation, an at least temporary loss of status, difficulty communicating, and most significantly, leaving behind loved ones. Dario's mother expressed her appreciation for the improved economic situation of her family and educational opportunities in the United States. But the many hardships she encountered in the new land gave her pause about her own future. At such times, her main consolation was the belief that she could provide a "better future and an education for my children." Dario's mother's focus on family is not unique among immigrants. Seventy percent of the immigrant parents we interviewed told us that they had come to the United States to provide better opportunities for their family, with

18 percent explicitly saying that their primary motivation for migrating was to give their children a better education.

Most children recognize the sacrifices their parents have made for them. As Arturo explained: "One of the most important successes in life is to study, because without a good education there's no life. That is why some of our parents have had to work in factories. They work hard to give us a good education so that in our lives we [will] have a good future—not a future like theirs. Their dream is to see us become lawyers so we can represent our family, our last name, our country."

These parental sacrifices propel many immigrant students to launch themselves wholeheartedly into their educational journey. In response to the true/false question "Does school prepare you to get ahead?" 97 percent of our participants said yes. When asked to complete the sentence "I know I can not succeed unless . . .," 86 percent provided a response indicating the importance of studying hard. Half the students in this study spontaneously offered "studying" as a response to the sentence completion task "In life the most important thing is . . ." Over the five years of our study, approximately three-quarters of our participants completed the sentence: "School is . . ." with a positive response.[2] These positive characterizations of schools included the answers "my second home," "wonderful," "terrific," "good and interesting," "very important for my future," and "very important because there you can become successful in life." In contrast, in a study we conducted ten years earlier, only 30 percent of white U.S.-born students responded to this same sentence-completion question with positive statements about their school.[3]

While some teachers may feel uncomfortable working with students who come from different language and cultural backgrounds, many others appreciate their immigrant students. When asked to compare their experiences working with immigrant and nonimmigrant students, one teacher said: "Immigrants have the desire to learn. They are more disciplined and value education." An administrator working with a diverse student body confided: "Immigrant students are nicer groups. They still have a greater desire to achieve. They tend to be more respectful and more motivated. Historically here, 99 percent of the honors society members were immigrants."

Similarly, a bilingual teacher shared these observations about newcomer students and their parents: "An immigrant child comes into classroom with a different attitude about education than those that have been here for a long time. For many students parents are encouraging them to do well because they value education because they did not have any. Parents often times go above and beyond [to help their children] to get there." Another described the drive to achieve that they often encountered among newly arrived students:

> There's an expression we use called "Americanization." Generally, immigrant children work harder and are more focused. As one child said, "if I do this, this, this, and this, then I go to MIT." They've got goals. The kids who are second and third generation—they get the idea of entitlement. Whereas you get the idea from a lot of the [immigrant] kids—not just the Asian kids— "All I have to do is work hard, save my money, go to school, and I can end up owning this place!" . . . In many cases I think the kids can see possibilities that many nonimmigrant students don't.

Indeed, the vast majority of our participants recognized that education was crucial for their success. Most hoped to go on to college—81 percent told us that they planned to attend college after completing high school. They were well aware that in the new economy, many who do not complete high school and go on to college are sentenced to work in the low-paying service sector, or may be more easily lured into the underground economy.[4]

Whether or not their dreams will be realized will be determined by a myriad of factors, including whether they learn sufficient academic English for high-level work, whether they master the intricacies of preparing for and applying to college, whether they are documented, and whether they can muster the considerable resources required to attend college in the United States. How they perform in high school will also, of course, play a critical role in whether they will have access to the more promising institutions of higher education.

The Long View

Although postsecondary education is increasingly important, there is mounting evidence that for all youth—immigrant and nonimmigrant, black, white, Latino, or Asian—motivation, engagement, and grades typically decline the longer students are in school.[5] This pattern was first documented among predominantly white middle-class students and the decline has been found to be even more precipitous among minority students.[6] As noted earlier, cross-sectional data comparing first-, second-, and third-generation students show a paradoxical pattern with second- and third-generation students doing less well on a variety of educational indicators.[7] Indeed a large-scale national study of high-school achievement found that while immigrants on the whole demonstrated greater engagement in school, the longer they attended American schools the worse they did academically.[8] Longitudinally, our data support such results: on aggregate, the longer the newcomer immigrant students were in school, the worse they did academically as measured by grade point averages, or GPAs (Figure 1.1).[9]

Country of Origin Patterns

Would the pattern hold true across the different immigrant groups? We found the familiar pattern of declining academic achievement over time, though this trend did not emerge for several years.[10] With the exception of the Dominican and Central American children, grades appeared stable during the first three years of the study. By the fourth year, however, almost all of the students began a significant downward trajectory that continued into the fifth year. (Significantly, had the study stopped after three years, we would not have detected this decline in performance.) The Chinese students were the only group to resist this pattern. Between the first and fifth years of the study, the Dominican and Central American students' grades

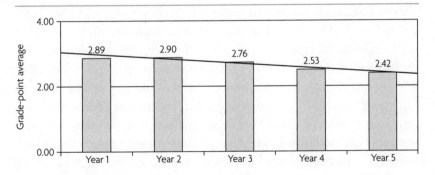

Figure 1.1. Grade-point-average trend for total sample.

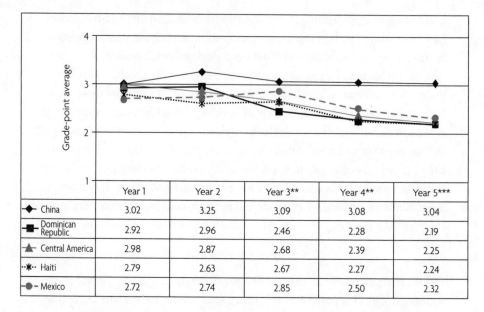

	Year 1	Year 2	Year 3**	Year 4**	Year 5***
China	3.02	3.25	3.09	3.08	3.04
Dominican Republic	2.92	2.96	2.46	2.28	2.19
Central America	2.98	2.87	2.68	2.39	2.25
Haiti	2.79	2.63	2.67	2.27	2.24
Mexico	2.72	2.74	2.85	2.50	2.32

Figure 1.2. Grade-point-average trends: comparisons by country of origin.

dropped three-fourths of a grade (from 2.92 to 2.19 and 2.98 to 2.25, respectively); the Haitian participants' grades declined slightly over half a grade; and the Mexican students' grades dropped just over one-third of a grade (Figure 1.2).

Profiles of Performance

This finding of a decline in performance across groups was disturbingly familiar, but did it tell the whole story? Were we losing the nuances of what was going on with regard to academic performance by grouping the sample by country and gender? To gain a better understanding of the differences between students, we examined whether children could be classified into groups based on their own individual trajectories of academic performance.[11] By examining the data in this way, five performance pathways emerged—consistently high performers (whom we have called high achievers); consistently low performers (low achievers); students whose GPA slowly drifts downward across time (slow decliners); those whose grades fall off precipitously (precipitous decliners); and students whose grades improve over time (improvers).

Disconcertingly, two-thirds of all the participants in this study demonstrated a decline in their academic performance over five years. Nearly a quarter of the sample (24.7 percent) were slow decliners, experiencing a steady decline of half a grade, from a 2.96 to 2.53 average GPA (a decline comparable with that found in the student population at large).[12] Another quarter of the sample (27.8 percent) were precipitous decliners, with GPAs sliding from a 2.9 average to a 1.67 average over the course of the study. Further, 14.4 percent were low achievers throughout the course of the study; they began with a lower average GPA (2.08) than any of their peers and dropped an additional half grade to an average GPA of 1.44. Hence, three of the five pathways of academic performance—slow decliners, precipitous decliners, and low achievers—pulled down the average GPA of the entire sample.

Yet two groups of students resisted this pattern of decline (see Figure 1.3). Nearly a quarter of the students in the sample (22.5 percent) were high achievers who maintained an average GPA of 3.5 across the five years of the study. And a last group, improving students (10.6 percent), made considerable strides in augmenting their GPA during this period. They began with a GPA of 2.29 (just above their lowest-achieving peers) but man-

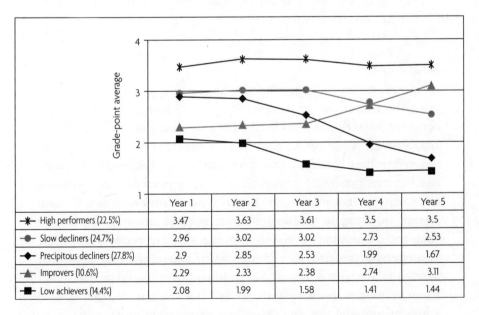

	Year 1	Year 2	Year 3	Year 4	Year 5
—✱— High performers (22.5%)	3.47	3.63	3.61	3.5	3.5
—●— Slow decliners (24.7%)	2.96	3.02	3.02	2.73	2.53
—◆— Precipitous decliners (27.8%)	2.9	2.85	2.53	1.99	1.67
—▲— Improvers (10.6%)	2.29	2.33	2.38	2.74	3.11
—■— Low achievers (14.4%)	2.08	1.99	1.58	1.41	1.44

Figure 1.3. Academic performance pathways: average grade-point average per year.

aged by the fifth year of the study to pull up their performance to a GPA of 3.11—a respectable B average.

Did girls demonstrate distinct patterns of performance when compared to boys? Indeed they did. Girls were significantly more likely to be high achievers or improvers than boys. And boys were more than twice as likely as girls to be found among the precipitous decliners and low achievers. (Girls and boys were nearly evenly distributed among the slow decliners.)[13]

We also found differences across groups related to country of origin. Two-thirds of the Chinese students were among the high achievers or improvers. Disconcertingly, over 40 percent of the Dominicans were found among the precipitous decliners.[14] We will explore these differences in depth in Chapters 5 through 8.

Predicting Academic Achievement

How can we explain the academic performance of immigrant newcomer students? Why are some immigrant youth falling through the cracks while others are outperforming their native-born peers despite the myriad obstacles they encounter? What are the most critical factors influencing an immigrant student's academic performance? (Figure 1.4)

Family Structure

It is well established that children who grow up in two-parent families tend to be at an advantage academically.[15] Two or more adult figures in the home are better able to provide financial resources, supervision, guidance, and discipline. They are also more likely to have the time and energy to be involved in their children's education. Immigrant children live in varied and complex household configurations. While some live in traditional two-parent families, many others live in extended families, in blended families, or with nonparental caregivers (such as grandparents, godparents, or aunts and uncles). We made the assumption that children who have more than one adult caregiver (like those who have two parents) are more likely to receive the financial support, supervision, structure, and guidance necessary to navigate a new context and facilitate academic engagement and achievement.[16] And our data show that having two or more adults in the home has a weak but significant relationship to grades.[17]

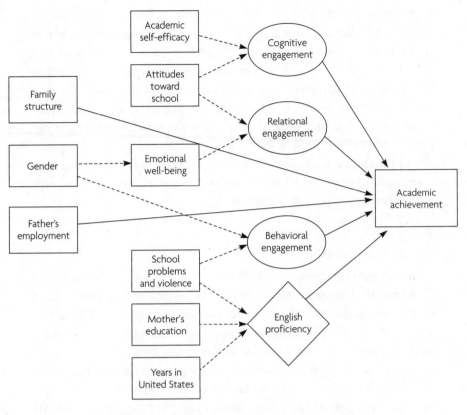

Figure 1.4. Academic achievement: conceptual model.

Parental Education

One of the most consistent findings in the developmental literature is the positive association between parental education and children's ability to do well in school. There is a close relationship between parental education and school readiness, performance on achievement tests, grades, drop-out rates, school behavior problems, and school engagement.[18] Parents with higher educational levels, when compared to parents who have lower levels of education, tend to provide more literacy opportunities, communicate with more sophisticated vocabularies, offer more access to computers, assist (productively) with homework assignments, provide private SAT instruction, offer knowledge about applying to and getting into college, as well as provide other academic supports.

The higher the level of education a mother attains, the better her children are likely to do academically. Further, higher levels of education often lead to higher earnings, which allow parents to place their children in relatively more advantaged schools.[19] Interestingly, our study shows that the educational attainment level of both the father and the mother had only a weak but statistically significant association with grades.[20] By contrast, both the mother's and father's educational levels influence the child's scores on the Bilingual Verbal Abilities Test. Our results also show a significant association between the father's education and the quality of the school the child attends, including what percentage of students there are performing at proficiency level (as measured by state tests) and the levels of segregation and poverty at the school.

Parental Employment

Parents who are earning an income are better able to buffer their children from the risks associated with poverty. As hypothesized, we found a positive association between the father working and the child's GPA as well as test scores.[21] There was no association, however, between the mother's working outside the home and the grades or test scores of the child. We also found considerable fluctuation in employment status over time. At the beginning of the study, we found greater levels of labor-market participation than at the end of the study. This trend may indicate the vulnerability of immigrants working in the service sector during the economic downturn that occurred after September 11, 2001.

Gender

In recent years, a significant gender gap favoring girls has emerged in the educational outcomes of students in schools both nationally and internationally.[22] Boys performed less well than girls and their grades declined more abruptly. This gap is more pronounced among minority populations—boys lag behind girls in academic settings across ethnic groups.[23]

A number of factors may help to account for the gender differences in minority educational adaptation. First, a critical difference between boys and girls is in the realm of social relationships. Compared with boys, immigrant girls were more likely to have friends who were serious about schoolwork and supportive of academics.[24] Girls also had better relationships with their teachers and perceived more support at school than did boys.

For immigrant students, school is a highly "gendered" institution.[25] Girls are more likely than boys to comply with the often tedious behaviors that are expected in classroom settings while boys are more likely to engage in disruptive behaviors.[26] Teachers are often less understanding of young men and more likely to discipline them harshly than a girl for the same infractions.[27] Boys of color, in particular, often face lower expectations, more stigmatization, and are subject to more blatant discrimination than girls and are thus at greater risk for academic disengagement.[28]

Peer pressure to engage in deviant behaviors is often stronger for boys than for girls.[29] Behaviors that gain respect with male peers may bring boys into conflict with their teachers. Immigrant boys from certain ethnic backgrounds are also more likely to perceive racism from mainstream society and thus are more likely than immigrant girls to develop an "oppositional relationship" with the educational system or to see schooling as a threat to their identity.[30] Expressions of "protest masculinity" coupled with structural obstacles seem to place boys of low socioeconomic status who belong to disparaged minorities most at risk of low educational achievement and delinquency.[31] Teacher interviews as well as field notes from the LISA study reflect that immigrant boys are more quickly recruited into their new social environments (which are often in deeply impoverished inner-city schools that do not foster cultures of high achievement orientation).[32] Further, because immigrant girls often have many more responsibilities at home than their brothers, they may be predisposed to finding school a more engaging social space.[33] Immigrant boys tend to be allowed more freedom by their parents, which may make them more susceptible to the lure of the street.[34]

As we predicted, we found that gender was robustly associated with GPA (Figure 1.5).[35] Girls in our sample exhibited higher grades and substantially outperformed boys in every immigrant-origin group for the duration of the study. This gender difference became significant in the last three years of the study as boys' GPAs declined more rapidly than girls'.[36] No gender differences were found in standardized test scores, however. The discrepancy in GPAs may be related to the relative importance of the behavioral component in predicting grades (discussed later in this chapter).

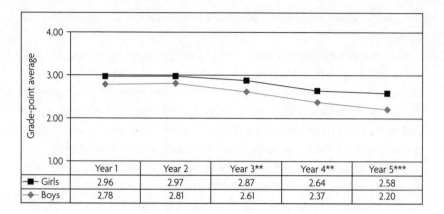

	Year 1	Year 2	Year 3**	Year 4**	Year 5***
—■— Girls	2.96	2.97	2.87	2.64	2.58
—◆— Boys	2.78	2.81	2.61	2.37	2.20

Figure 1.5. Grade-point-average trends: comparisons by gender.

School Contexts

Immigrant youth today enroll in schools that range from well functioning, with a culture of high expectations and a focus on achievement, to dysfunctional, with an ever-present fear of violence, distrust, low expectations, and institutional anomie. Unfortunately, poor immigrant youth who need the most academic help all too often enroll in low-quality schools.[37] We collected data made publicly available by states and school districts on a variety of indicators of school quality.[38] In addition to student self-reports on school problems, we considered four key predictors of achievement: (1) the percentage of poor students attending the school (with poverty defined as a student's eligibility for free or reduced lunch), (2) the percentage of nonwhite students attending the school, (3) the school's daily attendance rate, and (4) the percentage of students in the school scoring at the proficient or advanced levels on the state-administered English language arts exam. Each of these characteristics has been associated with student performance.[39]

Many immigrant children, especially those who live in urban neighborhoods with concentrated poverty, face daunting obstacles in their schools and communities.[40] Neighborhoods characterized by high unemployment, violence, and intense segregation by race and poverty tend to have overcrowded, understaffed schools that have high rates of turnover among teachers and other staff, are poorly resourced and maintain low academic expectations, and are plagued by hostile peer cultures and the ever-present threat of violence.[41]

The school environment has a tremendous influence on the engagement and performance of students.[42] It is hard to be open and eager to learn if you have to be constantly on guard against being attacked.[43] Exposure to and fear of violence also undermine the possibility of trusting relationships among students and teachers.[44] Since students of color and those attending urban schools are most likely to encounter violence, such concerns affect a disproportionate number of immigrant students.

To gain perspective on the student experience of school problems and school violence, we developed a scale to determine the frequency with which students perceived violence and bullying in their school and in the adjoining neighborhood (for example, with the statement "I do not feel safe in my school").[45] Not surprisingly, we found that students' perceptions of violence in their schools and neighborhoods were correlated with declines in not only academic performance (GPA and achievement scores), but also supportive school-based relationships, intellectual curiosity, cognitive engagement, academic engagement, as well as levels of proficiency in English.[46]

We also examined the relationship between the students' perceptions of school problems and the school district measures of such problems (segregation rate, poverty rate, attendance rates, and the percentage of students in the school who pass the state-mandated high-stakes English language arts test). Our data show a correlation between the students' perceptions of school problems, poor school average daily attendance rates, and high proportions of minority and low-income students, as well as poor school performance on the English language arts tests.[47]

English-Language Proficiency

Academic English-language skills affect students' abilities to adapt socially at school and are also highly predictive of academic success in the United States.[48] The ability to perform on multiple choice tests, to extract meaning from written text, and to argue a point both verbally and in writing are essential skills for high levels of academic attainment. In a large-scale study of five thousand first- and second-generation immigrant students from thirteen different countries, English-language fluency emerged as a key predictor of positive academic outcomes.[49] Most recently arrived immigrants, however, face the challenge of learning English at the same time as they struggle to adjust to a new school and become more skilled academically.[50] While conversational verbal proficiency can be developed within a couple of years, it takes, for most nonnative English speakers, five to seven years under optimal conditions to achieve the level of academic language skills necessary to compete with native-born peers in the classroom.[51]

We found higher oral academic English-language proficiency to be significantly correlated with higher grades and even more strongly related to achievement test outcomes.[52] Length of residence in the United States, maternal education, and the student's perceptions of school violence—as well as the school district indicators of educational quality (percentages of students achieving a proficient score on the English language arts test; segregation rate; poverty rate; and daily attendance rate) were all significantly correlated with students' proficiency in English.[53] (In Chapter 4 we look more closely at the factors that influence the acquisition and development of second-language skills and present an explanatory model.)

Academic Engagement

In recent years, a considerable body of literature has emerged pointing to the significant role of academic engagement for academic success. The extent to which students are connecting to what they are learning, how they are learning it, and who they are learning it with appears to play a central role in how well they do in school.[54] Highly engaged students are actively involved in their education, completing the tasks required to perform well in school. Somewhat engaged students may be doing "good enough" academic work, but are not reaching their full academic potential. Further along the continuum, there may be a significant gap between students' aptitude for intellectual work and their academic achievement. In cases of more extreme academic disengagement, a student's disinterest, erratic attendance, and missed or incomplete assignments can lead to failure in multiple courses, an outcome that often foreshadows dropping out of school.[55] Moreover, academic disengagement may not be immediate, but rather may occur over time in response to long-term difficulties in community, school, and family circumstances.

We considered various dimensions of academic engagement separately, and then in relation to one another as well as to our two achievement outcomes—GPA and the results of a standardized achievement test.

Cognitive Engagement

Our cognitive engagement scale examined the degree to which the students are engrossed and intellectually engaged in what they are learning.[56] Seventeen-year-old Rosa, for example, told us: "[I like] physics and calculus. It's interesting to me how planes lose altitude and how bridges are constructed." Rodney, a sixteen-year-old from Haiti, reported that "during the science fair, I did a project on looking at the effect of water on substances such as sugar and salt that I found really interesting." Yadira, a student from the Dominican Republic, told us about reading in an English class "a book called a *Taste of Salt* about a Haitian kid. I did a project on the book that was creative and original that I really liked." Cognitive engagement is the antithesis of the adolescent student lament of "being bored" in school, and our data show that attitudes toward school and academic self-efficacy were very important in fostering this kind of academic immersion.[57]

Surprisingly, when we examined the relationship of cognitive engagement to achievement, we found that it did not have a significant correlation to either GPA or standardized test scores. But cognitive engagement was a significant predictor of behavioral engagement (defined and discussed later in the chapter), which emerged as very strong predictor of the student-focused model of GPA.

Relational Engagement

Relational engagement is the extent to which students feel connected to their teachers, peers, and others in their schools. The immigrant students who are most likely to adapt successfully to school seem to forge meaningful, positive relationships at school.[58] Indeed, research suggests that such relationships are important for the academic adaptation of all students.[59] Social relations provide a sense of belonging, emotional support, tangible assistance and information, guidance, role modeling, and positive feedback.[60] The literature suggests that relationships in school play a particularly crucial role in promoting socially competent behavior in the classroom and in fostering academic engagement and achievement.[61]

Sixteen-year-old Dominican Yunisa explains: "When you come here, you don't know English. Your friends help you with English, with classes, and with showing you the school." Hence, peers can act as "vital conduits" of information to disoriented newcomer students. [62] Dario, a fourteen-year-old Dominican boy, echoed and elaborated on these sentiments, adding that peers can serve as buffers against the violence and drugs—dangers that particularly threaten boys in the low-income communities in which so many immigrants live:

> Other students from my country gave me courage to come to school because at the beginning I didn't like to go to school. I found it strange and different. When I missed school, they called to give me the new homework assignment. They would tell me who not to hang around with and they would tell me not to get into bad things like gangs and marijuana.

Peers can thus moderate the effects of school-related violence and provide support and relief from anxiety.[63] Moreover, by valuing certain academic outcomes and modeling specific academic behaviors, peers establish the "norms" of academic engagement.[64]

Connections with teachers, counselors, coaches, and other supportive adults in the school, which are important to the academic and social adaptation of adolescents in general, appear to be particularly important for immigrant adolescents.[65] Dario elaborated on the supportive role of teachers:

> [Some] teachers treat us well and watch out for our safety. When I came here, I didn't speak English and I didn't know how things were here. But a teacher helped me out and would explain things to me in Spanish.

Newcomer immigrant youth experience profound shifts in their sense of self and often struggle to negotiate changing circumstances in their relationships with parents and peers.[66] Positive relationships with school-based adults can provide immigrant youth with social support, safe contexts for learning new cultural norms and practices, and information that is vital to their success in school.[67] Moreover, positive relationships with peers and caring adults at school are associated with many positive outcomes for students: they become more social, motivated, academically competent, and high-achieving; they are more likely to attend school regularly; and they become more academically engaged.[68] Our finding of a dynamic relationship between the perception of supportive relationships and these positive outcomes lends empirical support to what parents and educators have long observed—students' motivation and effort in school require a meaningful connection between student and teacher.[69]

Teacher-student relationships are, of course, a two-way street. Teachers tend to be more nurturing and supportive toward students whom they like. We frequently heard during our fieldwork and interviews a sentiment that one teacher expressed this way:

> The thing I really love about teaching immigrant children is [that they] respect adults, teachers and parents, and older people in general. When they come here, they still have respect for authority figures like teachers and principals. They listen to you when you need to talk to them, and if you get serious about it they will respond to that. Children that have been here for many years have no fear of that . . . Immigrant children are easier to control and have better behaviors in the classroom . . . The other thing about immigrant kids is that it is easier to establish a teacher-student connection because they tend to talk to you and be friendly.

Relational engagement was established with a scale developed for this study that measured whether participants had meaningful relationships at school with peers and adults who could provide both emotional and tangible school-based support (for example, "I can count on at least one adult in school").[70] Relational engagement for the overall sample increased somewhat over time.[71] Girls tended to report more school-based supportive relationships than did boys.[72]

What factors contributed to students' relational engagement? To answer this question we considered emotional well-being, academic self-efficacy, and attitudes toward school.

Well-being (or the relative absence of psychological symptoms) influences a student's ability to focus on his or her studies. Experiences in schools appear to affect the health of nonimmigrants as well as immigrants.[73] A stressful school climate, in which a student experiences academic pressure, danger, discrimination, and/or the absence of supportive relationships, can undermine well-being, taxing the student's ability to cope.[74] Conversely, a more supportive educational context can help protect students' well-being.[75] Self-esteem, a close correlate of emotional well-being, is often compromised for disoriented, recently arrived immigrant youth. Among immigrant youth, low self-esteem has been shown to impair school performance.[76]

Significantly, girls were more likely report lower levels of emotional well-being.[77] While the well-being of boys improved the longer they stayed in their new homeland, the girls maintained similar levels of psychological complaints over the five years of our study.[78] This finding is consistent with results by Alejandro Portes and Ruben Rumbaut showing that although immigrant girls adapt better educationally than immigrant boys, they have higher levels of anxiety, sadness, and depression than do their male counterparts.[79]

Academic self-efficacy is the belief that one is competent and in control of one's learning at least to some degree. Research has shown that a child's academic self-efficacy contributes to her engagement in learning the new language, forging new relationships, and connecting with the academic tasks at hand.[80] Higher levels appear to be instrumental in fostering student learning as well as relational, behavioral, and cognitive engagements, which we will show lead to higher academic performance. While greater academic self-efficacy was not directly linked either to grades or test scores, it did play a significant role in students' level of cognitive and relational engagement.[81]

Immigrant students generally have very positive attitudes toward school. Indeed, a number of quantitative and qualitative studies have suggested that immigrant youth display more positive attitudes toward school than do their native-born peers. Sociologists of immigration Marta Tienda and Grace Kao have noted that immigrant attitudes are characterized by a general optimism about opportunities in the new setting that may partially account for their patterns of academic achievement.[82] Working in a different disciplinary tradition, psychologist Andrew Fuligni has found that immigrants in general share a positive attitude toward school that is central for understanding their motivation and achievement.[83] In our own previous research combining anthropological and psychological research strategies, we too have identified very positive attitudes toward schools among newly arrived immigrant youth from Mexico.[84] Further conceptual and empirical work is needed to examine the relationship between such schooling attitudes and academic outcomes.[85] Although attitudes toward school seem to be related to grades, they are even more strongly associated with cognitive and relational engagement (see Figure 1.6).[86]

While relational engagement was not directly associated with GPA, as we had initially hypothesized, it was strongly linked to behavioral engagement, a very important contributor to achievement that is explained later in this chapter. Students who reported better school-based relations were more behaviorally engaged in their studies.[87] Relational engagement also bolstered cognitive engagement. Students with better relationships in school with peers, teachers, administrators, and advisers reported finding their academic work more interesting and engaging.[88]

In terms of predicting relational engagement, as one might expect, we found that those students with more positive attitudes toward school and who felt emotionally supported were more relationally engaged at school. The result is a positive cycle in which students with better attitudes toward school elicit more caring interactions and support, which in turn encourage them to feel more optimistic about their school experiences. The same can be said about well-being—those students with fewer mental health symptoms are better able to engage adults and their peers.[89] A feeling of mastery over learning—academic self-efficacy—was also highly related to greater relational engagement. The more meaningful, nurturing relation-

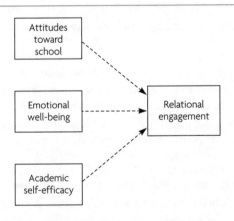

Figure 1.6. Predicting relational engagement.

ships a student had with teachers and peers at school, the more she felt able to tackle learning.

Thus, for immigrant youth, positive relationships at school can help bridge the gap between home and school cultures, creating important linguistic and cultural links to the new society.[90] Supportive relationships with caring adults at school can help strengthen immigrant children emotionally, and lead to these adults' offering practical assistance and advice. In particular, nurturing relationships with teachers may encourage students to explore new subject areas. They may also attenuate the effects of school violence and enhance students' feelings of belonging—positive emotions that, in turn, serve to enhance students' effort in doing their schoolwork.[91] (See Chapter 2 for a more detailed examination of how positive relationships at school enhance academic engagement and performance.)

Behavioral Engagement

Academic engagement and what we term behavioral engagement are often used somewhat interchangeably.[92] Behavioral engagement, in our view, is a component of academic engagement that specifically reflects students' participation and efforts to perform academic tasks. When students do their best on classwork and homework, turn in assignments on time, pay attention and behave appropriately in class, and maintain good attendance, we consider them behaviorally engaged (Figure 1.7).

Teachers often reported that they found newcomer immigrant students to be more behaviorally engaged in their studies than nonimmigrant students:

> Immigrant students seem to be more motivated to do well, because they look at it as an opportunity that they are going to make the most out of it. But sometimes students who are second generation, or who are native born, are not as motivated . . . [and] take things for granted. [Immigrant students] look at it as a great opportunity—let's make the most of it, which makes my job easier. They work harder . . . [and] they are diligent.

We assessed whether the students were completing the tasks necessary to be successful in school, including attending class, participating in discussions and classroom activities, and completing homework and course assignments.[93] Behavioral engagement is highly correlated with grades.[94] As we noted earlier, it is also associated with both cognitive and relational en-

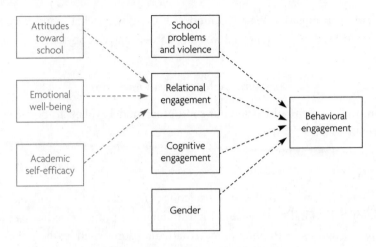

Figure 1.7. Predicting behavioral engagement.

gagement. Longitudinally, we found a distinct pattern of accelerating behavioral disengagement for the sample as a whole.[95] Interestingly, there was little difference in the amount of effort boys and girls expended in their studies initially. Over time, however, girls maintained their levels of behavioral engagement while boys were more likely to disengage.[96] As we expected, the consistently high achievers were significantly more behaviorally engaged in school than were the low or precipitously declining performers.

We examined the association between behavioral engagement and several key variables: relational and cognitive engagement, student perceptions of school problems, and gender. The greatest contribution to behavioral engagement turned out to be relational engagement, followed by student reports of school problems, cognitive engagement, and gender.[97]

Relationally engaged students—those with supportive school-based relationships—were more likely to expend greater effort on their schoolwork. Cognitive engagement also contributed to behavioral engagement— when students were curious and interested in their schoolwork, they were more likely to try harder. As expected, school problems interfered with behavioral engagement—the greater the student's perceptions of school problems, the less engaged they were in their studies, because it is difficult to concentrate and sustain the desire to work hard in a dysfunctional school environment. Students whose mothers were educated were more behaviorally engaged. We also found, consistent with what many teachers had told us, that girls reported working harder than did boys.

Academic Achievement Outcomes

How well do the predictors in our conceptual model explain academic performance?

Grades

Using GPA as our measure of academic performance, we considered the role of behavioral engagement, English-language proficiency, having two parental figures in the home, maternal education, whether the father is employed—all factors implicated in the research literature and by our models. We found that grades were positively correlated to all of these variables.[98]

The most robust predictors of GPA were English-language proficiency and behavioral engagement (in that order).[99] Students with stronger English skills were more likely to earn better grades, and the more the student engaged in the behaviors necessary to do well in school (such as attending classes and completing schoolwork and homework), the more likely they were to attain higher grades. (As we have already seen, students were more likely to engage in such behaviors when they had emotionally sustaining relationships in school, when they were interested in what they were learning, and when there were fewer problems at school.) Other student background characteristics (such as the mother's education and whether or not the student came from a household with two adults) were also linked to better grades in this student model of academic achievement.

Achievement Test Scores

It is well established that grades are highly influenced by teacher perceptions.[100] The student who is well behaved, regularly turns in assignments, and tends to achieve an at-least minimal level of academic proficiency overall, often receives better grades than a student who is less compliant. Further, there is considerable variation among schools; students receiving a comparable score on a standardized test who attend a less-high-functioning school may receive an A in language arts but a student receiv-

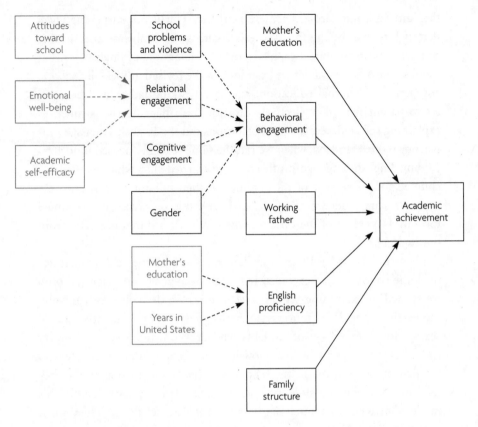

Figure 1.8. Predicting academic achievement: student-centered perspective.

ing the same score in an affluent, optimal school may receive a C or D.[101]

Would our conceptual model hold up if we used the more "objective" result of performance on an academic achievement test? To answer this question, we substituted the "grade" outcome of our model with a combined score derived from four subtests of the Woodcock-Johnson Test of Achievement-R, which we administered individually to our participants (see Figure 1.8).[102]

We used the same explanatory variables we had used to predict GPA—behavioral engagement, English-language proficiency, having a working father, maternal education, and having two parental figures at home. Of these factors, English-language proficiency was far and away the most predictive—the better a student's academic English proficiency, the better they did on a standardized achievement test. This is not surprising given that at least two of the four subtests (math word problems and reading comprehension) require a sophisticated understanding of English.

All of the other variables we examined in the revised model—behavioral engagement, maternal education, having a working father, and being in a two-parent family—collectively did not contribute nearly as much to explaining the achievement test outcome as did the English-language proficiency score.[103] Indeed, when we ran the same student-focused model excluding English-language proficiency, we learned that while we had accounted for 75 percent of the variance of the achievement test outcome when we had included the English-language proficiency score, we accounted for only 14 percent of the variance when we excluded that predictor from our model.[104]

Because student-level factors explained so little of the achievement test outcome (once we had excluded the English-language proficiency score), we turned to examining school-level factors. We developed a regression model that considered four variables that reflect school quality—school segregation (percentage of students who are nonwhite), school poverty (percentage of students who are low income), school attendance rate, and the percent of students in the school who had performed at proficiency level or above on the state-mandated English language arts exam. This model allowed us to predict 32 percent of the variance in the achievement scores (Figure 1.9).[105]

The best predictor of the achievement test outcome was the percentage of students attending the school who performed at proficiency level or above on the state's mandated English language arts exam; attending a school where other students were learning the skills necessary to perform well on the high stakes literacy exam seemed to provide an academic milieu in which newcomer students were also likely to do well on an achievement test. The lower the average daily school attendance rate, the less well our participant was likely to do on the achievement test. Further, the poorer the students in the school and the more racially segregated the school, the less well our participants were likely to do on the achievement test (see Chapter 3 for a more detailed discussion of how school-related factors affect learning outcomes).

It is fair to conclude, then, that English-language proficiency is the single best student-level predictor of academic outcomes as measured by an

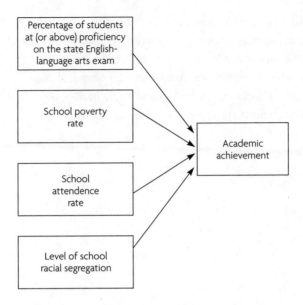

Figure 1.9. Predicting academic achievement: school-centered perspective.

achievement test as well as GPA. English skills have triple the predictive value of all the other student variables combined for the achievement score. Behavioral engagement (influenced by relational and cognitive engagement) was a very robust contributor to better grades, followed by characteristics of the student's family such as having two parental figures, a mother with a high level of education, and a working father. Further, school contexts were strongly linked to academic performance on standardized tests.[106]

FROM their very first days in a new school in an unfamiliar country, immigrant students are actively looking for ways to become acclimated and successful. Yet their level of academic achievement depends not only on their willingness to work hard, but also their ability to make friends, please teachers, avoid dangerous situations, find helpful mentors, and most of all, learn English quickly and well. Our research suggests that immigrant children and their families arrive eager to face any challenge, but too seldom have all the resources and skills to achieve academic success on their own. The disheartening decline in test scores and GPA for most immigrant students after their first three years in the United States shows that we are not doing enough as a society to nurture and sustain the initial positive motivation of these students. These students' resilience, enthusiasm, and work ethic will strengthen the American economy and culture. By making sure their best efforts help them achieve their hard-sought goal of a good education, we help them as well as ourselves as a society.

CHAPTER 2

Networks of Relationships

Much of the scholarly literature on the causes and consequences of large-scale international migration tends to be framed in the context of the economic incentives that make individuals search for better opportunities in another land. In this general framework, migration is seen as a rational choice an individual makes to maximize his or her interests—upon migration, he or she will earn higher wages, have better access to credit, and be better able to save money. According to this classic narrative, new arrivals are the archetypical "homo-economicus"—behaving rationally in accordance with economic principles of profit and loss, opportunity and disadvantage.[1]

But immigration is not just a financial decision; it is a profoundly social undertaking. Family and community-level factors exert tremendous pressure on the choices migrants make and the opportunities they seize. To see migrants as autonomous individuals motivated by self-interest foregrounds the tree at the expense of the forest. Indeed, it is safe to say that individuals do not migrate—families and other social groups do. Immigrants leave because others before them have left and forged the way. And when they arrive, immigrants enter social chains that have their own logic and momentum. For example, once a family from Governador Valadares in a corner of Brazil's Minas Gerais had successfully settled near Boston, they drew so many other Brazilians from this region that the group is now the most visible new ethnic community in Massachusetts.[2] But this story of immigrant social networks spans classes and ethnicities—the scenario is true for upper-class Ghanians in New York, Indian professionals in the Silicon Valley, working-class Ecuadorians in Long Island, and many other migrant enclaves.

This emphasis on social networks makes sense—the presence of family members, friends, and friends of friends in the new destination lowers the costs associated with one's arrival, and eases the transition in myriad ways. Migrant social networks make it infinitely easier to find jobs, establish a stable residence, locate schools, and to go about settling in the new land.[3] This alternative "homo-sociabilis" narrative of immigration claims that family and communities, rather than purely financial incentives, drive migration.[4]

In addition to providing practical on-the-ground help with the transition to the new country (such as running errands, making a loan, or picking up a child from school), those who have been in the new setting longer can provide newcomers with a general linguistic and cultural orientation to the new setting—acting as interpreters of the general social milieu and offering guidance and advice about good jobs, safe housing, and better schools. In addition to these tangible supports, experienced immigrants can provide companionship and a social support network, which help newcomers adjust to the new environment.[5] Likewise, social supports such as those provided by families, peers, mentors, and after-school community-based organizations are well-known to bolster academic success.

Family Relationships

Migration is first and foremost a family affair. Young men take the migratory voyage in order to earn enough money to purchase a home so that they can start a family. Older daughters and sons leave home to support their parents and younger siblings by sending remittances. Young fathers leave home to support their wives and children when the economy in their region does not provide jobs with living wages. Widows leave their children in order to feed them. Siblings join their brothers who went ahead some time ago. More often than not, family obligations and family ties are the very foundation of the arduous immigrant voyage.

The process of migration, however, inflicts tremendous stress on family members. Families often must endure long separations. The pressures to survive economically in the new land while sending back remittances to the family in the country of origin often lead parents to work multiple jobs and long hours. In addition, children acculturate more quickly than their parents, upsetting traditional family roles. These myriad pressures serve as both centripetal and centrifugal forces in immigrant families.[6] Given these losses and stresses of immigration, it is perhaps not surprising that many immigrant parents report feeling depressed.

Family Separations and Reunifications

Immigrant families are transformed by the process of migration.[7] In many cases, families migrate one or two members at a time in a "stepwise" fashion.[8] Historically, fathers migrated first, establishing themselves while sending remittances home, and only sending for the wife and children once they felt secure. Today, the first world's demand for service workers draws mothers from a number of developing countries to care for "other people's children."[9] Traumatic events prior to migration—the death of a spouse or political unrest—also can compel one member to go ahead, sending back remittances to loved ones while saving to send for those left behind. When mothers migrate ahead, they usually leave their children in the care of extended family members such as grandparents (or the father if he is still part of the family). In many other cases, both parents go ahead, leaving the children in the care of extended family. When it is time for the children to arrive, they may be brought to the new land all together or one at a time. Often reunification of the entire family can take many years, especially when complicated by financial hurdles as well as immigration laws.[10] Such migration separations thus result in two sets of disruptions in emotional attachments for the children—first from the parent, and then from the caregiver to whom the child has become attached during the parent-child separation.

Many psychologists believe that early parent-child relationships are the very foundation of our sense of who we are and our capacity for developing relationships with others.[11] Others emphasize that the capacity to develop and sustain relationships continues to develop into adolescence.[12] Attachment theorists maintain that disruptions in "affectional bonds" with parental figures can have profound psychological and developmental implications.[13] They argue that attachment figures are never interchangeable and that although they may become attached to other caregivers, they naturally will become distressed when they are separated from loved ones.[14] The attachment with the mother or primary caregiver is generally thought to be of particular significance, though parent surrogates, siblings, and peers also may become significant as attachment figures.[15]

The loss of an attachment figure may trigger a variety of physical, emotional, and behavioral responses.[16] Loss—which can result from death as well as a variety of other "exits"—is a transition that requires adaptation. Some argue that the loss of the individual (or individuals) triggers negative responses, while others claim that secondary losses, such as the changes in routines or emotional and financial security that accompany the initial loss, ultimately cause the distress.[17] The response to what Pauline Boss has termed "ambiguous loss" is particularly relevant for parent-child separations during the migratory process.[18] Ambiguous losses—as when a loved one is physically absent but psychologically present—may complicate the resolution of grief. Since the parent (or parents) that leave are not dead but simply gone for what is often expected to be a short time, "permission" to grieve may not be granted and the child's loss may go unrecognized.[19] Under such circumstances, the normal emotions of grieving—sadness, guilt, anger, and hopelessness—are intensified because there is no public arena in which to express them.

To understand how losses affect children, it is critical to assess the way in which the adults in the child's circle as well as the wider culture react to the loss.[20] Grief triggers a crisis in family development that affects all members in some ways as they attempt to accommodate the absence of a "vital member of an interdependent family."[21] Each individual family member's experience is intertwined with the grief reactions of the others.[22] If the remaining caregivers are feeling overwhelmed by their own losses, they may not be fully available to the child to help her manage her emotions. Critical to the child's well-being is maintaining some kind of relationship with the absent parent or caregiver.[23] If the child's current caregiver provides stable, loving care, as well as a connection to the missing loved one, most children will be able to understand the loss and adjust to it.[24]

Although it may seem unusual to middle-class Americans for someone other than the parents to raise children, "child fostering" is common in other parts of the world, such as the Caribbean, where children whose families are experiencing hardship may be sent to live with extended family members in order to have access to a better education.[25] This widely accepted cultural practice occurs within the native land as well as during family migrations abroad and is not viewed as unusual or deviant.[26] Some in fact argue that child fostering is an enriching experience for children and their caregivers because it provides all those involved with a wider network of supportive social relations.[27]

A number of clinical studies on Caribbean families in Canada and Great Britain, however, report that the practice may significantly strain family relationships even after family members have been reunited.[28] Indeed, within the clinical literature on parent-child separations that accompany migration, there is a general consensus that the experience is stressful and problematic. While apart from the parent, children may feel abandoned and may respond with despair and detachment.[29] Once reunified, children often miss those who have cared for them in their parent's absence as well as extended family members and friends.[30] Particularly when separations have been protracted, children and parents frequently report that they feel like strangers even after they have been reunited. Attachment difficulties between reunited parents and children have been noted: children often withdraw from their parents, and both children and mothers show signs of depression. Some youth may respond to the strain by acting out in a variety of ways.[31]

Much of the literature on this topic has been drawn from clinical practice—from families that were experiencing problems and thus sought care. Our research provided a unique opportunity both to consider the prevalence of family separations in a sample of nonclinical families as well as to assess the long-term consequences. Strikingly, we found that fully 85 percent of the youth in our sample had been separated from one or both parents—either biological or adoptive—during the process of migration (Table 2.1).[32] There were significant differences between the ethnic groups in how and when families were separated during migration. Families from the Chinese group were more likely than those of any of the other groups to migrate as a unit, while those in the Haitian and Central American group experienced multiple family disruptions during migration in nearly all cases (96 percent for both groups).

From whom were these children separated? As we can see in Table 2.2, nearly half of our sample were separated from both parents. Note that this includes separation as a direct result of immigration, as well as separation due to multiple factors, including immigration combined with divorce, the

Table 2.1   Patterns of separation, by country of origin (in percent)

Pattern	Chinese N = 78	Dominican N = 75	Central American N = 77	Haitian N = 71	Mexican N = 84	Total sample N = 385
Family comes all together	37	11	4	4	15	15
Family separated during immigration	63	89	96	96	85	85

Table 2.2   Percent of children separated from mother only, father only, or both parents at some point in the migration

Separation	Chinese	Dominican	Central American	Haitian	Mexican	Total sample
Mother only	23	64	80	69	42	55
Father only	48	86	96	86	82	79
Both parents concurrently	8	61	80	59	40	49

death of a parent, and so forth. Again, there are significant group differences. Separation from both parents was most likely to occur among the Central American families (in 80 percent of the cases) and was also high among Dominican and Haitian families.

Immigrant children today, just as they were historically, are most likely to be separated from their fathers—79 percent of the children in our sample were separated from their fathers at some point in the migratory process. This occurred in 96 percent of the Central American families, and in over 80 percent of the Dominican, Haitian, and Mexican families. Separation from the father was least likely to occur among the Chinese, but still occurred for nearly half of the children.

Fifty-five percent of the children were separated from their mothers sometime during migration and there are dramatic differences among groups. The Chinese children were least likely to be separated from their mothers, while most Central American, Dominican, and Haitian children lived apart from their mothers for a time. Nearly half of the Mexican children were separated from their mothers sometime during migration.

Significantly, 28 percent of the children in our sample were separated from their siblings as a direct result of migration. Bringing children to the United States one by one, or in some other incremental way, is more common among the Dominicans and Central Americans (about a third of the families used this approach). Because the child has been left in the country of origin, upon reunification other attachments are also disrupted, including those with another primary caregiver, such as an aunt, uncle, or grandparent, who took over the role of parent during the separation.

When they began the migration process, the families generally expected that establishing a home in the host country would not take long, that they would be reunited as a family soon. But delays often occurred for a variety of reasons, including financial obstacles, difficulties with legalizing immigration status, or personal reasons, such as the parents becoming legally separated or divorced (perhaps as an indirect result of the challenges of migrating). Thus the length of separation from parents often turned out to be unexpectedly long, with individual cases in our sample having been separated from one or both parents for nearly their entire childhood.

As mentioned earlier, if we group families by ethnic background, we can see dramatic differences in how long the children were separated from their mothers on average (Table 2.3).

Most Mexican youth were separated from their mothers for less than two years. Chinese children were rarely separated from their mothers to begin with, but when they were, it was usually for two to four years. Central American children, by contrast, experienced protracted separations: 49 percent of the children were without their mothers for more than five years.

When children were separated from their fathers during migration, it was often for a very long time—or permanently (Table 2.4). For those families who experienced father-child separations, 51 percent endured the situation for more than five years, with nearly three-quarters of Haitian families, on average, experiencing such lengthy separations.

Table 2.3   Percent of children separated from mother for various periods, due to migration

Period	Chinese	Dominican	Central American	Haitian	Mexican	Total N = 170
Up to 2 years	41	36	20	13	77	34
2–4 years	53	39	31	53	23	38
5+ years	6	25	49	34	0	28

Table 2.4   Percent of children separated from father due to migration

Period	Chinese	Dominican	Central American	Haitian	Mexican	Total $N = 223$
Up to 2 years	51	14	12	20	35	25
2–4 years	11	30	31	10	33	24
5+ years	37	57	57	71	33	51

What was the effect of family separation on children's psychological well-being? We found that children who had migrated with their families intact had significantly fewer depressive symptoms than those who were living in other types of family arrangements (although among these other arrangements we saw no such differences).[33] Put another way, children who were separated from their parents were more likely to report depressive symptoms than children who were not separated from their parents during migration.[34] Not surprisingly, children who came to the United States without either parent, or with only one parent, reported the most serious depressive symptoms.[35]

It has been well documented that the reunification of parents and children can strain family dynamics. During the separation, the family may have adapted so well to the absence of the missing family member that when he or she rejoins the family, relationships need to be renegotiated.[36] Parents tend to expect their children to be grateful for their sacrifices but instead often find that their children are ambivalent or even angry about joining their parents.[37] Parents can also have trouble reasserting their authority over their children—a process that may be complicated by parental guilt, leading to inconsistent or overindulgent parenting.[38] In some cases, a "continual pattern of rejection and counter-rejection" emerges, causing considerable distress within the family.[39]

Within our nonclinical sample, we found similar issues—some families underwent significant turmoil as a result of long separations and difficult transitions upon reunification. We asked our participants: "You have separated from your family for some time and it has taken a while to get used to each other. How much would you say that this is a problem in your family?" We found that there were significant differences by country of origin with fewer Mexicans (9 percent) and Chinese (11 percent) reporting that separations were creating family problems; perhaps significantly, these two groups tended to report the shortest separations. In contrast, Haitians and Central American students, who reported more and lengthier separations, were more likely to report that the separations were a cause of family problems (35 percent and 49 percent, respectively). Further, long separations followed by complicated reunifications were reported to be a serious problem most frequently by students who demonstrated a precipitous pattern of decline in academic performance; 26 percent of the group we defined as "precipitous decliners" reported that this was a serious problem, in contrast to only 2 percent of "high achievers."

In interviews and conversations with our study participants, their parents, and their teachers, it emerged that these separations were experienced as painful and complex by many of those affected. Children often spoke emotionally about separating from their loved ones. When the children were asked "What was the hardest thing about coming to the United States?" in the first-year interview, the response frequently reflected the emotional pain of leaving behind a loved one. As one fourteen-year-old Dominican girl lamented, "The day I left my mother I felt like my heart was staying behind. Because she was the only person I trusted—she was my life. I felt as if a light had extinguished. I still have not been able to get used to living without her."[40]

For most children, the departure is a time of mixed feelings. There is an excitement about the prospect of reuniting with loved ones and a new life. Yet migrating entails leaving behind caregivers who may have functioned for many years as the real attachment figures for the child. Many of our study participants spoke emotionally of the bittersweet nature of leaving. As an eleven-year-old Central American boy told us, "Once I was in the plane they told me to be calm, not to be nervous, not to cry. I was crying because I was leaving my grandfather. I had conflicting feelings. On the one side I wanted to see my mother, but on the other I did not want to leave my grandfather."

While reunification is usually described with relief and joy, contradictory emotions like disorientation can intrude. Sometimes the children report not recognizing the parent and poignantly describe feeling like they are meeting a stranger. As a thirteen-year-old Haitian girl shared, "I didn't know who I was going to live with or how my life was going to be. I knew about my father but I did not know him."

In several cases, the children expressed fear of the parent who they had not seen in many years. When the family has evolved in the child's absence to include new parental figures and siblings, the reunification process is further complicated. A ten-year-old Chinese girl recalled, "The first time I saw my father, I thought he was my uncle . . . I was really afraid when I saw my father's face. He looked very strict. I was unhappy. My father was a stranger to me. I didn't expect to live with a stepmother." The theme of forging a new relationship with a stranger is prevalent among immigrant children and complicates the future development of the parent-child relationship, with the sense of distance and unfamiliarity persisting for different lengths of time.

Parents also spoke poignantly of the sadness of separating from their children. In many cases separations occurred when the children were infants or toddlers. Many times, children were left behind because of extreme difficulties, such as catastrophic economic conditions, dangerous circumstances in the country, or the loss of a partner. The mother of a thirteen-year-old Central American boy shared, "I was a single mother and there we were at war. I talked it over with my mother and she told me that maybe [things would be better] on 'the other side.' It was very hard above all to leave the children when they were so small. [After I left] I would go into the bathroom of the gas station and milk my breasts that overflowed, crying for my babies. Every time I think of it, it makes me sad."

Parents and children often maintained contact by talking on the phone, and sending letters and gifts. But long-distance communication could be difficult, especially in long-term separations when the distant parent could become an abstraction to a growing child. The mother of a twelve-year-old Central American boy explained, "They lived with my mother in El Salvador (I left when they were babies). I spoke to the eldest once a month by phone. As the little one grew, I spoke to him, too. But since he didn't know me, our communication was quite short. I really had to pull the words out of him."

It is very important for the parent that the child understand why he or she left so that the child can appreciate the sacrifice. But children do not always feel appreciative. As the father of a thirteen-year-old Mexican boy confided, "My son and my daughter are not warm toward me. They are still mad that I left them and was separated from them for years. Even when I explain to them that I came here for them, they don't hear, they don't understand. My daughter acted strangely when she first got here, she got jealous when I hugged my wife. She just wanted my attention for her-self. Now, that's changed and things are getting back to normal."

When the caregiver in the country of origin supports the parental rela-tionship even in the parent's absence, the reunification is usually easier. As the mother of a thirteen-year-old Mexican girl told us, "In spite of every-thing, we have a good relationship because my mother always spoke well of me. She always told her where I was and that some day I would come for her. So there's a certain respect."

Other parents point to the difficulties of rebuilding relationships after reunification. When children have been separated from parents at a very young age, and for long periods, rebuilding the relationship is more com-plicated. The mother of a thirteen-year-old Central American girl admit-ted, "Our relationship has not been that good. We were apart for eleven years and communicated by letters. We are now having to deal with that separation. It's been difficult for her and for me. It's different for my son because I've been with him since he was born. If I scold him he under-stands where I'm coming from. He does not get angry or hurt because I discipline him but if I discipline [my daughter] she takes a completely dif-ferent attitude than he. I think this is a normal way to feel based on the cir-cumstances."

Parents, like children, reported that reunifications could be complicated for those children who had to adapt to a new family constellation in addi-tion to a new culture. In essence, these children are migrants twice—first to a new country and then to a newly constituted family. These chil-dren were frequently jealous of new siblings or their parent's new partner. The mother of a thirteen-year-old Central American boy disclosed, "We're getting used to each other. We are both beginning a different life together . . . [T]he kids are jealous of each other and my husband is jealous of them."

Parents also acknowledged that children suffer when they are separated from other beloved relatives who remain in the country of origin. The mother of a nine-year-old Mexican girl summed up this dilemma: "Before she came, she missed us. Now she misses her grandparents."

Observations by teachers of immigrant children echoed these findings. When we asked school personnel about their views of the challenges that immigrant students face, several mentioned family separations. For exam-ple, a high school counselor shared with us:

Did you know we have kids who are here whose parents are not here? They live with relatives or friends like neighbors, old neighbors of the parents, and they work to support the parents back home. So some of the kids are coming to school and working as well. [In other cases] the family has been separated for many years . . . so when they are reunited sometimes it's a mess . . . The mother doesn't know the child; she left him and he grew up with grandmother . . . The mother wasn't there and when he comes here the mother doesn't have the time to really build the relationship or maybe doesn't have the skills. Because she knows she's been working, sending money, caring for the child and everything—she's been doing her part. But now it is the child's turn, you know, to show understanding, to show appreciation . . . Sometimes you have the mother come first and the kids stay back home and maybe the father left home and has a new relationship, and the mother is in a new relationship. So that kids may be coming to a new family with other siblings and a step-parent.

A director of an international center at a high school shared:

I feel like I need to give [students] a great deal of personal and emotional support in the transition they are making. Talk with them, use our advising group to constantly talk about the problems of adjustment, adaptation, how are you feeling, what issues are coming up . . . Almost universally they say things like "I'm happy this year because I'm with my mother for the first time in 5 years but I miss my grandmother who still lives in El Salvador." Or "I don't see my dad anymore." You know, the whole issue of family separations. There are a lot of emotional issues which come into this . . . So, many students come here because one parent has brought them and all of a sudden they are confronted with a parent they don't know very well. Maybe they have a whole other family they don't know . . . We have people here from China, from Brazil, from Haiti, from Central America and what is interesting is that they are all [talking about] the same issues. "I don't know how to live with my parent."

During our study, we came to recognize that a number of factors could complicate and exacerbate the separation experience. Trauma arising from the death of a loved one; political, ethnic, and religious persecution; or warfare dramatically intensified the response. Difficulties were heightened if the parent who left was the primary caregiver. And associated traumas such as the concurrent loss of other critical supportive relationships or the disruption of predictable routines could make the experience much worse for the child. In fact, it was not the separation alone but rather the separation with its accompanying circumstances "before, during, or after" that led to intense psychological distress.[41]

To complicate matters, the parents' traditional or common-law marriage sometimes dissolved during the migration process.[42] The anticipation of the immigration sometimes caused these relationships to rupture; in other cases, a breakup led a parent to journey abroad in search of a stable income. Sometimes, especially following protracted separations, once the family had reunited the marital relationship came apart in the new context; women may have become significantly more independent, extramarital affairs may have occurred, or the more recently arrived partner may have found the adjustment too difficult.[43]

In other cases, after long separations, fathers (more often than mothers) married again, establishing new households with new children. In these cases, the reunited child had to adapt to a completely new family constellation. When we visited some of these households, we could sense a status hierarchy where the U.S.-born children occupied a highly privileged role when compared with the newly arrived, sometimes undocumented child. Sadly, the family system had replicated the narrative of the state, where "legal migrants" are romanticized and "illegal migrants" are disparaged as illegitimate.

The success of the reunification of parent and child can be helped— or hurt—by the quality of the relationships among the temporary caregiver, the child, and the parent.[44] Problems often emerged if the parent felt threatened by the caregiver or if the caregiver disparaged the parent.[45] When the parent and caregivers were able to work effectively as coparents, disruptions were much less likely to occur than when there was an ambivalent (or openly hostile) relationship.

Mei, for example, was a twin born to a middle-class urban Chinese family. She and her sister were largely raised by their paternal grandparents, who were openly hostile toward their mother who was often away for work. The family migrated when the sisters were ten. While the mother quickly found a job as a researcher, the father found the adjustment difficult. He returned to China with Mei, leaving her twin with her mother in the United States. After two years in China, they returned to the United States. There was tremendous marital discord. The mother and Mei's sister are openly hostile and disparaging of the father as well as of Mei, whom they associate with him. When we met her, Mei was withdrawn, depressed, and disengaged from school.

Similarly, Joaquin was a fifteen-year-old raised in rural Nicaragua largely by his maternal grandparents. An extremely contentious relationship developed between the grandparents and Joaquin's father. The grandparents had only negative things to say about the father who, along with Joaquin's mother, had left for the United States when Joaquin was very young. At one point, the father, in Joaquin's words, "kidnapped" him from the grandparents, a situation that culminated in a violent scene involving the brandishing of a machete. Four years after joining his parents in the United States, Joaquin names only his grandparents, still in Nicaragua, as significant people in his life. Joaquin was clearly socially isolated and longed desperately to return to Nicaragua.

By contrast, a cooperative triangle of caregivers (child, parent, and helping relative or friend) can enrich the child's overall experience. For example, Regine lived for five years with her single mother in Haiti until the mother migrated to the United States in search of a regular income. Recognizing that she could not work long hours and suitably care for her daughter, she left Regine in Haiti with a sister with whom she had a close relationship. Regine's mother maintained regular contact with both her daughter and the caregiving aunt and returned every year to visit them. Regine also visited her mother several times during summers. After she joined her mother permanently in the United States at age ten, Regine remained in regular contact with her aunt, who continued to be important in her life. Her adjustment was smooth and she reported feeling lucky that she had two mothers—her biological mother ("maman") and her aunt ("petite maman").

A caregiver's ambivalent relationship with the parent who has left often closed off for the child any possibility of having constructive discussions about the missing parent.[46] In addition, if the caregiver was grieving the absence of the missing parent, the child was more likely to hold back in talking about the loss. This reaction would make it difficult for the child to develop an understanding of the situation at the same moment that the caregiver was often less available psychologically to the child.[47]

Important to the child's success at navigating these transitions was the temporary caregiver's ability to project a sense of normalcy and high morale.[48] Maintaining a sense of family coherence, including parental authority, was also critical at each stage.[49] Keeping the communication going during the parents' absence was also linked to better outcomes; inconsistent or minimal contact was often interpreted by the children as abandonment.[50] Precious remittance monies sent by the immigrant parents could sometimes stabilize what might otherwise be a precarious situation. Phone calls, letters, tapes, photographs, gifts, and remittances, then, were critical factors in keeping the flame of the relationship alive.[51]

Despite these challenges, children often displayed remarkable resilience in the face of family separation. If the child was well prepared for the separation, the separation was framed as temporary and necessary, the separation was undertaken for the good of the family, and regular contact was maintained, the child was better able to make sense of what was happening and adapt.

In addition, our data suggest that for some families, after an initial period of disorientation, reunifications lead to an increased sense of intimacy. Indeed, some of our participants viewed the relationship between parents and children as having increased in intensity and closeness as they "made up for lost time."

The separation of children from their family members during immigration is a complex and long-lasting process that generates lingering long-distance emotional ties. We found that many immigrant youth, even several years after arriving, were likely to continue to turn to loved ones left behind in their country of origin for support and guidance. To investigate the prevalence of this pattern, we developed a sorting task in which we asked participants to write on cards the names of the most important people in their life.[52] We then asked them: Who do you turn to for help if you need it? Who makes you feel loved? Who respects you? Who do you turn to for advice? and the like. Amazingly, for a number of students, even years after migrating to the United States, loved ones in the country of origin continued to provide a number of crucial emotional supports. For the overall sample, 15 percent named someone left behind in the country of origin as a person who makes them feel loved, with Dominicans (34 percent) being more than twice as likely than participants from any of the other countries of origin to spontaneously name someone remaining back in their birthplace as a source of love (this may be because Dominican immigrants have especially strong transnational ties).[53] Likewise, 35 percent of the total sample (and a full 57 percent of Dominicans) named someone in their country of origin as the person who provided them with respect. Dominicans were also most likely to name someone back home as providing discipline, with 62 percent doing so; indeed, many of our participants (28 percent) internalized the sense that good behavior was expected by family members back home. Hence, for a sizeable number of the participants, transnationalism of the heart is evident. For these youth, those physically absent remain psychologically very present. Thus the same immigrant youth who had missed their parents when the parents left for the United States, years later still relied on loved ones they themselves had to leave behind when they joined their parents in the migration journey. Sadly, immigrant youth are perpetually missing someone somewhere—making the migrant journey almost always bittersweet.

Cultural Dissonance in the Immigrant Household

Immigrant parents face a daunting set of tasks—finding work, making a home, enrolling their children in new schools, grasping the new cultural rules of engagement, learning English, and establishing new social ties. Moves of any kind are considered by social scientists to be among the most stressful of events, but the stakes are higher and the process all the more challenging when a change of country is involved.[54]

Throughout our study we witnessed immigrant youth moving with increasing ease from their schools into workplaces, shopping malls, movie theaters, and other recreational spaces. While parents focus most of their energies on making ends meet in the new society, forging ties first and foremost with people of similar ethnic backgrounds or immigrant status, immigrant youth are out and about in the new culture, attending American schools, interacting with American teachers and peers, and watching American television. Thus, immigrant children today, just as in previous generations, learn the new rules of cultural expectations more quickly than do their parents.

Much has been written about the tensions that occur when parental cultural values clash with children's internalization of the new society's cultural expectations and values.[55] We found, however, that such conflicts were not as dramatic for families with newly arrived immigrant children as for immigrant households in which the parents are foreign-born and the children are born in the United States. Eighty percent of our participants readily acknowledged that their parents had different rules than those of American parents. This difference did not seem to create a lot of discord within our participants' families, however. We asked our participants: "Sometimes parents want their kids to behave the way they would in [their country of origin], but their kids want to behave more like Americans. How often do you think this happens in your family?" While 41 percent acknowledged that this happened from time to time, more than a third (38 percent) said that this never was an issue. Only 14 percent said that these tensions happened often and another 6 percent said it happened all the time. About half the youth (48 percent) said that their parents largely used the standards of expectations of their country of origin but an equal amount disclosed that their parents had adapted to using a mix of rules from their native land as well as from the United States. Interestingly, participants admitted that they would prefer be raised by a mix of both country-of-origin rules and American rules (64 percent); only 11 percent would prefer mostly American rules and 21 percent would prefer to be raised largely by the standards of their native country.

The less-than-expected tension around cultural parenting practices may have to do with our recently arrived sample—new arrivals are more likely to have internalized the expectations of their native culture and thus may be less likely to chafe against these rules than would immigrant-origin youth who have spent most of their lives in the United States or were born here. Interestingly, the amount of conflict created by any such dissonance differed by ethnic group. Nearly half (49 percent) of Chinese students and 45 percent of Dominicans noted that disagreements over household rules and family values were never an issue in their families. More than a third of Haitian students, however, reported that such tensions occurred often or all the time.[56] When there were conflicts about values, they tended to center around gender issues and were highly focused on dating patterns involving girls in the new society. While these responses point to interesting cultural differences, there was no direct link between reported acculturation tensions and academic performance.

Family Problems

Teachers were quick to attribute their students' performance to problems within their families. As one teacher dismissively put it: "These [immigrant] families are messed up." Certainly, there is research literature supporting the notion that family tensions and conflict can contribute to lower academic performance.[57] We were interested in establishing whether or not family problems and conflict indeed played a significant role in the lives of newcomer students. We asked students to describe how true the following statements were for their families: "Your parents work long hours and are not around much; Your parents are upset about your grades; Your parents don't understand what it is like to grow up in another country; You were separated from your parents for some time and it has taken a while to get used to each other; New people joined your family (like a stepparent or new kids . . .); Your parents don't like your friends; You disagree with your parents about curfews; You have too many responsibilities around the house; You want to do one thing in the future and your parents want you to do something else."

Reported family problems were less of an issue than we might have expected. In fact, most students responded to the bulk of the statements with "not a problem."[58] Interestingly, we found that there were no gender differences in reports of family tensions and problems. There were, however, country-of-origin differences—Chinese participants were less likely to report family conflict than the other groups, whereas Haitian students reported the most family tensions. Importantly, there was also a significant difference in reported family tension between each of the academic performance pathways. High achievers reported the least family tensions, while low achievers and precipitous decliners reported the most.[59] Not surprisingly, family problems were correlated with reports of lower levels of well-being and lower academic performance.[60] That is, children who reported fewer family problems felt better and did better in school.

While outright conflicts and problems were not especially an issue for most of these students, our qualitative data revealed a general long-term trend regarding intimacy and ease of communication within the family. As the children matured and spent more time in the United States, parents in particular complained of a growing gulf between them and their children. For some, this distance seemed to be a result of natural changes taking place in adolescence. For other immigrant parents, it was a culturally marked issue as the youth brought into the home behaviors (often fashions and dating) that surprised, or in some cases appalled, them. For still others, as the gap between the parents and their children's educational and cultural competence increased, they found less and less in common. Especially for families of youth who drifted away from school and toward gangs, tensions increased. Even some parents of high achievers eventually reported a bittersweet "be careful what you wish for" morality tale—the academic success of their children, which they had worked so hard to make possible, had over time led to a painful distance between them. Later in the book we will examine in more detail how these processes unfold.

Family Interdependence and Mutual Responsibilities

Our study revealed that recently arrived immigrant adolescents, by and large, were emotionally dependent on their families. Large percentages of our participants spontaneously named members of their family as people they "have fun with" (52 percent), "feel loved by" (83 percent), and "feel respected by" (85 percent). They were also far more likely to turn to their family members "for help if you need it" (72 percent) than they were to turn to peers (27 percent), adults in school (10 percent), or adults in the community (4 percent). This finding is consistent with others and shows that the dependence and closeness to family members among recently arrived immigrant youth is considerably higher than what we would expect to find among mainstream American teenagers.[61]

Immigrant families frame migration as familial project in which everyone shares responsibility. The bargain is that parents sacrifice to provide better opportunities for their children and children are expected to study hard and help around the home. To make ends meet, immigrant parents often work more than one job or take on afternoon, night, and weekend shifts when their children are most likely to be home. Many immigrant children, particularly first-born children and daughters, are expected to help their parents and families while their parents are away working.[62] We asked our students to tell us about the ways in which they helped around the home—doing household chores, babysitting, running errands, cooking, translating, and the like. Chinese students reported having fewer chores around the house; only 18 percent of Chinese children were expected to help around the house on a daily basis. By contrast, nearly 42 percent of Dominican, 37 percent of Central American, 36 percent of Haitian, and 40 percent of Mexican children reported daily family chores. Most of our participants reported translating for their families, with fewer than a quarter of students rarely or never translating; 42 percent translating once in a while, and a third translating daily (or nearly so). Mexican and Dominican students reported undertaking this responsibility the most frequently, and Chinese were the most likely to almost never have been asked to translate. High-performing students were significantly less likely to report that they had to miss school because they were called on to help their families (7.8 percent) than were low-achieving students (26.8 percent).

We developed a cumulative scale of family responsibilities and found, not surprisingly, that girls were asked more often than boys to help at home. In addition, there were significant country-of-origin differences, with Central American and Mexican students reporting the most family responsibilities. This difference may be in part because these students tend to live in households with more people as well as because of cultural expectations. Interestingly, there was no relationship between this cumulative family responsibilities scale and the academic trajectories. It seems that family responsibilities can have both positive and negative repercussions: children who are asked to be responsible at home may develop skills that help them at school—for example, a sense of responsibility and the ability to stay organized—but excessive demands, such as when children are asked to care for younger siblings instead of doing homework, or to miss school for family reasons, can distract from their academic performance.[63]

Students in the study repeatedly voiced their keen understanding and appreciation of their parents' struggles on their behalf.[64] Mia, a fifteen-year-old Dominican girl, offered this poignant and articulate interpretation: "One of the most important successes in life is to study, because without a good education there is no life. That is why some of our parents have had to work in factories. They work hard to give us a good education so that we can have a good future, not a future like theirs. Their dream is to see us become lawyers so we can represent our family, our last name, our country."

Many of the students spoke of the complex combination of love, affection, appreciation, gratitude, responsibility, and sense of duty that characterize their relationships with their families and influence their academic and behavioral choices.[65] They exhibited a keen understanding and appreciation of their parents' sacrifices and struggles on their behalf. Monica, a seventeen-year-old Central American girl, reflects on her parents' support: "My goal is to go to the university and get a career. I'm doing it for myself, for my family, to help them when I have my career. My parents think these are good goals so I can get ahead and earn money for happiness. But I have to do the work. My parents' support is the best inheritance they could give me."

The kinds of relational support that parents were able to provide varied widely among the participants. Many parents and students described the tangible and emotional support they gave and received in the form of homework help, advice, encouragement, and care. The Central American mother of seventeen-year-old Monica remarked: "To help my children succeed in this country, I keep up with their school life, help them study, and feed them good food." Of her parents, sixteen-year-old Graciela, who is also Central American, said: "My dad explains things to me if I don't understand. They always want the best for us. They leave us in peace after school so we can keep studying."

All too often, however, the immigrant family's struggle to survive economically derails educational aspirations. The mother of Wei, the fourteen-year-old Chinese girl introduced earlier, describes a common dilemma:

> Nowadays, parents are busy making a living, which is very important for them. They work long hours so they are alienated from their kids' schools. Basically, they don't know how their kids are doing in school, they don't know how the school operates. Education is very important for kids. But sometimes I feel that for Chinese families, they work very hard to get here so they don't give much attention to their kids' education. For them the most important thing is to make a living, to survive. How can you talk about education when you don't even have enough to eat? How can you talk about something else when you cannot maintain the basic living level?

Sometimes these economic pressures lead to competing goals within the family. Gina, an eighteen-year-old Haitian in her senior year of high school, told us: "[My parents] want me to get a job right after high school. They don't want me to go to college. My goal is to go to college, but my mom doesn't want me to. She wants me to get a job instead to make money so I can help them out."

Parents' Hopes for Their Children's Education

In the current ethos of American education, parents are viewed as important advocates and partners in the educational success of their children. Teachers in American schools share the belief that certain kinds of parental involvement, attitudes, and behaviors are necessary for a student's successful academic journey. But how do teachers working with immigrant children view the role of immigrant parents? To answer this question, our research team interviewed seventy-five teachers distributed across the seven school districts involved in our larger study: that is, each research assistant on our research team was asked to arrange three interviews in schools where they were conducting their ethnographies. They were asked to select one teacher whom they felt was exemplary, another they considered average, and another who seemed not particularly positive about working with immigrant students. In this way we hoped to capture a range of perspectives.

We asked teachers, "How do you expect parents to support their children's education?" Many of the responses were telling. One summed up the paradigm of parental involvement: "In American schools parents are expected to come to school and question the school. They are asked to be more active in the educational process." Another said she wanted "for parents, by their words and their deeds, to impress upon children that the education process is important." Coming to school was a critical symbol of parental involvement: "I expect parent[s] to find ways to come in to the school . . . The tendency and the assumption are that they should be more invested in their children's academic work. I want my bilingual student's parents to invest more so that their children can be better students." Supporting the students' efforts at completing homework was another theme: "When I send work home, please make sure the student does it." Another said, "I expect them to help their children with their homework."

Parents who came to school and helped with homework were viewed as concerned parents, whereas parents who did neither were thought to be disinterested and parents of poor students. A teacher shared with us: "Only a minimum percentage of parents get involved in their kid's education and usually the parents that are concerned and get involved are the parents of the students that are doing well in school. Parents that have kids with problems prefer to hide and not get involved."

In fact, immigrant parents were often found wanting in the teachers' eyes. "I would like to see them more than I do." Another noted, "Only a few [of these] parents show interest in their children's education, either by coming here to talk to me or by sending messages via their children. They don't know much."

Teachers also lamented their perception that immigrant parents had low expectations for their children. One confided her thoughts: "The parents of non-immigrant students, they understand that, like, education is the way to get ahead and they say, like, 'I want my kid to use his brain and not his muscles.' And my hunch is that might be different for the immigrant parents. Their goal may be more getting to this area and settling in here, as opposed to school. They are more interested in day-to-day things."

While overall teachers' assessments of immigrant parents were often patronizing at best and hostile at worst, looking into the eyes of immigrant youth we found a very different perspective. The vast majority of the children had internalized very high parental expectations for their academic performance. We asked students: "For my parents, getting good grades is . . ."[66] Seventy-one percent responded "very important" and another 22 percent answered "important." Likewise, students ended the statement "For my parents, finishing high school is . . ." with "very important" (86 percent) or "important" (11 percent). In the majority of cases, immigrant youth reported that their parents thought going to college was very important (73 percent) or important (20 percent). Students' perceptions of their parents' aspirations for them were fairly consistent with what parents reported to us separately—83 percent of the parents said that they hoped their children would attend college. The parents of high-achieving students had the highest aspirations—96 percent of those parents expected their children to go to college—though even 71 percent of low-achieving students' parents held this wish. These parental aspirations had no relationship to actual performance trajectories. Further, there were no significant differences by gender and by country of origin and only a small difference by performance trajectory. Put simply, the vast majority of immigrant parents, regardless of whether they had girls or boys, and independent of which country they came from, wanted their children to do well in school and go on to college.

This dream was a challenge for most immigrant parents to achieve, however. In particular, because many immigrant parents worked long hours in inflexible low-wage jobs, they often were not available to attend school meetings during the day or help their children after school with homework. Xie, a fourteen-year-old Chinese boy, remarked that he could not ask his mother for help with his assignments because she was "never home . . . I seldom see her." Dario, a fourteen-year-old Dominican boy, echoed the sentiment: "I don't ask my parents for help because they are always work-ing and when they get home they are tired and I don't like to bother them much." Similarly, when asked whom she would turn to for help if she were wrongly accused of cheating on an exam at school, Gina, an eighteen-year-old Haitian girl, remarked, "My parents are both very busy. I don't know. They can't really help."

Xie also expressed an oft-reported insight that many immigrant parents are ill-equipped to help with homework given their own limited education and unfamiliarity with English, confiding: "[My mother] isn't good at my schoolwork. It is impossible for me to ask her to help me with my English. She, herself, is going to night school right now. Her English is not that good." Indeed, only 38 percent of the students in the sample said they could ask someone in their family to help with their homework. Thus, un-like their middle-class peers—whose parents readily provide a computer with an internet connection and printer; correct errors in spelling, gram-mar, and logic; and help their child prioritize and organize their time—immigrant students are largely on their own when doing homework. And their homework grades show it. As we will see in Chapter 3, immigrant students are distinctly penalized for not having as much parental help with their homework.

When it comes to applying to college, immigrant students are also fre-quently at a disadvantage, because their parents often have very little un-derstanding of how to help their children navigate the college admissions process. Twenty percent of our participants told us they had no one to ask about how to get to college. Forty percent relied on their families, even though their families had little knowledge about how to help them gain ac-cess to college. While middle-class college-educated parents spend endless hours deconstructing college-admissions strategies at the sidelines of their children's Saturday soccer practice—which advanced-placement courses to maneuver their children into; the best volunteer activities for students; the most talented SAT coaches; and so forth—these approaches were impene-trable mysteries for many of the immigrant families.

Chinese families were somewhat advantaged in this regard. They came from a society where high-stakes testing is the norm—successful place-ment in each successive tier of the educational ladder provides a winner-takes-all scenario. Chinese parents arrive with a sense that there is an aca-demic game to be played and that figuring out that game will give their children an advantage. Further, because cohorts of successful, highly educated Chinese have paved the way, there is a well-articulated game plan available throughout the Chinese community by way of word of mouth, local Chinese newspapers, and an extensive ethnic tutoring network.[67] The other country-of-origin groups in our sample were far more trusting ("American schools are the best in the world") and naïve about the avenues to success in the American educational system.

Peers and Friends

The youth in this study often spoke about the importance of their peers as they acclimated to a new country, a new neighborhood, and a new school. Peers were described as providing a sense of belonging and acceptance, as well as tangible help with homework assignments, language translations, and orientation to school.[68] To newly arrived immigrant students, the companionship of friends from their country of origin seemed especially important; these peers were important sources of information on school culture.[69] "I hung out with friends from my country because they spoke Spanish, because they told me the things I didn't understand," noted Julieta, a fourteen-year-old Mexican girl. Similarly, a sixteen-year-old Dominican girl named Yunisa explained: "When you come here, you don't know English. Your friends help you with English, with classes, and with showing you the school." Hence peers act as "vital conduits" of information to disoriented newcomer students.[70]

In addition to offering guidance and protection, peers supported new arrivals emotionally, helping them to feel less lonely. Sixteen-year-old Graciela from Central America noted: "I have a lot of friends and I don't feel alone." Peers, for immigrant students, as with all other children, provide companionship, a sense of belonging, and a source of distraction from the harsh realities of life. For recently arrived immigrant students, peers were far and away the group to which students were most likely to turn when they wanted to have fun; in fact, 78 percent named peers as their source of fun. Peers also made them feel respected (reported by 57 percent of the students) and to a lesser extent, loved (18 percent). For newcomer immigrant students, however, family relationships still were by far the most important source of love and caring.

Learning is usually an intensely social act. As Frederick Erickson memorably explained, learning involves surfing at the edge of a wave of relative incompetence before new skills are internalized.[71] There is a social risk in learning—if one is made to feel ashamed for not knowing or understanding, the process can shut down. Conversely, generous and forgiving social supports can serve to fan the embers of learning. Our participants noted that their peers provided important emotional sustenance that supported the development of their learning, in many cases easing the shame that accompanied not understanding. Fourteen-year-old Dario from the Dominican Republic explained: "When I don't understand, I feel stupid when I ask my teacher. Sometimes even when it's explained several times, I just don't understand how to do it. It makes me feel bad. When I ask my friends, I don't feel as bad because they are my friends and they show me I can do it."

Many peers were described as modeling positive behaviors; others, however, distracted their classmates from performing optimally in school.[72] Consuelo, a seventeen-year-old Mexican girl, summed up the problem—"They try to get us to cut class, use drugs, and tease us for wanting to study"—articulating how peers may undermine new arrivals' academic aspirations.

About a third of our students' parents reported that they worried a lot about the possibly bad influence of their children's friends. More Mexican parents and Central American parents reported worrying "a lot" than did Chinese and Haitian parents. As would be expected, parents of low-achieving students worried more than did the parents of the other children.

We developed a scale to determine the extent to which peers were a source of academic support or, conversely, a distraction. Students were asked to respond to the following statements: "My friends are serious about their schoolwork"; "When I do well in a class, my friends tease me"; "I can count on my friends to help me in school"; "My friends think school is boring"; "My friends talk to me about college"; "My friends ask me to cut classes with them"; "My friends explain things that I do not understand in class"; and "My friends encourage me to do my best in school." Not surprisingly, the students in the lowest-achieving academic pathway reported the least academic peer support. Further, while there was no difference between four of the five country-of-origin groups represented, Mexican students were less likely to report academic peer support than any of their other peers. There were no gendered differences on this scale.

We also found that 26 percent of all students relied on their peers for help with homework. Improving students were more likely than other students to turn to their peers for help with homework.[73] And when country of origin was considered, Chinese students were the most likely to rely on peers for academic help.[74]

The newcomer students in our sample were disconcertingly segregated. They reported few opportunities to interact with native-born peers—let alone white middle-class youth—and told us that they were most likely to spend time with other newcomer youth. Indeed, on the card-sorting task used to describe students' networks of social relationships, only about a third named a friend who was born in the United States. All immigrant youth long to be accepted by their peers, and the pull of acculturation is an inevitable part of migration.[75] The fashions they wear, the accents they develop, and the behaviors they emulate are influenced by the models to which they are exposed. But few immigrants today come in sustained and close contact with white middle-class youth, which means it is very unlikely they will internalize the white middle-class Protestant ethos that served as the point of reference in previous waves of migration.[76] Remarkably, only 4 percent of all informants reported having close friendships with white American peers, after an average of six years in U.S. schools. While neither Mexican nor Central Americans reported close friendships with white American youth, almost 14 percent of Chinese participants reported having such relationships (Table 2.5).

Because most immigrant youth attend highly segregated schools and live in segregated neighborhoods, when immigrant youth refer to their

Table 2.5 Percent of children saying that the majority of their close friends come from a particular group

| | Child's country of origin | | | | | |
Background of friends	China	Dominican Republic	Central America	Haiti	Mexico	Total
Same country of origin	43.1	46.7	3.5	68	44.3	40.8
African American	0	3.3	0	22	0	4.2
White American	13.9	3.3	0	2	0	4.2
Asian	43	0	0	0	1.4	10.4
Latino	0	45	80.7	0	51.4	35.2

Note: Chi-square (24,308) = 297.87, p <.0001

"American" peers, they typically mean not the white American majority but the African American minority group. Moreover, as we will see in more detail in Chapter 3, their relationships with these African American peers are ambivalent at best and hostile at worst. While many newly arrived immigrant youth (consciously or not) end up mimicking the dress and linguistic styles of inner-city African American youth, they nonetheless report negative attitudes toward these peers, whom they all too often have experienced as intimidating and hostile. Few immigrant students (only 4 percent) reported close friendships with African Americans. Notably, nearly a quarter of Haitian students reported having close African American friends while no Mexicans, Central Americans, and Chinese students reported having friends with this background (Table 2.5).

According to a growing body of literature, academically successful African American students can be socially penalized by their peers when they engage in academically focused behaviors. Behaviors required for academic success, including getting good grades, turning in homework, and engaging in the behaviors that please teachers, may lead to accusations of "acting white."[77] Such performances seem to indicate a general lack of "cool," "being out of it," and in the worst cases, racial treason in the sense that one is rejecting one's identity in favor of the majority white culture.

Is there any evidence that newly arrived immigrant children of color struggle with this issue? Are they teased or sanctioned by their peers for doing well in school? Neither our ethnographic nor quantitative data suggested the existence of this phenomenon in newly arrived immigrants of color. By contrast, our data imply that this issue is of little or no relevance for them. When we asked our students what their friends' reaction was when they received good grades, 67 percent told us that their friends "mostly congratulated" them, and fewer than 2 percent reported that their friends would "tease them" for getting good grades.[78] There were no gendered differences on this point. Further, our black informants (such as those born in Haiti) were most likely to report that their peers would congratulate them for getting good grades (80 percent). These immigrant youth retain a faith in education as the primary way to improve their social status. Being engaged in school did not seem to compromise these children's sense of ethnic belonging and identity.

As first-generation immigrants, these youth maintained very strong country-of-origin identities during the entire five-year study. We asked students to describe whether they felt "Completely from your county of origin"; "Mostly from your county of origin and a little American"; "Somewhat American and somewhat from your county of origin"; "Mostly American and a little from your county of origin"; or "Completely American." Even in the last year of the study, nearly 59 percent of all students maintained a sense of identity completely linked to their country of origin. Another 26 percent identified themselves as "mostly" from their heritage country but also a little American. Approximately 14 percent identified themselves as feeling somewhat American and somewhat from their country of origin. Notably, fewer than 2 percent of the students considered themselves mostly or completely American. There were no gendered differences in ethnic self-identification nor were any of these differences linked to the academic trajectories identified in Chapter 1. But there were differences among country-of-origin groups, with Mexican students most strongly identifying with their heritage country (75 percent), and Chinese students much less likely to exclusively identify themselves with their country of origin (32 percent). In addition, the Chinese students were the most likely to report feeling mostly from their heritage country but also a little American (42 percent).

New immigrant students tend to form friendships with others like themselves—particularly those who share their immigrant background. Around 41 percent of the students in our sample reported that the majority of their close friends were from their country of origin (Table 2.5). The exception to this general trend were the Central Americans, who tended to enroll in schools where most of their peers were of Mexican origin or were African American; in their case, 80 percent reported that most of their close friends came from the pan-ethnic Latino group. For Mexican, Chinese, and Dominican students, most friendships fell into two categories—either others from their country of origin or members of their other pan-ethnic group (Asians for Chinese and Latinos for Mexicans). Haitians, by contrast, overwhelmingly identified the majority of their close friends as Haitian (although they also reported many more African American friends than any of the other groups—Table 2.5).

Immigrant students' segregation from their more acculturated peers has significant educational implications. Other immigrant students, while often more positively oriented toward school than native-born peers, tended to have only limited abilities to help their newcomer friends.[79] Their English-language skills are usually not as well developed as those of native-born students. They often live in homes with parents who are not highly educated and are not highly proficient in English. They often attend schools that fall short in providing a quality curriculum, adequate resources, and high academic standards. Indeed we asked our participants: "Some kids have friends who help them with homework and others do not. What would you say most of your friends do?" Only about a third (36.9 percent) reported that their friends help them with academics. When we asked them why they did not rely on their peers more, most students confided that their friends did not know how to help them with their homework. Further, like most first-generation-to-college students, these peers did not have a nuanced understanding of the intricacies of how to get into college.

Community and Mentor Relationships

Mentoring relationships can make a tremendous difference in adolescents' lives in a variety of ways.[80] In stressed families with limited social resources, they support healthier family and peer relationships by alleviating pressure on the family.[81] In addition, college-educated mentors can help their protégés to perform better in school by helping them with schoolwork and by providing informed advice about college access. Research has also established that mentoring relationships help reduce substance abuse, aggressive behavior, and delinquency.[82]

It seems that mentoring relationships could be especially valuable for young immigrant newcomers.[83] Because immigrant adolescents' parents may not be available given their work schedules, mentors can help to fill the guidance void and ease intergenerational conflicts. A bicultural mentor can be a bridge between the old and new cultures. An acculturated mentor can act as a fount of information about the new cultural rules of engagement.

There are a number of well-established formal mentoring organizations such as Big Brothers/Big Sisters of America or Youth Friends with proven track records of effective mentorship for at-risk children. We found, however, that none of our newcomer immigrant participants were connected with these kinds of formal mentoring organizations. Instead they had to forge nonfamilial adult relationships on their own.

Broad-based community organizations can also help foster these healthy mentoring relationships. Community-based youth development programs—such as the YMCA, YWCA, Boys and Girls Clubs, as well as local church, sports, and after-school organizations—were developed to help steer children away from drugs, gangs, and delinquency.[84] Their organized, supervised after-school activities help structure the time of restless adolescents. Further, in the context of activities and conversation, natural links can evolve between adults and youth. After-school community organizations, therefore, provide the opportunity for informal mentoring relationships. Unfortunately, only a small portion—7 percent—of the participants in our study reported regularly spending time in community centers.

By and large, however, immigrant youth are not left unsupervised. Seventy-eight percent of the participants claimed that an adult knew where they were most of the time and that they were under some kind of supervision. The vast majority reported spending the bulk of their after-school time with family members—either parents, siblings, or extended family members such as aunts, uncles, or grandparents. Twenty-eight percent reported that they spend some of their time outside of school working, and 18 percent spent time in church-related activities (girls were twice as likely as boys to be involved in church organizations).

Only 9 percent of the students in this study reported participating in after-school classes or other academic enrichment programs like Upward Bound, although many more of the high-achieving kids were enrolled in such programs. Ethnographically, we observed that the Chinese students were more likely than their Latino counterparts to be involved in after-school tutoring (which often were ethnic niche organizations) or college preparation activities like Upward Bound. Latino students, by contrast, were more likely to be involved with "keep them out of trouble and off the streets" kinds of organizations. Not surprisingly, the more scholastic activities seemed linked to more positive academic outcomes than were the behavior-based programs.[85]

After-school and tutoring programs can be of critical importance to immigrant students needing homework help.[86] Fourteen-year-old Jeanne from Haiti noted: "They help you with your homework a lot. When you come home your parents don't have to check it because it's already corrected." These programs also provide information to newcomer students about the American higher education system that immigrant parents, unfamiliar with education in this country, cannot offer. Rosa, a seventeen-year-old Mexican girl, commented about Upward Bound: "They told me all I needed to get into the university."

Informal mentors can be a source of both tangible and emotional support to immigrant youth. As Camila, a sixteen-year-old Central American girl, explained about the adults in her community-based after-school program: "They ask me if I need anything for school. If we go to a store and I see a notebook, they ask me if I want it. They give me advice, tell me that I should be careful of the friends I choose. They also tell me to stay in school to get prepared. They tell me I am smart. They give me encouragement."

Nonparental adults in the school and community can ease the cultural transition for newly arrived immigrant students. But unfortunately, our data show that most students in our sample missed this opportunity. Few immigrant students named nonfamily adults as playing a significant role in their lives; instead, most spent the bulk of their time within their extended family network. In response to our question "Other than your parents, is there an older person whom you turn to for support and guidance?"—only 35 percent named an extended family member. Further, none of the students in our sample named a mentor provided by a formal mentoring organization. Only 14 percent of the total sample named a nonfamilial adult—3 percent named a community leader and 9 percent named someone in a school. Girls were twice as likely as boys to name a nonfamilial supportive adult. Notably, high achievers were twice as likely as the other students to have developed a supportive relationship with an adult outside of the family.

We also asked students to tell us who they were most likely to turn to when they needed academic support. Thirty-eight percent relied on their family for help with homework, 13 percent found such help from people in school or after-school activities, and 16 percent reported having no source of help with homework. Ninety-six percent reported that family members expected them to get high grades, whereas only 18 percent reported that people in school or at after-school sites held these expectations for them. Seventy-eight percent reported that parents talked to them about the future, while only 14 percent reported that people in school or at after-school sites did so. Forty percent reported that they received information about how to get to college from a family member; only 28 received this information from a logical and probably more knowledgeable source—counselors and teachers in school or at after-school sites. Alarmingly, 20 percent of the participants reported having no source whatsoever for information about applying to, and attending, college.

IMMIGRATION is an intensely social process that ideally involves a healthy synergy among newly arrived families, their communities, and established institutions in the host society. But for too many new arrivals, family members—both those in the new country and those left behind in the country of origin—seem to be their sole island of solace and support. Addressing immigrant families' needs through partnerships among after-school groups, community organizations, schools, and churches would go a long way toward expanding these networks of supportive relations and easing the transition for these families. For although immigrant families are highly resilient, there are clear limits to the assistance that immigrant parents can offer their children—especially given the less-than-optimal educational environments that their children so often experience.

■ ■

CHAPTER 3

Less-Than-Optimal Schools

AMERICAN EDUCATION matters more than ever before. While a hundred years ago immigrant youth could (and routinely did) drop out of school without hampering their futures, today the costs of so doing are substantial.[1] The stakes are high because the global workplace requires much more than the simple, rote memorization idealized in twentieth-century education. Instead, it demands the capacity to think analytically and creatively both within a single discipline as well as in an interdisciplinary manner, the ability to work with people from diverse backgrounds, and an understanding of both historical and global perspectives.[2]

We all want our children to attend schools that are rigorous and engaging, as well as safe and welcoming. We wish for schools that maintain high standards and expectations for all students. We want our children to learn how to learn so they may become lifelong learners, as they need to be in order to succeed in our new economy. Ample research demonstrates that effective schools have strong leadership and high staff morale; high academic expectations for all students regardless of their backgrounds; respect for students' heritage cultures and languages; and a safe, orderly school climate.[3]

In recent years, the Melinda and Bill Gates Foundation has been calling for a reappraisal of the oft-referred-to "three Rs" of education. Until the waning years of the last century, students needed to be grounded in reading, 'riting, and 'rithmetic. The Gates Foundation argues that in order to engage learners and prepare them for the new economy, schools must provide a new group of characteristics: *rigor* in challenging classes, *relevance* to engaging topics that "relate clearly to their lives in today's rapidly changing world," and *relationships* with adults "who know them, look out for them, and push them to achieve."[4]

Principals play a critical role. A charismatic leader articulates a vision of the school's mission and projects a collective sense of purpose to the entire school community—teachers, students, and parents. An effective instructional leader maintains high expectations (and makes it clear that teachers are expected to do the same) for all the students in the school, making sure that the students are provided with rich, engaging, and relevant curricula. A successful principal reaches out to parents and makes links with community organizations, creating strategic alliances with local businesses to invest needed resources in their schools. A strong principal fosters a warm, safe, and inclusive school climate where students can focus on learning. In short, principals who are able to provide this kind of transformational leadership can substantially improve school performance.[5]

But such principals are as few and far between as are exemplary schools. Our data demonstrate that most of the newcomer immigrant students in our sample attended schools that fell far short of these ideals. In fact, most of the children in this study attended schools that not only obstructed learning and engagement but also were, in many ways, toxic to healthy learning and development. Rather than providing "fields of opportunity," all too many were "fields of endangerment."[6]

Fields of Endangerment

Most of the students in our study attended highly segregated schools where more than three-quarters of their peers were of color and many were from poor families. In recent years, despite legislation passed in the 1960s designed to reduce segregation, our schools have become increasingly resegregated. This new pattern of segregation tends to be not just about color but also about poverty and linguistic isolation—so-called triple segregation.[7] This development is of deep concern because these types of segregation have proven to be inexorably linked to negative educational outcomes—including climates of low expectations and academic performance, reduced school resources, lower achievement, greater school violence, and higher drop-out rates. As a recent report from Harvard University's Civil Rights Project establishes: "The strong relationship between poverty, race and educational achievement and graduation rates shows that, but for a few exceptional cases under extraordinary circumstances, schools that are separate are still unquestionably unequal."[8]

Poor children clearly face particular challenges. Although some immigrant youth come from privileged backgrounds, large numbers of immigrant youth today, especially those who come from Latin America and the Caribbean, face challenges associated with poverty. Immigrant children are more than four times as likely as native-born children to live in crowded housing conditions and three times as likely to be uninsured.[9] Children raised in circumstances of poverty are more vulnerable to an array of psychological distresses that impair educational outcomes, including difficulties concentrating and sleeping, anxiety, and depression.[10] Poverty has long been recognized as a particularly significant risk factor for educational access. It limits opportunities and frequently coexists with a variety of other factors that augment risks—such as violent neighborhoods saturated with gang activity and drug trade, as well as schools that are segregated, overcrowded, and understaffed.[11]

In such settings, students' opportunities are hemmed in on all sides. Resources are scarce and the buildings are thus often run down, with peeling paint and litter all about. Classrooms are typically overcrowded and the curriculum is outdated and irrelevant. Classroom routines can be mind-numbingly unengaging—often consisting of below-grade-level worksheets or outdated videos. In many classrooms we studied, "non-teaching" or "teaching to the talented tenth" was prevalent. Instruction is often tracked, especially for English-language learners who are put into dumbed-down classes in which they fall further and further behind their English-speaking peers. Few students go on to four-year colleges, so college counseling is only minimally available. In such settings, teachers tend to be inexperienced, teaching outside their content area, or uncredentialed. Morale is low and turnover of teachers and principals is high.

The climate in these schools challenges even the most dedicated and focused students. Such settings promote neither learning nor a sense of safety.[12] A recent report noted: "If an adult had to work in an environment where disrespect, bad language, fighting, and drug and alcohol abuse are practiced by a relative few, but tolerated or winked at by the management, it might be considered a 'hostile workplace.'"[13] Yet this is precisely the environment that many immigrant students and students of color encounter at school.

Parents often voiced concerns about the violence they perceived at their children's schools. The mother of Rolando, a fifteen-year-old Central American boy, remarked: "The role of the school is to educate the students the best that they can so that they can have a better future. But unfortunately, there are many terrible things going on in schools, many delinquent students killing others. It is very sad because the students feel unsafe." Students often told us how their peers contribute to unsafe school and community environments. As sixteen-year-old Graciela from Central America remarked: "Sometimes there are fights in school. This causes problems for me because I think about these fights instead of my work." Fourteen-year-old Jean from Haiti likewise said: "I don't like it when kids are bad at school—like to the teachers, when kids don't listen and try to beat up the teachers."

Such contexts undermine students' capacity to concentrate, their sense of security, and their ability to experience trusting relationships in school, as well as their ability to learn. When we asked students to tell us about their perceptions of school problems and violence, an alarming number of them spoke of crime, violence, feeling unsafe, gang activity, weapons, drug dealing, and racial conflicts.[14] As we saw in Chapter 1, student perceptions of school violence were highly related to their academic engagement. Students who attended schools where they perceived such problems were more likely to disengage—"low achiever" and "precipitous decliner" students reported the most school violence and problems. We also found a strong correlation between students' perceptions of school problems and a variety of "objective" indicators of school performance available through school districts' public access websites.[15]

Statistics for Schools in the Study

School districts make public information available about a variety of indicators of school quality, including percentages of students attending the school who are poor (assessed by whether they are eligible for free or reduced lunch); segregation rate (the racial and ethnic composition of the school); percentages of inexperienced teachers (or out-of-subject certification rate); greater than average school size; drop-out rate; daily attendance rate; whether suspension rates and expulsion rates are higher than average; percentage of students performing below proficiency on the state-administered English language arts (ELA) or math standardized tests; and a significant achievement gap on the standardized exam between one or more ethnic groups that attend the school.[16] Each of these characteristics has been linked to lower student performance.[17]

What kinds of schools were the participants in our study attending? By the last year of the study, 74 percent were attending high school, with 96 percent of our students attending public noncharter schools. Though there is a growing body of evidence that students learn better in small schools of five hundred or fewer students, only 12 percent attended such schools. The majority of our participants (65 percent) attended large schools with more than a thousand students, and 22 percent attended a school with between five hundred and a thousand students.[18]

Most of our students' schools were also highly racially and economically segregated. Eighty-six percent attended schools in which more than half of students were of color, and 54.2 percent attended schools where more than 90 percent of students were minority students. Nearly 60 percent attended schools where at least half of students were classified as low income.

There were significant differences in segregation patterns by country of origin. Dominicans were most likely to attend low-income schools, followed by Mexicans. Fewer than half of the Chinese students in our sample attended schools where most of the students were of color, whereas nearly all of the other immigrant students attended schools of this kind. The Latino students in our sample—Dominicans, Central Americans, and Mexicans—were much more likely than either Haitians or Chinese students to attend "intensely" segregated schools where more than 90 percent of the students were of color (Table 3.1).[19]

Not surprisingly, different academic performance trajectories, as defined in Chapter 1, were linked with different levels of segregation. "Low achievers" and "precipitous decliners" attended the poorest and most racially segregated schools. "High achievers" were least likely to attend low-income and racially segregated schools; even so, a sizeable proportion did so (Table 3.2).

Most of our students, then, were attending schools that provided a "separate and not equal" educational environment.[20] Eighty-nine percent of

Table 3.1   Percent of students in segregated schools, by country of origin

Country of origin	N	Segregation by income[a]	Racial segregation[b]	"Intense" racial segregation[c]
China	68	43.1	47.2	27.8
Dominican Republic	47	98.3	100.0	83.1
Central America	51	42.1	98.2	61.4
Haiti	54	44.0	98.0	30.0
Mexico	62	69.6	95.7	68.6
Total	309	59.2	86	54.2

Note: For all categories of segregation, p < .001.
a. Fifty percent or more of the students are from low-income families.
b. Fifty to 100 percent of the students are from racial minorities.
c. Ninety to 100 percent of the students are from racial minorities.

Table 3.2   Percent of students in segregated schools, by academic trajectory

Academic trajectory	N	Segregation by income[a]	Racial segregation[b]	"Intense" racial segregation[c]
Slow decliners	70	58.6	88.6	42.9
Precipitous decliners	79	65.8	96.2	63.3
Low achievers	41	68.3	97.6	75.6
Improvers	30	60.0	83.3	56.7
High achievers	63	47.6	58.7	38.1
Total	283	59.2	86.0	54.2

Note: For income segregation, p is statistically insignificant. For both types of racial segregation, p < .001.
a. Fifty percent or more of the students are from low-income families.
b. Fifty to 100 percent of the students are from racial minorities.
c. Ninety to 100 percent of the students are from racial minorities.

our sample attended schools with a significant achievement gap between white students and minority students on standardized performance tests.[21] Predictably, many of these schools had higher than average dropout and suspension rates.[22] Their teacher-student ratio was also higher than the state average and they had a lower-than-average rate of teachers who were accredited and teaching in their specialized subject areas.[23]

How did the schools our students attended compare to other schools in the Boston and San Francisco metropolitan areas, where we drew our sample? In order to contextualize our school data, we compared the school statistics for the schools our participants were attending to those of all the

Table 3.3 Aggregated district contextual data

Characteristic	San Francisco area[a]				Boston area[b]			
	Our sample		Metro area		Our sample		Metro area	
School statistics	Mean	(SD)	Mean	(SD)	Mean	(SD)	Mean	(SD)
Percentage of school population that is low income	49.9	(23.7)	57.8	(9.0)	49.1	(23.5)	51.8	(23.3)
Percentage of minority students	85.8	(17.4)	88.0	(5.2)	73.9	(25.1)	67.7	(26.1)
Percentage of school population that is Limited English Proficient or English Learners	36.1	(16.5)	30.2	(3.9)	17.3	(13.9)	18.3	(8.5)
Student/teacher ratio	20.2 to 1	(2.3)	18.3 to 1	(1.0)	16.0 to 1	(4.4)	13.1 to 1	(2.3)[c]
School avg. daily attendance rate (in percent)	95.3	(4.7)	94.4	(.2)	90.2	(5.3)	93.4	(1.1)
Suspension rate (in percent)	24.1	(22.7)	15.3	(18.8)	16.0	(9.8)	11.9	(3.2)
Percentage of school population at proficiency or above on state English language arts exam	15.4	(13.8)	29.1	(9.4)	36.5	(26.7)	43.1	(15.7)

Note: Unless otherwise noted, all district data are taken from the 2002–2003 school year due to availability of complete public data.

a. School districts include Oakland Unified School District, San Francisco Unified School District, and West Contra Costa School District.

b. School districts include Boston Public Schools, Cambridge Public Schools, Lawrence Public Schools, and Quincy Public Schools.

c. 2003–2004 district data.

public schools in the same districts. Thus we compared the schools our Mexican and Central American participants were attending to those in the same San Francisco metropolitan area districts, and the schools our Chinese, Dominican, and Haitian students were attending to the public schools in the same Boston metropolitan districts (Table 3.3).[24]

Several facts stand out in these comparisons. First, our sample students attended schools that, according to the criteria we used, were similar to other public schools in the same districts. There was only a small percentage difference for poverty and diversity (with a bit more of a gap in Boston), and our participants tended to attend schools with somewhat higher teacher/student ratios and suspension rates. The greatest difference between our participants' schools and schools in the general area was on the rate of passage of the high-stakes English-language test. Strikingly, too, the schools in the Boston area fared better on all the school statistics than did schools in the San Francisco area districts. (The Mexican and Central American participants, then, were attending schools that presented the least optimal learning environments to their students.)

As might be expected, the indicators of school quality were consistent with poor performance on the standardized testing indicators. Fewer than one-third of all the students in these schools, as reported by the districts and the states, reached proficiency level or higher on the states' English language arts exam. Students in our study from different countries of origin attended schools that had different exam results. While Chinese students attended schools where 59 percent of the schools' students performed at the proficient or above level on the state English language arts standardized exam, only 37 percent of Haitians, 20 percent of Dominicans and Central Americans, and 16 percent of Mexicans did so. Not surprisingly, using our trajectories of performance as a lens, we found that a higher percentage of high achievers attended schools where more students pass the exam (47 percent), whereas low achievers and precipitous decliners attended schools where only a small percentage of their students passed these tests (21 and 25 percent, respectively).

We found a highly significant relationship between schools that were both poor and racially segregated, and our participants' grades during the last year of the study.[25] There was an even stronger relationship between those schools and students' Woodcock Johnson Test of Achievement scores.[26] Students who attended these kinds of schools received lower grades and did less well on the achievement test we administered. The inescapable reality is that schools matter for the performance of their students. Many newcomer immigrants enter poor and segregated schools, and are consequently at a significant disadvantage as they strive to adapt to a new culture, learn a new language, master the necessary skills to pass high-stakes tests, accrue graduation credits, get into college, and attain the skills needed to compete in workplaces shaped by the new global economy.

School Ethnographies

Quantitative data from the school district provide an index of the discrepancies between schools, but offer little insight into the day-to-day realities of school life for immigrant children. To more fully understand their everyday experiences, we spent long hours in our participants' schools, and here we present ethnographies from four of them—two middle schools and two high schools. We picked these particular sites after our first year in the field, once we understood the range of schools our students attended. Each of these four schools had fifteen or more of our participants in attendance at some point in the study. We selected two "less than optimal schools" and two "better than average" schools, in order to capture the range of experiences that our participant students were encountering in their schools.

Quentin Middle School

Quentin Middle School is in northern California.[27] The city of "Quentin" lies between two sites of natural beauty—a spectacular bay to the west and rolling hills to the east. Incorporated in 1905, Quentin's economy boomed through the first half of the last century and reached its zenith during the 1940s and 1950s. During World War II, Quentin served as a major shipbuilding center, but today most of its industries stand idle. The one exception is in the hill area to the north, where a large, active oil refinery is a source of ambivalence for the community. While the refinery provides many jobs, it spews toxins into the air; occasional explosions leave an oily stench.

Accompanying the downturn in employment, this city of now just over 100,000 experienced a marked rise in drug- and gang-related violence during the 1980s. By the early 1990s, it had a homicide rate of seven times the national average, with more than sixty homicides during 1998, the year our study began. That year, the police department responded to 911 emergency calls every seven minutes. On average, calls reporting "shots fired" came in seven times a day, for a total of 2,640 such calls during the year. Despite increased police patrols, even today this city is one of America's fifteen most dangerous.[28]

Driving along Main Avenue, a dilapidated stretch of road leading to the school, we pass commercial establishments in various states of decay: a liquor store here, a used-car lot there, a gas station beyond. The businesses that are open seem neglected. Many storefronts are empty or abandoned, with broken windows, peeling paint, and garbage strewn about. Flamboyant graffiti covers entire buildings, proclaiming the presence of local gangs: the Black Crips and Bloods, the Mara Salvatruchas (a brutal and widespread Salvadorian gang), and various Norteño and Sureño Mexican gangs. There are few homes along Main Avenue. The streets are deserted, save for isolated groups of men. The feeling of decay and disrepair is inescapable.

The remaining businesses cater to the area's diverse ethnic groups. African American women frequent the nail salons and the hairstylists who specialize in hair extensions and braiding. Mexicans run restaurants and grocery stores with Spanish names—Carneceria (meat market), Frutas y Legumbres (fresh produce), Jugos y Licuados (juices and smoothies). There are Thai and Vietnamese stores and restaurants, too. These are locally owned businesses, and many of the proprietors are parents of children enrolled at Quentin Middle and other neighborhood schools. Right by the school are liquor stores, bars, and adult-video stores. Even some establishments that do not identify themselves as "adult-oriented" have pornographic material on display. We often spotted Quentin Middle students entranced by the adult videos playing on the store monitors.

At Quentin Middle School, more than three-quarters of the students are either Latino or African American: specifically, 45 percent are Latino, 31 percent are African American, 15 percent are Asian, 7 percent are white, 1.5 percent are Filipino, 0.3 percent are Pacific Islander, and 0.2 percent are Native American. Mexicans make up by far the largest immigrant group in the school: nearly 90 percent of all immigrant students there are Mexican. The remaining immigrants came from Asia, Africa, the Middle East, and

Central and South America. The school is deeply segregated by language (Spanish and English) and by race and ethnicity (African Americans and Latinos). Eighty percent of the students are designated as low income. Only 7 percent of the students who took the state high-stakes English language arts exam scored at or above the minimum state standard.

On our first visit, Quentin Middle School looks uninviting; impersonal, dreary, austere. The school covers a full city block. The schoolyard fence encloses five basketball courts and a grassy area of equal size. The main two-story building houses classrooms, offices, library, and a large cafeteria. Its walls are painted industrial gray and green, but they are covered with large blue and black graffiti letters. At the front door, an ominous sign greets visitors: "The site is equipped with metal detectors."

The dim, monochromatic classrooms along the long hallways, with their metal doors, are distinguishable only by their room numbers. The ethos here is decidedly institutional: correctional rather than educational, it strikes us. Scrawled on some doors are the sorts of graffiti usually reserved for bathroom stalls. The bathrooms themselves are filthy, dark, and trash-strewn. The mirrors are cracked, the soap dispensers contain no soap, there is no toilet paper, and the toilets are often backed up. The fetid smell is overpowering. Graffiti covers the walls: "Paola is a slut," "She does blow jobs," and, perhaps, an answer from Paola: "*Hijas de puta* [sons of a whore]. Tell it to my face." Outside the bathrooms, the drinking fountains—two on each side of the hall—are clogged with gum and debris. The school library on the first floor is closed more days than not because the librarian comes in only twice a week. It has just seven shelves of books.

During our time at Quentin Middle School, the administrative personnel changed. The vice-principal, Oscar Rangel, was appointed principal in 1998. Apparently, Rangel experienced adjustment problems during his transition from vice-principal to principal. Many teachers told us they were disappointed by his promotion, and they displayed little confidence in his ability. While he was always positive toward and accommodating of our research project, he often seemed remote, removed from the life of his school.

After his promotion to principal, we rarely saw Rangel in the halls, in the cafeteria, or in front of the school at the beginning or end of the day. He was almost always secluded in his office behind mounds of paper. It was the new vice-principal, Tamika Washington, a no-nonsense woman with a severe demeanor, who became the most visible administrator. She often monitored the halls, harshly directing students back to their classrooms. Some Mexican students confided that they felt Washington did not like Mexicans and played favorites with the African American students because "they are from the same race."

As the school bell sounds, chaos explodes. Students rush from their classrooms, swarming through the halls and the schoolyard. Most of the students run, there is a lot of pushing and horseplay, and the noise is deafening. Other students—mostly boys—strut languidly, as if to broadcast a challenge: "Just try to make us get to class on time."

One day during our second year at Quentin, as we walked with two immigrant youngsters on their way to the cafeteria, we came upon a group of five African American students running and pushing each other against the hallway walls. The Mexican immigrant students tensed—one told us that this same group of students had recently shoved her against the wall, almost breaking her wrist. The nearby guards were involved in a private conversation with each other and did nothing.

Inside the cafeteria, we cannot find a single racially mixed group. The segregation here is absolute: Asians sit with Asians, blacks with blacks, Latinos with Latinos, whites with whites. The seating arrangement is a near-perfect reflection of the school's social organization. In our two years at the school, we seldom saw students from different ethnic groups working together on projects. When groups come together, it is usually to fight.

IMMIGRANT CLASSROOMS

Immigrant Spanish-speaking children who are limited in English proficiency often take all their classes together. Typically, they take English as a Second Language (ESL) classes for reading and language arts and bilingual classes in math, science, and social studies. Some children may take higher levels of ESL classes. While most of the teachers in this program are identified as bilingual in Spanish and English, after the implementation of Proposition 227—which banned bilingual education in California—the teachers have been directed by the administration to use Spanish for clarification only, not as a language of instruction.

In many of these classrooms, we found a culture of "goofing off." In Mrs. Fidel's ESL I class, for example, horseplay made up much of the classroom interactions. During our observations in three ESL classes, we saw only a quarter of the students, or fewer, working on task. The rest talked, rested, napped, or fooled around. Girls gossiped. Boys traded comic books or put together picture albums of their favorite soccer stars; others overturned trash cans onto one another's heads or challenged and even fought with boys seated nearby. Joking and physical activity were the currency that earned capital—laughter and approval—for the disruptive boys. Asked about his frequent goofing off, José, a Mexican eleven-year-old, told us: "I try to pay attention, but if the teacher starts talking in English, I kind of get lost, and the next thing I know I am thinking of something else or doing something that is not part of the class. Then I am lost and want to have fun."

The large concentration of Mexican-origin students created a special dynamic, and Mexican culture dominated the ethos of the school. ESL teachers consistently drew from Mexican culture and not from the cultural backgrounds of students of other nationalities, including Salvadorian, Guatemalan, Peruvian, and Vietnamese. One morning in late October, Graciela Fidel passed out copies of skeleton puppets *(calaveras)* by José Posada, a twentieth-century Mexican artist who drew skeletons as political statements about the inequities of the Mexican social system. When we mentioned to her how many students decided to decorate their puppets with the colors of the Mexican flag, she replied, "Oh, yes. Students like to do things with Mexican themes, even the non-Mexicans." For example, Julio, a boy from Peru, decorated his skeleton with a Mexican flag motif. Mrs. Fidel commented: "There is a lot of pressure to be 'Mexican' in this school. He has no identity as Peruvian, but as Mexican he could be recognized."

Such immersion in Mexican culture was common. Mexican Spanish was the most common language spoken. Students' clothing, binders, and book covers sported Mexican soccer-team colors or Mexican flags. Girls exchanged pictures of Mexican soap-opera stars and talked about the previous night's episodes of the shows. Quotes from TV shows on Spanish channels such as Univision became the punchline of classroom jokes. For example, a popular comedy called "Ay Maria, que punteria" (Hey Maria, you hit the nail on the head) depicts the life of an indigenous woman from rural Mexico who moves to Mexico City. In the newcomers class were several girls named Maria. Often, when the teacher called on a girl named

Maria, the boys yelled, "Ay Maria, que punteria." Other Mexican items exchanged included chili-flavored candy, teen magazines from Mexico, and clips from the sports section of Mexican newspapers. Some of these items were available in the nearby Mexican markets, but students or their family members also brought them directly from Mexico.

The enormous social distance between the immigrant children in this school and white middle-class American youth was dramatic and pervasive. From the point of view of the Mexican children in this school, white American middle-class youth might as well have been in Oslo, Paris, or some other distant city, rather than just on the other side of the freeway. Here, where Mexican culture reigned supreme, supporting newcomer Mexican students became a sign of solidarity and membership and a source of empowerment in student rivalries. Most Mexican newcomers made friends immediately, an acceptance based more on regional and national origin than on language. For example, a Mexican girl and a Salvadorian girl started school on the same day. The teacher asked them to introduce themselves to the class. The Mexican girl got a cheer from the crowd when she said she was from Guadalajara, Mexico. Nobody said anything when the Salvadorian girl introduced herself as being from San Vicente, El Salvador. This reaction was typical whenever new children came into a classroom. During recess, the Mexican newcomer was already talking with a group of five Mexican girls while the Salvadorian girl sat alone on a bench.

Yet over the years we discerned tensions among the Mexican students. Newcomer youth, whom the teachers generally viewed as more studious and obedient, were mercilessly teased by their peers. Sometimes these students were called "putos," "maricas," and "jotos" (disparaging names for homosexuals) by more acculturated peers. During a visit to one ESL classroom, we overheard three Mexican boys who were sitting in the back calling another boy "puto" while he sat quietly doing his work. One of the three explained: "The thing is that he is a coward. He doesn't like to fight." Another said: "He doesn't even seem Mexican. He's giving us a bad name."

Newcomer Mexican immigrants had their own grievances about their more acculturated Mexican-American peers. Laura, a twelve-year old new immigrant from Michoacán, explained her dislike of Mexican-American girls: "Chicanas are stuck-up. I don't like them because they feel they are from here and not Mexicans, even if they are as dark as we are. They speak

Spanish, but they pretend they speak only English and they don't talk to you if you are Mexican."

LEARNING FEAR

"Slaying fugitive arrested," read a headline in the local paper. The article reported that a murder suspect had broken into the school while classes were in session and had been chased by the police inside the campus for almost two hours before he surrendered. This episode shook up everyone at the school. A teacher, Janice Smith, told us: "The police were here chasing a black man who came in the school. We didn't realize what was going on. When my fifth period was in session, I heard a lot of noise in the hall. I asked a student to go outside to see what was going on. When he opened the door, I heard somebody yelling, 'Get the hell back in the classroom and lock the door.' The boy came back and said that there was a police officer pointing at a black guy with a huge gun, maybe a rifle. Truly, it was the worst day of my life." Armida, a twelve-year-old Mexican girl in Smith's class, recalled the day's events with the same fear: "That man came into the school. It was so ugly. The teacher got so scared. She sent a boy to take a look and the boy said that the police officer was outside with a huge gun. We were all afraid."

Newly arrived immigrant students at Quentin learned to manage fear by staying in groups and by avoiding certain spaces known to be especially dangerous: the stairs, the bathrooms, and the natural creek in the schoolyard. "The Creek" was officially off-limits to students, but they congregated there anyway, engaging in behavior that was harder to get away with in the school buildings: fighting, smoking, drinking, heavy petting, and using drugs. Never once did we see a school guard near the creek. Alicia, a twelve-year-old Mexican girl, warned us, "Don't go to the creek; the *cholas* go there to smoke pot or to be with their dates. I am better off if I don't go over there." *Cholos* and *cholas*, as gang-affiliated youth are called, are said to dominate the creek, the site of ritualized interethnic fighting described in greater detail later in this chapter. In the fall of our second year at Quentin Middle School, three African American male students allegedly raped a twelve-year-old African American girl at the creek. Two of the attackers were rumored to be Quentin Middle School students, while the third suspect was said to attend a nearby high school.

Two months later, another tragedy struck when an African American student was killed in a motorcycle accident. The student was riding with his father, who was drunk. They were traveling at high speed in a slow lane and crashed into the freeway wall. The student was killed upon impact. His father, who survived the crash but sustained many injuries, was charged with involuntary manslaughter in his son's death. The dead boy's friends covered the walls of the school with banners that bore his picture, signatures, and heart-wrenching messages from schoolmates.

Then there was the school's violent tradition of "Rice and Beans," a recurring, ritualized form of fighting between Asians ("Rice") and Mexicans ("Beans"). During recess on a winter day just before Christmas break, an episode of "Rice and Beans" broke out by the creek. Some Asian students we met at the counselor's office told us that an Asian boy had beaten up the boyfriend of a Mexican girl, which had led a group of Mexican girls to attack the Asian boy. In retaliation, Asian boys had attacked a group of Mexican boys and girls.

After lunch, the principal made an announcement over the public address system: "From now on, any students involved in 'Rice and Beans' or 'Beans and Rice,' whatever you call it, will be receiving a five-day suspension. Again, no more 'Rice and Beans' will be tolerated on campus. Students involved will receive a five-day suspension."

One ESL teacher was furious that the principal had actually used the term "Rice and Beans" to refer to the fight, fuming that doing so legitimized negative stereotypes. That day, we learned that some thirty students, both boys and girls, had been involved in this latest episode of ethnic fighting, that there had been some injuries, and that all those involved had been suspended. Some students glorified these ritualistic fights, telling and retelling their "war" stories with exaggerated relish.

On another racial front, social barriers between black and Mexican children fostered suspicion, fear, and stereotypes. Many of the newcomer students found their African American peers intimidating; they reported regular bouts of bullying in the cafeteria, in the bathrooms, and when changing classes. José said, "I don't feel so good in school because most children in this school are black and some are fighters. When you are eating lunch, they go by you and take your stuff away from you. Black children attack everybody—the Chinese, the Arabs, and the Mexicans."

In both informal conversations and structured interviews, newly arrived immigrant students shared their fears. Safety came up spontaneously much more often than learning. In one conversation, Regina, Alicia, Pablo, and Oscar, all newly arrived twelve- and thirteen-year-old immigrants from Mexico, said they felt threatened by fights, by people offering them drugs, or by sexual advances.

> *Regina:* "There are a lot of drug users here and *chola* people. The *cholos* are the gang members who kill people."
> *Pablo:* "The worst place is the bathroom. In the boys' bathroom, when you get in, it smells like cigarettes. The other day it smelled like marijuana. Somebody offered me some. I was afraid and ran out."
> *Alicia:* "I knew this *chola* girl who went to The Creek during P.E. with a boy and she let him touch her private parts."
> *Oscar:* "The stairs are very dangerous. You can get beat up there any time."

Many Mexican immigrant children said their parents had come to view the school as a "bad place" where children were at risk of getting pregnant or becoming drug users and gang members.

> *Regina:* "My mom told me that when I finish this grade, she is going to send me to Mexico. She does not want me to go to the high school here because in the high school all children became bad. The girls get pregnant."
> *Alicia:* "My parents are afraid that I might become a rebel, a *chola*, or a drug addict."
> *Regina:* "My parents are afraid that in this school I might become a gang member."
> *Oscar:* "My parents are afraid that I might smoke marijuana."
> *Pablo:* "My mom told me that if I hang out with *cholos* in school, she's going to call the police."

During our two years at Quentin Middle School, we saw no sign of clear procedures for dealing with the oppressive air of fear and discontent. Following highly public incidents that traumatized the entire school population, administrators, faculty, and staff addressed problems only superficially. A culture of silence engulfed the school after each trauma. There was little follow-up after the rape of the girl by the creek or the boy's death on his father's motorcycle. A few posters went up announcing that counseling was available for students, but when we tried to speak with the school leadership about the fear, violence, and grief we saw the students struggling with, teachers and staff alike avoided such discussions. When we told Mrs. Fidel that her students seemed troubled by the rape and the death, she rationalized: "I don't know much about it. About the rape, I heard it was not a Latina girl, but African Americans were involved. About the kid who got killed, I don't know him. Actually, I really don't know these [non-Latino] students. I never see them, and I don't interact with them. To me, QMS students are the Latino students."

Mrs. Fidel's comment reflected what we had come to understand about Quentin Middle School: there was a pervasive culture of segregation and little sense of community. Fear, anomie, separation, and disengagement were rampant.

Putnam Middle School

Putnam Middle School is in "Putnam," a small city in Massachusetts. To its south lie a series of well-to-do residential towns; the eastern edge of the city borders the Atlantic Ocean. Putnam occupies fewer than twenty-seven square miles and is less densely settled than its neighbor (a population density of 5,062 per square mile versus the big city's population density of 11,860 per square mile).

Putnam is a historic town, home to signers of the Declaration of Independence and early American presidents. It was first settled by immigrant traders in 1625, established as a town in 1792, and incorporated as a city in 1888. Beyond trade, Putnam was an agricultural city that added fishing, shipbuilding, and granite quarrying over time. At the turn of the twentieth century, immigrants from Italy, Sweden, Finland, Scotland, and Ireland came to work in the shipyards and granite quarries, diversifying the original Yankee population. At the beginning of the twenty-first century, Putnam's economy remained strong. It had a slightly lower unemployment rate (2.9 percent) than the neighboring big city (3.3 percent) and the state as a whole (3.2 percent); many Putnam residents have attended some college or have a bachelor's degree.

By the mid-1980s, large numbers of Asian immigrants had begun to arrive, altering Putnam's demographics. In 1980, there were sixty-four students in the city's English as a Second Language/Transitional Bilingual Education (ESL/TBE) program, representing 0.6 percent of the total school population. Twenty years later, there were 996 students in the program citywide, representing almost 11 percent of the total student population. The district offers bilingual programs for Cantonese speakers (now 60 percent of all ESL students) and Vietnamese speakers (now 14 percent of all ESL students), to comply with the state's mandate for bilingual education.

During our study, the student body of the school was 55.9 percent white (versus 77.1 percent statewide), and approximately 40.6 percent of students were Asian (compared with 4.2 percent across the state). African Americans represented a smaller share of total enrollment in Putnam than in the state as a whole (1.4 percent in Putnam versus 8.6 percent statewide); Hispanics also represented a smaller share (1.4 percent in Putnam versus 10 percent statewide). Thirty-seven percent of all students at Putnam were eligible for free lunch.

Let's set the scene. Built in the mid-1950s, Putnam Middle School is a plain, boxy, two-story yellow-brick structure surrounded by athletic fields. The school door stays locked, and students enter en masse when the doors open in the morning. Visitors must ring the doorbell and identify themselves through an intercom before the door is electronically unlocked and entry to the school is granted. These security measures seem excessive, given the tranquility of the school's surroundings: the neighborhood looks neat, trim, and orderly. Adjacent blocks contain modest single-family homes on small, tidy lawns; the streets are empty of people.

Entering the school building, we step into a wide central space, bright from the light reflecting off shiny, stone-colored floors. A red-brick wall to the right displays a banner made from brightly colored pieces of felt that reads "Student Alliance against Racism." To the left, a freestanding partition displays pages of student poetry and artwork on its three tall walls. This central space is the hub into which flow the school's corridors and stairwell. Just off this central space is the main office, where all visitors to the school must check in. Receptionists sit behind a long counter running the length of the office, greeting visitors with a polite hello and courteous inquiries into the purpose and nature of their visit. Visitors are asked to sign the logbook.

The office is in a constant bustle as student helpers run about fetching and sorting, teachers hurry in to check their mailboxes or make photocopies, and guests mill around near the counter or sit expectantly in chairs by the door.

With 580 young adolescents in the building, the noise rises to a deafening level when students change classes. Students pour out of classrooms, some walking quickly and others bolting through the corridors. They have only two minutes to rush to their lockers, exchange hasty greetings with friends, and arrive at their next classes. The air is filled with shouts, laughter, and taunts, punctuated by the slamming of locker doors.

During those boisterous breaks, we often see the principal or assistant principal directing traffic, issuing firm orders to students to walk not run, or standing in intense conversation with a student, giving a stern lecture about the use of rude or foul language. At the start of each class period, when the halls are suddenly drained, the quiet hum of muffled voices murmurs through closed doors. The hallway floors shine; they are amazingly free of debris. Walls of glazed tile and brick reflect light through the corridors, which are decorated with boards displaying student artwork. Several photo collages of former students line the wall across from the main office. Along one corridor, the walls are covered by large painted murals depicting figures and backdrops from stage musicals such as *Oliver Twist*.

At precisely 11:30 each morning, students line up outside the cafeteria doors before they pour into the large, bright, clean room with tall ceilings and bright lights overhead. Clear rules and a strong teacher presence keep lunch in the cafeteria organized and under control. The room buzzes with hundreds of conversations, but it remains orderly as students patiently line up for food or sit at their tables eating and chatting. Teachers stand throughout the room, their firm yet warm presence helping to maintain order and ensuring that students dispose of their trash properly.

In the cafeteria, we find that students segregate not only by race and ethnicity, but also by gender. Asian students tend to cluster with other Asians, while white students cluster together. In both groups, girls and boys tend to sit separately from one another. One table might have only Asian boys, another only white girls.

On the second floor, above the cafeteria, is the school's library, called the "media center." Low bookcases define different spaces within the bright, inviting room. Books fill the shelves, colorful educational material lines the walls, and there are a couple of TV monitors on wheeled stands. In the middle of the room is a cluster of rectangular and circular tables surrounded by low metal chairs with smooth glazed seats. The school's staff of approximately fifty teachers and staff can fit quite comfortably around the tables in the center space; indeed, we were asked to give a presentation about our project to the staff here. The media center is a colorful, comfortable, and welcoming space used by staff and students alike.

Across the hall from the media center is a smaller classroom filled with computers. About ten brand-new iMac computers with green translucent covers sit on desks around the edges of the room. In our visits to the school the previous year, we had seen ESL students learn to use computers in this space under the direction of a young math teacher, Julie Masseratti. Using grant money she had been awarded, the teacher helped the mostly Asian students learn not only to navigate pull-down menus and save and edit word-processing files, but also to create their own on-screen scrapbooks of photos and text illustrating different aspects of their identity. Masseratti would walk around the room, offering gentle support and encouragement to the contemplative students busy writing at their stations. These immigrant students wrote creative pieces about their best friends in China, their favorite activities in the United States, how they felt about their families, and their feelings about their new country and their native countries. Masseratti's goal was to offer limited-English students another form of self-expression while teaching them basic computer skills; the project was a great success.

On a frigid yet sunny day in early winter, we entered an art class in a room on the second floor of the school where a number of our student participants were working. The walls were decorated with posters, artwork, and reproductions of famous paintings. The room was clean and organized, and a radio played soft music in the background. Some twenty students worked quietly and autonomously on their drawings. Everyone appeared deeply engaged in the work. Once in a while, students looked up to ask a question or chat softly. The art teacher greeted us warmly and walked around the tables, giving thoughtful suggestions and encouraging each student. Her demeanor was kind yet authoritative: this was a woman in total control of her class. At one point, she called the students' attention to the front of the room and reviewed different genres and styles of art that spanned several different eras and cultures. One by one, she described how each student's drawing reflected some of these significant genres and themes. This teacher was able to engage her students both in producing their own artwork and in thinking about broader artistic themes. She made thoughtful connections between her students' works and master works, thus elevating her students' efforts and achievements. We observed how comfortable many of the Asian immigrant students seemed to be in this class. It was a place where speaking English was not always necessary, where the students could express their talents and receive praise.

The principal, Maria Bonaso, is a no-nonsense granddaughter of Italian immigrants who worships at the altar of education. She has a clear sense of her mission—"student learning and engagement" is her mantra, one she used in nearly every exchange we had with her, formal and informal. This small but powerful woman seems to be everywhere at once. During class transitions, she is in the hallways, telling students to walk or tuck in their shirts, or wishing them good luck on a test. During lunch periods, she is in the cafeteria. When we wish to speak with her, we have to schedule appointments, and as time goes by, we learn that it is best to catch her while she is walking around the halls. We often saw Mrs. Bonaso standing in the middle of a hallway before a line of teachers waiting to speak with her: she made herself available to teachers and students alike. She is warm, firm, and utterly in control.

At the end of one school day, we watched as Mrs. Bonaso stood outside, shepherding students toward the buses that had pulled up by the school's entrance. Mrs. Bonaso waved to a bus driver; the next moment, she told a bunch of rowdy students to watch their language; and in the next, she rolled her eyes and shot a fleeting smile at a passing teacher. We tried asking her a question, but suddenly she darted across the schoolyard, intent on picking up trash. All the while, she called out to loitering students, telling them it was time to go home.

With never a moment to spare, Mrs. Bonaso makes it her business to know exactly what is going on in her school. A hands-on administrator and focused leader, she is curious about current research and thoughtful about new initiatives outside the school. She expressed generous support for our research project, and early on invited us to present it to the teachers and staff.

If its principal sets Putnam Middle School's intellectual agenda and climate, the school's bilingual counselor, Cindy Cheng, shapes the immigrant students' emotional lives. Ms. Cheng is the principal's right-hand woman; the two have now worked together for eleven years. Ms. Cheng is herself an immigrant: she was a schoolteacher in Hong Kong before coming to the United States. When she first started working at Putnam she was a bilingual education teacher, but eventually she became the guidance counselor for most of the school's foreign-language and immigrant students. Today she is a major figure in the school. She is one of three guidance counselors on staff, and the only one who speaks Chinese in a school where 20 percent of the student body is of Asian descent. In five elementary schools across the city, she assists parents with their concerns and counsels Asian students who have limited English-language proficiency.

Because she is such a key person, Ms. Cheng has her own office on the first floor of the building. It is decorated with photos of current and former students, thank-you and Valentine's Day cards, and handwritten or photocopied inspirational phrases, such as "Well-begun is half done" and "It is never too late to learn." A hanging wind chime bears the message: "Love is Gentle, Love is Kind." A list of values is written across a whiteboard, and some of these words are circled: honesty, kindness, friendship, good grades.

Students stop by her office throughout the day. Some ask her to sign a form; others ask her to help straighten out a scheduling problem; still others come by merely because her office is welcoming, a place where Asian students find a kind, gentle adult who talks to them in their own language. Once, when we were in her office, Ms. Cheng called out a hearty hello to two Asian boys as they walked by. When they came in to greet her, she complimented them on their new haircuts. She turned to us and said how "gwei"—good, sweet, and well-behaved—these students are. The boys smiled. She noticed that one of the boys, a recent immigrant from Vietnam, had very chapped lips. Concerned, she asked if he had any lip balm. Speaking no English and only a little Cantonese, he shyly nodded yes; she patted him on the shoulder and sent the two off. No small detail seems to escape Ms. Cheng's kind attention.

When Ms. Cheng is in her office, she usually is catching up on administrative work, speaking with parents on the telephone, or counseling students who have come by to look for her. Occasionally she meets with Asian parents who come in with various concerns. But more often we found her in the hallways, moving from one classroom to another, surrounded by Asian students. She meets with the school's ESL teachers each week and monitors student performance. She mentors the new Chinese-speaking ESL teacher, offering advice and helping with assignments. She believes that the Chinese students should maintain their written Chinese language as they are learning English. She encourages the new Chinese ESL teacher to have the Chinese students keep a journal in Chinese. The new teacher cannot read or write Chinese, so she took it upon herself to read, correct, and write comments on the students' journal entries.

Because Ms. Cheng is conscientious and capable, the principal asks her to help with larger administrative tasks. Following the administration of the eighth-grade state standardized testing, both Mrs. Bonaso and Ms. Cheng were occupied with collecting and reviewing student answer sheets. They examined hundreds of student test booklets to ensure that basic identification information had been entered correctly.

Ms. Cheng works long hours, often well past regular school hours. One afternoon, she explained modestly that she is one of the first to arrive at the school each day and one of the last to leave. Parents have often asked her if she would tutor their children privately in English; she said that because she has to set some limits on her working hours, she has declined these requests. She does make herself available, however, to tutor students who are willing to come to school before classes begin.

Ms. Cheng also extends herself to help parents who have difficulty understanding or conducting personal affairs in English. Once she accompanied a new immigrant couple by subway to a downtown government office to assist them with their Social Security papers. In addition, we learned that Ms. Cheng plays a leading role in Asian student affairs throughout the city. Whenever Asian students get into fights or there is an issue involving Asian students, she is called in to help translate, interpret, and mediate.

Both inside and outside school, Ms. Cheng concerns herself with the moral and character development of her immigrant students and worries that they are subject to unhealthy cultural influences. She notes how many students remain unsupervised when they go home from school because most of their parents work long hours in restaurants, factories, or hotels in the city. Knowing that students watch a great deal of TV and have access to a wide range of information from the internet, she often lends students videotapes containing what she believes are more wholesome messages. These tapes include *The Sound of Music,* as well as Chinese-language dramas that focus on the importance of family relationships. A self-described Christian, Ms. Cheng attends church regularly and once organized a trip for Chinese students and parents to watch a play at the nearby Christian college.

At Putnam, the students range in age from eleven to fourteen. While some claim to be dating or are seen flirting, most look awkward with or act uninterested in members of the opposite sex. Chinese girls seek each other out in the hallways or congregate in the cafeteria, speaking Cantonese. Boys, too, sit and talk with each other in Chinese—sometimes alternating among the more widely spoken Cantonese and other dialects such as Fukienese or Taisanese. Only those Asian students who have lived in the United States for many years or who take mainstream classes seem to have interactions with the white students in the school. On a day we visited, two Asian girls who were not taking ESL classes sat with a group of white girls in the cafeteria. The Asian girls and their white counterparts dressed and spoke alike. They talked about pop stars and sat at the opposite end of the table from several ESL girls who discussed what they would wear for their school choir concert that evening.

Ms. Cheng told us that while the school has its racial tensions, they are subdued. Bullying is an occasional problem however, with white American students aggressively accosting Asian students. She noted that white students complain about Asian students who speak in their native languages; the white students fear that the Asians are saying bad things about them. Ms. Cheng also noted the tensions among ESL students from different countries. For example, some Albanian students become irritated and resentful when Chinese students speak to each other in a language that other ESL students cannot understand. Some Chinese students have also complained, asking Vietnamese students not to speak in Vietnamese.

New students from overseas who enter the school district attend a city-wide registration session, held every Monday and Thursday at the district's pupil personnel service office. There they take tests that assess their English proficiency. Those assessed as having limited English proficiency are assigned to schools with ESL classes to serve them. Putnam Middle School is the only one of four junior high schools in the city with an ESL program.

At Putnam, ESL classes are divided into three levels: basic, intermediate, and advanced. When a new student arrives, Ms. Cheng studies the results of the English proficiency test and information about the student's background. She assembles the student's schedule, provides the student with a school orientation, introduces the student to his or her teachers, and holds an initial meeting with the parents. Throughout the year, the three ESL teachers and Ms. Cheng meet weekly to discuss individual students' progress and to decide whether to move specific students into more advanced

ESL or mainstream classes. Such moves usually occur after report cards are issued. At the end of each year, students take an English proficiency test that helps teachers gauge their progress.

Asian parents typically want their children moved into regular education classes as soon as possible, Ms. Cheng said. Some of the more assertive parents insist that their children be moved into regular classes immediately, even if their English is limited. Many parents know little English themselves and want their children to help the family by learning English as quickly as they can. To ensure that their children maintain fluency in Chinese, many parents send their children to Chinese schools on the weekends.

Ms. Cheng noted that some students, including some who were born in the United States, spend years in ESL classes. Many teachers have questioned this practice and blame the ESL program for fostering it, fearing that students will become dependent on their native languages and escape learning English. Ms. Cheng said that many of these children live in households and communities in which only Chinese is spoken. They have little exposure to English outside school; with little chance to practice outside the classroom, they make little progress. Most students want to leave the ESL program as soon as possible, she said. Those who stay longer than three years tend to feel "no good" about their schoolwork; only "lazy students" want to linger in the program because it is easier, she said.

Much of classroom ethos depends on teacher character and style. At Putnam, Chinese students in the beginning ESL class were often talkative and inattentive, sometimes rude. These students may have felt emboldened because they knew that the teacher understood Chinese and because Chinese students were a majority in the class. Others may have acted up because the teacher was new—fresh out of college and unsure of herself.

In a mainstream social studies class with a majority of white students, an older white male teacher stood at the front of the room, commenting on a video about ships. The white American students ignored the teacher's questions, making rude comments and turning their backs to him. Two Asian girls read at their desks, paying no attention to the video, while three Asian boys chatted quietly in a corner. One white girl read a novel, while another emptied the contents of her purse on her chair before slowly putting each item back, one by one. Ms. Cheng told us that this teacher often evaded real instruction by showing videos, which bored the students. The day we sat in his class, he appeared unconcerned or oblivious to the students' inattention or to their facetious replies to his questions.

Yet in other classes, students were fully engaged and absorbed. In a reading class, a young white teacher filled the class period with participatory and collaborative activities. She began with a few minutes of free writing while classical music played from a radio in the corner. She used an ingenious strategy to help develop attention and respect in the classroom. She would ask a question about the week's reading, then throw a fuzzy ball to whoever raised a hand. It was a rule that the rest of the class gave its full attention to whoever held the ball. She followed the question-and-answer period with short, competitive activities in which student teams took turns challenging each other to define vocabulary words. The class ended with a small-group activity during which groups worked together to prepare a skit on the book they were reading that they would perform for the rest of the class. The class generally was characterized by respectful and thoughtful interchanges between the teacher and the students.

Other teachers were also able to manage the students and gain their affection and respect. The same students who were loud and unruly in the beginning ESL class were obedient and attentive in the ESL tutor's class. This tutor was a middle-aged white woman with a kind but firm manner. Only those students who appeared to need the most help with their English were pulled out of their ESL classes to attend sessions with the tutor. She typically gave the class simple, entry-level worksheets with pictures of basic terms, such as items found in the house or in nature. She would ask the students to color the objects according to different criteria: yellow for objects that began with an "h," blue for objects that began with a "p," and so on. Students talked quietly to each other in their native languages to find the right answers or to exchange crayons. Strolling around the tables and attending to students' hesitant English, she maintained an engaged, quiet, and relaxed atmosphere in the class.

Another teacher who was able to keep her students' attention was the young, white, advanced-ESL teacher. She appeared to be in her thirties and led her class with the firm manner of a sports coach, as well as with a warm sense of humor. Like the young reading teacher, this teacher filled her classes with a mix of writing, drawing, and discussion exercises to keep the students engaged. During one class, she showed a short video of a musical reenactment of the signing of the U.S. Declaration of Independence.

Joking with the class about the silliness of the songs, she followed the video with a serious question-and-answer session about the historical figures and activities surrounding that event. Like the reading teacher, she had high expectations for her students and expected them to hand in their homework on time.

Putnam has support groups and programs that promote student achievement and social development. These include a morning homework center, a peer-mediation program that teaches conflict-resolution skills, and a program called "Making it in Putnam," which aims to promote students' self-esteem, attendance, and achievement. A student organization called Alliance against Racism, whose colorful banner hangs in the central hub of the building, meets weekly with staff advisers to discuss issues of racism and violence. The school sponsors an International Week that celebrates its diversity.

With grant funding, the school offers tutoring for state-mandated tests both after school and on Saturdays. Another grant-funded program offers computer classes for teachers in partnership with a nearby college. The school also works with the local YMCA to provide extracurricular programs for students, such as street hockey, babysitting courses, and "Mountain Movers," which takes students on Saturday bike trips into the hills nearby. A glance at one of the school's brochures reveals other school partnerships. One program focuses on teaching about the New England coastline; another brings seventh-grade students to an Outward Bound camp experience on the shore. A partnership with the local newspaper allows students to learn about journalism and newspaper production, and a collaboration with the local police department teaches students about the dangers of drugs.

Extracurricular life at Putnam is rich and varied. Listed among the school's club activities are a language club, a nature club, the student council, the school yearbook, and a literary magazine. The main office displays recent issues of the magazine, which has won awards and national recognition from teacher groups. Other activities include the school chorus, band, a drama program, and a dance ensemble. School sports include soccer, swimming, wrestling, volleyball, basketball, and track and field.

A recent policy change that Cindy Cheng tells us has troubled Putnam's faculty is the institution of the controversial new statewide test. Results from the spring 1999 test showed that the school performed very close to average levels across the state.[29] Most teachers in the school say that preparation for the eighth-grade test gobbles up valuable class time. Moreover, the test worries Ms. Cheng. She fears that many of her immigrant students will fail the exam because their English skills are still at basic levels.[30] Both she and the principal fear that low scores among ESL students will affect the students and the school. As it turns out, 67 percent of the students performed at or above proficiency on the high-stakes English language arts test. This is a considerably higher rate than most of the schools in which we conducted research.

Over the course of our ethnographic work at Putnam, we watched the school adapt to the growing influx of Asian immigrant students. This change is occurring at a majority white school where students have expressed unease with foreign languages and cultures. Despite tensions, the school allows students to express their different backgrounds and encourages them to learn from each other's diversity. This approach is apparent between classes and during each lunch hour, when students in the hallways or cafeteria freely speak in a variety of languages. It is also apparent through school-sponsored events like International Week, when students bring in food from their native lands and put on performances that share elements of their cultures.

The school administration has carefully built a well-structured and functioning school environment by establishing and enforcing a climate aimed at promoting learning. The school's dominant narrative is student engagement, and most teachers, staff, and students seem to have internalized the idea. Engagement, learning, and school achievements are ritually celebrated in public events, classrooms, and hallways. The principal plays a visible role in enforcing clear rules, and many of the school's teachers follow her lead. Within individual classrooms, students receive quality instruction using multiple teaching and learning strategies. With an active and attentive school administration, the school as a whole challenges most of its students to grow both socially and academically.

For immigrant students, who face some of the greatest challenges, the school provides valuable support. Three ESL teachers in a structured ESL sequence help students learn both the English language and American culture, while Cindy Cheng is an ever-present source of kind help and sure guidance to students, teachers, and parents. In the end, too, the students have each other. The school has welcomed so many Asian immigrant children that most can find friends who share the same background and language. Chinese immigrant students who face difficulties with English or with schoolwork have a good chance of finding ethnic peers with whom they can communicate easily and who share the experiences of adjusting to life in a new country.

Monroe High School

"Monroe" is one of Boston's most historic neighborhoods. Originally settled in the 1620s, Monroe was incorporated into Boston in 1874. Situated on a small peninsula between two important rivers, its citizens figured prominently in the making of early colonial America. The attractive architecture of this historic neighborhood includes Federal, Greek Revival, and Queen Anne styles. During World War II, its navy yard employed 50,000 workers.

At the end of the nineteenth century, Irish workers escaping the potato famine of the 1840s settled in Monroe in large numbers, driving the earlier English Protestant settlers to the suburbs. Today, a "townie" identity still dominates the ethos of Monroe. Beyond the original English-Irish tensions, this "townie" identity has been reinforced by the relative isolation of this special peninsula neighborhood from the greater city. It is not uncommon for people from other neighborhoods to believe that Monroe is a separate town altogether.

The neighborhood today is divided into two sections: one is elegant, with many chic restaurants, stylish boutiques, and beautiful old-fashioned streetlights. Its less-graceful section features potholed streets, rundown mom-and-pop grocery stores, and old triple-decker homes with beat-up paint jobs inhabited by a mostly working-class and low-income population. There we find the Monroe Housing Development, one of the first housing developments in the United States and the largest in the city. It has 1,108 public-housing units; to live there, tenants pay approximately 30 percent of their income in rent.

Monroe's Irish have historically had tense relations with black and Italian neighbors in nearby towns. Its homogeneous white population has also been cold to newcomer immigrants of color. According to the 2000 census, Monroe's racial composition is nearly 90 percent white, with residents who have mostly Irish, English, and Italian ancestry. There are very few blacks,

Asians, or Hispanics. In fact, in 1988, the city's housing authority began to desegregate the developments by assigning more blacks to Monroe's housing development, but the locals resisted. In 1996, the U.S. attorney filed a civil action suit against the housing authority for failing to investigate, protect, and take action to solve discrimination and harassment against thirteen tenants from Trinidad, Haiti, Nigeria, and St. Thomas, and others who were Latino and African American. The tenants complained that their white neighbors had harassed them with racist graffiti, physical violence, threats of physical violence, and destruction of property. Racial tensions are common throughout Monroe.

Monroe High School sits right next to the huge housing development. It is an imposing five-story building with the capacity to hold 1,230 students. The school was restructured in the 1990s but was on probation for three years, until early 1999, when it was fully reaccredited. As the principal explained to us, the school is divided into the Upper School and the Lower School. The Lower School (ninth and tenth grades), comprising four "units," is independent and can set its own academic emphasis and schedule. The Upper School (eleventh and twelfth grades) consists of school-to-career pathways, such as communication technology, law and justice, finance and economics, and conference and events planning, in addition to the core courses. Today, the school is 41 percent black, 30 percent Latino, 20 percent Asian, and 9 percent white. Sixty percent of the students qualify for free or reduced school lunch, and 50 percent of the students come from homes where English is not the first language. Eighty percent fail the annual high-stakes state test of English language arts. Only a small percentage go on to four-year colleges.

A large, litter-strewn ramp leading to the main door dominates the entrance. Just inside, someone is stationed at a small desk, but does not seem especially interested in either welcoming visitors or challenging them. We often observed the ostensible monitor reading a newspaper, talking on the phone, or listening to sports on the radio. As often as not, we walked right past the desk and directly into the classrooms without anyone greeting us, requesting identification, or asking about the nature of our visit.

On our first few visits, we find the secretaries in the main office rude. They make us wait, sometimes for entire class periods, before considering our request for directions or helping us make an appointment with the principal. As they get to know us, they warm up, but we cannot help wondering how parents must feel about this reception when they first come to the school.

The hallways have no student artwork hanging on the walls, no decorations celebrating student achievements, no references to athletics or special events. The walls are bare, save for some barely painted-over graffiti that reads "Fuck you." We find our way to one of the two stairwells, which is littered with trash. Students who are skipping class, usually in groups of two or three, congregate on the stairs to hang out—and to deal drugs, drink, and gamble.

Across the street, connected to the main building by an elevated pedestrian bridge, are a modern auditorium and the school's gymnasium. The athletic facility is well kept, with a roofed basketball court, two volleyball courts, a pool, and a large outdoor football field. Sports are a priority at Monroe; students, we are told by a proud coach, often choose the school for its renowned teams. A Dominican student explains that he chose the school because he wanted to play professional baseball. The courts are the only place in the school where we see students of all races and nationalities, immigrant and native-born alike, come together amicably.

The library, in the main building, is organized and well maintained. It boasts a large collection of English books, but books in other languages are conspicuous by their absence. The librarian says that although she asked the bilingual teachers to choose Spanish and Chinese books for the library collection, they did not respond. The principal tells us that the school's budget for books is minuscule. Moreover, he says, 85 percent of the books in the library have never been checked out. Students visit the library primarily to use the computers; once in a while, we see students studying there. Part of the reason the library is so rarely used may be its irregular hours: it doubles as a classroom and opens only when classes are scheduled there.

The school cafeteria is big and, unlike the rest of the school, clean. During lunch, teachers attempt to maintain order by shouting at their charges. Teachers and staff eat in their own space—a small room next door to the cafeteria where they can escape from students.

We dread going into the bathrooms. The odor is overwhelming. The stalls rarely have toilet paper; soap is a luxury. We learn to bring our own paper and soap when we visit. Because bathrooms are regularly the site of drug dealing and fighting, they are under surveillance.

We rarely see the principal, David Lee, interacting informally with students. He comes across as remote, cold, and brusque. Students complain that he does not know them, that he screams a lot, and that he is careless and arbitrary with discipline. One Dominican student confides that he has no respect for Mr. Lee, explaining, "He doesn't even remember the names of students who he has disciplined." In one case, we're told, Mr. Lee forgot that he was going to suspend a student and passed her without comment in the hall the very next day.

The immigrant students avoid the ineffectual Mr. Lee but are drawn to the competent and caring Monica Sandrini, a young Dominican woman and a proud recent graduate of a nearby Ivy League school. As the school's only Spanish bilingual counselor, she was overworked the instant she started working at the school, but she has become an important source of emotional support for the many immigrant students who gravitate to her. She remains highly invested in their emotional and academic well-being. Before Miss Sandrini joined the staff, we saw no signs of basic supportive services for immigrant students, such as bilingual tutoring services or preparation for TOEFL, the Test of English as a Foreign Language that nonnative speakers must take as part of their college applications. Eventually she organized and ran an after-school program that tutored immigrant students. Two of the students in our study named her as one of the most important people in their lives. She even helped one of our participants find housing. Soon word got out among many of the white mainstream students, too, that she was the person to go to for real help: many who had been assigned other guidance counselors went to Miss Sandrini for help with their college applications.

RACIAL AND ETHNIC TENSIONS

Early efforts to desegregate the city's schools sparked fierce battles, most famously in Monroe. The city's desegregation was implemented in two phases, though these efforts did not affect Monroe High until phase 2 began in 1975. With strong opposition to "forced busing," the community banded together through its local committee on education to voice—and act on—its disagreement with the desegregation order. While not all residents shared the antibusing sentiment, most did. Protesters took to the streets, and tension grew between outsiders imposing the ruling and the community. In anticipation of violent outbreaks on the first day of busing, a convoy of police officers followed the school bus, filled mostly with black children, to the school. Those images flashed around the country, leaving indelible marks on the city's, and particularly Monroe's, image and identity.

Soon after, white residents who could afford to moved to other towns or enrolled their children in more expensive, often Catholic, private schools. But even before busing, teachers and staff had believed that Monroe High drew the town's weakest students. Busing, many teachers told us, only aggravated the situation.

At Monroe High today, whites, blacks, Latinos, and Asians occupy separate social spaces. Immigrant students, mostly Latinos and Chinese, are relegated to the bilingual program. Decades-old patterns of distrust and mutual disdain continue. Tension and disrespect permeate the school environment. At best, students from different groups pointedly avoid each another. Daily, we hear taunting and racial epithets and see pushing and bullying. Fighting and threats of violence are ever-present. Only on the school's sports teams do students from different groups work together congenially.

Administrators barely address these overt tensions, denying that racially motivated fights occur with any frequency. We see no systematic attempts to deal constructively with the violence and noted several incidents of bullying that adult bystanders simply ignored. According to one white teacher who is seemingly oblivious to the evident tensions, "This generation of children is used to being together."

The bilingual teachers and counselors are more attuned to the school's complex racial dynamics. A counselor explains that white students, who over the years have been outnumbered by minority students, tend to hang out together. A bilingual teacher notes: "The white kids have a feeling of privilege and entitlement, like how they walk around the hallways. They have their own little space in the corridors and they walk like they are the kings. But the real power is in the black kids." Another bilingual teacher sums it up this way: "There is a clear and visible racial divide among students, whereby blacks and Latinos, Asians, and whites hang out separately. Even when there are not violent outbreaks, there is clear separation and mistrust."

The forbidding racial dynamics adversely affect students who have friends from different ethnic backgrounds. A Dominican student tells us that her Latina friends pick on her because she hangs out with the black girls. A white student says that having a Latino boyfriend led to tension with her friends. Several students explain to us that Puerto Ricans and Dominicans do not get along, because Puerto Ricans, who tend to be lighter-skinned, "think they are better." As a Dominican student tells us, relationships are "awful between *Boricuas* [Puerto Ricans] and Dominicans. My Dominican friends talk about the Puerto Ricans, and don't like me being friends with them." This student describes the divide between Dominicans and whites: "Some white students are very racist. They hate Dominicans, and Dominicans do not get along with whites."

FEAR AS THE DOMINANT ETHOS

Personal safety is a theme of conversations with students and staff alike. All define their school experience around the fear of violence: when to be afraid (going to and from school), how to cope with fear (always walk in groups), where it is safe (bilingual classrooms), and where it is especially dangerous (the stairways). A parent volunteer notes, "Students disrespect each other and many of the teachers and staff members, and [I have seen] students screaming and hitting at each other and calling each other derogatory names." Pushing, shoving, and punching are routine in the hallways, the stairways, and on the way to and from school. Weapons are not uncommon.

On a cold February afternoon in 1999, one Vietnamese student stabbed another. It happened the day of the school's Valentine's Dance, on the eve of a school vacation. In a pattern that we came to associate with the management of violence at Monroe High, the school dance was abruptly cancelled. Students were told that the disc jockey had pulled out at the last minute. Instead of initiating a dialogue about the trauma and consequences of this horrific incident of school violence, the administration chose instead to dissemble. The students, of course, knew very well what had really happened and were outraged by the administration's lie.

One afternoon, walking down the stairways, we witnessed a fight involving two African American girls and two Latina girls. The girls were hitting, punching, and kicking one another, surrounded by a shrieking crowd. A teacher standing a few steps away reacted by screaming, "That's enough!" When the fighting continued, the teacher approached the group, still screaming, "That's enough!" The fighting stopped, and the group drifted down the stairway as though nothing had happened. The teacher, too, walked away. There was no discussion. There were no consequences.

During our interviews, the boys in particular commented on the tension between the blacks in the mainstream courses and the Latinos in the bilingual program. Fourteen-year-old Leonardo, a Central American immigrant, said the constant conflict between blacks and Hispanics made him feel unsafe. Another student explained that the *tigradas* (a Dominican term for fights) in the stairways worried him. He added, "This year more than last year because more blacks have entered [the school]."

Girls, too, worried about the racial tensions. Thirteen-year-old Norma, from the Dominican Republic, said, "I think the blacks are racist with the Latinos . . . they used to scream at me and tell me ugly things." Another student, twelve-year-old Stefany, described the following incident: "A few weeks ago during gym class, a friend of mine from the bilingual program slapped a girl from the regular program because they were talking badly about them. Regular students want us to speak English, and we tell them to learn Spanish. Those kids, the only thing they know in Spanish are bad words and they say them to get into fights. But one has to ignore them." In general, though, girls were less likely than boys to report feeling besieged. As a twelve-year-old Dominican girl said, "It is safer for me because it's boys who want trouble and get into trouble."

Another source of anxiety at Monroe High is the fire-alarm system. Not long after September 11, 2001, when tensions were running high, a cherry bomb exploded, and in an orchestrated prank, three different fire alarms sounded simultaneously, causing chaos throughout the building. From then on, teachers were posted in the hallways, sometimes trying to conduct their classes while keeping an eye on the alarms, sometimes meeting or doing their prep work. After the prank, there were always three or four school guards walking the halls, moving the students between classes, and following them up and down the stairs. In spite of the new surveillance, we still saw students cutting classes, wandering in the halls, and hiding from adults in the stairwells.

Students said that vandalism sometimes triggered racial tension. A Central American student complained that Latino students were always blamed: "One day someone set a fire in the stairway between the fourth and the fifth floor. Everything could have blown up. They blamed us [Latinos], even though we were on a field trip and did not do it. They blamed the

Hispanic students because they found a Goya can [Goya is a brand sometimes associated with Latinos]."

Increased surveillance made the students feel safer, but also oppressed. As a fourteen-year-old Dominican student confided: "It's more safe now. There's a lot of police now. It's good . . . but it's also annoying because you can't play or anything. They've become too serious, always watching over you." At first, interactions between students and the new guards were surprisingly relaxed. Students approached guards in a spontaneous, friendly manner, seeming respectful and appreciative. Over time, however, the guards' constant presence elicited other feelings. "It feels like a jail in here," one student said during the last year of the study. A parent volunteer added, "The students feel they are always being watched, as if they are ready to commit crimes—so much so that many students simply want to get out of there."

Fear and violence followed the students home from school. Many said they felt especially vulnerable on their way home, when drinking, drugs, beatings, and robberies were common. A staff member shared her concerns about a fight that was supposed to take place between two rival gangs after school one day, an event she was anxiously trying to avert. Though individual teachers sometimes tried to get involved, we were struck by a culture of administrative silence regarding violence in and out of school. As a thirteen-year-old Dominican student said with resignation in her voice: "De eso no se habla" (We don't talk about that).

BILINGUAL PROGRAMS

Relations between the bilingual and mainstream teachers and administrators are another source of division at Monroe High. While bilingual teachers often feel irrelevant to the school's larger mission, mainstream teachers tend to see them as sheltered and overindulged, with special privileges that include smaller student-to-teacher ratios. As in many of the other schools in which we conducted fieldwork, the bilingual staff describe the Latino and Asian teachers as "warmer" and "more caring" toward immigrant students, while characterizing mainstream teachers as "cold, harsh, and tense." Over the years, and not just at Monroe High, we often saw Latino immigrant students greet teachers with kisses and hugs, whereas with mainstream white teachers, they were more formal and distant. The language barrier and different interpersonal styles seem to hamper relationships between mainstream teachers and staff and the immigrant students. One bilingual teacher, for example, felt that the white cafeteria workers were impatient and rude when immigrant students had trouble understanding them.

The school has had a well-established Chinese bilingual program since 1979 and a Spanish bilingual program since 1981. It offers literacy classes aimed at those newly arrived students who come with limited schooling. In the literacy classrooms, basic reading and writing skills are taught in English.

Over the years of our study, the structure and personnel in Monroe High's bilingual program changed. During our third year of fieldwork, the bilingual faculty consisted of two counselors (one Latino and one Chinese), seven ESL teachers, six Chinese teachers, and five Spanish-speaking bilingual teachers, along with one Spanish bilingual aide. The director of the bilingual program was a Chinese woman. By 2000, there were 115 Spanish and two hundred Chinese-speaking students. The Chinese group had an almost equal mix of Cantonese and Mandarin speakers. The bilingual program had four levels, ESL I (for students with the lowest level of proficiency) to ESL IV (for students with the greatest competence). Placement depended on the score on a language proficiency exam, and students were expected to move out of the bilingual program in three years.

Though the bilingual program prided itself on offering electives that mingle bilingual and mainstream students, those electives were open only to students in the top two levels. Students at lower levels were assigned additional ESL skill classes, leaving no room in their schedules for electives. Sports remained the only activity that routinely brought bilingual and mainstream students together. During the 1998–1999 school year, there were fourteen immigrant students on the soccer team, seven on the volleyball team, three on the swim team, and nine on the softball/baseball team.

The bilingual teachers told us that they received far less attention and fewer resources than the rest of the school. They reported that their program was marginalized, their students rendered invisible, and that they rarely met with the mainstream teachers. The head of the bilingual program used the word "ghetto" to describe the bilingual program and regularly cited what she considered evidence of second-class citizenship. When the position of the beloved bilingual counselor, Monica Sandrini, who so tirelessly and effectively advocated for her students, was cut for budgetary reasons, the staff saw the move as yet another indication of the administration's lack of support for its growing numbers of immigrant students.

Monroe High School is characterized by raw contradictions. Despite its violence, barren walls, and filthy stairways, many students choose to attend because of its celebrated athletic program. It is a school in which academics are defined by the pressures of statewide testing, a place where few strive for scholastic excellence and where few adults seem to care about learning or mentoring. The bilingual program is the school's only refuge for newly arrived students, a place where students feel nurtured—where teachers advocate for them, and where, at least for a while, they have a skilled and loving counselor to look up to. Yet in another paradox, the cozy bilingual program offers academic rigor and leads to educational excellence for only a few of the Spanish-speaking students. The lack of a strong curriculum, and the struggle students face when they move out of the bilingual program, place many students at a high risk for eventual academic failure.

In this environment of squandered opportunities, however, immigrant students at Monroe who are not in the bilingual program may be at an even greater risk for academic failure and further social isolation.

Reade High School

Reade High School lies in a small city in Massachusetts. With a population of approximately 100,000, this city is home to two prestigious universities and two smaller colleges. Its residents are a combination of "town and gown" folk: many are academics in the universities, colleges, and research centers that abound in the area, while others have jobs that support the academic enterprise: janitors, clerical staff, and so on.

Reade became a single school in the 1970s upon the merger of two older schools, a vocational school and a classics-based high school founded in 1648. It is the only public high school in the city and serves slightly fewer than two thousand students. The student body, like the city, is diverse in class and race. The student population is 35.9 percent white, 41.7 percent African American (including foreign-born black, many of whom are Haitian), 14.4 percent Latino (many of them immigrants), and 7 percent Asian (again, many of whom are immigrants). About 22 percent of the students are classified as having limited English proficiency.

The school comprises two large buildings joined by a glass passageway. In the front is a large lawn that is shared by the municipal library next door. In the spring, we find students of many nationalities playing softball, Frisbee, and soccer there. In contrast to the library's colonial aesthetic, the high school's architecture is distinctly modern. There is a welcome sign at the entrance, next to a bulletin board listing upcoming trips, lectures, plays, and concerts. Entering the building, we are greeted by student art projects and photographs from recent field trips, carefully displayed in glass cases along the walls. The hallways are clean and the building is well maintained.

The main office buzzes with activity. The three secretaries, all middle-aged white women, simultaneously answer calls, direct visitors, and dispatch questions and complaints in a blur of voices and motion. The office seems efficient and courteous, if not particularly warm and welcoming.

Rarely is anyone seated at the security desk. The security guards usually walk the halls, chatting with teachers and students and keeping an eye out. Many are friendly, always ready to answer a question or give directions. Some issue directives to the students: "Take off your hat," "Get to class," "Settle down." A couple of the guards have warm relationships with their charges and know not just the students but also their families and the community.

The school cafeteria is spacious, inviting, and fairly quiet even at its busiest, when hundreds of energetic teenagers are chatting, joking, and rushing to get their lunches. Students of all races and many nationalities are, for the most part, friendly with each other and respectful toward the cafeteria employees and the watchful teachers and guards. Students clean up after themselves and leave calmly. During our five years in the school, we never witnessed a scuffle in the cafeteria, though they occasionally erupted in the hallways or in an area immediately outside the school.

The highly diverse student body of Reade generally coexists well. Unlike in many schools we observed, when fights erupt, they tend to be between students of the same racial groups rather than between students from different racial groups. On our visits, we saw a fair amount of what Beverly Daniel Tatum refers to as "Why are all the black kids sitting together in the cafeteria?" behavior, but we also observed a number of mixed-group tables.[31] That is, students often group themselves by interest and shared activities—basketball or drama for example—in addition to the oft-encountered racial segregation found in most schools. Immigrant students, especially the newly arrived, however, tend to keep separate from other students—perhaps in part because they do not fully feel comfortable with their English skills and in part because native-born students clearly have little interest in befriending them.

Many immigrant-origin students who have been in the United States for a number of years, however, do mix comfortably with native-born students. Second-generation Haitian students, for example, tend to dress and talk in ways that make them virtually indistinguishable from African American peers whose parents have been in the country for many generations. They often have friendships with other black students from a variety of backgrounds. The students who seem to have the most social difficulty are those who have not yet assumed a comfortably ethnic and racially hyphenated American identity yet are no longer a part of the "newcomer immigrant" group.

The bathrooms at Reade are clean and well maintained, with soap and toilet paper in good supply. Mirrors are intact, and the walls are free of graffiti, aside from a few romantic proclamations. During class time, the hallways are usually empty, except for the occasional student going to an office.

The school has several computer rooms, each one of which has been reassigned to one of its "houses," which are described later. There is a "writing center" staffed by a language-arts teacher, and most classrooms have computer stations with internet access. Several students and teachers have their own web pages. A technology-proficiency program is being designed; the goal is to make it a requirement for graduation.

The two-story library is large and well lit. The upstairs is reserved for teachers. Computer stations, most in frequent use, take up half of the downstairs space. Students come in during their study periods to work on projects, browse the internet, check e-mail, or simply chat with their friends. There are three full-time librarians and several part-time employees, some of them student aides. Funding for books and software comes from an allotment from the city public school system, grants from various technology companies in the vicinity, and from a discretionary fund managed by the principal. About 10 percent of the books are in languages other than English; in the world literature section, Spanish and French predominate. We see just a handful of books in Portuguese and none in Haitian

Kreyol, though many students speak these languages. "We follow teachers' requests," Janice Klein, the senior librarian, says. "We have catalogs from [Haitian] publishing companies, but we don't know what to buy. There are no requests for Kreyol, not even for a dictionary."

During class time, students need a pass from their teachers to enter the library. After the last period of the day, the library fills with students doing homework, exchanging the day's gossip, and socializing until closing, an hour and a half later. The library staff does not seem to mind, though there is much shushing.

The school has after-school programs in athletics, arts, and cultural interests. For example, several Haitian students in our project belong to the Haitian club, which meets weekly. A Haitian teacher presides over the club, and its board is composed entirely of seniors, most of them second-generation immigrants.

Reade was completely restructured after the first of our five years of fieldwork there. In the culture of the school, everything is divided between the time "before" and the "after" this tumultuous period of restructuring.

"BEFORE"

From 1990 to June 2000, Reade was divided into five smaller learning communities—"schools within schools," referred to as "houses"—each with its own management structure, pedagogy, and curriculum. In freshman year, the students were placed in a house through a Byzantine process of "choice" and "lottery" and took most of their core courses in that house. Although the stated purpose of these separate houses was admirable—to "create smaller communities and respond to the individual needs of students," as an official pamphlet announced—there was a lamentable de facto segregation by race, income, and national origin among the houses. There was also a clear pattern of ability tracking.

The houses were physically separate, which made the school's segregation obvious. Walking from one building to another, or from one floor to another, was like visiting schools in different neighborhoods. In the hallways of the ESL-bilingual house, immigrant students chatted in Spanish, Portuguese, Haitian Kreyol, or Cape Verdean Creole. The floor that housed the "basic skills" house and special-education students was the most austere, least decorated, and most poorly maintained. The "traditional" house looked like what one would expect of an urban high school: a great deal of public space was devoted to athletics; announcements on bulletin boards gave updates on forthcoming games and social events. Most striking was the "alternative" house, founded as a pilot school in the 1960s by an eminent psychologist to reflect his theories of morality. Sitting on the top floor, symbolically the jewel in the crown, it looked more like an art department in a private college than a public high school. Its walls were adorned with student projects on subjects such as science, theater, and community outreach. Students bustled about, working on projects or preparing presentations. Elaborate posters were displayed in a large common area. Students confidently called teachers—many of whom held doctorates from prestigious universities—by their first names. When the house was dismantled as part of the redesign, teachers, students, and parents alike were outraged, concerned, and sad. The alternative house was the only viable public school setting for families who could not afford to send their high-achieving children to one of the many private schools in the area.

Although the dismantling of the system brought much protest and resulted in the demise of a couple of vibrant and well-functioning houses, many teachers and students agreed that the distribution of students and academic achievement had previously been inequitable. Indeed, the number of students failing courses was vastly different among houses. In the alternative house (where 52 percent of the students were white), 21 percent of the students were failing a class each semester. In the basic-skills house (where only 37 percent were white), the failure rate was a whopping 51 percent. Only one of the immigrant students in our study was in the elite alternative house and, although she enjoyed being there, she complained about having little contact with her immigrant friends from other houses. She also recognized that she had much higher standards to meet: "I always have a project to research," she once said. "They"—her friends in other houses—"don't have as much homework."

When immigrant students "placed out" of the ESL-bilingual program into mainstream classes, they literally "crossed over" from one building to another in a sort of mini-migration. This crossing metaphor was not lost on the immigrant students, who looked to the "other side" with apprehension. Many ESL teachers were reluctant to send their immigrant students to the "other side," worrying that they would feel lost in what was seen as a cold and alien mainstream environment. Interestingly, many teachers in the other houses scorned the bilingual program for coddling the students and not allowing them, in the voice of one critic, "to sink or swim."

"AFTER"

The architect of Reade's restructuring, Ellen O'Leary, was controversial from the start. She took over Reade after the well-regarded principal of twenty-five years retired. Coming from the academic world, she had little sense of the school's culture or social structure. Brusque and arrogant, she imposed her redesign soon after her appointment, seeking little input from teachers, staff, parents, or students, and setting out to break up the school's "house" structure as fast as she could. Teachers and parents alike complained that O'Leary was tactless, authoritarian, and "undemocratic." Her decision to freeze out the highly educated parents who had been active in school affairs—many of them professors at local universities—was a strategic disaster. These parents, whose sense of entitlement includes close involvement in decisions affecting their children, were alienated and angry.

Teachers were frustrated that their input was scorned and skeptical that this reform would benefit the students. "The principal has good intentions," a seasoned teacher with a Ph.D. said, "but she will not achieve anything by antagonizing teachers. Our old house was a magnet program for Reade. Parents who can afford it will be taking their kids out and sending them to private schools." There were several heated meetings among parents, teachers, and the principal. Some teachers and administrators quit in protest. Many middle-class parents, as the teacher had predicted, voted with their feet and enrolled their children in prestigious private schools nearby. The top floor, formerly the alternative house, blended into the rest of the school. The energy and creativity that used to emanate from its hallways and classrooms vanished.

The school was now divided into five newly constituted houses, each serving approximately four hundred students, each with its own dean and teaching staff, and each with a cross-section of students of different abilities. In theory, the new houses promised to better integrate the school's highly diverse population. The principal said she hoped the better-prepared and most highly motivated students would raise the standards and increase the engagement of their peers. But the effect of the restructuring on the school's sense of itself seemed superficial. A full year after the transition, the new schools had yet to name themselves. They continued to be called "School 1," "School 2," and so forth.

Before the old system was dismantled, Spanish, Haitian Kreyol, and Portuguese were spoken only in the hallways of the bilingual building. After the restructuring, the school felt more integrated; the sounds of immigrant languages penetrated every corner. But the immigrant students and staff from the bilingual program reported feeling lost in the new system. The abrupt changes had upset the treasured warmth and rhythm of the bilingual-ESL program. Teachers murmured that the system was dismantled precisely to stop bilingual students from connecting with each other and with the bilingual faculty. Their students shared this feeling. "We don't have our own house any more," one Haitian student told us sadly. "It's harder to see the other [bilingual] kids." Students who had been mainstreamed also complained about the change, which made it difficult for them to see their old teachers. Soon, however, students and teachers began finding new ways to recreate their old networks. "We have to make sure we can regroup," an ESL teacher said to us shortly before the end of the school year.

CREATING A SAFE PLACE AND FIGHTING INVISIBILITY

Although Reade is a large urban school, the environment was peaceful, compared with most of the schools we observed. Though fights occasionally broke out, they were rare and quickly resolved. Students seemed happy and well behaved. Regardless of race or class, many students favored the popular "urban hip-hop" look: boys wore baggy pants, oversized jackets, and expensive sneakers; some girls wore fashionable tight pants or short skirts and knee-high boots. The recently arrived immigrants usually looked less flashy, but the newcomers quickly learned to dress, walk, and talk as their American-born classmates did.

While most teachers were white Americans, many in the bilingual programs were immigrants, some European (Greek and Portuguese), and some South American or Haitian. Most of the adolescents we worked with during our sojourn at Reade were in the bilingual program and developed warm, strong relations with many of their teachers. The teachers grew involved with their students' academic and social lives. They considered themselves different from the mainstream teachers and, as mentioned earlier, sometimes kept students in the bilingual program to protect them from the anonymity of the larger school. The teachers who largely worked with immigrant students often told us that they felt that the "real" mandate of the school was to focus on its large middle-class student body and that the immigrant students were generally invisible—an afterthought that only served to add color and spice.

The intentions behind the redesign effort—minimizing inequity and closing the achievement gap—were laudable. Unfortunately, Ellen O'Leary's leadership style alienated most everyone in the school community. She rarely met with students and communicated with the teachers mainly via officious, formal, written announcements and memos. She closed out parents who had considerable social capital and energy. As a result, she was not able to effectively lead her community of students, teachers, and parents to support her redesign efforts. After three years in which much was changed, though seemingly little for the better, Ms. O'Leary left her position as principal.

Relationships between Teachers and Immigrant Students and Their Families

What kinds of relationships exist between newcomer students and their teachers?

Students' View

Every year, through "the sentence completion task," one of our projective methods, we asked our participants to complete the sentence: "Teachers are . . ." These data reveal a very positive attitude toward teachers among newly arrived immigrant youth. Across the five years of the study, nearly three-quarters of the participants completed the sentence with positive answers such as "caring," "helpful," "people who respect others," "smart and understanding," "very nice to me and really helpful to me," and "perfect."

Even so, our students rarely named teachers or an adult at school as someone they would turn to for help (a role measured by what we call the "network of relations card sort task").[32] Only 10 percent of the students named a teacher as someone they would go to for help generally, and a mere 6 percent said they would go to teachers if they had a problem. Only

21 percent named a teacher as someone who respected them and an abysmal 3 percent named a teacher as someone who was proud of them. Surprisingly, especially given the challenges these students face in getting help with homework or accurate information about college access (as we described in Chapter 2), only 13 percent said they would ask teachers for help with homework. Only 28 percent indicated they would ask teachers or an adult at school for help in learning about how to get to college.

Some of our participants complained about the indifference and cultural insensitivity they experienced while interacting with some adults at their schools, including their teachers. Some of them spoke longingly about wanting closer and more understanding relationships with their teachers. Carl, a fourteen-year-old boy from China, reported: "Most of my teachers are quite cold. I wish they would care more about my feelings." Another student, in response to the question "How do teachers and administrators treat most students?" responded: "Not much. Teaching is just a job. Teachers just try to get by day by day and get salary at the end of the month, whether you learn things or not, it's not their business."

Teachers' Perspective on Immigrant Students

By and large, teachers reported liking the immigrant students precisely because they tended to arrive to the United States with behaviors that made classroom management easier.[33] As one teacher put it: "Immigrants have the desire to learn, are more disciplined, and value education." Many other teachers agreed with her:

> In working with immigrant children, you don't have the discipline problems that you would have working in a regular monolingual school, Many of immigrant children come with the cultures and the values of a strong, tight, family, and respect for elders that are taught early. They value education.

> I find that a lot of immigrant students were raised to be very focused on their studies.

> Recent immigrants kids are trying their best. They are aware that their parents have sacrificed a lot. They don't want to let it go to waste.

> Honestly, I'm like, why can't I have a class of only immigrant students? . . . Because if I only had to deal with this, I would be in heaven, because there

are no discipline problems, I have never run into an discipline problem with them. So it's a pleasure.

Teachers often noted that immigrant students were more motivated than native-born peers attending the same school:

> There seems to be a motivation to do well because the [newcomer] student they look at it as an opportunity and they are going to make the most of it, but sometimes students who are second generation, or who are native born, they sometimes are not as motivated . . . So maybe some of the students from here take things for granted. [Immigrant students] look at it as a great opportunity and let's make the most of it, which makes my job easier; they work harder.

> You know, the immigrants, even though they don't have much education, they have such a willingness to learn—such a strong desire to learn.

> The immigrant students are the hungrier ones. They seem to be going for the awards and the academics where some of your mainstream students, or your traditional students, they are just taking their C and fleeing—you know?

Teachers report, however, that as the newcomer students acculturate—as they become more like their native-born peers—their behaviors begin to change for the worse.[34]

> In the beginning, immigrant kids are more respectful, more disciplined because of stricter schools they had in [their] home country. Later, as they become Americanized, which takes between 3 to 4 months to a year, they become unruly, Then they become like the American kids—they lack discipline and [do] things to get attention.

Our ethnographic data highlighted extensive differences between the newcomers and their native-born peers in a multiplicity of ways: from how they dress, to how they walk, to how they sit in classrooms. A perceptive principal mentioned how over they years he had noticed the profound changes especially as his immigrant students moved out of bilingual classrooms and into the monolingual environment. "The new immigrants show up in very formal dress—some of the boys from the Caribbean even wear white starched shirts during their first weeks in school. Everywhere you see them, they are carrying big sacks of books. But over time they get the point. They become more Americanized. They begin by dressing differently—more hip, you see the boys wearing baggy pants and un-tucked shirts, sticking together, imitating each other's every move, and never carrying book packs with them; it is not cool." It does not help, as we saw in the school ethnographies, that the more acculturated peers mercilessly teased newcomer students for any social transgressions.

Dress codes are just the tip of the iceberg of acculturation. As children from the old country come into contact with those from the new, they begin to internalize new behaviors, manners, and attitudes, including negative attitudes toward school and school authorities. Those who worry that the new immigrants are not acculturating should not worry. As in previous generations, immigrant origin youth today do Americanize over time. In the case of attitudes toward school, however, this may be a case of "be careful what you wish for."

How Teachers See Immigrant Parents

While teachers tended to be quite positive about immigrant students, they did not think much of immigrant parents. They tended to see them as uninterested in their children's academic welfare and reported that immigrant parents were often absent and uninvolved, without taking into consideration their difficult work schedules and language barriers. Judgments about immigrant parents were often harsh:

> Part of our problem is that parents don't support their children . . . Even
> just to come to school to check and make sure, you know, if they get a poor
> report card, that they show up, or come even. We have open houses for re-
> port cards. We have 1,200 students, and if we have 100 parents, we think it is
> a good year. So that's what I mean, there isn't that interest there.

Another said: "Education may not be the number one priority in their country but it is here. Sometimes, I get the sense that it is not important to them."

Teachers frequently complained about the low expectations they thought immigrant parents had for their children. With disdain, one confided:

> [The best way for parents to support their children] is for them to be a
> model. You want your children to be educated, you have to educate yourself,
> so your kids can do the same. The best way is to learn English. Many parents

never try to learn the language. In this community, many of the Mexican immigrants are not educated when they come to the United States. For them coming to the U.S. is the goal. Once they get here, it is "mission accomplished" for them. That was their dream to come to the United States but once they get here there are no more dreams. They go from paycheck to paycheck. They do not understand that you have to have goals in order to go places in America.

There is a resounding irony in these views. Children, most would agree, internalize their values—including those about education—largely from their parents. How, then, can we reconcile that recently arrived immigrant students "value education" but their parents do not? These misconceptions seem to be born from a lack of meaningful contact and cultural misunderstanding. The optimism and drive that teachers see in the eyes of their immigrant students is most often the result of enormous parental sacrifices and dreams.

The Importance of Teacher Expectations

Fieldwork places the participant observer into contact with individuals at all levels of the educational hierarchy—from students, parents, and teachers, to janitors, principals, and district superintendents. In one meeting with a superintendent serving a highly diverse district with a large proportion of immigrant-origin students, we asked, "What is the hardest thing about your job?" Without hesitation he responded: "To get the teachers to believe these children can learn." On another occasion, we walked into a conversation in the teacher's lounge in one of the middle schools where the students were predominantly Dominican and Puerto Rican. A teacher was asking her colleagues: "What do they expect me to do with these kids? Within the next few years, most of the girls will be pregnant and the boys are going to be in jail." This comment, met by knowing looks and nodding heads from the three colleagues she was speaking with, was made by a teacher working with fifth graders—ten- and eleven-year-olds.

Rhona Weinstein has beautifully demonstrated how teacher expectancies shape the educational experience and outcomes of their students.[35] She shows that these interactions tend to be manifested in repeated interpersonal exchanges between students and their teachers and other adults in the school—exchanges that corrode self-confidence for those students held in low esteem. Further, these dynamics "are always driven and reinforced by institutional arrangements."[36] She argues that classrooms and schools typically sort students into those who are thought to be talented versus those who are thought to be less so. These expectations are made based on impressions of individual student traits as well as stereotyped beliefs about their backgrounds (for example, "Asian students are smart" or "Latino students are not as bright"). Students who have extensive vocabularies, easily express themselves in the language of instruction, stay focused, work fast, grasp new concepts quickly, and turn in carefully completed homework are viewed as more capable. Students are well aware of the perceptions that teachers have of them. Well-regarded students receive ample positive social mirroring (or reflections and feedback) about their capacity to learn and thus are more likely to redouble their efforts.[37] Students who are found wanting on any combination of these characteristics, however, tend to either become invisible in the classroom or are actively disparaged. Under these circumstances, only the most resilient of students will remain engaged.

We are sometimes asked to reflect on what we want for our students (or indeed our own children). Not surprisingly, as intellectuals, we are biased toward a love of learning, but as realists, too, we also recognize that in order to thrive in the new global economy we all need to be lifelong learners. The optimal educational system, then, should build on children's natural early curiosity. Classrooms and schools that foster cognitive engagement—that is, students who are engaged, curious, and eager to learn—is the standard we have come to look for. But in the schools where we encountered our student study participants, most of the teachers did not seem to have this goal. Only in one case—among the seventy-five teachers we formally interviewed—did a teacher characterize a good student as we would: "Someone who is interested and engages with what is going on . . . and [is] willing to push [herself] to the next level . . . Kids who are curious." Rather, when we asked teachers to define a good student, we found that intellectual curiosity was almost never mentioned. Instead, most teachers' definitions emphasized compliance:

> Attentive in class. Does homework. Asks questions when they need help. Is polite.

> One who follows rules, is punctual, does homework.

My ideal student is just someone who comes to class, is attentive, works hard, tries to do the work, comes prepared with their homework every day.

Do you have your pencil and paper, your books, and dictionary? Did you do your homework?

A good student is someone who comes to class prepared.

Has materials ready to work. Never asks for a pass. Sits in a different way in class than someone who has mentally checked out. Has good attendance. On task all the time. I don't separate behavior from academics.

In fact, we found that whether or not students did homework was a primary marker of how teachers graded them. Amazingly, the strongest correlation between any of our measures and grades was the teacher's report that they regularly completed their homework.[38] Thus, students who did their homework received much better grades than those who did not. Completing homework, however, had little to do with performing well on standardized achievement tests.[39] Hence teachers appeared to be overly reliant on homework as an indicator of whether or not a child was a good student. Moreover, as we noted in Chapter 2, emphasis on homework places immigrant youth at a disadvantage when compared to their middle-class peers; immigrant students are able to draw on far less homework support from their parents and friends than are their more middle-class peers. Hence an overemphasis on homework perpetuates inequities between advantaged and disadvantaged students.

GENDERED EXPECTATIONS

As we demonstrated in Chapter 1, immigrant boys, like boys from other groups, do considerably less well academically than their female peers.[40] Teacher frustrations with boys' behaviors and the related expectations about them, we have come to believe, have much to do with this discrepancy in academic outcomes.[41] During our study, we learned that teachers report that boys were more likely than girls to demonstrate poor or very poor attention in class, whereas girls were more likely than boys to demonstrate good or very good attention.[42] Teachers also reported that boys were more likely than girls to demonstrate poor or very poor motivation and effort, whereas girls were more likely than boys to demonstrate good or very good motivation and effort. Similar patterns were reported for behaviors such as compliance with teacher requests: 13 percent of boys were perceived by the teachers to demonstrate very poor or poor behaviors compared to 9 percent of girls, whereas 61 percent of boys compared to 77 percent of girls were rated as demonstrating good or very good behaviors. Teachers also reported that girls were more likely than boys to demonstrate very good attendance, very good punctuality, and were more likely to complete homework. Boys, however, were more likely to have very poor ratings for each of these dimensions of academic engagement.[43] Overall the teachers perceived the girls in a much more positive light than the boys. One teacher's response summarizes well the general outlook of many of the teachers: "Girls, in general . . . tend to be more willing to buckle down, do their work, get all of their homework in. With boys, lots of times, there is more of a tendency to get distracted, to take as a role some anti-social types of behavior."

As we have emphasized throughout these pages, relationships make a difference in the academic experience of students. Again there is a gendered pattern—boys were more likely to report that they were less engaged than girls in school-based relationships.[44] Our structured student interview data revealed that boys also tended to report more conflict with school administrators and teachers than girls. Boys were more likely than girls to report experiencing or witnessing their male friends' negative interactions with the security guard at school. Boys were also more likely than girls to perceive schools as a "prison." Fifteen-year-old Gonzalo from El Salvador told us: "[At school] I don't like them taking electronic devices [pagers, cell phones] away, it's ridiculous; [our school] is a closed campus . . . They want to put cameras; we're going to be prisoners . . . [It is] not good when security wants to catch you. They are rude and rough with the students. The security often throws you to the ground; not me, but I have seen it."

Leonaldo, a fourteen-year-old Dominican boy, in response to the question "How do teachers and administrators treat most students?" confided: "Bad. One time, a security guard threw my friend to the ground to search him because he saw my friend had a pen knife in his pants pocket. Another example is the teachers who always screaming 'go to class' and threatening you with suspending you from school. They say all these yelling at you. Everything is bad, if you talk, if you listen to music, etc." Similarly, a fourteen-year-old Chinese boy who later dropped out of high school responded to the question "What do you not like about school?": "Of course the security guards. They always stop me and ask me many things, probably because of my appearance."

The interview data also suggested that boys experienced more blatant racism at school than girls. For example, when asked about his feelings toward his school, one Dominican boy told us: "The school environment is fine. The majority of the teachers are friendly, but some never let go of their racism against Hispanics. What I like most is to share with people and to learn. What I like least is the teachers' racism, and that some teachers do not care about the students . . . When I asked a teacher to speak more slowly because I didn't understand much English, he asked me why I had come to the U.S. and told me that if I didn't understand English I should just go back to Santo Domingo."

Similarly, another boy reported: "Sometimes I don't like some of my teachers. One teacher used to call me racial slurs in a joking manner. I used to hate those comments and told him so but he continued doing so. I got picked on by a teacher so much that once I acted like I was going to hit him. I got suspended for eight days for it and he never got even reprimanded."

The immigrant boys in our study were more likely to lack connection with adults in school, and reported more hostile and racist experiences in school. The boys appear to respond to these largely negative interactions with teachers by "checking out" of the academic process.

COLLEGE ACCESS

Most of the students in this study would be the first generation in their families to apply to college. Students whose parents have never gone to college are highly disadvantaged when it comes to playing the "how to get into college" game, because their parents do not know themselves what is required beyond "good grades." Even if an immigrant parent went to a university in another country, the rules of engagement for college entry are very different in the United States.

Further, many recent immigrant students are attending schools where this kind of information is provided in only a limited way. Few of the students attending poor, segregated schools are college bound. College guidance counselors often have absurdly large numbers of students for whom they are responsible. Not surprisingly, many internalize the low expectations of the school settings in which they work and often steer students away from applying. In some cases, they even actively discourage college recruiters from pursuing minority students who are managing to do well despite the school context they are in. During a talk one of us gave at an Ivy League school, an admissions recruiter confided that this kind of thing "happened more often than I can count."

Indeed, our data showed that students were unlikely to turn to teachers, counselors, or other adults at school for advice on getting into college. Only 28 percent said that they had learned about how to prepare for and apply to college from an adult at school. Indeed, very few of the students had accurate information. We asked them to tell us step by step what it takes to go to college, but few were able to articulate the strategies that most middle-class students of college-educated parents know well: "get good grades, take honors and AP classes, do well on the SAT, do lots of extra-curricular activities, get good letters of recommendation, write strong essays." Many of the high school students recognized that good grades were important (93 percent), but very few were able to point to other requirements for entry into a good college. Only 35 percent mentioned the SAT; 16 percent recognized the importance of extracurricular activities; and just 7 percent noted either AP courses, or essays or letters of recommendation.[45]

For many of these students, community colleges or junior colleges become the default strategy for accessing college. Under the best of circumstances, these two-year colleges offer newcomer students the opportunity to overcome their lack of knowledge about how to get into more selective schools. This route also offers the opportunity to strengthen English-language and other academic skills in a setting that costs significantly less than the first two years of private college. Ideally, once these first two years of college are completed, students can transfer to a four-year college. While some do, the transfer rate to four-year colleges is surprisingly low and the drop-out rate for students who pursue this route is appallingly high, especially for students of color (including immigrant-origin students).[46]

Over the years, all too often we have encountered a number of students who undergo a particular challenge as they end high school and try to move on to college. It is estimated that there are approximately 1.8 million children under age eighteen who are undocumented, with approximately 65,000 graduating each year from U.S. high schools.[47] Many of these students—who may have spent much of their lives here, have worked hard in school, and are eligible to enter college by virtue of their accomplish-ments—instead find themselves encountering a jarring reality: these un-documented students are unable to access state and federal financial assis-tance or benefit from in-state tuition rates; thus the vast majority are unable to continue their studies.[48] Poignantly, eighteen-year-old Joao told us:

> I was brought over to the United States . . . when I was seven years old . . . I did very well in high school and worked incredibly hard. I was on the foot-ball team, the wrestling team (captain), lacrosse team, key club member as well as treasurer of the outing club. I was enrolled in honors English, honors science, AP American history and advanced French. I had worked my entire life to accomplish all of that, but when time came for me to apply to college everything changed. I had expected to be able to receive a scholarship to at-tend college but found out in my junior year of high school that illegal im-migrants aren't eligible for scholarships. So while all of my friends went off to school, I have been stuck in my hometown desperately trying to find a way to live the American dream.

We wondered whether working would be an impediment for academic success for some of our participants. It was possible, for example, that working too many hours could interfere with students' completing their homework, which would result in lower grades. But when we analyzed the grades of working and nonworking students, we found no statistically sig-nificant difference between the two groups. Our ethnographic data re-vealed that for some children work kept them motivated; taught them skills such as responsibility, timeliness, self-confidence; and kept them from be-ing lured into counterproductive behaviors like gang life, drug use, or the underground economy. In these cases, work actually enhanced academic performance.

Other students, however, turned to work as an alternative to school be-cause they felt so unsuccessful in school. At work, they often felt more ac-complished and productive than they did in school. For such students, leaving school was not only a seemingly sensible economic strategy, but also an ego-preserving tactic. As we know, however, in the new economy dropping out of school sentences the student to significantly lower wages and limited possibilities for upward mobility.[49]

MANY immigrant families come to the United States in search of a better education for their children. Lamentably, however, all too often their children attend the worst schools America has to offer—schools where no student is being optimally educated, and where vulnerable newcomer immigrants, who in fact need extra support, end up being "overlooked and underserved" academically.[50] These schools, as we demonstrate, are often highly segregated by race, poverty, and language. It is precisely in such school contexts that we see the American's lack of commitment to teach "other people's children."[51]

As we learned from our ethnographies, immigrant students' experiences in school are shaped by several common factors. First, the emotional tone and academic expectations of a school, set by the school's leadership, matter to students' success in school. Deeply engaged, omnipresent principals; thoughtful counselors; and demanding teachers make a powerful difference in setting a tone of respect, high expectations, and intolerance for intolerance. This is what we found in the Putnam Middle School—a culture of engagement where there prevailed high expectations for all students and a sense of collective ownership of the school.

The more toxic schools, by contrast, were deeply divided spaces characterized by tensions and barricades. At both Quentin Middle School and Reade we found no sense of school community, but rather a culture based on divisions (between the races, between immigrants and native-born, between more acculturated immigrants and newcomer immigrants, between the bilingual program and the mainstream program, between the administration and the teachers, between the teachers and the parents) that fed a sense of anomie and lack of belonging.

In these cases, immigrant students found refuge in the school's bilingual programs. But because of longstanding ambivalence about bilingualism in the United States, these programs are often far from ideal. They tend to be starved for resources and lack up-to-date materials. Further, while newly arrived immigrant students nearly universally found emotional supports and social belonging in these programs, we detected a certain Faustian bargain at work: the tradeoff for social warmth seemed all too often to be a lack of academic rigor. In many of these schools, too, this barrier was hard to break through because the programs are divided physically as well as socially. Typically students in these programs did not share classes, and there were no structures provided by the schools for healthy interactions between new arrivals and native-born students. Most often the programs had different staff and students, who exhibited distinct behaviors and attitudes in school. There was almost no sustained contact between students from the bilingual programs and the mainstream programs, which severely constrained opportunities for newly arrived students to practice their English with native speakers.

Most disturbing of all were the general violence and culture of fear that pervaded many of the schools in our study. In nearly every violence-plagued school we visited, we found the same bad-faith arrangement: the school leadership was all too often complicit in the covering up of events, as well as denials of the problem. In far too many schools, most of the day's energy was devoted to managing fear and staying safe, with little energy left to engage in learning.

■ ■

CHAPTER 4

The Challenge of Learning English

Aₗₜₕₒᵤgₕ ₜₕₑ Uₙᵢₜₑd Sₜₐₜₑₛ was founded by immigrants and has as part of its identity the notion that it welcomes the "poor and huddled masses," Americans are ambivalent about immigration.[1] In particular, when large numbers of newcomers choose one area in which to settle, those who live there already tend to have two main areas of concern: (1) How will the new immigrants affect our economy—that is, will they take away our jobs or burden our social service system? and (2) How will they affect our culture—will they assimilate and, above all, learn English?

Indeed, concerns about immigrants' supposed unwillingness to assimilate and the "threat" they may pose to the local culture and language are often cited in nativist vigilante meetings where locals mobilize in response to the newcomers' arrival. In addition, such concerns are fodder for vituperative outbursts on the internet, underlie legislation to make English the official language of the United States, and are even the source of intellectual debate. In a recent controversial book, Harvard professor Samuel Huntington, a political scientist, voices the worries of many. He claims that Mexicans have no desire to learn English and that they are in fact "contemptuous" of American culture and its language. He suggests that large-scale Mexican immigration poses a profound risk of "a bifurcated America, with two languages, Spanish and English, with two cultures, Anglo-Protestant and Hispanic."[2]

How grounded are these concerns? At the dawn of the new millennium, English has become the lingua franca of business and diplomacy (as the official language of the United Nations). There are over 500 million English speakers across the globe, and English has become the most widely studied second language worldwide.[3] In the United States, Alejandro Portes and Ruben Rumbaut have shown that by the second generation, 40 percent of a large sample of five thousand no longer felt competent in their parents' language and 95 percent claimed to be English dominant.[4]

What attitudes did the newcomer students in our study have toward English and how did they view the challenge of learning a new language? How quickly did students in our study acquire academic English? And what factors contribute to higher levels of academic English proficiency? As part of our five-year study of the immigrant education experience, we set out to find in-depth answers to these essential questions.

The Importance of Learning English

When we asked students during the first year of the study whether they thought that English was important to learn, fully 99 percent responded affirmatively. During the fourth year of the study, we asked them whether they thought English was important for being successful in school—again, the vast majority agreed (94 percent). Further, 93 percent indicated that they liked learning English. Although it has been argued that positive attitudes toward learning a language are predictive of new language mastery, we did not find a relationship between these positive attitudes and better English-language proficiency.[5]

We asked students to complete the sentence: "English is . . ." Nearly half spontaneously answered in a way that demonstrated their clear understanding of how important it is to learn English. Their responses included: "very important to speak [in this country]"; "a language that I have to learn and to know because it is the most important language in the U.S.": "very important to get a good job"; "important for the future"; "very important for everything, for opportunities"; "important to succeed"; "important to get ahead."

At the same time, many (20 percent) responded with an answer that made it clear they found learning English a challenge: "hard," "very hard," and "difficult" were typical responses.[6] We also asked students to tell us how much this statement applied to them: "For some people learning English is easy but for others it is hard." Thirty-eight percent responded that learning English was hard.[7] (Significantly, students who responded that learning English was hard were more likely to score below their peers on the English-language proficiency test.[8]) We then tracked answers to this question over three years. About a quarter never responded that learning English was hard, whereas 31 percent responded at least once that it was hard; another 28 responded twice (that is, for at least two of the years) that it was hard; and an additional 15 percent responded every year that it was hard. There were interesting differences by country of origin: none of the Haitian participants responded all three years that learning English was hard, whereas 24 percent of the Chinese students did so. There was also a range within the Latino origin groups—13 percent of Dominicans, 14 percent of Mexicans, and 22 percent of Central Americans noted all three years that learning English was hard.

Concerns with learning English were often reflected in the narrative prompts that we asked students to respond to (that is, the Thematic Apperception Test). One picture that showed a boy pensively looking at a violin particularly seemed to elicit stories that belied the students' preoccupation about how difficult it is to learn English. Sometimes, in fact, the participants explicitly superimposed the task of learning English onto the task of learning to play the violin:

> The boy is sad. He looks sad. He doesn't look very happy. He has a problem with his parents or someone in his family. Or he is sad because Proposition 227 [ending bilingual education in California in 1997] passed. Perhaps he doesn't know how to speak English. Perhaps now he can't learn English. It becomes harder for him. Perhaps in the future he could speak English. But he can't do math or science in English.

> This story is about a boy that had to study a problem in English. Since he did not know English, he asked for help from his mother. She could not help him, so they called a friend of his. He explained and the boy understood. The boy was frustrated, but the story ended well.

> There is this boy named Manny who has been in the U.S. for four years. He is in his last year of high school and he thinks that he won't make it to college because he doesn't speak English too well. One day while reading a book, he finds this character, the man, who is going through the same problems and decides to stand up for himself and try to make it in the U.S.
>
> Manny says to himself that that can be him too and applies to college. He still thinks that he won't make it but he has hopes, dreams, and faith that he'll make it. Two months later, he receives a letter from the college that he

applied to that says, "Congratulations, you have been accepted to get into our college and get an education."

In other cases, though the students talked about learning to play the violin, their profound desire to learn English, and feelings of inadequacy about doing well at that difficult task, emerged in their narratives.

> There's a person in the picture. He came to the U.S. from China as well. When he was in China, he liked to play violin, and he played well. People liked to listen to him play. But after he came to the U.S., he doesn't know how to read the scale/music. That is why he hates American English and he doesn't play violin anymore.

> This person didn't know how to play the instrument. He was thinking of what to do. He asked others to teach him. He practiced often and finally learned how to play violin. He was feeling that it was very difficult in the picture.

> This Latino boy really wants to learn his violin well. However, he does not have any talent for it. Also, his parents force him to learn the violin. He feels really overwhelmed. He does not know what to do. He just sits there. Earlier on, this boy was yelled at by his violin teacher. His parents want him to learn. He also wants to learn but he still does not do well even though he has tried hard. He is thinking how he can play it well. In the future, he should play the violin well.

> There is a boy who is studying, he was having a lot of problems [a very hard time] studying. His mom told him to try, try harder. Then, he tried harder. Then he was getting better and better and he was learning. Then, he became a professional book writer.

The second year of the study, we asked students, "What do you think are the main obstacles to getting ahead in the United States?" Fifty-six percent spontaneously responded "learning English"—singling out not knowing English as a greater impediment than even discrimination, lack of resources, or not being documented. We then listed a number of obstacles that over the years we have learned are concerns for new immigrants. Fully 90 percent of our participants responded that learning English was a challenge they needed to overcome to get ahead.

In the last year of the study, we also asked students what they perceived were obstacles to getting to college. Of those who thought they would go to college, 45 percent responded that their English fluency presented a problem. Our respondents were realists: those who were concerned about their fluency scored lower than others on the English-language proficiency test.[9]

Despite their recognition that learning English was both important and difficult, newcomer students maintained feelings of loyalty toward their first language: "It is my language"; "It is rich; I like it more. It is my native language and you can express more emotions"; "It is important not to forget from where we come." Besides being "a language I have to speak at home," several recognized the practical value of bilingualism: "It is very important since being bilingual is important." Others noted that their own language had cultural value ("[it is] an ancient and important language") as well as marketplace value ("[it is] complicated but cool, because everyone wants to learn it.") Adolescents being adolescents, one even admitted that it was "good to know—you make fun of someone who doesn't speak it."

Eighty-nine percent of our participants indicated that continuing to speak their native language was important. Most spoke in their native language at home and many continued to speak with their siblings and friends in that language.[10] By the fifth year of the study, a clear gap had emerged between the students' oral communication skills in their native language and their writing skills. By the last year, when asked in what language they felt they read and write best, 36 percent responded that their literacy skills were better in English than in their native language, 33 percent felt equally adept in both languages, and 30 percent felt their literacy skills were better in their native language.

English-Language Proficiency and Academic Performance

In Chapter 1, we noted that the English-language proficiency score our participants attained on the Bilingual Verbal Ability Tests (BVAT) was strongly predictive of their academic achievement—both on grades as well as on the achievement test scores. But what does this mean? With an average of seven years in the country, were our participants academically proficient in English?

The Nature of Bilingualism

Bilingualism, as we define it, means that a person is able to use two languages at a minimal level of proficiency. It is important to note, however, that bilingualism is a relative concept.[11] Although a person may be a fluent speaker and writer in her native language, in the second language, she may only be able to carry on a simple conversation and may be unable to write or read anything but the simplest text. Conversely, a "dormant" bilingual, while being capable of political discussions and writing sophisticated essays in the second language, may understand his native language but have difficulty expressing anything but the simplest of thoughts in it.[12] Some are best able to express emotions and feelings in their native language but are better able to read, write, and argue in their new language. Still others are "balanced" bilinguals, equally adept at expressing any and all levels of communication in more than one language (although this "native-like control over both languages" is a very rare accomplishment).[13] Language acquisition is a dynamic, fluid process that is highly dependent on both the context in which it is developed and the range of opportunities that one has to use it.

Another distinction is worth noting. "Elite" or "elective" bilinguals already speak the dominant language of the land and acquire a second language as a matter of choice in order to enhance their general profile of skills.[14] "Folk" or "circumstantial" bilinguals, by contrast, often speak a lower-status language and must acquire the dominant language of their new country as a matter of survival.[15] For these circumstantial bilinguals, the native language is often neglected and atrophies over time. In fact, they are often discouraged from maintaining it, even though it is an important way to communicate and maintain emotional ties with their families. Ironically then, while the children of the elite are encouraged to study a second language as a marker of competence and as a skill for succeeding in the global economy, children who enter the United States adept in the use of another language are often urged to let go of this ability.

It is also very important to distinguish between those language skills necessary to carry on a conversation and to go about taking care of the daily transactions of life, and those language skills required to be competitive academically. The first dimension of language skill—termed basic "interpersonal communicative skills"—can, with adequate exposure, be readily learned within a year or so.[16] "Cognitive/academic language," however, takes an average of seven to ten years of systematic high-quality training and consistent exposure to achieve.[17] To get to the point of being able, in a second language, to argue about the relative merits of an issue, write a quality essay, read quickly enough to be competitive on a timed test, or detect the subtle differences between multiple choice items on the SAT, simply takes extensive time as well as high-quality education. It is to this academic language to which we now turn.

The Bilingual Verbal Abilities Test

The Bilingual Verbal Abilities Test (BVAT) was designed to assess bilingual students' academic readiness.[18] The BVAT comprises three individually administered subtests:

1. The picture vocabulary task. The student names a pictured object. This is an expressive language task that assesses the ability to retrieve single words and measures comprehension/knowledge.
2. The oral vocabulary task. The student hears and sees a word, then supplies a synonym or antonym.
3. The verbal analogies task. The student is asked to recognize the relationship between two words and then identify a word that has the same relationship to a third word (for example, hungry is to eat as tired is to sleep).[19]

The test is first administered by a bilingual researcher in English, then the test-taker is given the opportunity to respond in his or her native language. The test provides both an English-language proficiency (ELP) score as well as a so-called Gain score, which indicates the student's academic conceptual knowledge when allowed to access both of his or her languages. The ELP score combined with the Gain score yield a bilingual verbal ability (BVA) score. The BVAT, which uses U.S. English-language norms as well as test protocols developed for each of the native languages of our study participants, was the best available instrument to establish cognitive and academic language abilities.[20] We administered this test in the third and fifth years of the study.

ENGLISH-LANGUAGE PROFICIENCY SCORES

Strikingly, by the fifth year of the study, we found that only twenty students (7 percent of the sample) scored at or above the normalized mean for English speakers of the same age on the English-language proficiency subtest (the normalized mean was a score of 100). Instead, the mean score for our entire sample was 74.7 (with students' scores ranging from 31 to 156).[21] On average, then, our sample had academic English proficiency scores equivalent to the lowest two percentiles of native English-speaking peers. The Chinese students scored, on average, nine points higher than did the students from the other ethnic groups, but this was not a statistically significant difference.[22]

More than three-quarters of our participants' scores were more than one standard deviation (fifteen points) below the mean. Only 22 percent of the total sample fell within one standard deviation of the average native English speaker of the same age. Moreover, the country-of-origin differences were dramatic. While 37.8 of the Chinese students achieved a standard score of 85 or above, only 9.3 percent of the Dominican students did so. The other three groups—Central Americans, Haitians, and Mexicans—all scored close to the total sample average, with only 22.6, 17.0, and 18.6 percent, respectively, earning scores of 85 or greater.

Grouping the students by our previously defined academic performance trajectories demonstrated a clear connection between the English-language proficiency score and performance. More than half of the high achievers scored within one standard deviation from the mean score, whereas 22.9 percent of the slow decliners did so. Only 11.3 percent of precipitous decliners, 10 percent of improvers, and 7.3 percent of low achievers scored within one standard deviation of the mean. While the mean score for high achievers was 91.3, the low achievers, improvers, and precipitous decliners scored more than two standard deviations below the normed mean.[23]

USING BOTH LANGUAGES: THE GAIN SCORES

We examined whether the assessment of our participants' overall academic cognitive ability changed when they were able to draw on both sets of language skills. Indeed it did. On average, the students' scores rose over a standard deviation when they were able to use both their languages. This gain suggests that the students' conceptual knowledge is greater than it would appear based only on their use of English. Interestingly, there was no statistical difference in the Gain score across the five academic performance trajectory groups (Figure 4.1).[24]

There were differences in Gain scores, however, when the student's country of origin was considered. The Chinese students demonstrate significantly higher skills when they are able to draw on their native language,

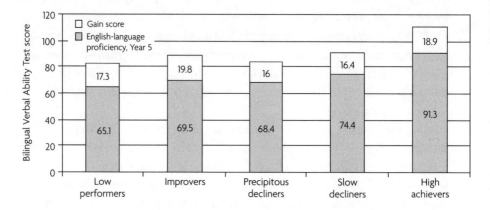

Figure 4.1. Bilingual verbal ability, by academic cluster.

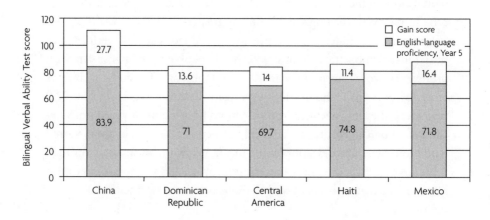

Figure 4.2. Bilingual verbal ability, by country of origin.

whereas the home-language advantage was smaller for the other groups (Figure 4.2).

INCREASES IN ENGLISH-LANGUAGE PROFICIENCY SCORES OVER TIME

Did our sample students' English-language proficiency increase over time? Indeed, it did—for the total sample, the standard score went up an average of eight points between the third and fifth years of the study. Note that the standard score uses age norms; this increase in fact represents a significant gain. Mexicans demonstrated the greatest increase in English-

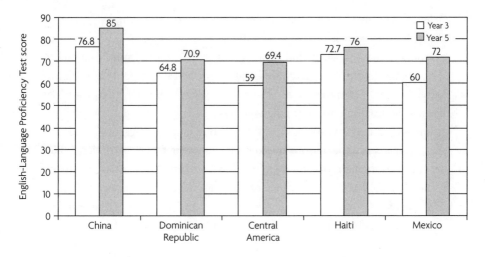

Figure 4.3. English-language proficiency, by country of origin.

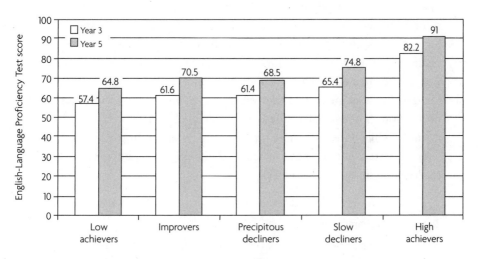

Figure 4.4. English-language proficiency, by academic cluster.

language proficiency over time, while Haitians showed the least improvement (Figure 4.3).[25] Interestingly, English-language proficiency increased at the same rate for each of the academic performance trajectories (Figure 4.4).[26]

While the participants demonstrated a significant gain in English proficiency over time, nonetheless, when compared to native-English speaking students, they still lagged significantly behind in academic English proficiency. Hence it is clear that it takes longer than most would imagine to develop the English-language skills necessary to be competitive academically. By most, we mean those who have not gone through the process of intensively learning another language—the average voter, teacher, or politician—who make naïve assumptions about language learning and impose unrealistic expectations based on a lack of first-hand experience. Researchers in the field of language learning have long known that acquiring an academically competitive level of language acquisition takes a significant period—from seven to ten years of strong academic environments and frequent second-language exposure.[27] Our data support these claims.

Challenges to Learning English

There is a fertile field of research addressing the factors that influence second-language acquisition. Drawing from disciplines within and across linguistics, psychology, anthropology, and education, researchers tend to focus on (1) background factors such as prior education and literacy, as well as previous experience with learning another language, (2) aptitude for learning a language, (3) motivation, (4) exposure, and (5) quality of instruction. Some scholars focus on contextual variables that influence learning, while others are more interested in understanding individual differences. Based on our study, we believe that both play an important role in the learning of a second language.

Background Characteristics

There seems to be a clear link between parental education and how well a person learns a new language.[28] The mother's education in particular seems to facilitate the child's learning in this area. Children with more educated mothers are advantaged in two ways: they are exposed to more academically oriented vocabulary and interactions at home, and they tend to be read to more often from books that are valued at school. Indeed, home literacy is another variable associated with greater ease in learning a second language.[29] There also appears to be a link between the number of years of education in one's home country and the ease of learning a second language. When students are well grounded in their native language and have developed reading and writing skills in that language, they appear to be able to efficiently apply that knowledge to the new language when provided appropriate instructional supports.[30]

Age

A general assumption is that the younger people are when they arrive in a new country, the better they will learn the new language. The evidence on this issue is complex and debated. Older learners, who have developed literacy in their native language and have greater cognitive maturity, seem to learn the rules of language more efficiently than do younger learners.[31] Indeed, perhaps counterintuitively, assuming an identical quality of instruction, older learners learn a second language more quickly (though younger learners catch up over time). Younger learners generally acquire better pronunciation, however, which makes them seem more fluent and competent in the second language.[32] Further, adults must master a larger vocabulary in the second language to appear "fluent." There continues to be a debate about whether one's age of arrival is more or less critical than one's length of exposure to a new language. For adolescents, language learning does not fit neatly into the ongoing debate about age-related capabilities.

For our sample, the age of arrival and time in the United States were significantly correlated—that is, the younger the participants were when they arrived in the United States, the longer they had been in the United States by the fifth year of the study. Both age of arrival and length of residency were correlated with higher levels of proficiency.[33]

Cognitive Aptitude

There is no doubt that some people simply have more of a knack for learning languages than others.[34] Are they more intelligent? In a word, no; there is no evidence to link traditional measures of intelligence to second language acquisition.[35] There do, however, appear to be traits or skill sets that are linked to better second-language learning, such as the ability to discriminate between sounds; the ability to recognize the role and function of various parts of speech; the capacity to detect and generalize grammatical rules; and memory for language.[36] While there appears to be a general agreement that these skills facilitate language learning, it is a challenge to reliably and validly develop sound assessments of these linguistic capabilities.[37]

Motivation

Some argue that whether or not someone really wants to learn a second language will strongly predict how quickly and how well they will learn it.[38] While this concept is intuitively appealing, it is, like aptitude, difficult to measure systematically.[39] For example, is the student motivated in a general, casual way (it would be nice to learn another language) or does he feel it is a matter of survival (I must learn another language in order to thrive in my new context)? Researchers studying motivation distinguish between various kinds of motivation, but like with aptitude, there is no consensus regarding either what the components of motivation may be or how to measure them.[40] As indicated earlier, we learned during our study that newcomer immigrant students arrive convinced that learning English is important for their future well-being. This is hardly surprising given the influence of English fluency on one's social, cultural, and economic experience in the United States.[41] And because their level of motivation was so universally high—across different country-of-origin groups as well as across the various academic performance trajectories—it seems that a student's stated motivation is not a particularly useful indicator for predicting language learning over time.

Exposure to Native Speakers

The maxim "less contact, less learning" succinctly summarizes the arguments supporting students' exposure to quality language models and instruction.[42] To learn a language well, one must have sustained interactions with educated native speakers of English, as well as good language instruction. Students can only learn the new language in the style to which they are exposed. If an English-language learner lives and talks daily with English speakers in a boarding school in London, she will learn a very different kind of English and sound very different than if she had been immersed in a public school in Atlanta, Sidney, or Toronto. Likewise, someone hoping to improve their Spanish-speaking skills will sound very different after an extended study-abroad stay in Madrid, Mexico City, Santo Domingo, or Buenos Aires.

Regardless of regional differences or styles, however, all language learners benefit from sustained support in a linguistically rich and cognitively engaging environment.[43] Students learn more quickly and attain higher levels of academic language proficiency when they participate in high-quality bilingual education than when they are placed in mainstream classrooms without any language support.[44] Teachers with an in-depth understanding of the needs of language learners are key to the success of any bilingual program, as are the school and social context.

What kinds of exposure to English did our participants experience? Opportunities to listen to radio and watch television varied significantly by language group. Spanish media is a booming industry in many parts of the country.[45] As a result, we found that many of our Spanish-speaking participants spent more than half of their radio-listening or television-watching time tuned into Spanish media. Indeed, for our Latino participants, watching television was often a family event. Watching the current popular *telenovela* (serial soap operas) was a cross-generational practice—grandmothers, parents, and children would tune in each evening for such hits at *Yo soy Betty, La Fea* (Betty, the Ugly), a twist on the Cinderella theme with a huge viewership that later spawned a U.S. adaptation. In contrast, only about 20 percent of our Chinese participants watched television in Cantonese or Mandarin, and none of our Haitian students watched Haitian Kreyol television (which tended to be local, low-budget talk shows focusing on political concerns). Similarly, significantly more Latino-origin students listened to radio in Spanish than did either their Chinese or Haitian peers.

We asked students to tell us what percentage of their time they spent speaking in English at their schools (which could include classrooms, the playground, hallways, and the cafeteria). Seventy-eight percent told us that they spent more than 75 percent of their time speaking in English at school, while 23 percent told us that they spent less than half of their time interacting in English at school. Almost all students, however, spoke nearly exclusively in their native language to their parents. And in nonfamily and nonschool situations (like work and neighborhood contexts), the students demonstrated a range of language-use patterns. Forty-four percent used English more than three-quarters of the time, while 30 percent told us that they used English more than half the time. By the third year of the study, just under half of the students told us that they spoke primarily in their native language with most of their friends, roughly a quarter spoke with their peers primarily in English, and another quarter used both languages. More than a third of the students in our sample told us that they had little opportunity to interact with peers who were not from their country of origin, which no doubt contributed to this pattern. Interestingly, we found that students who claimed to have at least one friend with whom they predominantly speak English performed somewhat better than did students who had no friends with whom they spoke primarily English.[46]

Quality of English-Language Instruction

There are many approaches to English-language instruction. The types of programs that are offered depend in part on the beliefs of those who develop the programs about language learning and cognitive development, the composition of the class (for example, if only one or two native languages are used by the class as a whole), and access to resources (such as bilingual teachers). Some believe that language learning and cognition are deeply intertwined, and that to develop second-language skills without attending to cognition places students at a clear disadvantage both short- and long-term. Others take the position that these two aspects of learning are independent, and that immersion in the second language will best facilitate adaptation to the new environment.

Under the rubric of bilingual education we find a wide array of practices and programs.[47] The vast majority of research on bilingual education focuses on elementary rather than secondary educational practices, contexts, and outcomes, though nearly half the students who need services arrive during secondary school.

English as a Second Language (ESL) programs often consist of limited pull-out instruction and academic support with the rest of the day spent immersed in regular classes; in ESL classrooms, most often there are learners from many different countries speaking many different languages.

Transitional bilingual programs focus on providing academic support while students transition out of their language of origin into English. In one-way developmental bilingual programs, students of one language group are schooled in two languages (for example, English and Cantonese) so that they can keep up with academic material in their native language as they learn English. In structured immersion programs, the curriculum is simplified and is taught more slowly, and with a great deal of repetition, in English. And in sheltered English programs, all lessons in every subject are at least in part a second-language lesson; thus a science class is also an opportunity to learn new vocabulary.

Dual-immersion classes, the state of the art of bilingual education, involve students' learning half of the time in English and half in their native language (most often Spanish), with half of the class being native speakers of one language and the other half native speakers of the other language. This kind of program offers greater opportunity for students to truly become bilingual—they develop their second language while maintaining their first. They also develop and expand their academic skills by drawing on both languages.

Studies of the relative merits of such programs find that dual-language programs most consistently produce the best results. Excellent results as measured by high performance of students are also found in one-way development programs offered in high-achieving districts.[48] There is no doubt that in addition to the range of kinds of instruction that fall under the general bilingual education rubric, there is also a great disparity in quality of instruction between settings. While high-quality bilingual instruction yields excellent outcomes, low-quality, erratic instruction leads to far from optimal results.

Nearly the entire sample (93.8 percent) began their education in their new country in some form of bilingual instructional setting (including pull-out programs, sheltered instruction, ESL, and dual-language instruction). Over time, many of the students transitioned out of their bilingual settings, though there seemed to be little rhyme or reason to the transition.[49] Our study began the year before Proposition 227—the Unz initiative that mandated a transition to a mainstream class after one year—was voted into existence in California. The proposition took many educators by surprise and there were huge disparities among districts, schools, and classrooms in how the initiative was implemented. In Massachusetts there was also a great disparity among districts and schools in how English-language learners received instruction.[50] Often neither the school records nor the students themselves were clear about whether or not they were receiving bilingual or ESL instruction or language learning supports.

Because of the disparities between programs, the lack of systematic definition of programs by district, the wide range of settings in which our students received their education, and the poor recordkeeping about the kinds of programs students were actually assigned to, it is impossible to provide hard data on the relative merit of different kinds of English-language-learner programs—it is simply beyond the scope of this study. Ethnographically, however, as we saw in Chapter 3, many of the school settings in which newcomer students found themselves left much to be desired. The schools tended to lack adequate resources and offer a poor quality of instruction, and the contexts of learning were frequently neglectful, disengaging, and even hostile. All too often these were schools in which very few students—whether they were native-born Americans or newly arrived immigrant students—thrived. Further, the bilingual students were segregated from the native-born peers by being relegated to the basement or a wing of the school. The mission of the school was generally not focused on meeting the needs of newcomer students—at best they tended to be ignored and at worst they were viewed as a problem contributing to low performance on state mandated high-stakes tests.

By the fourth year of the study, nearly three-quarters of the students had begun taking classes outside of the bilingual programs and 41 percent were enrolled entirely in mainstream classes. Notably, many students spoke about how difficult it was to make the transition to mainstream classes. Many missed their friends and the nurturing, sheltered environment that had served them well as they were adjusting to a new country and educational environment. Students often lamented that when they first transitioned, they did not know any of the other students and were scared, or missed their friends. Many students also told us how inadequate and "stupid" they felt as they struggled to express themselves and academically compete with a less than fully developed vocabulary and still-evolving grammar skills. As one student shared, "It was harder because of my English. Sometimes the teacher spoke fast and sometimes I couldn't understand her."

Other students, however, appreciated the greater rigor of their mainstream classes. "I knew it would help me improve my English, even if it was hard," said one student. Another told us, "I liked the challenge—the bilingual classes were too easy; you had to start over when new kids came." Students also appreciated the opportunity to interact with American peers. "[I can] make new friends, like American people," said one; "[Now] I was talking to different people that don't speak Haitian," said another. Students also appreciated not being singled out: "It just makes me feel normal again."

While some students ended up doing well in mainstream contexts, clearly others struggled and could have used more support than they received. There seemed to be little rational planning and follow-up regarding placing students in a particular program. There also was a surprising amount of haphazardly moving students among bilingual, ESL, and mainstream classes. Sometimes these shifts had to do with changes in funding or programs within a school; what was available one year was not available the next.[51] Sometimes a student was transitioned into mainstream classes before they were ready and then moved back into a sheltered environment. Other times students were left in ESL courses long after such classes appeared to help them. Sometimes, too, students moved about from school to school and were placed in different kinds of programs depending on what was available in each school. By and large, in most cases, there was no clear strategy to place students into a progressive program of instruction that would (1) identify the student's incoming literacy and academic skills, (2) provide high-quality English instruction, (3) continue to provide instruction in academic subject areas such as math, science, and social studies in the students' native languages, so they would not fall further behind their English-speaking peers, and (4) offer transitional academic supports—like tutoring, continued language instruction, homework help, and writing assistance—as the language learners integrated into mainstream programs.

Predicting a Student's Success or Failure in Learning English

Why do some students learn English more efficiently than others? Based on what the literature in the field tells us, we developed a model to predict our participants' English-language proficiency score the last year of the study.[52] We examined the role of several variables: parents' assessment of their own English skills during the first year of the study; how many years the students had been educated in their country of origin; how many years the students had been in the United States; students' reports of how much English they used in informal situations; measures of the school's poverty and segregation levels; and the percentage of students in the school who were learning English. Understanding this combination of characteristics

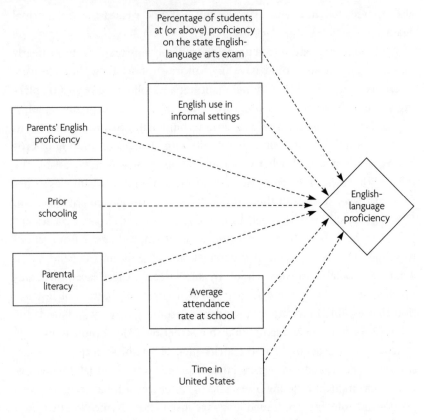

Figure 4.5. Predicting English-language proficiency.

allowed us to predict nearly half of the variance of the last year's English-language proficiency score (Figure 4.5).[53]

The two school characteristics we included in this model—the percent of the students attending the school who reached at least proficiency level on the state-mandated English language arts exam, as well as the daily average school attendance rate—were highly predictive of the English-language proficiency of our students. Thus students who attended schools where a higher percentage of the students did well on the state's English language arts exam did significantly better than students who attended a school where a substantial number of its students did not reach proficiency. We surmise that in those schools where more of the students performed well on the English language arts exam, the quality of instruction as well as the language models were substantially better than in school settings where few students performed well. Likewise, schools with higher daily average attendance rates tend to have better school climates and more efficacious monitoring of their students than schools where fewer students come to school regularly. In such settings, newcomer immigrant students have a substantially better chance to learn English.

Students' personal backgrounds also mattered. Parental literacy was strongly predictive, as were the parent's English skills. The number of years that the student had been educated in his or her country of origin (an indicator of general educational level and literacy) contributed to English-language proficiency, as did years in the United States (an indicator of exposure to English).

The students who spoke with others in English in informal settings had better English-proficiency outcomes. Many of our students, however, lived in ethnically segregated neighborhoods and either attended segregated schools or were segregated within the school. Thus many had limited opportunities to make friends with native English speakers.

NEWCOMER students arrive highly motivated to learn English. They recognize that speaking the language of the new land is essential for them to make friends, do well in school, and have a "better future." Consequently, during their first years in the United States, newcomer students are often preoccupied about the challenge of learning a new language. But learning a second language is very difficult, especially when immigrant students feel pressured at the same time to succeed academically and socially at a new school. Sadly, as they approach graduation, many recognize as well that their limitations in academic English proficiency will likely hamper their ability to enter or achieve in college.

We also learned that becoming proficient in English takes a long time. Even after, on average, seven years in the new country, very few of our participants (2 percent) performed comparably to their normed average peers who were native-born English-speakers. Yet while most immigrant students performed well below average when compared to native-speaking peers, all groups showed improvement between the third and fifth years of the study. Our analyses demonstrate the critical interplay of the skills the students bring with them and the linguistic and educational contexts in which they find themselves. The less access that newcomer students had to rich models of academic English and high-level instruction, the less likely they were to demonstrate strong proficiency in academic English during the last year of the study.

Clearly, if we are to expect newcomer students to learn English, as they and we would like them to, our schools need to do a better job of developing educational contexts that will make it happen. Our focus at the beginning of the study was very student-centered; we considered the resources the students brought with them, the engagement they brought to the task, as well as the educational contexts they encountered. But while these factors certainly contribute to language acquisition, the schools also play a fundamental role in whether students learn English. Our findings parallel those of Gary Orfield, Guadalupe Valdés, Laurie Olsen, and others who have insightfully described the intense physical and linguistic segregation that many newcomer immigrant students encounter.[54] While there have been some attempts to address the needs of students coming in at the elementary level, there has been a lamentable and disconcerting absence of efforts to meet the needs of English-language learners arriving at the secondary school level.[55] This gap absolutely needs to be addressed if we wish to harness the energies of all of our newcomer students.

The alternative to supporting immigrant children while they learn academic English is to allow them simply to sink or swim; that is, to stand by while some stay afloat, and many others become weary and drown. Our dilemma is compounded by our culture's emphasis on standardized and often high-stakes exams, which most newcomer students are unable to pass within three years of arrival as is currently required. Indeed, we have become very concerned about the wisdom of using high-stakes tests to assess the progress of newcomer immigrant students. It is important to recall that many newcomer immigrants attend highly segregated and high-poverty schools, where very few of the students—whether native English speakers or immigrant students—are adequately prepared to do well on a standardized English test. Given that even in the best circumstances, with the highest-quality English-language instruction, it can take seven to ten years to gain academic proficiency, how can we expect the average newcomer student to become proficient in just three years? To be fair to them, we must develop alternative strategies of assessment that are linguistically and culturally appropriate.

■ ■

CHAPTER 5

Portraits of Declining Achievers

MOST IMMIGRANT CHILDREN arrive with great hopes for the future. They view their migration as a route to new possibilities and opportunities. They throw themselves determinedly into the enterprise of crafting their future, recognizing that an education is essential for a prosperous life. For many, however, these initial hopes and dreams are difficult to sustain. Some experience a slow decline in skills and opportunities over time, while many others are jarringly derailed from what could have been a promising future. More than half of the students in our sample started off with approximately a B average, but declined over the course of five years. Approximately half of these declining students slipped about half a grade point.[1] The other half demonstrated a precipitous slide of a grade and a half, to a C-minus average.[2] (See Table 5.1, which relates to all the portrait chapters.)

Who are the students who disengage? Disengaging students were distributed among all of the countries of origin that we studied.[3] Statistically, among all the groups, Central Americans were somewhat more likely to slowly disengage and Dominicans were the most likely to take a precipitously declining path.[4] Interestingly, unlike some other areas of academic performance, girls were just as likely as boys to disengage from school over time and were equally likely to follow the slow as well as precipitous paths of decline.

There are important distinctions between the slow decliners and the precipitous decliners, however. The slow decliners in fact follow national patterns for all students (whether or not they are of immigrant origin), in

Table 5.1   Characteristics of students, by academic pathway (Part A, in percent); this table refers to Chapters 5–8

Characteristic	Slow decliners 24.3% N=70	Precipitous decliners 26.8% N=79	Low achievers 14.4% N=41	Improvers 10.9% N=30	High achievers 23.6% N=64
Originating country—China *** [N=68]	16.12	10.3	7.4	19.1	47.1
Originating country—Haiti *** [N=47]	27.7	36.2	19.2	6.4	10.6
Originating country—Central America *** [N=51]	31.4	25.5	19.6	5.9	17.7
Originating country—Dominican Republic *** [N=54]	25.9	42.6	11.1	7.4	13
Originating country—Mexico *** [N=64]	25	29.7	17.2	10.9	17.2
Gender—males * [N=122]	23.8	30.3	21.3	8.2	16.4
Gender—females * [N=162]	25.3	27.2	9.3	12.4	27.2
Two-parent home **	71	52	63	74	82.5
Problematic separation *	11.8	26.4	13.8	16.7	2.2
High-school graduate mother *	35.3	19	29	38	46.8
High-school graduate father (n.s.)	19	16.9	27	26.9	32.8
Working father **	64.2	51.4	63.2	75	82.3
Working mother (n.s.)	79.7	70	68.6	65.4	75.4
Household income (n.s.)					
< $20,000	32.1	31.3	23.5	24	18.5
$20,001–$49,999	50	43.3	44.1	44	42.6
> $50,000+	17.9	25.4	32	32.4	38.9
Low-income students in school (50% +) (n.s.)	58.6	65.8	68.3	60	47.6

Note: The academic pathways were established using Nagin cluster analysis—see Chapter 2; the data reported below is the basis for our descriptions of differentiating characteristics of the pathways at the beginning of Chapters 5 through 8.

The number of students in this trajectory sample is slightly smaller than the sample of 309 at the end of the study because we had missing data for some key variables [N = 284].

For categorical variables we report percentage and establish significance with chi squares. [Significance levels: n.s. = not significant, * <.05, ** <.01, *** <.001] For continuous data we report least square means and establish significance with analysis of variance. [Significance levels: n.s. = not significant, * <.05, ** <.01, *** <.001]

Characteristics of students, by academic pathway (Part B); this table refers to Chapters 5–8

Characteristic	Total sample		Slow decliners 24.3%	Precipitous decliners 26.8%	Low achievers 14.4%	Improvers 10.9%	High achievers 23.6%
	Mean	(SD)					
School segregation rate***	77.9	(23.61)	76.5	84.74	87.33	77.81	64.8
Percent of schools' students passing state high stakes English test***	31.98	(25.68)	32.07	25.19	21.33	32.5	46.88
Reported school problems, Yr3***	24.05	(5.69)	23.99	25.70	25.96	21.45	22.13
Reported school problems, Yr5***	20.23	(5.56)	19.71	20.88	24.12	18.63	18.14
Age of arrival n.s.	9.92	(1.96)	9.54	10.16	9.98	9.9	10.02
Psychological symptoms, Yr1***	19.28	(9.09)	18.16	21.45	21.24	20.17	16.19
Psychological symptoms, Yr5***	18.61	(9.76)	16.23	21.49	19.49	21.13	15.90
Family problems scale**	10.83	(2.95)	10.35	11.37	11.82	10.67	10.11
Relational engagement, Yr3 n.s.	26.2	(2.24)	22.37	21.23	19.28	21.41	23.41
Relational engagement, Yr5 n.s.	36.20	(5.02)	36.39	35.89	34.93	36.57	37.03
Behavioral engagement, Yr3***	21.76	(3.29)	22.37	21.23	19.28	21.41	23.41
Behavioral engagement, Yr5***	20.84	(4.37)	21.50	20.24	17.25	20.37	23.38
Cognitive engagement, Yr3*	11.88	(1.99)	11.93	12.38	11.23	11.17	11.92
Cognitive engagement, Yr5*	11.60	(1.97)	11.53	11.69	11.17	11.47	11.92
Schooling attitudes, Yr5**	5.99	(1.38)	6.06	5.71	5.56	6.03	6.44
Motivation, Yr5***	12.20	(3.55)	12.56	11.31	11.63	12.10	13.29
Reported peer support*	33.83	(5.22)	34.50	34.23	31.29	34.22	33.98
English-Language Proficiency SS, Yr3***	66.79	(19.64)	65.62	61.54	58.64	60.93	82.37
English-Language Proficiency SS, Yr5***	74.68	(19.32)	74.4	68.37	65.15	69.53	91.25
Bilingual Verbal Abilities Test SS, Yr3***	88.57	(17.96)	85.16	82.93	82.48	85.57	104.47
Bilingual Verbal Abilities Test SS, Yr5***	91.98	(19.75)	90.75	83.99	81.64	89.00	110.36
Woodcock-Johnson Test of Achievement (combined score)***	90.46	(16.6)	89.47	84.49	80.14	88.09	106.85

Significance levels: n.s. = not significant, *<.05, **<.01, ***<.001.

which they drop approximately a half grade in GPA as they transition from middle to high school.[5] Much more alarming is the precipitous decliners' grade-and-a-half decline in GPA over five years.

Acquiring academic English was often a profound impediment for students who showed a decline in performance over time. While at first most of our students attended bilingual or English as a Second Language (ESL) programs, more than 80 percent of them were transitioned into mainstream classes after only a few years. At this point, we all too often saw grades fall. In a few cases, a student's stellar performance had led to his or her premature transition into rigorous exam schools—where even non-immigrant students also often show a decline in grades (because these programs are much more competitive). In most cases, however, the students were placed in regular mainstream classes, which were often in low-achieving, strife-ridden schools where it is difficult for anyone to flourish. In both kinds of transitions, without appropriate academic support, students often floundered, finding that their English reading and writing skills were simply not strong enough to succeed.

The students who declined slowly also shared a number of personal and family characteristics with those who declined more precipitously. In most cases, their parents did not have much educational experience and were not able to provide tangible educational supports to their children. Many families had been strained by protracted separations and complicated re-unifications.[6] Often, the parent's authority had become disconnected and ineffective and there were other reported conflicts within the family. In addition, while these students usually reported that they had made good friends, usually those friends were no better informed or equipped to navigate the educational system than our participants. Relationships with supportive adults were rarely reported by declining students, and when they were, the adults tended to be negative rather than positive influences.

Those who showed the steepest decline were most likely to have more strikes against them. They were more likely to come from single-parent homes. Their mothers often had less education. They were more likely to be undocumented than their peers who had declined more slowly.[7] Their English skills were weaker. They reported the highest levels of psychological symptoms and unlike students from all the other groups, those levels did not decline over time. They attended the worst schools and reported greater violence and discipline problems at their schools. By the last year of the study, the precipitous decliners were reporting that they felt significantly lower behavioral engagement: they were less motivated and less willing to participate in class or in school-based activities. Many of the students who gave up most completely had personal, family, and situational obstacles that only the most resilient of individuals could possibly overcome.

In this chapter, we introduce five students from a number of countries who lost ground in the struggle to overcome challenges to education. The subject of our first portrait, Lotus, is at first highly engaged in school, but suffers from transplant shock and an isolated social network; without the necessary supports she becomes overwhelmed with anxiety and cannot sustain her initial accomplishments. In the next portrait, we see how a premature and unsupported transition from a supportive bilingual environment to a demanding English-language school setting derails Henry's initially promising academic trajectory. We also meet Mauricio and Andrés, two young men who without adequate family or community supports flounder in and disengage from their toxic school environments. And in Marieli we see how a host of disruptive factors—a traumatic childhood, extensive family separations and problematic reunifications, undocumented status, and a toxic school and neighborhood—come together in a perfect storm of disruption and failure.

Lotus: Seventeen Years of Solitude

It is a late October day, very cold, when Lotus appears in the distance, walking with her only friend, Mei. Lotus shivers in the thick yellow sweatshirt she wears with an old pair of faded jeans and worn sneakers; others on the street are bundled in jackets with mittens and scarves. She hugs her arms tightly against her chest, but asked whether she is cold, she replies simply, "[I am] okay." Both girls are about five feet tall and have slight builds. Their huge backpacks overwhelm their small fifteen-year-old bodies.

Lotus's migration to the United States followed a broken path from a coastal city in China. Her paternal grandmother had lived in the United States for several years and helped Lotus's father apply for a green card. When Lotus's father first immigrated in the early 1990s, he brought Lotus and her younger brother, but upon learning that local laws forbade leaving young children unattended at home, and feeling that "people here are cold," he soon sent the children back to China. Two years later, when Lotus was twelve, her father decided they were old enough to take care of themselves when necessary, so he brought them back to the United States, this time to stay.

The family's finances are precarious because Lotus's father is the only worker in the household. He had worked as a technician in China, but since coming to the United States, he has often switched jobs, working either in kitchens or on construction sites, with frequent periods of unemployment during which he wanders around Chinatown looking for work. He speaks no English.

The story of Lotus's mother remains somewhat elusive. When the father took the children back to China, he left them in the care of his sister, not their mother. And during our interviews, we learn that Lotus's mother remained in China far longer than Lotus. She worked as an accounting clerk and cared for her own mother and a younger daughter who stayed with her. It turns out that the parents are divorced, but for her father, Lotus's mother remains "my wife," and he visits her in China several times a year. Lotus maintains regular contact with her.

After her arrival in the United States, Lotus began living with her seventy-year-old grandmother and younger brother in a dark, gloomy, and poorly furnished one-bedroom apartment in a housing project for senior citizens in Chinatown. The three of them share a small bedroom, their humble belongings jammed together. The apartment has no heat. It is furnished with a few old, worn-out pieces. To keep warm, Lotus wraps herself in whatever clothes she can find. The only new object in the apartment is a Hewlett-Packard computer the father bought for his children. Lotus describes the home as crowded and noisy because of her grandmother's yelling and her brother's video games—it is difficult to concentrate and study there.

In this home, the grandmother is the head of the household, and she is strict and demanding. She frequently yells at Lotus about the way she does the housework. (Lotus remains silent during these tirades.) The rules at home are explicit. Lotus can recite them mechanically and in detail: "Squeeze the kitchen towel dry after washing the dishes. If I get the floor wet, my grandmother will scold me to death. Turn off lights, TV and the VCR before going to bed. No reading when eating. Don't pull the sofa cover down. Put the shoes away." She is very preoccupied with following rules, perhaps because her life is organized around rules, both at home and at school.

Her father rarely stays with them. Mostly he lives where he works—usually in the restaurant—but between jobs or on his day off, he joins them in the senior housing project. Thus Lotus shoulders most of the responsibility at home—cooking, cleaning, and taking care of her grandmother and younger brother, including helping him with his homework.

After a five-year separation, long compared with most Chinese families, Lotus's mother and younger sister arrived in the United States on an immigration visa and the family was reunited. Now the entire family would live in the small apartment. Lotus was delighted at their arrival—having been burdened with adult family responsibilities since the age of twelve, she was relieved and grateful that her mother could take over. Now there was someone to make her breakfast in the morning.

A Girl Turning Inward

During one conversation, Lotus clenches her fists and sits anxiously on the edge of her chair, responding indecisively, changing her mind, and asking how she should reply. She had tried calling the research assistant before the interview in order to confirm the time, but could not get through.

> "Have you changed your phone number?" she asks.
> "No."
> Disbelieving, she objects, "But your number did not work."
> "Sometimes when I am home, I do not turn on my cell phone. You can call my home number if you need [to]."

She is encouraged to call if she needs someone to talk to, but she never has believed that her calls are truly welcome. She is afraid of being a bother, that others are "always too busy" and "don't have time for me," that she is "not important at all" and should not "waste our time." Though clearly wanting to reach out for help, she never takes the step, afraid that others will confirm her low self-worth by ignoring her call for help.

In the early years after migration, Lotus maintained a close relationship with her father. Though she did not live with him, she would sometimes confide in him. As time went on, she spent less and less time with him. Given the absence of her mother, it is quite possible that she was pained by her father's decision to live apart from her; she may have felt abandoned. After her mother and sister arrived, more conflicts emerged between mother and daughter, although Lotus considers them minor. She sums up the consequences of the separation precisely: "My mother and I have separated for many years. There have been many changes between us. Our thoughts and beliefs have changed. Our daily lives have changed."

Over time, Lotus started withholding much of what she thought and felt, protecting her parents from her distress to prevent them from worrying about her. Lotus says she refrains from sharing the depths of her emotions with her parents, fearing they might think that she has abnormal or irrational thoughts. But she also refrains from sharing with her parents or siblings any of her secrets or thoughts because she finds them unsupportive.

Lotus's family is very traditional, particularly concerning gender roles and expectations, even though in most areas of China such traditional gendered ideas have become less rigid. Lotus's father's concern and high expectations for his son are apparent, but he has low expectations for Lotus's future, framing her education as needed to help her brother with his studies. Marriage or a job as a clerk is what he sees in her future. Lotus's father repeats that he would prefer that Lotus not go to college because he does not want to work to earn money for her tuition. Yet there is a mismatch between the father's expectations and the children's achievements in school: Lotus is a good student while her brother performs poorly.

Lotus is keenly aware of this contradiction. "They don't have any expectations for me," she says flatly. When asked how her life would be different if she were a boy, Lotus says, "If I were a boy, my family would care more about me. Also my parents would pay for my college tuition if I were a boy. But since I am a girl, they expect me to work for my tuition fee if I want to attend college." She is pained by her family's lack of respect for her work: "[My grandmother] always throws my homework away or uses it as a placemat. She thinks my homework is useless and throws it away." Yet these low expectations fuel her determination to prove herself.

Mastery and Control through Studying

Lotus achieved high grades in her six years of education in China, and after coming to the United States, she maintained a high level of motivation. Academic success, high grades, graduation from high school, and attending university are all very important to her. She maintains this drive to achieve almost exclusively on her own. Her father is unavailable, and when she encounters questions with her homework, she cannot seek help at home. Partly because of his hectic work schedule, and partly because he feels incompetent, he prefers to stay uninvolved and leaves his children's education in the hands of teachers and other school personnel. Lotus's father describes how in China the educational process is stricter and "uses the 'feeding duck' method," which means rote memorization (or force feeding). "I like the 'feeding duck' method better," he continues. "Here, it is more relaxed . . . I do not know much about things my daughter learns. I let the school nurture her." Her mother is a phantom in the background of this story, her role in Lotus's academic life unclear.

Despite the lack of support from her family, Lotus remains strongly self-motivated to perform well in school. Lotus sees education as the way to ensure a better future for herself, her family, and the community. "If I decide to do it and study hard every day, I will succeed and miracles will appear," she says. Lotus believes that individual effort is a more critical factor than race or ethnicity in determining how successful one is at school and in a career. She seems to think that by working hard she can overcome most problems.

Lotus's tremendous motivation to achieve translates into a devoted, persistent approach to schoolwork. She is anxious about her grades and spends a lot of time and energy studying. During the first year of our study, when she was in seventh grade, she spent two to three hours a day on homework, but by the third year, after entering high school, she was spending seven to eight hours on homework, often staying up until 1:00 A.M. Her conversations with her best friend, Mei, are always about schoolwork—comparing test results and their answers. Everything in Lotus's life is related to school, and she does not have time for, nor does she dare devote time to, anything else, because she considers it to be a distraction from what is truly important—her schoolwork.

To Lotus, her heavy workload is a joy, not a burden. She likes school; she loves learning and the feeling of accomplishment. Lotus shows a strong sense of curiosity, and the more complicated the task, the greater she works to overcome the challenge and the more the confidence she gains in herself. Yet she finds the amount of time she devotes to homework increasingly exhausting, and she worries whether she can sustain this schedule through the twelfth grade.

Lotus went to a middle school that had few resources but a well-developed bilingual program. The school had five hundred students, about 15 percent of whom were Asian. At first, she found the school stressful, and she particularly hated "being bullied by others. There are students (most are blacks, some are whites) that throw things—they throw them at people, throw them around, crumple the paper and throw it, or throw cereal. Sometimes when we are having lunch they throw things. I see many people scold others or kick others." Later, Lotus felt more comfortable, having built a supportive social network. As it does for many immigrant children, the bilingual program functioned as a supportive "holding place" that sheltered Lotus from the unknown.[8] These "holding places" can be powerful, providing children with psychological space to deal with the multiple losses inherent in immigration. They also provide the necessary skills—educational and cultural—for a successful transition to the American school system. But the transition from middle school to the high school can be equally traumatic, a sort of secondary migration.

As a result of her persistence, Lotus was accepted to the competitive exam high school in her city and entered the school's college track. We visit her in this school, planning to stay with her for several of her classes. Lotus comes down the cafeteria stairs in a white shirt and pair of blue jeans, and when she sees us, she literally freezes on the spot, looking very nervous and uncomfortable. She walks in, puts down her bag on a bench, and asks us to wait for her there while she gets her tray. We share the table with her best friend, Mei, and other Chinese girls. Lotus does not exchange a word or make eye contact with her friends. The two other girls are talking while Mei, Like Lotus, eats her lunch quietly.

The atmosphere of tension persists as Lotus sits upright and rigid, eating her pie bit by bit, her jaws making the least possible movement. We try to initiate a conversation to break the ice: "How's your lunch?" "How are your classes?" She only nods or gives one-word answers. Since Lotus is so self-conscious and uneasy in our presence, we make plans to catch up with her another time and cut this visit short. Her social awkwardness is painful.

Lotus has maintained A and B grades with a steady improvement throughout the years as her English has improved. For four consecutive years, she had straight A's. But there is a drop in the last year of the study. She has felt more isolated and more pressured in this much larger school of 2,400 students. Even now, the English language remains her biggest challenge, and she avoids participating in class: "I don't have much to say in class. I'm afraid to raise my hand. I worry that I would say something wrong and people will laugh at me." Tests and evaluations in English provoke particular anxiety. While taking a test in school, she squeezes her hands into fists, frowns, and stares at the questions. She takes out a tissue paper and holds it in her hand, gradually crumpling it during the exam.

Tests given to Lotus in eleventh grade reveal that she is intellectually gifted. Her verbal ability, assessed by combining English and Chinese, is in the very superior range for her age (99th percentile). Her English-language proficiency score, however, remains just slightly above average, at the 58th percentile.[9] This discrepancy is a source of frustration and dissatisfaction for her, because she is aware of her abilities and how the language suppresses them. While her English is not as weak as she perceives it to be, she is self-conscious and reluctant to speak English both in and out of class. Her English teacher says that Lotus has good skills in writing and reading but avoids speaking in English and does so with difficulty. "Lotus is a delightful girl," the teacher says. "She is still rather silent in class, does not speak very often, but still does very good work. I encourage her to speak up, but she is very shy about it. She needs practice in speaking English out loud." At one point the teacher referred her to after-school tutoring with the hope of immersing her in an English-speaking environment, but Lotus felt uncomfortable and quit the program. She is convinced that English will prevent her from pursuing a satisfying career. But her determination is evident in her insistence that if she tries hard, she will overcome this obstacle. And a year later, her English teacher remarks: "Lotus's work has been good. There are certain language obstacles, but over the years she has overcome many of them through persistent effort and intelligence."

Lotus tells us that she is dissatisfied with her performance at school; she feels that she is "never doing well enough." Her academic achievement fails to boost her self-esteem; rather, it invokes further strife, dissatisfaction, and anxiety. She strives for straight A's, and her educational goal is to get onto the honor roll. Her inability to maintain her goal of straight A's leads to painful self-doubt and self-deprecation.

Lotus is unwavering in her desire to go to college after high school. She wants to major in business and be a "banker, teacher, or a hero." She explains that bankers "earn a lot of money" and a teacher could "help [her] students," "learn many things," and have "a high salary." It seems that money is of great concern: She sees the effort she puts into her studies now as a way to help her family be comfortable financially in the future. Lotus's wish to become a teacher also seems to be a way to make up for the pressure and powerlessness she is experiencing now. She envisions a future in which she would have more control. In fact, she says that she wants to be a teacher because teachers "obtain satisfaction by taking revenge on her students. My teachers are giving us too much homework. I have worked so hard as a student all these time. When I grow up, I should become a teacher and 'show' my students what hard work really means. I will give my students as much workload as I am having now."

Lotus's expectations about school and her future are ambivalent. On the one hand, she holds high expectations about her future, framing it in terms of success in the United States. She consistently expresses the wish and the determination to go to college, saying, "Five years from now I will be in college and be an American citizen." On the other hand, she also feels overwhelmed by what she sees as huge obstacles and by the effort she devotes to overcoming them.

Living in Her Own World

On one occasion when we meet with Lotus, we discuss for a while where we should sit down to talk and suggest going to the library. Lotus refuses, however, because she lacks a pass to the library and believes that the staff will reprimand her for being there when she is not supposed to be. We decide to go back to the study room, and along the way, Lotus sees her counselor approaching from the opposite direction. She freezes on the spot, her body tight. Her head bows slightly as the counselor passes with a warm smile and greetings. She asks Lotus how things are going, but Lotus cannot formulate a response; she stays frozen until the counselor has passed.

We arrive at the study room. Lotus stops at the door, reluctant to enter. She says several times that the teacher will "scold her to death" because she does not have a pass. We reassure her over and over again that we will explain the situation to her teacher, and finally, we enter the study room, where a dozen students are reading quietly. A friendly teacher welcomes us and invites us to use the room now and in the future.

The social support available to Lotus is limited. Insightfully, she describes herself as "alone by myself. Very lonely, very shy." But she has developed relationships with teachers and school counselors, which are generally positive. Lotus says she talks more often with her teachers in the United States than she did to her teachers in China. Here she feels she can ask them questions, but only "when others have finished asking." She is frightened by authority figures, however, because she has carried with her from China the image of the teacher as a second and punitive parent. She therefore seeks less support from adults at school than she could, particularly from her American teachers. Her guidance counselor is especially important to her, because she is the only one telling Lotus what she needs to do to get into college. The counselor is the one adult whom Lotus names as really important for her besides her parents, yet, as we saw, this person instills a seemingly unwarranted fear.

Lotus interacts minimally with a couple of students at school and avoids the other students. She knows that she hangs back from meeting new people and trying to make friends. She has joined no extracurricular activities or after-school organizations. Lotus simply does not find school to be a place where she can talk to people about her troubles. As we follow her throughout the years, her definition of success changes from a relational one when we first met her, of "having many friends," to one of mastery, of "doing well in school." She appears to have given up on the notion that she will be able to elicit and sustain nurturing relationships.

When she was in middle school and enrolled in the bilingual program, Lotus had more social contacts, particularly more friends from China. Since she started high school, however, she has made only one good friend, a girl who went to the same middle school and was the top student in the class. Lotus always eats lunch alone. There are only two students who sit alone during lunch hour, Lotus and a Native American boy. The boy has tried on occasion to start conversations with Lotus, but she does not respond. She is isolated from her peers; a telling example is that even at seventeen, she uses her e-mail only a few times a year and has never used instant messaging, which is hugely popular among teenagers in the United States and abroad.

Lotus is further isolated socially because she eschews all extracurricular activities. She explains this decision by noting the time her homework consumes; she's always staying up late at night to complete it. She has no paid or volunteer jobs. She quietly acknowledges that colleges expect students to have had extracurricular activities. Over the last year, Lotus has joined the Bible club at school, but only because it was the easiest club to join and required the least time away from studying.

Indeed, Lotus has come to view all extracurricular activities as distractions, as evidenced by her changing attitude toward Buddhism. She had been involved with Buddhism; she found the teachings reasonable and reading them calmed her. But she began to worry that believing too much in those teachings might influence her work ethic. Buddhism teaches people to be accepting and not to fight, and she worries that accepting such an ideology might affect her motivation to learn and to work hard, to fight for success. After coming to this conclusion, she gave up reading Buddhist philosophy.

Lotus is wrought with anxiety and she always appears nervous whenever we meet. She admits that she often feels nervous, shy, sad, and physically or emotionally tense; has trouble concentrating; and believes that she is not as good as other people.[10] Her low self-esteem comes through in all of her social interactions. She feels intense stress and pressure from school. Lotus's father is concerned that Lotus might become introverted because of what she perceives as her poor ability to communicate and her lack of friends. It is also obvious that Lotus's parents are concerned about her workload at school and the pressure she feels. Lotus's father says that he would rather Lotus get a lower grade than work so hard. In these conversations, a family concern around suicide surfaces. Lotus says that one of the things parents from China worry about most in raising a girl in the United States is that the girl might commit suicide. An Asian girl in Lotus's school recently killed herself, at least partly due to the pressure of academic expectations.

Lotus's day is predictable: "I go to school every day. When I get home, I do my homework. When I'm done with my homework and revision, it is time for bed already." Lotus is acutely aware of her disconnection from the "outside world." She believes that she doesn't know anything about U.S. society. She says that although she has been in this country for a long time, she does not fit easily into American society and lives instead in her own little world.

Through the years, we observe changes in Lotus's ethnic identity. Initially, she identified herself as Chinese, said she felt uncomfortable in the United States, and disliked everything about her new country. Because she had few relatives in the United States, and one of them was a demanding taskmaster of a grandmother, Lotus longed to return to China. Over time, however, she started to enjoy her new life and said that she wanted to stay in the United States for a while before returning to China. Lotus has preserved a strong sense of Chinese identity, which is perhaps unsurprising given that she has learned little about American culture. She attends ethnic cultural festivals with her relatives, her limited friendships have been with Chinese peers, and she clearly feels most comfortable with Chinese people. She observes that students from different countries or backgrounds cannot communicate with each other, stating that there are no common topics to talk about across ethnic lines. She points out that although students from different backgrounds have known each other for a long time, they remain distant. By the end of the study, Lotus identifies herself as "American Chinese," saying she feels "somewhat American and somewhat Chinese." But this self-identification might be a mechanical combination of taking into account her nationality (she is now an American citizen) and her ethnicity, which she continues to identify as Chinese.

Everything about Lotus's behavior invokes a sense that she has never truly immigrated. Consciously, she knows that she is in a different place and must adapt to new circumstances, but Lotus's phenomenological world has remained in China. She maintains the habits of a Chinese student, and she would likely behave in exactly the same manner if she were attending a high school in China.

High Achievement as a Life Jacket

Despite receiving almost no support from her family and having nearly no friends, Lotus continued to demonstrate very high levels of motivation and engagement in her schooling during the first years of the study. She performed well academically, receiving above average grades. But the situation changed in eleventh grade. At that point, her grades began to drop significantly and she began to show signs of psychological distress as a result of the extreme academic pressure she was placing on herself as well as possibly her unstable family circumstances. We can't help but wonder how long Lotus can go on like this, with limited support, great pressures academically, and a strong determination to be a high achiever.

Compared with many other Chinese children, Lotus faces huge disadvantages because of her poverty, immigration history, and home circumstances. She is further hampered by limited social and parental support. As mentioned earlier, her father has said he will not pay college tuition for her because of her gender. These factors have contributed to her anxieties and made it difficult to adapt to her new homeland.

In spite of these obstacles, Lotus remains strongly motivated to achieve. In fact, studying may have become her only coping mechanism, because it is the one aspect of her life over which she exerts control, whereas everything else during the immigration process has happened to her. Lotus is very sensitive and reacts negatively to change. The only thing that is stable for her and that she controls is her studying, which is why even minor fluctuations in grades are deeply worrisome for her. When we show her the picture of a boy and a violin and ask her to tell a story about it, Lotus's responses lend insight into her academic identity as it has changed over the years:

> He was a violinist who was in an inter-schools competition. He was going to compete very soon. His violin was broken. He could not compete. He was very poor, and he could not buy another violin. He went to many stores; he finally found someone to repair [his violin]. On the competition day, he overslept. He could not go to the competition at the end. (Year 1)

> This Latino boy really wants to learn his violin well. However, he does not have any talent. Also, his parents force him to learn the violin. He feels really overwhelmed. He does not know what to do. He just sits there. Earlier on, his violin teacher yelled at this boy. His parents want him to learn. He also wants to learn but he still does not do well even though he has tried hard. He is thinking how he can play it well. In the future, he should play the violin well. (Year 5)

In Lotus's stories, we see a shift in the way she explains her struggles with academics, which resonate with her own struggle with the English language. In the first story, the problems are framed mostly as external and manageable. With time and accumulating tension, however, the source of the problem shifts to an internal one—the absence of "talent"—mirroring Lotus's doubts about her own capabilities and skills. According to Lotus, she can overcome this self-doubt only by trying harder.

When reading Lotus's second narrative, it is impossible to ignore her internal frame of reference. At a superficial level, her social adaptation seems adequate and she seems to be adjusting well to the United States. She attends a school with an excellent reputation and earns high grades during most of the years that we work with her—she seems securely on the college track. But her psychological world is in turmoil. She internalizes everything, turning her doubts, her confusion, her rage, and the unfortunate circumstances of her migration in on herself. She is alienated from family and peers, though ironically, at least initially, this alienation and anxiety propel her motivation to achieve.

By the last year of the study, Lotus's grades have plummeted from largely A's to several C's. Though she is behaviorally and cognitively engaged in school, she lives in a socially isolated capsule in her universe of one. Difficult family relationships and a lack of emotional support at school (in part due to her self-imposed isolation) cause her to become overwhelmed by anxiety and depression. With so little nurturing by others, over time Lotus is simply unable to sustain her initial impressive levels of motivation, engagement, and performance.

Henry: "I Can Think for Myself"

When in the fifth year of our study we asked Henry to create a story about a drawing of a young woman with books overlooking a farm scene, he tellingly offered this narrative:

> She has a family who owns a farm. She wants to have a certain education.
> Her mother doesn't like or want her to get the education. She wants to learn
> just to satisfy her own curiosity. She gets ahead anyway, regardless of what
> her mother says.

As his story suggests, Henry, a lanky youth with a perennial smirk, has an independent streak. He's always hard to pin down. Each of our meetings entails multiple attempts to reach him by telephone, long waits at the arranged times, and frequent rescheduling. The first time we manage to sit down for a talk, he is fourteen years old and seems exhausted. His formal necktie contrasts sharply with the wrinkles in his faded white shirt as he leans against the table, propping up his head with one hand. Our conversation flows freely despite his occasional struggles to express himself. When we offer to talk only in English, he declines, insisting that he prefers to continue in Chinese, although his native language is slipping from him.

When he was ten years old, Henry and his mother arrived in the United States after leaving their previous home, a coastal city in China. Many years earlier, Henry's mother, who was married at the time, had remained in China while Henry's maternal grandparents emigrated to the United States. After incidents of domestic violence broke the marriage apart, Henry's mother decided to join her parents, who were able to sponsor the immigration of both mother and son. Henry's father stayed in China, and they have no contact with him. The history of violence has had a lingering effect: Henry, who witnessed his mother's humiliation, vividly remembers the fear his father provoked and how he would run away when he saw his father coming. Henry's mother has remained single since her divorce, and she notes that she values her freedom as a single parent.

Henry's mother studied rubber technology and received a degree from a technical college in China. After graduation, she worked in a rubber factory. When she immigrated, she worked for a while in a Chinese restaurant, but she made it her goal to escape what she saw as the trap of working for a Chinese business in an ethnic enclave. She succeeded, starting as a temporary worker in a state government office and becoming a permanent worker after two and a half years. She takes great pride in her job at a mainstream workplace, which for her signifies her full participation in American society.

Henry's mother seems to enjoy her life in the United States, and, unlike many immigrants, she has regained the living standard to which she was accustomed in China. Although Henry's mother works full-time and earns a decent salary, she continues to live simply. She intends neither to make any major purchases nor to move to a new place. Since shortly after their arrival, she and Henry have lived in a subsidized housing project. His mother likes the location, for it is right next to a subway line that goes directly to Chinatown. She feels safe in her neighborhood although she knows few people in her building. Henry, in contrast, feels uneasy. He complains about the neighborhood's many Latinos. He reports seeing many fights and says he feels unsafe walking around.

Doors Closing between Mother and Son

On a Saturday morning, near the end of our study, we visit Henry's home. His mother greets us warmly at the door, and we settle into a armchair in the living room for what turns out to be a rich conversation as Henry sleeps the morning away in his bedroom. The house is inviting, adequately furnished, and neatly kept. The dining table is covered with textbooks and Henry's homework in progress. A cat silently wanders across the room, enhancing, as cats do, the sense of comfort and homeliness. It is a pleasure to talk to Henry's mother, who is friendly, takes time to consider the questions in depth, and answers thoughtfully. She has an engaging sense of humor and finds something to smile about in many of her comments, throwing her head back slightly and breaking into lighthearted laughter every once in a while. She comes across as resilient, resourceful, and optimistic.

Poignantly, she laments the increasing alienation and estrangement between mother and son. For years, she says, they shared many activities, though even then Henry rarely shared his feelings. When they argued, Henry would go into his room and close the door, or, if he stayed in the living room, he would rudely turn up the television to drown out his mother's voice. His mother sees Henry as stubborn, a son who responds better to gentle guidance than to force and authority. The mother complains that Henry has been difficult to control since they moved to the United States. Henry won't listen to advice or respond to her directives. He often tells her: "You don't have to reprimand me. I can think for myself."

Henry recently started working two nights a week from 4 P.M. to 2 A.M. at a Chinese take-out restaurant. He shocked his mother when he announced that he would use his earnings solely for his own entertainment. She found it unfathomable that he felt no obligation to contribute to household expenses. This disagreement has exacerbated the tensions in their relationship. She believes that his greater financial independence erodes her authority. One time, when he came home very late, his mother scolded him and told him that she had almost called the police. But he retorted that legally she could not report him as a missing person until he had disappeared for a full forty-eight hours. On another occasion, "when I said that I could throw him out, he informed me that I am not allowed to do that under the U.S. law. I was very shocked when I heard that. Here they have classes on law but not on values."

When we talk to Henry at age seventeen, it becomes apparent that he admires his mother's strength, but thinks she does not understand him. It's clear he would rather not discuss their relationship. He says he rarely sees her, rarely talks to her, and doesn't follow her rules. This distancing veils his concern for her. He shifts between being protective of her and minimizing her importance. He laments his mother's hard work and wishes he could to do something to help her, yet he shares neither his earnings nor his time. (He tells us he spends about twenty minutes a day with her.) "No, I completely won't [talk to her]," he says. "It is because she would not understand how I feel and think. I was a child in the past. Now time has passed. I think that she does not understand how I think." When asked his definition of a good family, Henry answers, "more care and warmth . . . but this is the textbook answer. Personally, I think I value my friends more than my family. That is why I put my friends in the first place and my family in the second. So it does not really matter whether I have a good family or not."

His mother is heartbroken about the direction their relationship has taken. She feels that as Henry has become older, her authority has completely deteriorated. Her words nearly echo his: "He does not listen to me; he does not follow my instructions any more." They argue, but the next day both act as if nothing had happened. Thus their conflicts are never resolved but pile up, ignored by both. She is resigned to the fact that he simply will not listen to her, and whenever she tries to speak to him, she says, he either remains mute or yells back. These days, it is she as much as Henry who avoids the verbal fights; she hides behind the closed door of her bedroom. It is not surprising that she knows virtually nothing about his academic life. When she tries to ask him about his homework or examinations, he simply ignores her, and she sees his report cards only when she happens to come across them in the mail.

She attributes Henry's growing independence and disobedience to her having treated him as a friend rather than as a child. She reasons that since she never assumed the role of an authoritative figure, she never cultivated the respect that she deserves as his mother. "A while back I read this newspaper article, and I realized that I might have done something wrong that will not only hurt me but also my son," she says reflectively. "All along, I have always treated my son in ways that one would treat a friend. But now I think this was wrong. I have lost the respect granted to a senior person, and it is very difficult to make him do things or listen to me. If he doesn't like it, he would just talk back to me just as he does to his friends." She regrets that she did not discipline Henry more while he was younger, and she thinks that they will both suffer the consequences of her lenience. She also blames negative messages in the popular media as well as the U.S. approach to childrearing, which, she believes, grants children too much freedom. U.S. schools, she goes on, do not offer *sixiang jiaoyu,* or moral education.[11]

In addition, Henry's mother seems to accept Henry's facade of intellectual superiority as the truth. Henry portrays himself with great self-confidence; he describes himself as extremely smart, intellectually superior to those around him, and destined to become a great scientist. His mother knows that Henry's grades have been low for the past few years. Instead of recognizing that he is neglecting his academics, she attributes his poor grades to his frequent absences from school. She believes him when he says he skips classes because the material is too easy and the teachers too slow.

Ivy League Aspirations Unshaken by Failing Grades

When we started the study and Henry was a newly arrived seventh grader, he had voiced ambitions to attend an Ivy League university and become an architect, genetic engineer, or scientist. In the early years, he appeared to be on track to reach these goals. At his Cantonese/English bilingual middle-school program, he received high grades in all his classes; he also received crucial guidance from a bilingual counselor who was a fierce advocate for her students. Henry was one of only two students from this program to gain entry into an elite high school that required a competitive exam for admission.

Henry's academic performance, however, has plummeted ever since he entered this high school. His math skills are strong, but his English-language ability has lagged, fettering his ability to negotiate the high school's academic and social demands. Although his verbal ability in the tenth grade (using both his English and Chinese skills) was in the high-average ability range for his age, his English-language proficiency was low.[12] His reading skills in English are far below what he needs to have to perform in a highly competitive academic environment.[13]

Henry found the pressure from high-school-level schoolwork overwhelming. To protect himself from his growing sense of inadequacy, he began to disengage. He started cutting classes and refused to do schoolwork. His grades nosedived. In his bilingual middle school, Henry had felt comfortable asking his teachers and counselor for advice. In the English-only classrooms of the high school, however, Henry felt exasperated and isolated, and he stopped asking questions.

His teachers note that Henry lacks enthusiasm, is passive in class, and refuses to interact. Henry says he avoids asking questions or seeking help because to do so would cast doubt on his intellectual abilities. He fears triggering suspicions like "You say you are smart—then why you can't you do the homework?" One of his teachers in the ninth grade described how Henry becomes impatient and won't listen to explanations. Another teacher says Henry is "reticent, answers in monosyllables, does not complete assignments in a timely fashion, and is often absent." His history teacher writes that Henry "is not personally disrespectful, but he tunes out, often with headphones hidden under his hair, which causes him to miss a lot." The teachers are concerned and believe that he is capable of doing much better, but his absences hamper him; his calculus teacher exclaims: "Henry is excellent. He does have an attendance problem, however, and it has gotten worse lately." In fact, the teachers referred him to the guidance counselor due to his poor performance. Henry's teachers also comment frequently on his condescending behavior toward his peers, saying he criticizes them, making them uncomfortable.

As Henry's disengagement evolves, no one at the school is able to help. In middle school, he defined school as "a place to learn"; in high school, he comments, "School is a boring place."[14] By the end of the ninth grade, he has received failing grades in nearly every course for "attendance failure." He earns a D plus in one subject and F's in the rest. Consequently, he must repeat ninth grade. Even so, he continues to flounder, and in January of his second ninth-grade year, he is transferred to a regular urban public high school.

The new high school is much smaller and much less demanding. While his old school had 2,400 students, the new one has four hundred. On standardized tests, 37 percent of the students in the tenth grade, where Henry is placed, have scores at or above proficiency level in English/language arts and 41 percent are proficient in math, compared to 99 percent and 98 percent respectively at his former school. Sixty-three percent of students are eligible for free lunches in his new school, compared to 28 percent in his former school. And here 68 percent of the students are college-bound versus 90 percent at his former school.

Henry is dismissive of the academic standards at his new school, feeling that he isn't challenged. He persists in cutting classes, rationalizing that the materials are too easy and sap his motivation. He is officially a tenth grader, yet because he took advanced classes at the exam school, he has been placed in many eleventh- and twelfth-grade science classes. He has already taken the SAT and received a very high score. He sent his SAT scores to the Massachusetts Institute of Technology and other competitive engineering schools, from which he received positive letters, telling him that he is exactly the kind of student they are looking for—although they have yet to see his transcripts.

Despite his academic disengagement, Henry's interests have become more focused. When he was younger, he spoke in general terms of becoming a lawyer, doctor, scientist, or geologist, but now his plans are precise and elaborate. He wants to finish both college and graduate school. His eyes light up as he discusses his plans: he definitely wants to study biology as an undergraduate. He'll attend an Ivy League college. He'll pursue graduate study in genetic engineering at Harvard Medical School or architecture or biological engineering at MIT. Harvard, MIT, and the University of California–Los Angeles: those are his dream schools.

Back to Reality

Henry is eighteen years old and in the tenth grade when he confronts a choice that preoccupies him: he could either try to finish at his new school and then apply to a four-year college, or he could quit school and get a GED (the general education development credential, a high school equivalency certificate). As usual, his side of our conversation is conducted with dismissiveness, but a floodgate opens when we ask about his current academic standing. His dilemma is almost palpable as his thoughts rush from one path to another:

> I'm actually working to try to get into college now. I could drop out now at tenth grade and get a GED. But I actually have a very good SAT score. Everything is great. The only thing upsetting about my situation is my transcript, my GPA. Today I saw my transcript for the first time, and it is practically all F's because I didn't attend the classes for a whole month since I've transferred to the new school . . . So I am trying to figure out some solutions. I really want to go to college. I did really well on the math part. And you know, since I am a foreign student I don't have to pass the English part. I

could take the TOEFL. That's why I got accepted to every single school that I've tried to apply to. I am perfect, but I only don't have a good GPA to show off to people . . . I don't think I can really fix all the straight F's. I don't think I am going to try really hard. Maybe I can just get a GED, so I won't have to waste two more years. I might not get ahead, . . . but everything I did was ruined—my good SAT score. So it seems to be meaningless if I do the GED, but if I don't do it, I will have to stick with high school for two more years and my GPA is not going to be good. But perhaps this way I could get to a better college, although I'll be two years behind. I'm still struggling.

Language barriers and the burdens of being a single working parent—not to mention the alienation between mother and son—prevent Henry's mother from helping him with his schoolwork. Henry describes his mother's lack of involvement in a way that simultaneously preserves her image of scientific competence and explains her inability to tutor him: "I seldom see her. Even though she may help me, but as far as I know, she isn't good at my [schoolwork]. It is impossible for me to ask her to help me with my English. She herself is going to evening school right now. Her English is not that good. In terms of math—science and math—Chinese people are good at math, but my mom is really good. However, sometimes when I ask her, I don't know if it is because she doesn't want to or what, she just looks like she doesn't know much. That's why I don't ask. In addition, I seldom see her." Indeed, Henry regularly misleads his mother about how school is going. When she asks whether he has finished his homework, he always says that he has. She believes that the system has to take greater responsibility. She thinks teachers in the United States use their hearts to teach the students but lack a method to reprimand students who do not complete their assignments.

Despite Henry's inflated self-image and his obvious intelligence, he has been failing classes since the beginning of his high school career. His low grades are largely due to his continual absences in virtually all his classes; his absenteeism is, possibly, fueled by his sense of inadequacy and the frustration caused by his poor English abilities. He continues to believe in his talent and ability, maintaining that the far-too-elementary class materials simply cannot sustain his interest. As his doubts about his chances of getting into college grow, he defends against them by saying: "If a school does not admit a genius like me, it's the loss of that university. It's the university's failure."

Henry lives in the impossible place between the extremes of "I am perfect" and "I am failing school." His insecurity blocks him from seeking help, so he persists in trying (and failing) to solve his problems alone. "When I have a problem, I think about it myself. If I cannot solve it, then I quit . . . Just kidding. Sometimes I won't ask teachers because they would say to me, 'You said that you are very smart, but you cannot do it yourself.' Thus I will solve the problem myself, most of the time." Rather than face shame, Henry takes himself out of the game entirely.

Caught between Two Worlds

The family seems completely cut off from the Chinese ethnic community: the mother has no close Chinese friends who could offer advice about raising her son, and although she is close to some of her American coworkers, their experiences as parents are, naturally, quite different. Her and Henry's main source of social support is their extended family, particularly the grandparents who live nearby and whom they see weekly. The grandparents picked Henry up from school when he was younger and helped their daughter in various ways, but she won't turn to them for financial support. She consciously declines to share her feelings with others because she believes everyone has different life experiences and no person can fully understand another. Sometimes she feels desperate.

One measure of Henry's sense of isolation is that he names his aunt as one of the important people in his life—but near the end of our conversation we find out that she died eight years ago. In middle school, he had many Chinese friends. They spoke Chinese, played ball together, and hung out watching television. These relationships faded, however, because very few of his friends from middle school made it to the exam high school Henry first attended. At that school, too, he couldn't communicate well with the American students; his English was too weak. One of Henry's teachers noted that he always ate alone in the big cafeteria. At his second, smaller high school, he was placed in science classes with juniors and seniors, though officially he was a sophomore. This schedule made it hard for him to establish relationships either with people in his own grade or with the upperclassmen. His fellow sophomores seemed to sense his belief that they were somehow at a lower intellectual level. His condescending attitude toward his peers, which he uses to compensate for his own self-doubts, has isolated him.

Henry's self-doubts hinder him from making friends with boys; in these relationships, he constantly and convincingly needs to affirm his superiority. He tells us that most of his friends are girls whom he tutors in math. While he is comfortable in the role of teacher, he gets competitive with girls whom he perceives as his intellectual equals. His teachers note that while he shows respect for male teachers, he pushes away and discounts the authority and efforts of his female teachers.

Henry has not returned to China since he immigrated to the United States, and there is no one, relative or friend, whom he keeps in touch with there. His mother once offered him an airplane ticket to go back, but he declined. He seems determined to stay here without trying to stay connected to his country of origin, which poses an interesting contradiction: although over the years Henry has consistently identified himself as "completely Chinese," both he and his mother keep their distance from everything Chinese, whether in the United States or in China. His mother doesn't want to live or work with other Chinese people, and neither will travel to China or keep in touch with people there. Henry is caught between two worlds—he can't yet fully enter the mainstream American world because he does not have the English-language skills, yet he won't reach out to his Chinese peers. He is caught in many ways: between the extremes of high intellect and failing grades, between his marginal performance in high school and his conviction that he will enroll in an Ivy League college, between his concern for his mother and his alienation from her.

The Fragmented Self of an Immigrant Youth

Henry's journey of escalating disengagement is painful to witness. He is a capable student with high potential and very high educational and professional expectations who seemed to be thriving in the first years after immigration. The transition from a bilingual middle school to a mainstream exam school was traumatic for Henry, almost a second migration—this time from the comfort and safety of his bilingual classes to the anomic environment of a huge, competitive, English-based high school. Rather than intensifying his efforts to cope, however, Henry gave up. He would rather skip school and allow himself to believe that he is failing because of his absences than admit that he has stopped trying. He finds it difficult to integrate his smart self with the self whose severe academic difficulties are caused by the language barrier. In addition, his independence and off-putting attitude isolate him from those who might offer help. He is estranged from both his peers and his teachers, and his mother can neither offer support for his academics nor meaningfully influence him.

Henry's unshakable confidence in his academic capabilities is glaringly inconsistent with his performance. Projected arrogance comes through as a defining feature of Henry's behavior, his way of protecting himself from his growing inability to deal with the academic requirements he encounters. His tremendous belief in his own intellect masks and defends against his escalating self-doubt. It is possible that his mother has overcompensated for his witnessing her husband's abuse of her by striving to bolster his self-esteem. In middle school, his smooth adaptation in the bilingual program and his easy mastery of the material led him to set very high goals for himself. He started speaking of entering Ivy League colleges to study genetic engineering even before he entered high school. When he entered the exam school, he soon became overwhelmed, but instead of admitting that he had to work hard to master the material, he used his overconfidence as a shield and began manufacturing excuses for his failing grades.

As we end our five-year relationship with Henry, we sense his growing awareness that regardless of how intelligent he might be, his failure to perform adequately in school and the resulting F's on his transcripts mean he will be rejected by the colleges he has long dreamed of attending. He sees himself as a genius caught in an institutional predicament. When he talks about his college plans, he says that he wants to study biology at the University of Chicago, where the biology department is very strong. "If I can't get into the University of Chicago, then I will go to Brown," he says airily. "If not, then I will go to Harvard. Harvard's undergraduate program is not that good. I only rank it third on my list." During the same conversation, however, near the end of the study, when asked to complete the sentence "My future will be . . ." he fills in "very lost."[15] When trying to identify his goals for the next five years, he is certain only of his humanity, without being able to specify any actions or other identities: Five years from now? "I will still be a human being. Of this I am sure."

Mauricio: Alternative Pursuits

Whenever we ask the "Professor" for an interview, his round face flashes a fresh and generous smile. Mauricio was given his nickname by his friends because he always has a clever response at the tip of his tongue. He takes our meetings seriously but also with a touch of humor, and he enjoys joking with his friends about being taken out of class for the interviews. When we talk in private, he is serious, almost confessional. Mauricio addresses us respectfully, in the way that Dominican youth are taught to address older people. He sports a hip-hop style, his hair cut very short.

The members of Mauricio's family came to the United States separately. His stepfather arrived in the late 1980s and settled in the Northeast without a clear idea of whether he would stay. Mauricio's mother followed two years later. The children stayed with their grandmother in Bani, their hometown, for another four years, and then they, too, emigrated. Mauricio was eleven. "They came here to have a good future," Mauricio says of his parents, "and for us, their kids, to have the opportunity to study."

After four years, Mauricio says he likes the United States because it offers "many opportunities for studying," although, as we learn, his efforts don't match his rhetoric. What he finds most difficult is coping with racism and violence. He thinks some Americans are "very abusive and jealous; they want to be better than others." He likes going to the Dominican Republic every summer for vacations. "Here I can't get into the discos because of my age, while in the Dominican Republic I can get in," he says, revealing his true priorities, at least at age seventeen. "If they see me with designer clothes there, they let me in."

Like Mauricio, his mother sees the United States as a land of opportunities. She pictured the United States as a "paradise, a very pretty place about which I didn't have references before . . . especially for somebody who only knew about Bani and Santo Domingo." Mauricio's mother knows fellow Dominican immigrants who have bought houses in the United States and made important changes in their lives. "But life is hard here, one lives just for working," she says wistfully. At first, her main goal for her U.S. sojourn was to save enough money to build a house in the Dominican Republic, to which she plans eventually to return. Now, however, her most important goal is educating her children. The eldest daughter has excelled academically: she attends an Ivy League university on scholarship and plans to become a professional.

In the Dominican Republic, both the mother and stepfather worked as tailors. (We never learn anything about Mauricio's biological father.) Here, the stepfather works as a mechanic. Mauricio's mother had an eighth-grade education; when she arrived she started working as a cleaner and later worked full-time in a textile factory. She appreciates the state support that parents receive for raising their children, especially Medicaid. What she cannot adjust to is the "locked-up life . . . There is no freedom, you can't stay in the street and see or talk to people. You can't hang out late in the street. Here, is it very rare to do that." Mauricio's mother also appreciates that anyone can become an American. "Even though I am not American, I could have a child here that will enjoy the benefits and rights, for instance, of voting," she says, adding, "Of course, American citizens have more rights than residents."

Early in the study, Mauricio lives with his mother, his stepfather, and two sisters. He is the middle child. The elder sister is three years older than Mauricio, the other three years younger. They live in a mixed neighborhood where the population is predominantly white and black Americans. Few Hispanics live nearby; most of Mauricio's friends live elsewhere. Although he knows there are gangs in his neighborhood, he says it is safe.

The bond between parents and the children is tight when Mauricio is in middle school. His mother feels that their relationship has been unaffected by immigration, but Mauricio sees it differently, saying that the family spends less time together than before the move. His mother, he says, "works too much here." Mauricio's social support network includes his family, particularly his mother, and his friends, in whom he places great confidence, believing they will always help him with problems by trusting his judgment or giving him advice. When he lived in the Dominican Republic, his grandmother, grandfather, aunts, and uncles were also his confidants.

Mauricio sees his mother as providing discipline in the family, but he also considers her his guide. She is the one who knows where he is and usually what he is doing. When they disagree on something, he usually obeys her, he says. He follows her rules: come straight home from school and call if running late. Mauricio believes a good child is one who "respects his parents and follows their advice."

Mauricio gets along with his sisters. He speaks admiringly about his older sister's academic success: "She always gets good grades and always gets good scholarships. She applied to several good schools and she was accepted by Cornell, a very good university. She is very smart." This sister embodies Mauricio's own expectations for achievement. In general,

Mauricio's home life fulfills his ideal of parenthood and family: "To me, a good family is one where everyone helps each other and where people don't fight." Together, the family goes to the park and plays baseball; they go to the supermarket; they watch TV; they eat together every day. He talks to his parents about his day at school, the problems he is having with other students or teachers, and his plans. He is well aware that his parents want him to get good grades, finish high school, and enter college, and for now, these are his aspirations, too.

Mauricio and his parents often call their relatives on the island. Since her arrival here, Mauricio's mother has traveled to the Dominican Republic at least four times, staying for less than a month each time. She went to get the children and bring them back with her; she also went back when her father died. Like many Dominicans, her family relies on the money she sends; sometimes she sends letters and clothes with people who go back to visit. She keeps an eye on events in her country through the news or through her relatives. The family socializes weekly with Dominican friends in the area. They have no American friends.

In his baggy pants, Mauricio looks like a typical urban teenager, but he strongly identifies as Dominican, describing Dominicans as "happy people." To Mauricio, being a Dominican means being astute and acute ("*vivo*"), in contrast with the "dumb" image that Americans project. He sees himself as a person of color from the Caribbean, distinct from the black people of the United States. Ethnic and racial issues are important to him; for example, friends warned him to be careful with African Americans: "Some people told me that Afro-Americans were abusive with Latinos and with new students," he says. All his friends are Dominicans and he speaks Spanish with them. (At home, he and his sisters speak English.) After all, he says, his friends "are from my country. We understand each other better because we share the language, and we came from the same place." To him, "a good friend is one that is with me through the good and the bad times." He also keeps in touch with friends on the island, whom he sees on summer vacations when he travels back to Bani. He appreciates his country as a place where he can always return when he feels lonely, constrained, or bored—as he did in tenth grade, when he went back in the middle of the school year, missing a large part of the curriculum: "I was tired and I wanted to be with my extended family there, so I went to the Dominican Republic."

The family has a transnational mindset, which for Mauricio translates into a continuous duality of experience. Throughout our study he experiences himself as belonging to two worlds. He wants to live in the Dominican Republic, though he recognizes that for the moment, his family and school keep him in the United States.

The Initial School Years

When during the fifth year of the study we asked Mauricio to interpret the ambiguous picture of a boy playing the violin, he wrote:

> He tried to play the violin, but it seemed that he didn't do it well, and he was disappointed with himself. He was going to get motivated, and he was going to do it better.

Mauricio's big brick high school, a couple of blocks from the train station, looks like an arsenal, dominating the solitude of an industrial area. For most of the day, teachers guard the main entrance. As we sign the visitor log, a student enters and asks the teacher to let him in "just for a minute to get the weekly homework." We find out that he was suspended last week and is not supposed to enter the school, but the teacher gives him some leeway and lets him in.

The five floors of the building shelter 1,200 students speaking thirty languages, predominantly English, Spanish, and French. "The school's growing diversity reflects the political crises in other parts of the world," the headmaster tells us. "We know that we can expect children coming from countries in war, which start expelling people as refugees, but also from very poor places. Somalia is one example."

The school is highly segregated, and its statistics tell the story of the challenges the students contend with: poverty, language barriers, ineffective management. Around 5 percent of its students are white. Nearly two-thirds of the students qualify for free lunch. More than 50 percent report having a first language other than English, and another 39 percent are classified as having limited English proficiency. The school's attendance rate is 10 percent lower than the district average and its absenteeism rate is more than double; its reputed dropout rate is a high 5 percent. The school is rife with tension. It is common to see adults screaming at students and fights between black and Latino students or between immigrants and U.S.-born teenagers.

During the short breaks between classes and at lunchtime, students cluster in the hallways according to nationality. Dominican girls and boys chat in familiar and relaxed Spanish jargon about the answers to a recent test, their schedules, and homework—some things remain the same in any high school.

We pass the library and stop at the guidance office to meet with one of the bilingual counselors. When we ask her what kind of problems the students bring to her, she responds, "Everything—from not having a place to sleep to feeling homesick for their countries." While she answers a parent's phone call, we look at the walls, decorated with attractive pictures of Old World–style college campuses in an attempt to motivate potential college students. When she finishes her call, we ask her to describe how the bilingual program works and how the students adjust.

Some of the Dominican students are in ESL (English as a Second Language) I and II, where classes are taught in Spanish, she tells us. Another group is in ESL III and IV, where classes are taught in English, though health and Latin American history are considered "cultural" courses and are taught in Spanish. Mathematics belongs to the multicultural program, which means that the classes are taught in English, but the teachers speak Spanish and can help the students if needed. This alternation between bilingual and multicultural groups has been implemented during the last three years and has helped to increase the students' proficiency in English. When the students first begin the bilingual program, they don't feel overwhelmed because they all share more or less the same experience, the counselor says. "The most stressful experience for them, however, is when they are transferred to the regular courses, where the group is predominantly African-American and some racial tensions enter into the picture," she adds. A history teacher tells us that the climate in the bilingual program is much more positive than in the regular program downstairs. She says: "Downstairs is another story . . . *Alla abajo es una perrera* [Down there it is a kennel]."

Mauricio feels that he was a better student in the Dominican Republic. "I never failed a grade," he says. Here, he considers himself an average student: "Sometimes I do my homework and sometimes not. Sometimes I participate in classes, but sometimes I get distracted." The teachers are more lenient, he says; here "one is left free, there aren't any consequences"; students "don't have to study hard." In the Dominican Republic, he recalls, teachers responded swiftly and harshly to infractions of discipline, slapping students who erred. There, if someone did not want to study, he or she was expelled; here, the student has a chance to change his or her attitude.

Mauricio's mother sees positive and negative aspects to the U.S. educational system. She approves of the schools' providing transportation and following up on where the students are: "If the students don't go to school, someone calls me right away," she says. "They also help them with their studies, academically, [and provide] counseling and job searching." She disapproves, however, of teachers complaining to parents about the children's bad behavior rather than disciplining the students themselves. In the Dominican Republic, she says, echoing Mauricio, the teachers are stricter and have more control.

When he first enrolled in a U.S. school, Mauricio was placed in the sixth-grade bilingual program. He continued in the bilingual program when he moved up to the high school, but he doesn't like it. "They don't prepare you well enough for English," he says. "I know that from friends in other schools where ESL programs are more effective." Despite this, his grades show considerable progress in English proficiency: within three years, he lifted his grade from a D, to a B plus, to an A minus.

Mauricio also raised his math grade from a C to an A and improved in social studies. His ninth-grade algebra teacher considers Mauricio's understanding of class material, including his reading of the English-language math textbook, to be excellent. "He has improved this year because he cares about his grade, although he talks a lot in class," the math teacher says.

Mauricio feels confident in mathematics, science, and social studies because he considers himself an intelligent person—and because his parents, sisters, and teachers are willing to work with him. But his performance is inconsistent, and everyone, including Mauricio himself, says he struggles to maintain adequate motivation and effort. "He is a bright student but a medium to low achiever," his ESL teacher writes. "He needs a push! Very capable of doing excellent work but doesn't seem to feel the need to do so."

Mauricio, like most of his friends at school, has always planned to graduate from a four-year university, which is what his parents expect, too. He dreams of getting a scholarship to study computer sciences and imagines that money is his only obstacle to a college degree. Thanks to his sister, cousins, friends, teachers, and counselors, he has a general knowledge of the procedures necessary for applying to college, such as filling out applications, taking the TOEFL (Test of English as a Foreign Language) and SAT exams, getting good grades, and taking advanced-placement classes.

Mauricio and his family value education highly. Year after year, he makes positive statements about school, but after a while this stops translating into motivation and engagement. The more he becomes alienated from school, the more exaggeratedly positive these assessments become, so that by the end of the study he is stating that school is "super important." His assessments of his future also begin to sound artificially optimistic, especially considering his performance in school: he says he will have a "super-excellent" and "brilliant" career. Through the years, he sustains his optimism but not the academic engagement necessary to achieve his goals. In high school, a significant mismatch becomes apparent between Mauricio's potential and his behavioral engagement in academics.

The Later Years

The lunch bell rings, and everyone jumps up to rush from the classroom. A mixed group of young men and women lingers in the hall instead of heading to the cafeteria, which is against the rules. Dominican students, some in the camouflage uniform of the Junior Reserve Officers' Training Corps Program (JROTC), pose for pictures, gesturing expansively, their arms entwined, their bodies hanging from one another. We ask them why they decided to enter the JROTC, which the school offers as an elective. Most say it teaches them discipline and how to relate to other people. We ask whether the uniforms give them some cachet with the girls; they just smile at each other. In an environment where there are few avenues to prestige and hope about the future, the JROTC appears to be a place where students with few options can attain some degree of both. Wearing a uniform for young men is a way to signal that they are members of their new homeland; the JROTC creed states, in part: "I am proud of my country and its flag. I will try to make the people of this nation proud of the service I represent, for I am an American Soldier." Further, since the armed forces promise job training and money for education, this organization provides hope for access to college, a possibility that otherwise would simply be unattainable for many. It is not surprising, therefore, that this organization is attractive particularly to young men, but also to young women, who want to become members of their new society.

Mauricio joined the JROTC, and for a time, his classmates were the group of peers that seemed most important to him. That changed after he got a job as a cashier in a downtown restaurant. He says he no longer admires his JROTC friends and does not want to be like them. "I don't think that they help me at all," he says. "I used to like them, but now I find that class and the group boring." Mauricio's coworkers, who are also Latino, have become his good friends. "They treat me well," he says. "I like how they relate [to] each other."

As mentioned earlier, Mauricio's academic engagement has fluctuated during the years that we have known him. In eighth grade his grades ranged from A to D, resulting in a B average; in ninth grade and tenth grade they dropped, ranging from A to F and resulting in a C average. His math and science grades are his strongest, but he has done particularly badly in his JROTC courses, receiving D's and F's—which is ironic because he has decided to continue his schooling through the army. In a development that says as much about the school as about Mauricio's abilities, he was among the only 20 percent of students in his grade to pass the state standardized test.

In eleventh grade, Mauricio begins to cut classes frequently and then to skip school entirely. His teachers see him very differently than in previous years. His history teacher says: "He is frequently absent—he has 30 or 40 unexplained absences. He is totally . . . [un]interested in class. His behavior is appropriate only when a strict class regimen is established from above, and sometimes not even then." His typical classroom behavior became "ridiculing other students, incessant joking, challenging authority, cutting class." His teachers still see him as bright and capable, but they say he is totally disengaged. Before eleventh grade is over, Mauricio has dropped out of school.

Later, he explains his decision to leave school as immature. "I would say [I did it] for stupidity, for mistakes that the youth make," he says. "I was doing really well. I don't know what happened from one moment to the next, I don't know what happened with me, it just happened . . . When I am not in school, I do everything—going to parties, messing around in the street, everything fun."

After he drops out, he realizes that he is deeply disappointed that he will not finish school. He mentions his sister, who has a full scholarship at Cornell University, with admiration. And he has decided he wants to be an engineer. Mauricio is trying for a second chance. He has begun the process of joining the army, where he plans to earn a high school equivalency degree.

Dropping out of high school has strained his relationship with his family because they strongly disagree with his choice. Further, Mauricio's mother feels that she has lost all control over him. She confides that though she establishes rules, Mauricio decides whether or not to follow them. "Right now, I'm in disagreement with Mauricio because he does not want to go to school," she tells us. "He says he is smart enough, he just doesn't want to go. He is lazy. He doesn't want to go. They have called me a lot from school, saying he doesn't pay attention, he plays in class. So this semester he brought me a note saying finally he is not going back."

They argue frequently about whether he should return to the high school. His mother mulls her tactics: "He is bright. If he wanted to study, he would do well. If I push him too hard, he will rebel more. I have to let him come to see how he needs school." His mother believes his job spurred his decision: He saw what it meant to earn an income, he became enamored of having money in his pocket, and he decided that school was dispensable. She also thinks that his friends were a negative influence, and blames his having a girlfriend whom he wants to impress.

One thing his mother doesn't tell us is that his family context has changed.

Needing an Extra Push

At the end of the study, Mauricio explained the picture of the girl with books gazing over a field in this way:

> She is on her way to her school, and her family is working hard to survive.
> She is searching for the hope of the future of her family.

From a passing comment his mother makes at the end of the study, we find out that she and Mauricio's stepfather have divorced. All along, the stepfather has been nearly invisible in Mauricio's story, and there has been no mention at all of his biological father. This separation must have affected Mauricio's well-being, but it is unclear exactly when and why it happened and what the effect might have been. In general, interactions among Mauricio's family members have become strained over the years. The close relationship Mauricio enjoyed with his mother in the beginning is gone. While he denies any family problems, he says that he now makes all of his decisions on his own and does not tell his mother about his activities.

His mother hates the way American laws limit parental authority and their ability to discipline children, a common concern among Dominican parents. She feels that if the laws gave more autonomy to parents, she would have had a tighter hand and continued control. "You know here that they, they monitor the parents so much," she sputters. "The children have too much support here. Even if one wants to correct them, one cannot. In the Dominican Republic, you can. They have more fear there. You can't raise them how you would like to without bringing problems. Of course, I don't let them stop me from raising my children; I do what I have to, but you do what you can. In the Dominican Republic, you can maintain your family on your own. I'm not saying I would maltreat them, but what happens here is if you try to do [anything], they can go to the telephone and say 'No.'"

More parental authority might have helped prevent Mauricio's precipitous academic decline and eventual dropping out, although his mother attributes his "laziness" about school to the seductive lure of the material culture. He works long hours to support his pursuit of fashionable clothes, discotheques, parties, and girlfriends.

Mauricio's academic fate has been strongly influenced, however, by his inadequate education. Eighty percent of his school's tenth-grade students score below the proficiency level on the state's high-stakes math and English language arts tests. Mauricio was one of few in his class who passed the state standardized testing in tenth grade despite his erratic effort and engagement. This fact speaks volumes about the school's standards and its inability to serve its students. Indeed, the school has low expectations, an impoverished curriculum, a climate of violence, and an overloaded guidance counseling staff that can only haphazardly provide advice to a very needy student body. No serious effort has been made to intervene and reengage Mauricio in order to prevent him from dropping out. Mauricio's history teacher attributes the problem to the difficulty in contacting Mauricio's parents and that they simply "do not care." Falling prey to a common stereotype about immigrant parents, the teacher assumes that

Mauricio's parents are simply not interested in their child's educational outcome.

No one in Mauricio's life seems to be able to influence him during this critical time in his development. His stepfather has disappeared and his biological father has been out of the picture for most of his life. His mother toils long hours in a sewing factory, which seriously limits the time she has for school meetings. (In fact, she has no control over Mauricio's pursuits.) Mauricio's JROTC teacher, a potential mentor, gave up on him. And although a couple of parent-teacher conversations took place over the phone, no vigorous attempt is made to put Mauricio back on a path to academic success. While his teachers consistently state that Mauricio is bright and capable of excellent work, they often mention that he needs a "push." Sadly, no one specifies from where this extra push might come.

Andrés: Longing to Return

Andrés's mother came searching for better jobs and higher wages so that she could send money back to her parents and make sure that her two children would always have enough food and a school to attend. "I came to push us forward," she says. She imagined that the United States would be very pretty and green, that work and help would be as abundant as the trees. She was sad to find that the land is sometimes dry and the work sometimes scarce, but she finds the situation here much better than what it was in Mexico, and she is grateful.

Andrés's mother stayed in the United States for almost two years before going back to Mexico for a six-month break. She returned to the United States, but despite repeated trips home, she was not fully reunited with her children until six years after her initial migration, when they joined her in the United States. Andrés has few recollections of his mother's original departure, because he was only six, but one has remained vivid. When we ask him "Did your family talk to you about coming to the United States? When your mom came, did she tell you why she was coming?" he replies: "I don't remember. She didn't say anything. She said she was coming. She said, 'I am going to the United States,' and that's it. I don't remember very well what she said. The only thing that I remember is that I saw her walk out the door, and that is all."

When their mother left, Andrés and his sister stayed with their aunts, a time Andrés remembers happily. He does not know his biological father, who left when he was five months old.

As soon as she felt confident that she would able to provide for all of them, his mother sent for Andrés, who was then eleven, and his younger sister, who left their grandparents' house and made the trip together. He still feels attached to his aunts' home after five years in his new country, possibly idealizing it in the context of the problems he now faces. He talks of his family in Mexico warmly, saying he was torn apart when he had to leave. We sense that Andrés is a caring and emotional boy, closely connected to his relatives and his childhood surroundings, now far away. He tells of becoming numb when he realized that he was leaving the place he so loved.

> "Andrés, how did you feel when you left Mexico?"
>
> "Well, I felt bad. At first I was kind of happy because I was going to see mom again. But on the other hand, I felt sad because I was leaving my grandparents and my aunts and uncles. I didn't want to leave. My mom called me and I told her that no, that I was going to stay in Mexico. She said come. No, I am not going. So it's like my aunts and uncles convinced me to go. So I said, all right all right, I am going . . . It was the next day, I felt very strange. I didn't feel anything. I didn't feel like walking. Outside my house, it was going to be the last time that I was going to walk on my grandparents' house. It was a big house. It was real big. And it was the last time that I was going to be there and then a tear fell from my eye. So that was when I started crying and crying and I felt like I was leaving my grandmother. And when they took me to the plane that was when I said goodbye to my aunts. They were crying."

Andrés describes a plane ride from his hometown, but it is not clear where the flight landed. With pride, Andrés describes how he was entrusted to take care of his little sister during the border crossing. He recalls their fear they experienced *pasando la linea* (crossing the border). Andrés's family is one of an estimated 11 to 12 million individuals who are undocumented. While more than half of "illegal" immigrants have overstayed their tourist, student, or working visas, most Mexican and Central American undocumented persons steal across the southern border of the United States. This is a treacherous and expensive journey; indeed one or two people die every day attempting to cross this border. For many undocumented children, the crossing is nothing short of traumatic.

Andrés and his sister joined their mother and her partner in a Latino neighborhood in California. Andrés loved the place and the people he encountered: "It's better than Mexico," he said. The household always has people coming and going: two uncles lived with the family from the start, and later their household is joined by family friends. Especially at first, Andrés's mother worried about the neighborhood and kept her children indoors, to keep them away from the *borrachos* (alcoholics) and the drug users. Their car was broken into three times. The atmosphere improved when the police started to patrol more aggressively and the threatening presence of gang members diminished.

After a couple of years, the family moved to a small two-bedroom apartment in a complex where they enjoy more space, nicer facilities, and a better neighborhood. We talk to Andrés's mother in her attractively decorated, homey living room. A huge Virgen de Guadalupe hangs on one wall and a painting of Jesus on another; nearby are certificates of appreciation and acknowledgments of perfect attendance honoring the mother at her workplace. Plants and a fish bowl enliven the space. A puzzling adornment is a painting of the Mona Lisa with a marijuana joint in her hand. The mother could not explain its presence, and states she is certain that her children do not smoke marijuana.

During this interview, in the first year of the study, the mother is radiant. She is pregnant and extremely happy about the new baby. This pregnancy symbolizes a new beginning, a new attempt to reconstruct her family after they have been apart for so long. Her happiness highlights her genuine warmth and caring; she is reminded, however, of how her parents ostracized her when they found out she was pregnant with her second child eleven years ago, just when she was separating from her abusive husband. Now, she is content. The best thing about being in the United States has been "to find my partner and that he accepted me with my two children. He has been a great father for [the children]. They love him."

About a year after the family was reunited this baby sister is born. The family has grown in other ways: an uncle, also named Andrés, joined the household. He is a big influence on our Andrés, though as we will see, not a constructive one. Andrés tells us that besides his parents, Uncle Andrés is the most important adult in his life. Andrés's stepfather had seven years of schooling and was an agricultural worker. Andrés's mother had eight years of education and was a factory worker for a food company before moving to the United States, where she was a kitchen aide in a home for the elderly until the baby was born. Her partner, who paints houses for a living, is now the family's only source of income.

Relatives and friends live nearby. They get together for holidays, birthdays, and other social events. Because all but the newborn sister who was born in the United States lack legal residence documents, the family has not traveled to Mexico since "Operation Hold the Line" at the end of the 1990s made the crossing significantly more arduous and dangerous. Andrés has never returned since arriving in the United States. Using prepaid telephone calling cards, Andrés talks to his grandparents often and maintains a warm, idealized relationship with them. In a childlike way, he holds on to the grandparents' images as though they were frozen in time. We ask him what their conversations are about:

> "When you call your grandmother, do you talk to her or does your mother? What do you talk about?"
>
> "About how we are, when we will return. I told them that [I will return] when I am 18 years old. They joke and say that when I return my grandmother will not be there. That maybe she will be dead. How can she be dead?"

A Commitment to Family

The family's relatively smooth reunification was helped by the mother's diligence in maintaining contact with the children and her parents during their six years apart. Andrés tells us that his reunion with his mother was happy, though his words seem to reflect some ambivalence: "There were lots of pictures of her in my room. It didn't seem weird [reunification] but I didn't remember how she looked. I would only see pictures of her."

Gradually, it dawns on us that the family never talks about its long separation. The years apart do not figure in the family narrative as an issue that needs to be dealt with specifically. Life is presented as uneventful, as having flowed smoothly since reunification; what life was like before is left unsaid. His parents, Andrés says, "never talk about any bad things, only the good things." Sensing that there might be an unvoiced agreement that certain topics—the separation, the appearance of the mother's second partner— are off-limits, we wonder whether Andrés has suppressed his concerns about these issues and what effect this might have. We suspect that the family harbors elements of mourning that have largely not been discussed or processed. This sadness seeps through his mother's words of regret: "I never learned English because my kids were there [in Mexico], so in my mind, I was there too. I cried and cried. It was ugly and sad."

Perhaps the family avoids these discussions to preserve a superficial sense of harmony. There is no mention of conflict, even when Andrés starts to dramatically disengage from school. His mother emphasizes that she creates a nonthreatening atmosphere of trust; Andrés confirms this, saying, "Mother never argues." The Mexican familial values of respect for adults and parents, of helping and obeying elders, are evident in this family, as they are in the projective narrative, which Andrés tells during our first meeting:

> A young girl helped her family cultivate the land. When she became older, she had to go to school. She left her parents to do the work alone. Their hands became very hurt. She was sad, but in time she could help her parents with things they didn't know. The story ended happily.[16]

Andrés is happy that his family is together. Even later on, when he joins a gang and begins to run afoul of the law (and as it becomes increasingly clear that other family members are also involved with gangs), Andrés upholds the ideal of family. Clearly, though, it is his mother to whom Andrés stays loyal. His resistance to and jealousy of his mother's second partner are apparent when we first meet. Eventually, however, Andrés accepts him because "he turned out to be good people." We ask Andrés:

> "And who did you live with when you first got here?"
> "With my mom and my step-dad and little sister."
> "Only the four of you?"
> "Yes."
> "And did you get along well with your step-dad?"
> "Yes."
> "Had you met him before?"
> "No, I had never met him."
> "Had your mother talked to you about him? What did she say?"
> "That she was together with another guy. That was when I came. Because the first time that she told me I got mad. I told her that I didn't want to have another dad. Because I never met the one I had. But I told her that I didn't want another one. She got sad and was crying when I said that to her. I was

almost coming here. And I told her that it was fine. If she was happy, she can have another guy and that is that."

"So she didn't say anything until you were about to come?"

"No, she had told me, but I didn't want to believe her. I didn't believe her. It wasn't until I saw that it was true. Before she would tell me 'I am going to get together [with another man], son.' OK, I would say. And because my mom is good people, she never says anything to me when I do something wrong. She simply says, 'Just don't do it again' and that is all. She never argues. I tell you I didn't believe her. And finally, when she was telling me that he lived with her, I didn't want to have another dad. Later I told her that it was OK, if she was going to be happy. It is with him that she is going to be, not with me. And in the end, he turned out to be good people."[17]

Andrés's mother reflects on how she nurtures her relationship with her children. She wants them to feel comfortable confiding in her, saying, *"Platico, aconsejo, muchos consejos"* (I chat with them, advise them, lots of advice). She tells her children: *"Si tienes un problema, dime. No te voy a regañar al contrario. Puedes confiar en mi"* (If you have a problem, tell me. I won't get mad at you. On the contrary, you can trust me). In general, the family has cushioned the stress of acculturation and protected, perhaps overprotected, the children.

A Fascination with Gang Life

As we follow Andrés during the first year of our study, we see that he gradually appropriates the symbols of the middle school's Sureño gang, wearing baggy clothes and a long blue belt, his hair half-shaved and greased back. Sometimes his friends make fun of him because he wears his pants so low that walking is difficult. Unlike his counterparts, however, who almost always dress in dark colors, Andrés prefers to stand out in white clothing.

One day, when he is in the seventh grade, we ask Andrés to explain the gang culture. He tells us that there is no territorial base to the gang system in his city, whereas in San Francisco the gangs have well-defined territorial claims. He explains that people choose to join for various reasons, though he can't articulate them clearly, saying merely that some people join and some do not. In addition to the Norteños (made up of those who originated from the northern regions of Mexico) and Sureños (originating from the south), Andrés mentions the Salvadoran Mara Salvatrucha gang and a Vietnamese gang whose members wear yellow. Andrés confides that he hopes to enter the gang "big leagues" when he goes to high school.

Gang identity is a way of constructing masculinity. Membership confers status, and Andrés, like many young men, sees gangs as a way of impressing girls. The young girls at Andrés's middle school, who bring blue bandannas and belts to class, like Sureño boys because they are "cute and brave . . . because they stand up for what they believe . . . the blue." Andrés makes distinctions between the girls who embrace gang culture and those who do not. He tells us that he has two girlfriends, one in the girl gang and another who is "nice." One girl who belongs to the female counterpart of the Sureño gang is often with him, but he says he doesn't have a serious relationship with her. She is only someone with whom to have fun.

Andrés's fascination with gang life is catalyzed by what we and some of his teachers begin to suspect are the gang affiliations of the older men in his family. His stepfather is a *veterano* (a veteran former) gang member, though apparently he never discusses this in the presence of the children. Andrés's nineteen-year-old namesake uncle, however, has introduced him to older gang members and tells him he could enter the gang's big league one day. This uncle also bails him out when he gets in trouble so that his parents do not find out and become upset. As we are talking one day, Andrés shows us a big chain he carries in his pocket, explaining that his uncle gave it to him for protection.

It is not clear how much the mother knows about all of this. A breakdown of family as the mechanism of social control has been identified as the main predictor of gang involvement.[18] For Andrés, this dynamic is not completely relevant: the family is cohesive and a reliable source of support and nurturance for its members. Yet two of the men in the family appear to have gang connections—with one actively encouraging Andrés to enter this world and another projecting an unspoken sentimentality about his former involvement.

Inconsistencies

When we visit his middle school for our observations, Andrés always says hello in the hallways or comes over before class to shake hands. On our first few visits, he greeted us with "Hi, *morra!*" (chicks); after he realized we dislike this term, he began calling us by name. A likable, friendly, and obviously bright young man, Andrés jokes and flirts with the girls in the classroom, who like him because he is both handsome and witty. Everyone who works with him likes him, too. His politeness, wit, sense of humor, and intelligence endear him to many people. This is not a "typical" gang member; indeed his upbeat demeanor may well distract those around him from recognizing the trouble he is sinking into. His personality and maturity instill in others a false sense of confidence; they believe that even if he is drawn into some negative behaviors every once in a while, it is experimental, not serious, and he will soon have the sense to reengage in school.

According to both Andrés and his mother, Andrés was a good student in Mexico: she heard no complaints about him, and he always had good grades. When we visit his mother during the first year, his report card has just arrived, and she tells us proudly: "The teacher congratulated me. She says Andrés raises his hand a lot." The report card contains all A's and B's, but the mother tells us she does not know how to interpret it and asks us for help. Andrés finished his first year at middle school with a high grade-point average, but by the end of the seventh grade it is unrecognizably low. The more the gang culture exerts its pull, the less motivated he becomes in school. He begins to neglect his homework and scores low on most of his tests.

His teachers are sad to see him disengage because they see how capable he is and that he understands the class assignments. Andrés's seventh-grade English teacher tells us that Andrés wrote an essay in ten minutes that would have taken the average student many hours to write, adding how impressed he was with the thoughtfulness and clarity of Andrés's writing. Andrés's behavior in class is always respectful; he is never disruptive. He helps classmates who ask him for assistance, even though doing so disrupts his concentration. His inconsistency, however, garnered him failing grades in several classes.

When Andrés first immigrated, his English-language skills were limited, as indicated by the Bilingual Verbal Abilities Test (BVAT). With English and Spanish combined, he was in the average ability range for his age (54th percentile). This combined verbal-ability score was much higher than his English-language proficiency score, which was in the fourth percentile. While with time his language skills improved, he encountered other obstacles to educational progress.

Andrés hangs out with his homeboys during lunch. They eat quickly and then begin their pilgrimage to the baseball field, far from the eyes of school staff. Most of Andrés's classmates are immigrants like him, though with time his group of friends has become more diverse and now includes second-generation as well as recently arrived immigrants. Mexican boys seem to have few social options at the middle school, where most of the "cool boys" belong to a gang. There is not a single immigrant boy who is both high-achieving and popular among Latinos at this middle school.

With time, Andrés becomes more and more disruptive, more involved in gang activities. He is charged with vandalism and drinking in school. In addition, his teachers suspect that he is smoking pot, and sometimes during our interviews his eyes are glassy and he has a goofy grin. Things whirl quickly in a downward spiral: the vice principal warns Andrés that he will be transferred to an alternative school unless his behavior changes. The threat is enough to force him to concentrate on his studies, but not for long. The school schedules a meeting to decide whether Andrés and two other students will be transferred.

No one shows up to defend Andrés at the meeting. It turns out that Andrés has been lying and hiding his problems from his parents, and his uncle has been covering for him. At the last minute, Andrés asked his mother to attend the meeting about the transfer, but by then it is too late: the school confirms the decision to move him to the alternative school after eighth grade. Andrés's teachers, who believe in his potential but have made only feeble attempts to contact his parents through the bilingual counselors, are frustrated and upset. They suspect that the school used his low achievement as an excuse for the transfer, and that the administration's real fear was related to his gang activities.

The transfer is a vivid example of a failure of communication among administrators, teachers, parents, and the student. This kind of failure can be devastating for a child's future. In Andrés's situation, we get the sense that if only someone from his family or a designated advocate had come to the school meeting, his transfer and many of its consequences could have been avoided.

Andrés's stay at the alternative school has mixed effects. He seems to like this school, particularly because the teachers give him more individual attention and require little homework. He likes all but one of the teachers, whom he calls "racist" because "she doesn't help Latinos." The only thing he dislikes about his school is the "lack of women." At the same time, Andrés now has more support than he has ever had from the school staff and counselors. Every Wednesday he attends counseling and a group therapy session at a community center, missing the whole day of school. Some of the groups that he attends go on weekend-long camping retreats and other trips.

Andrés has changed since our first meetings with him, which were held only two months after he arrived in the United States. Still bright, friendly, and polite, he is now impatient and fidgety during the interviews, eager to finish quickly. His appearance has also changed, because he is not allowed to wear gang-related clothing and symbols such as the color blue. Nevertheless, Andrés manages to wear the extra-large shirts and baggy pants that subtly identify him as a homeboy. (Some boys dress in this homeboy style without having close ties with a gang; it can also be a fashion statement that sets them apart from less "cool" new immigrants.) The gangster image still fascinates him and a lot of his friends, but he no longer talks about becoming a gang member in the big leagues.

During his year at the alternative school Andrés behaves better and talks about continuing to do so, attends counseling sessions seemingly without resentment, and enjoys the hiking trips he takes with his therapy group. External guidance and limits may have offered some relief from the pressure to maintain the identity of gang-related power and confidence. But in the long run, his time at the alternative school has been detrimental. The quality of the education is low, and he loses academic skills and habits. An identity of marginalization, deviance, and exclusion has been reinforced: in fact, at the alternative school he learns and perfects deviant and criminal behaviors. He begins to associate with drug dealers, uses drugs in school, and fails most classes.

After a year at the alternative school, Andrés graduates from the eighth grade and enrolls at a public high school. Alas, he dislikes the school, despite his many positive social contacts. He has friends and feels at home—though most of his peer contacts are probably gang-related. His teachers like him—but he is not close to any of them. He has sources of counseling and support—but they seem to be formal and have not given him a sense of belonging. The change in his academic engagement, compared to middle school, is dramatic. He fails all of his classes except algebra, in which he earns a B plus. He tells us that he never has homework assignments, while his teachers say he never turns in the work. Andrés's science teacher thinks that Andrés simply does not care about his future; he blames Andrés's choice of friends for his attitude. "Andrés showed great apathy for the majority of the year," the science teacher said. "I suspect he has been using drugs at school and I told him so. I encouraged him to find work, but he was not easily reached. He was not disrespectful, but he did not participate and often sat speaking to his friends."

Andrés's Mexican identification remains strong. He prefers all things Mexican. Like most Mexicans, he is aware that others classify him by nationality. He mentions racism frequently, relating several instances in which he and other Mexicans felt discriminated against. "A white guy wrote an article about Latino immigrants in the school newspaper that was negative," he tells us, though the rest of the story seems to omit details. "We stepped out of class in protest. The superintendent was called in. The student is now saying something about freedom of speech."

Andrés says that only he and a couple of his friends stand up to the "white boys" who jeer at them. He takes pride in having instilled fear in some of his tormentors. The high school seems to be a hostile environment that has pushed him to adopt even more fiercely the oppositional identity that he had begun to take on during middle school. Here, however, he feels he must separate himself not only from "whites" (and their cultural markers), but also from many of his Latino peers, whom he sees as meek, spineless, or "sellouts."

Andrés's identity has become racialized—he feels discriminated against and marginalized—and he has become passionate about protecting Latinos against discrimination. His gang involvement and oppositional identity have taken on a sociopolitical flavor. While Andrés may be passive in some ways, when it comes to this "fight against racism" he is passionately active. Unfortunately, the methods he has chosen have cost him his academic future.

Starting Out with High Promise

Andrés started middle school highly motivated, but somewhere along the line he got lost. At certain points in his journey he began to realize that he needed to change course, but he never quite made it happen. Now it is quite possible that if he does not change his academic performance he could again be transferred to an alternative school. As he himself foresaw, his gang involvement has deepened since he got to high school, and this involvement is responsible for much of his academic disengagement.

Andrés exemplifies an oppositional identity, which, though similar to the concept as developed by John Ogbu, incorporates elements specific to immigrant youth: anger at discrimination and opposition to aspects of U.S. culture and institutions.[19] The immigrant oppositional identity, however, is not explicitly oppositional toward school and academic values. It does not associate academic success with white values, and thus does not call for rejection of educational goals. Quite the opposite: immigrant youth continue to claim that a good education is very valuable to them. But often, the schools fail to engage these young people, who in turn disconnect from their studies, finding their schoolwork boring, constricting, and irrelevant to their lives.

Initially, Andrés's oppositional identity had more to do with romanticizing the gang than alienating himself from academics. But although he continues to reaffirm the importance of education, he displays anger toward the school through vandalism and fights with other groups. While his relationship with academic values is positive, he rejects school.

An immigrant oppositional identity can also include discouragement about the opportunities available after high school. The immigrant youths we studied initially described in optimistic terms their high expectations for future success, yet over time, many lost hope. Andrés talks about becoming a pilot or a lawyer, yet he is forced to evaluate the chances of this happening in light of his academic and undocumented status. In addition, in Andrés' case, racial conflict leads to his determination to stand up for Latino rights, maintain a "fierce" attachment to a Mexican identity, and fight with Latinos who have "given up the cause." Feeling like he does not belong in his new homeland only adds to his anomie and intensifies his search for other alienated compatriots.

This form of oppositional identity does not translate to pushing away his family; indeed, Andrés's familial ties and sense of responsibility remain high. He tells us he plans to work after he graduates. He wants to help his family financially, telling us during one session, "When I am 18, I want to get a steady job to help my family, get married, and have a stable life." Yet though dutiful and connected, Andrés hides an important part of his life. Further, his parents' are in denial about how their son is doing in school, and his mother, in particular, seems oblivious to the gang involvement of several men in her family. Her concerns that her son will get involved with gangs and drugs are phrased as something abstract and distant; to us, who know details about Andrés's actual involvement, her statements sound surreal.

An Immigrant's Existential Quandary

Andrés longs to return to the idealized land of his childhood, the "big house," the grandparents, and the aunts who nurtured him. This longing has caused him to create an alternative plan to working and getting married: he will hold on in the United States until he is eighteen so that he feels he has fulfilled his obligation to his mother, then he will attend college in Mexico. No one, however, has really talked to him about college, and his knowledge of college requirements is limited. Ultimately, Andrés's plan seems like a fantasy that reflects his disillusion with the United States. He feels that if he had stayed in Mexico, he would have never gotten in trouble.

During the last year of the study, in his projected narrative about the girl with books overlooking a farm, the setting is unclear:

> A girl arrives from the city to study in the farm and sees that everything is different. [There is] more land, more things, more nature. And she's seeing what is there, where she is at. What's going to happen in the future is that she will adapt to the place and she will be more . . . I don't know . . . how do you say . . . she will adapt more to that place and become more like them.

This ambiguity about whether the story takes place in Mexico or in the United States captures Andrés's troubling existential question about whether he belongs anywhere.

Marieli: Giving Up the Dreams, One By One

Marieli is a tall, severe-looking girl who is passionate about soccer. She never appears without her Adidas soccer shoes, and almost always wears a soccer jacket and pants or an Adidas sweat suit; occasionally, she dons black jeans and a denim shirt. While talking about soccer, telling us that she would like to play professionally, she grows animated, vibrant.

When she feels comfortable, Marieli is sweet and polite, laughing and joking freely. But in a large group, she rarely smiles. Teachers and other students find her intimidating, and perhaps with good reason. She is quick to defend herself verbally from perceived attacks, and with people in positions of authority, she tends to be even more hostile and aggressive, especially when she sees injustice.

Behind this pose of coolness, we sense a constant disquietude in Marieli. She tells us that she gets angry and upset easily and argues too much. She suffers from frequent migraines, which keep her home from school about once a month. She feels that people don't really understand her, nor do many like her: "The rest of the world does not accept me," she says. Occasionally, she feels sad; she says she cries easily and has trouble concentrating and sleeping.

Marieli wears her "tough" facade like a second skin, reminding us of the "cool pose" of many young black men who hide behind it to mask fear, pain, and insecurity.[20] As we get to know her, we learn that Marieli has had more than her share of fear and pain in her young life. Every once in a while, she tells us, frightening events from her early childhood flare into her conscious mind.

A Traumatic Beginning

Marieli and her family lived in a small city four hours from the capital of Guatemala. In the 1980s, when Marieli was very young, her father was assassinated in front of his family. Marieli's mother tells us: "They killed the girls' father and I got scared. I couldn't raise my daughters and my younger brothers, who are like my sons, alone." A widow living in abject poverty, she decided she had to move to the United States to earn a living. She left her two daughters with their grandparents, and after Marieli's grandmother passed away, Marieli's mother hired another woman to care for her children in their hometown.

After arriving in the United States, she found a job with the help of a childhood friend. Despite leaving her girls, she had been excited about going to the United States because "everything seemed easy": money would come easily, life would be good, and one would never grow old. Yet seven years passed before the mother was able to arrange for Marieli and her sister to join her. At last they arrived—without documentation, which they still lack. Interestingly, when we ask Marieli why her family immigrated to the United States, she mentions only economic reasons, perhaps preferring to repress the memories of violence.

Marieli claims that she felt no emotions upon rejoining her mother at age eleven, but that seems like just another tough pose. Her mother had borne a third daughter in the United States, though she never remarried, and the mother believes that her older daughters resent this child's existence. Indeed, Marieli relates that when she arrived at her new home, she was shocked to meet this child, seven years younger than herself, and the sense of betrayal has lingered. This bitter feeling, along with the resentment that the daughters feel because they were left alone for such a long time in Guatemala, makes the atmosphere at home tense.

Marieli speaks as though she were indifferent about coming to the United States, but it is easy to detect that her feelings are in fact very negative. She did not want leave Guatemala, and now she finds the United States limiting and "too boring." "You can't go anywhere or leave your house because something might happen to you," she complains. For a long time, Marieli wanted to return to her home country because she felt she was poorly treated in the United States. "It stinks here," she says. Seeming to forget the death of her father, she adds: "In Guatemala, there was less danger, more freedom." Considering the brutality she witnessed in Guatemala, her current circumstances must seem very disheartening to evoke such a statement. The negative perception of American society persists as she spends more time in the United States and sees white Americans acting as though they are better and smarter than Latinos. She specifies that most of the discrimination is aimed at people who lack residency papers and cannot speak English, and that such people are not given a chance to succeed.

Cloistered Alone at Home

In the one-bedroom apartment where Marieli has lived since she first came to the United States in the mid-1990s, we have our first meeting with her mother. The conversation is one of the most heart-wrenching we have experienced during our study. The mother, an articulate and sensitive woman, breaks down in tears several times, sharing intimate, sorrowful experiences. She feels utterly abandoned and hurt by what she feels are her daughters' rejection and resentment. Her work is exhausting, yet she manages to rush home to make lunch for her daughters daily. She cannot afford to take time off; she works until she gets sick and then is forced to stop. The list of symptoms she recites suggests depression: she has chest and stomach pains, is always nervous and shy, feels withdrawn, gets angry easily, feels tense, and has trouble sleeping. Occasionally, she feels guilty about her absence from her daughters, and she weeps. She doubts that anyone understands her or truly likes her.

At first, Marieli lived in this apartment with her mother, her two sisters, and her mother's two younger brothers, but now it is just Marieli, her hardworking mother, and her young half-sister. The uncles recently moved to their own apartment. Her sister, who is a few years older, is now married and has moved out, though the sisters continue to be close. In fact, her older sister is one of Marieli's crucial resources. This nurturing relationship developed when the two sisters were alone in Guatemala and needed each other, something that their mother seems unable to understand. She senses this alliance between them and seems jealously critical of how the older sister supports and "spoils" Marieli.

Marieli's neighborhood houses whites, Chinese, and most of all Latinos, of whom a majority are of Mexican and Central American origin. Many of the retail stores in the area cater to these immigrant groups. Although Marieli's neighbors get along, she doesn't feel safe: two major gangs are active nearby, and more than once strangers have tried to break into her house. Since her mother works late, Marieli is usually alone or with her younger sister, locked inside for most of the day. After school, she says, "I go home; I take a shower and bore myself to death watching TV."

Marieli's mother had very little schooling, but she was trained in Guatemala as a pharmacist's assistant, which allowed her to find good work in a pharmacy and in a doctor's office before she emigrated. She has been unable to find similar work in the United States, and her social status has declined. She struggles just to get by. She first found work cleaning rooms in a hotel, then in a restaurant. Now she babysits for a Japanese family, cleaning houses in the late evenings or on weekends to earn some extra income. This is the plight of many immigrant women from Central America, who have little choice but to participate in "outsourcing the heart"—taking care of other people's children while being absent for their own. Marieli is bitter that her mother takes care of someone else's children but is not at home to nurture her. "I almost never see her," she complains.

Marieli's attitude toward her mother is fraught with ambivalence and has worsened over the years. She resents her mother in many ways and is often angry with her. Yet she acknowledges that she owes everything to her mother, admires her mother for being a hard worker, and says often that she wants her family to stay together forever. "Mom feels bad sometimes because she doesn't speak English, which makes work difficult," Marieli says. "She can't always pay the rent." In the first year we knew her, Marieli said there was nothing she would want to change about her mother and that she appreciated everything they did together. But she noted that when they argued, they could go days without speaking. At a later stage, when asked whether she admired anyone in her family, she said no. She admits she does not get along with her mother, complains that her mother is never home, says resentfully that her mother favors her younger sister, and adds: "She yells for any little thing. She yells quite strongly." In some ways, she sounds like almost any American teenager: on the one hand, she says that family is the most important thing in her life, while on the other, she describes her family members as weird.

Her mother sees the conflicted nature of their relationship as resulting from the seven-year separation. Their physical reunion failed to renew their emotional bonds. "What has gotten worse [since the girls immigrated] is my relationship with my daughters," she says. "I don't think it will ever improve." Now that Marieli is eighteen, the mother fears she has lost all control over her. Discipline has always been a problem; the grandmother had been the disciplinarian after the mother's migration, and Marieli and her mother never fully adjusted to their new relationship after the reunion. Marieli knows that her mother wants her to do well but says that except for attending classes, "there are no rules."

Marieli's family has a few friends and relatives in the neighborhood and none in Guatemala. Neither Marieli nor her mother has returned to their hometown since arriving in the United States—mostly because they lack documentation but also because there is no one left to visit.

An important source of social support for the family comes from their church. Marieli and her sisters were born into a Catholic family and baptized soon after birth, but their mother converted to a Pentecostal religion and is now very devout in her faith. Religion seems to offer the mother much-need solace from her overwhelming exhaustion from work, what she perceives as the uncaring attitude of her daughters, and palpable loneliness. The church has also been a continuously stable presence for Marieli, who attends almost every night and on weekends and is president of the church youth group. Marieli spends about twenty hours a week at church. She comments that although she's not sure she is wild about religion, she is drawn to the comfort that the contact with others offers, and by the fun activities, such as field trips and soccer games.

Frustrated Educational Aspirations

In the last year of the study, Marieli, like other student participants, saw elements of her own story in the picture of the boy with the violin:

> It's a boy. The boy is at school. He is reading a book, which he doesn't understand. He is frustrated, bored and just wants to go home. He is hungry, too. He wishes he could be in a fun class.

We first meet with Marieli when she is in the tenth grade—at her high school, high in the hills overlooking the city's downtown and beyond to a magnificent view of San Francisco Bay, with its bridges and islands. A guard keeps visitors waiting until he has checked their names with the main office. The first thing we notice when we enter is an antismoking campaign: student-created posters about the harm of smoking line the hallways. One poster reads: "10 things to do instead of smoking: Read, play sports, watch TV, listen to music, sing, party, vacation, church, school, and nothing." This is one of the better academic high schools in the area. Admittance is based on the results of an exam, and many graduates go on to college. Nonetheless, like many of the region's high schools, it is plagued by gangs and racial tension. Marieli says she knows of several funerals held for students who had died in gang-related violence.

The student body is 51 percent Asian, 21 percent Hispanic, 18 percent African American, and 2 percent non-Hispanic white.[21] Ethnic tensions seem inescapable. If she is in a class with other Spanish-speaking Latino students, Marieli says, she can't ask students of other races for help with classwork because her Latino friends will turn on her. Five security guards roam the halls, but Marieli warns that school can be dangerous if you are in the wrong place at the wrong time. "A lot of things can happen to you in school," she says. "A group of kids can still beat you down. There are only five security [guards] and they can't cover the whole school. Last week, there was a fight and a female teacher stepped in to separate them and they hit her. Cut her face. Lots of blood."

Marieli attended a public school in Guatemala through the fifth grade. After immigrating, she attended middle school for three years, where she was assigned to a sheltered bilingual program and was lucky enough to have the same caring, dedicated teacher for the sixth, seventh, and eighth grades. Marieli says this teacher treated all her students well, regardless of race. The teacher herself was Puerto Rican and had learned English as a second language. She insisted on giving Marieli and the other students a solid foundation in English and in the way U.S. schools work.

Like many of her peers, Marieli has seen her academic engagement and performance suffer since she left the more nurturing middle-school environment for high school. She continued in bilingual classes but found that the teachers were neither as committed nor as understanding. "I think there are some teachers with attitudes, and some are racist," she says. "My third-period teacher is a hater . . . She hates everyone. She yells for any little reason. She is really harsh." Marieli says she has learned nothing in high school compared to junior high. "School is boring but important," she says, adding, "I don't like school. It is a closed campus so you can't get out."

Marieli says that learning English was hard, but she is more English-dominant than most of her peers. When we gave her the first language assessment of our study, Marieli was in the tenth grade and had been in this country for four years. Her English-language proficiency score was rather low (17th percentile), while her verbal ability (English and Spanish combined) was in the average ability range for her age (66th percentile).[22] On the Woodcock Johnson Test of Achievement subtests, Marieli scored at age-equivalency levels on the Broad Reading subtest (72nd percentile) and on the Broad Math subtest (65th percentile). The second BVAT assessments two years later indicated that her English had improved significantly, and she was in the average range of ability for her age in English-language proficiency. She now speaks both Spanish and English comfortably, and her English grammar is excellent. But her mother says that Marieli's aptitude for English is yet one more barrier to communicating with her daughter.

Overall, Marieli thinks that Guatemalan schools were better because the teachers were more careful about teaching. "In the U.S., they pass you even if you didn't learn," she says. "In Guatemala, they actually teach you the material." Marieli speaks from experience: at the end of her junior year, she is failing nearly every class. This is a significant change from her earlier performance.

Marieli earned all A's in middle school and continued to do so as a high school freshman. Then her grades began a steady decline, dropping through C's and D's until in the spring semester of her junior year, she has received F's in all her subjects. She explains this change with reference to vague and unspecified "problems" she has been having, without wanting to elaborate. She admits that she often skips classes, which leads to arguments with her mother, though she accuses her mother of indifference toward her grades: "My mother doesn't care, so I don't care." Her absences increased, too. Sometimes she skipped school altogether for several days in a row for no apparent reason. In her junior year, she had as many as seventy-seven absences in some subjects. Her trigonometry teacher writes: "Marieli is a very smart young woman. Unfortunately she does not come to class and this, of course, affects her grades." "I think I am a bad student," Marieli tells us. "I don't care . . . I don't like anything about school. It sucks."

Marieli's mother cares about how her daughter does in school, and she blames the teachers, at least in part, for Marieli's loss of interest: "Marieli told me of this class: algebra. She was really mad because it is a difficult subject. Her teacher told her that she was never going to need that class in life, but that it was a requirement she needed to graduate. I don't think it is good to tell kids that. They told her to take a class that she was never going to need. She then didn't want to try hard." Marieli's mother's naiveté about the rules of engagement for applying to college makes it hard for her to encourage persistence in seemingly "useless" subjects. Though she tries, her limited education, poor English skills, and relentless work schedule keep her from helping Marieli with her homework. Marieli can't see past her own needs and longings; she can't empathize with her mother's limitations. She experiences her mother's inability to help with schoolwork as another abandonment and accuses her mother of not caring. Because she doesn't know where to turn to for help, she gets frustrated and throws her homework away. "If I don't understand, there isn't anybody in the house to help me. So why bother?" she asks.

Several adults at Marieli's school have tried to keep her engaged. Those who seem to care about her are her bilingual counselor (the one adult in school to whom she is close) and her soccer coach. Her coach says that

Marieli is one of the most talented players she has ever seen, though she can be difficult and sometimes throws tantrums. Knowing her passion for soccer, the counselor has talked to her about college soccer scholarships. This possibility evaporated as her grades dropped during her last two years of high school, however. Marieli now hopes to attend a community college, though with her failing grades the prospects for achieving this goal are slowly fading as well. An equally high barrier is her undocumented status. Even if she had sustained her high grades, she has little or no access to scholarships without documentation. And without scholarships, she cannot afford to pay for college.

As it dawns on her that her undocumented status will hold her back, Marieli gives up her dreams one by one: she forfeits first an early desire to become a veterinarian, then her soccer dreams, and finally any aspirations of going to college. The more familiar she becomes with the school system and U.S. society, the more she sees that her lack of documentation will be a significant barrier, and she pulls away in anger.

Yet while Marieli's academic disengagement has been dramatic, she is bright and has a healthy passion for those activities to which she has managed to stay connected. She enjoys creative projects such as artwork and can even become actively involved in school if the subject catches her imagination: for example, she talks enthusiastically about a paper she wrote describing how she thinks soccer will change in the new millennium. Clearly soccer is her real love, and the one thing that could have kept her motivated to do well in school would have been staying on the team and winning a soccer scholarship. More than anything, Marieli's identity is constructed around her image of a Guatemalan soccer player. She projects this identity through her clothes and her one accessory, her backpack, which has "Guatemala" and "soccer" written all over it. Marieli identifies herself as Guatemalan and Latina. It frustrates her that North Americans think all Latinos are Mexican. She favors Mexican and South American soccer and scorns the U.S. version: "Americans can't play soccer," she proclaims.

Through soccer, school, and church, Marieli has a supportive group of friends, mostly boys and mainly Latinos from Mexico and Central America. They speak Spanish together and help each other navigate through school. They assist each other with homework but do not push each other to achieve their dreams. Few of them are highly engaged in school. Marieli's mother feels that Marieli's friends are a negative influence. She explains: "For example, she didn't go to school for two days. I asked her why she wasn't going to school. 'No, mami,' she says, 'because we, all the Latinos, we aren't going to school.' And why, I ask. 'We aren't going to do anything,' she says. 'Only stupid Chinese go to school.' Her friends influence her."

Many of the students at Marieli's high school are of African American descent, and Marieli feels they get away with "stuff." For example, students are required to wear certain colors as part of the school uniform. If a student is caught out of uniform, he or she is sent to the detention room all day. Marieli says African American students get sent to detention far less frequently than do the Latino students. These and other remarks attest to Marieli's perception that there is a great deal of racial tension and stereotyping at her school.

Multiple Losses

Many events have made Marieli's adaptation to the United States difficult. A bright, curious young girl with a lot of potential, Marieli becomes one of our saddest examples of academic disengagement by the end of the study. This was a student who was involved in school, who had excellent grades, who was liked by her peers, who played soccer, and who is now virtually disconnected from any academic activity. Despite her own efforts to stay connected and involved, Marieli is slowly pulling out of the system. She feels cheated. The school itself has given up on her. Her lack of documentation papers precludes many choices. With little personal attention, she is slipping through the cracks.

Some of the anger Marieli harbors toward adults and people in authority seems to emanate from anger she feels toward her mother. After their seven-year separation, a time when she felt abandoned in Guatemala, Marieli is still antagonistic toward her mother, and yearns for her mother to be there for her in ways that she herself cannot define. While she identifies some positive aspects about being in the United States, she feels that through the immigration she has lost her mother—that in spite of the reunification, her mother continues to be gone, both physically because of her work hours, and psychologically because of the unresolved conflicts.

Marieli has other sources of social support. She has friends, and she is very close to her older sister, her soccer coach, and her bilingual counselor.

She also finds support at church. She has become more outgoing socially as she has mastered English. With those who connect with her, Marieli is sweet, thoughtful, hardworking, and fun. With others, she can often become hostile. For some students, alternative sources of social support are adequate in the difficult transitions associated with immigration. For Marieli, however, the repercussions of her separation from her mother are longstanding, and other sources of support have not compensated.

Marieli's story is one of multiple losses, traumas, and unresolved mourning. Marieli has lost her father to violence, her grandmother has died, her mother is "ambiguously" lost, her sister has married and moved away, and now Marieli herself slowly has let go of her passion for soccer and her dreams of college. She dreams of becoming a veterinarian, but her uncle even takes away the animals that she brings home and becomes attached to—every contact she makes is broken. Only the church remains, and it becomes increasingly important to her because of the relationships it offers.

Everything seems to slowly collapse for Marieli. Having started high school with straight A's, now she is not even sure she will graduate. Having started with dreams of going to college with a soccer fellowship and continuing to play soccer professionally, she has now virtually let go of the idea. This outwardly tough and hostile young woman also had dreams of spending her life taking care of small animals. But with time, much of her enthusiasm has dissipated. This process of demotivation has been driven by her increasing awareness of how her undocumented status will prevent her from achieving her goals in the United States. Today she truly does not know how to envision her future.

THE portraits in this chapter reveal the many missed opportunities, gaps in emotional and academic support, and institutional failures that have led to the derailment of immigrant youths' dreams of creating a better life in the United States.

In every one of these cases, the adolescents have grown increasingly distant from burdened parents who do not have the resources—psychological, social, or financial—to guide their children's journey through dysfunctional schools and neighborhoods and around structural and symbolic violence. Significantly, all of these children told us about painful encounters with racist teachers and peers in schools. Facing this kind of hostility, with only fragile and tenuous home relationships as support (relationships

that themselves have often been complicated by long separations and ambivalent reunifications), has exhausted the parents and led the children to
disengage from school.

With each missed opportunity and failed engagement, with each affront
to the children's struggle to maintain a coherent sense of self, the youngsters become angrier. The boys tend to mask their anger with ever more
grandiose posturing (think of Henry's growing bravado even as his grades
plummeted). The young women, by contrast, tend to manage their frustrations and broken dreams with anger turned inward—Lotus, for example, is
a deeply depressed young woman who is struggling in a sea of loneliness.

The human journey is punctuated by fundamental turning points—
transitions that promise both risk and opportunity. With proper social
supports, academic scaffolding, and guidance, these transitions can lead
to greater mastery, potential, and self-realization. When poorly managed,
however, such transitions can be debilitating and derailing.[23] Immigration
is a profound transition that involves dramatic, sudden changes in geogra-
phy, culture, language, and relationships. Perhaps not surprisingly, then,
any smaller transitions that follow for immigrant children—from middle
school to high school, from a sheltered English class to a mainstream class,
from an average school to an exam school—tend to reactivate many of the
issues that had emerged during the transnational move. For those immigrant youth whose migrations were fraught with loss, disruption, and feelings of helplessness, and whose later transitions within the community
and school are mismanaged, it is nearly impossible to maintain the motivation and inner strength needed to succeed in school and beyond.

■ ■

CHAPTER 6

Portraits of Low Achievers

WHILE THE DECLINING immigrant students arrive with abundant optimism and do well before fading away, another group arrives with coping abilities taxed beyond bearing. These students' grades start out low and slide downward the longer they live in the United States. These low achievers, 14 percent of the students in our study, come from all countries of origin, though fewer come from China. Boys are more than twice as likely as girls to be found among the perpetual low achievers.

What are the distinguishing features of these low-achieving students? They were more likely than their more highly achieving peers to live in a single-parent home, and their mothers tended to be less educated. Their English-language proficiency was lower than that of the other groups, and they reported high levels of psychological symptoms upon arrival. They often attended the very worst schools, schools deprived of resources and plagued by conflict. These schools failed to draw the students out of the initial shock of migration and were unable to elicit or nourish their engagement. In such settings, low-achieving students reported the least academic support. These students simply had too many counts against them. Overwhelmed and chronically unsuccessful in class, they reported more negative attitudes toward school, lower levels of motivation, and more indifference than their higher-achieving peers.[1] (See Table 5.1.)

As the schools fail them, other avenues offer alternative rewards. Some derive a sense of self-worth in the camaraderie and financial compensation of the workplace. Others are drawn to the mystique of the streets and find financial rewards in the underground economy. Attractive girls who flounder in school may find rewards in cultivating their beauty. Eliciting little teacher support and with limited access to caring, supportive adults who could help them navigate the rocky educational waters, these students give up on their education.

In the narratives that follow, we see how limited resources lead some new immigrants away from a focus on school. With Civic, we see how a premature transition to a mainstream class in a school that seems "like a prison" leads him to develop an oppositional identity and search for alternative sources of positive social regard that are not conducive to school success. Myriam must leave her mother and join a cruel father who disparages her at every turn; she has limited psychological energy to focus on school. Léon, never much focused on academics to begin with, attends a school where survival is much more of a priority than the pursuit of education; he finds that the world of work adds both to his wallet and to his self-esteem.

Civic: A Toxic School Derails a Student

To Civic, it is all about "style." A driver since age fourteen, he now zooms around in a brand-new Honda, which his parents bought him recently. He also loves to wear dark clothing. Today he sports a black jacket, black pants, and a black shirt. His hair falls below his earlobes and parts in the middle. Civic admits that his clothing and hairstyle give people the impression that he is a gang member. In fact, he says he usually dresses differently if he goes to Chinatown because he does not want to be mistaken for a gang member and killed. He smokes. When he goes to school, which is not often, he does not carry a book bag. He keeps only his wallet, keys, and the latest-model Nokia cell phone in his pockets. He walks in and out of school "bag-free" and boasts that he has never brought any books or papers to classes.

When we first met Civic, he was fourteen years old and had been in the United States for three years. At the time, he was an eighth-grader in the bilingual program of a local middle school. His academic escapades are hard to follow. Because of failing grades, he had to repeat eighth grade. After that, he entered high school for ninth grade, but was truant for much of the year. The next fall, he enrolled in ninth grade again and remained enrolled for three months, during which time he cut classes regularly and was suspended several times. Finally, at age seventeen, he was expelled from school. Now he spends most of his time in the family-owned restaurant with his parents, with no immediate plans for finishing high school or earning a GED.

Civic's father first arrived in the United States in the late 1980s. He lived here alone for ten years before he could help his family apply for green cards and join him. While his father was working in the United States, Civic, his mother, and his elder brother lived together in Macau. Though he and his father were apart for more than ten years, their reunion seems to have been smooth, and Civic says that they are happier than before.

Macau consists of a peninsula and two small islands, Taipa and Coloane, in the South China Sea, close to Hong Kong. The Portuguese settled Macau in 1513, and it prospered as an important port for more than a century. Recently, Macau's economy has been dependent on casinos and tourism, with gambling bringing in more than 40 percent of its income. When in 1984 the British handed over Hong Kong to China, China initiated similar negotiations with Portugal, and Macau became a special administrative region of China in 1999. Under its new governance, Macau has significant autonomy and will preserve its previous economic and legal structure for the next fifty years. Its economy is growing, with expanding foreign investment and increasing tourism. Civic, however, remembers Macau as a chaotic and poverty-stricken place.

In Macau, Civic's father was a manual laborer at the pier and his mother did not work. Neither parent had any formal schooling. In the United States, his parents own a small Chinese take-out restaurant. Both work long hours, and though the restaurant doesn't look like it is thriving, the family is fairly comfortable financially. While he was in school, Civic helped at the restaurant, and since his expulsion he has devoted much more time to working there, particularly as a deliveryman so that he can drive his car. His mother is happy that Civic is helping more in the restaurant because the business is doing well.

Civic is close to his family, particularly his mother. After being separated from his father for so long, he says "the most important thing in life is having both parents." He feels his mother is like "his elder sister." He explains, "My father is very nice and my mother is a goddess," adding jokingly that his mother has become "more beautiful" after immigration. Both Civic and his mother agree that they have a healthy and amicable relationship, so much so that they never have any arguments. He repeatedly reports feeling close to his parents. For instance, he would not consider attending a college far from home, even if it were an excellent school. And if he were accepted to a college near home, he would not consider living in a dormitory. In short, he simply does not want to live apart from his parents, and he very much wants to stay emotionally close to them.

Civic's parents are generous and tolerant. They give him an allowance, and his mother refrains from giving Civic chores at home because she does not want to "have him laboring"; she just wants him to live comfortably. He reports that they accept his poor grades and behaviors, such as talking back to his teachers and in one instance hitting another student in self-defense in school.

The family dynamic has been shaped by the father's long absence. In situations where one parent has been absent for an extended time, the remaining parent is likely to develop a closer relationship with one of the children. This seems to be the case with Civic and his mother. And though Civic feels that his relationship with his father is happy after the reunification, his father remains absent from the story, playing no discernable role in Civic's education or development.

Because neither of Civic's parents had any formal education, they cannot help him with his schoolwork. In the beginning, they expected him to go to college and get a good job, but now they seem to have given up on those goals. Asked how his parents respond to his bad grades, he answers, "They scold me at first. After a while, [I] get used to it. When I am used to it, my parents stop scolding me. They just say, 'Do better next time.'"

While the mother is the disciplinarian at home, there is a gap between what she says she hopes for Civic in terms of his behavior and academic performance and what Civic perceives as her expectations. For example, she says she checks his homework and follows his assignments, but Civic says she doesn't. Furthermore, his mother says that she expects him to finish college sometime, but Civic thinks she does not really care what educational level he attains. One way to make sense of these conflicting answers is to see the mother's statements as representing her ideals but not what she actually demands of Civic. For example, after Civic was expelled, his mother was very worried and tried to arrange for Civic to enroll in another school; later, however, she appeared resigned to his being a dropout. His mother continues to believe that American schools are too lenient, and blames the schools for turning Civic into a poor student. Although she says she wants him to finish high school somehow, she is glad that now he can help out more at the family restaurant; she happily reports that they make more money than when he was a student.

Interestingly, Civic believes his parents would have different expectations for him if he were a girl—"for a girl, they would demand her to study better and be more obedient to them. For a boy, [these] things don't really matter."

When Civic and his mother first arrived, the family had regular contacts with friends and relatives in Macau, and his mother returned twice after their migration to visit relatives. Civic, however, has no connection with anyone there. Initially their social support in the United States came mainly from their coworkers in the restaurant, but those friendships seem to have withered. They have no relatives in their city, and after the maternal grandmother passes away, they have no more relatives back in Macau; the mother's only sister now lives in Taiwan. Over time Civic's mother ceases to maintain regular contact either with her only sister or with anyone in Macau. She says she has made some acquaintances in the United States, but when she needs to talk to someone, she goes first to Civic and his brother. Essentially, her social world is confined to her immediate family.

Passion and Talent Redirected Away from School

During the year he dropped out of high school at age seventeen, in addition to "playing and sleeping," Civic worked in his family's restaurant and at odd jobs. We call him to set up a meeting, and he says he is free any time. We agree to meet him at the subway the next day at 2 P.M. And we do. And we wait and wait. After fifteen minutes we call his cell phone, and he apologizes for having lost track of time. A few minutes later he drives up with his friend Vick in his green Honda Civic to pick us up. The Honda has a large new muffler that roars when he applies the gas. He has changed the wipers and the stereo. He has added an amplifier and lots of figurines that dangle around the dashboard. He drives everywhere, and he particularly loves to drive on the highway at seventy miles per hour, without a seatbelt. He drives aggressively, horning his way through traffic jams, squeezing between two lanes of cars to preserve his speed.

Today, he takes us to the house he and Vick have been renovating. It is

large, with four levels, including an unfinished basement and a spacious attic with two bedrooms. They have been hired to paint the walls and lay car-
peting in the attic. They start to work, and we notice that Vick is doing the
work while Civic gives orders and makes comments. They began the project three weeks ago, and today is their last day. They must finish laying the
carpet and return the keys to the owner tonight. Civic explains that they
have worked on similar projects before but on a smaller scale. Their ama-
teur craftsmanship is evident as they patch pieces of irregularly cut carpet
together and staple them to the floor.

We ask Civic about his plans to return to high school. He sidesteps the
question by saying he will think about that after the summer. "Summer is
for fun and play," he says. We ask whether he has any preference for a high
school, and he responds that he would go to any school that accepts him.

Before immigrating, Civic had finished six years of education in Macau,
where he was a successful student. His mother says he ranked seventh or
eighth among seventy students. Here, however, his engagement has steadily
slumped, as he himself acknowledges. At first, in middle school, he earned
C's and D's, but in high school a straight column of F's rips through his report card. His educational goals and motivation to achieve have plummeted. Civic makes sense of this decline by concluding that his appearance
leads people to view him as a gang member and a bad person. Civic argues
that he is not a gang member and has no intention of becoming one because he does not want to be stabbed or gunned down. He prefers to be an
"ordinary" person.

"In Macau, [we have to] study all the time," Civic says. "Here, if you like
to study, you can; if you don't, you can go to bed. In Macau, [we] study
from morning till night and from night till morning." When he was still in
school, he says, he spent five minutes on homework each day and only occasionally bothered to submit his efforts. When he didn't understand an
assignment, he would not ask for help but simply chose not to submit that
homework. This lighthearted attitude toward homework expanded until
finally he stopped doing any homework at all because, he says jauntily, "It
wastes too much time. My time is for playing and sleeping." At the end, he
would submit only one out of about ten homework assignments.

In Civic's defense, much of his speedy disengagement might be attribut-
able to a mistake he made in the paperwork when he moved from middle
school to high school, a mistake that might have led directly to his drop-

ping out. He inadvertently registered as a mainstream student in the high school instead of as a bilingual student. There were no other Chinese students in his classes. Though he said he managed to follow the lessons, he understood superficially at best, and as a result the classes were boring and he lost interest. School administrators wanted to help him switch back to the bilingual program, but could not because of the school system's procedural requirements. Only a few months later, Civic, feeling disengaged and ignored, decided to drop out. In one of our conversations in the third year of the study, when Civic is seventeen years old, we sense that he felt let down:

> "Civic, did anyone at school talk with you about your future? If so, what did they tell you?"
> "No one. Nothing."
> "Did anyone from school speak with you about your decision to stop going to school?"
> "No. No one."
> "Was there any one at school who took a special interest in you? Can you tell me about them?"
> "No one. I look like a bad person. Who cares about me? Everybody calls me 'big brother Civic, big brother Civic.' I had some fights in the middle school; even after I left the middle school, people still remember my fights clearly. They just think I am bad."

When Civic first stopped attending ninth grade, nobody from his high school—Monroe High School, described in detail in Chapter 3—ever followed up on his case, which is not surprising considering that the school has only one counselor per class. The following academic year, he enrolled once more as a freshman. Three months later he was out of school again following a heated argument with a school security guard. Though the dispute was limited to bitter verbal exchanges, Civic and his mother told us that school officials felt that Civic was a threat to school safety. The principal decided to dismiss him. Civic sees this decision as biased because of his earlier behavior: in middle school, he was involved in several big fights and was labeled a troublemaker. He insists that he has not been fighting at the high school, that his only offense was cutting classes. After the expulsion, school administrators mentioned alternative solutions, but none were tried. His mother feels manipulated by the system. She was asked to sign Civic out of school with the understanding that this would be "in exchange" for school officials' finding an alternative program in which Civic could finish his degree or earn a GED. She made multiple calls to the principal and counselor seeking to hold them to their end of the bargain. Her calls were not returned, and the situation remains unresolved.

In spite of his disengagement from school, Civic still has high aspirations. He defines a successful person as someone who has a good education and who can make money. His vision for the future is upbeat: "I will be well-off and carefree."[2] His self-esteem remains high, unscathed by his academic failure. He believes that he is talented in virtually everything except academics. He describes himself as smart. He believes that education is the way to get ahead in this country, so he wants to attend a two-year college. His goal is to start his own business, and he believes that he must finish college to attain it. Though he has lost interest in graduating from high school, he still feels it is "important" that he go to college. Moreover, he said, he is "certain" that he will go to college, and he even has specific technical schools in mind. But he's vague about when that would be, and he shows little knowledge about the application process. He has no plans to obtain a GED. His main passion is cars, and he becomes excited only when we ask about them. "[The only interesting thing is] changing car components, changing the body, engine, everything," he says.

A School Like a Prison

Looking back over Civic's early experience in school helps us to understand how and why he so quickly disengaged and ultimately left school. As his engagement with school dwindled, Civic's in-school behaviors worsened. Asked how he would describe himself as a student, he says, "A bad student. Things that people don't dare to do, I do them all . . . throw a trash bin with friends, cut classes, and walk out of school through the main door. I hate to do things sneakily." One week during ninth grade, which was his last year in school, he was late to class four times and cut class five times—one month, he missed eleven days of school.

Fighting has become a theme in Civic's school persona, in the context of ethnic conflicts. "In Macau, there aren't 'black ghosts' [an often used disparaging term used for blacks] and 'white ghosts,' [a disparaging term applied to whites]," he says. "In Macau, I didn't have to fight. Here, I have to fight. [In Macau,] I never fought, not even once. Here, because there is this bad guy, he provokes me to fight all the time. He would call a whole bunch of people, then they fight with me one by one." When he was an eighth grader, Civic fought both black and white students who teased his friends and was suspended several times.

Civic perceives Monroe High School as hostile and lonely. He sees it as "dark," "garbage," "a prison," and "very dangerous."

> "When you walk down the corridor, you never know whether some one will stab you with a knife in the back."
> "Has that happened before?"
> "No, not yet. But people bring in weapons—knives, baseball bats, glass bottles. Home is the safest place."
> "So who fights with whom?"
> "Usually it is the Vietnamese versus the Latino, or the Chinese versus the Latino. But never Chinese versus Chinese. Usually it is fist fights."

He continues, "Teachers are correctional officers, like those who supervise inmates in prison. Teachers are like policemen who have a whip and whack when they feel like it."[3] The atmosphere in the school is definitely uninviting, and the school loses many of its students each year.

What Civic at first liked most about life in the United States was "getting to know many friends." His friends were all Chinese, some born in China and others here. In the first couple of years, Civic spent many hours with his friends each day, playing basketball, talking at home, or going to the arcade to play video games. They communicated in Chinese. Repeating eighth grade, however, meant that he stayed in middle school while his friends moved to another grade and another building. It was "terrible": "Many of my brothers have left. It's more boring than before. I feel bad. I am still in eighth grade. All my friends are in high school now. I'm the only one here."

After he quit school, he began to spend more time with his family and less with his friends. Most surprisingly, he no longer sees Vick, who used to be his very best friend and who has also dropped out; now, Civic does not even have Vick's phone number. Civic belongs to no social or religious organizations. Like his mother, Civic has let his social world collapse. Now he sees only his immediate family.

Civic has a strong attachment to the Chinese culture and consistently identifies himself as Chinese. "Chinese people are the greatest people in the world," he says. "Most Americans think Chinese people are trash . . . Most Chinese people think Americans are trash."[4] He feels "completely Chinese"; it is inconceivable to feel even "a little American." He thinks Chinese are the "cleverest, greatest, most lovely" people. He favors Chinese songs and Chinese pop culture. He mingles mainly with Chinese. He uses Cantonese in his daily conversation. And he has always tried to pick a school with a largely Chinese student body. He distrusts other ethnic groups, especially Latinos and African Americans. But he also says that America, not Macau, feels most like home to him. And he believes that he can get rich in the United States. Macau is a backward country, in his view, and he remembers his life there as plagued by poverty. He has not traveled back to Macau since coming to the United States at age eleven, and he has no intention of returning any time soon.

From Top Student to "Notorious Troublemaker"

We talk to Civic in the family's Chinese take-out restaurant. It is dark, poorly ventilated, and cramped, with just three small tables. The kitchen occupies two-thirds of the floor area. Customers are rare. The table where we sit is greasy and sticky. Someone is deep-frying pork in the kitchen, and from time to time the odor hits us so strongly that we must draw a deep breath before continuing. When we finally leave, we smell like fried dumplings ourselves.

Civic is open and easygoing, with an engaging sense of humor. Our conversations proceed naturally even when the topics are difficult, and he is quick-witted and funny, throwing in slang words that add color to his descriptions.

"Civic, what are the reasons you left school?"

"I feel bored. Nothing to do in school. All my classes were in the mainstream, no bilingual classes. I used to study in Chinese and I was not comfortable with the mainstream."

"You think the mainstream classes are too hard for you?"

"No, not really. I could manage the classes, but I felt bored because there weren't any Chinese students in my class. All the classes were in English and I found that boring."

"You mentioned many times that you feel bored in school. What kind of things would excite you?"

"If the school could teach something that I am interested in, such as cars."

We talk about Civic's reasons for dropping out. From an above-average student in Macau with good behavior, after starting school in the United States, Civic has transformed into a "notorious troublemaker" and "fighter." Later, after only three years of our study, he has become a school dropout. What happened? At a school like a "prison," with no support and no caring, he failed to make a connection with any school personnel or with the work itself, and the school failed to connect with him. The bureaucratic error that assigned him to the regular program instead of the bilingual one contributed to his disengagement. In addition, the intensity of ethnic conflict discouraged him from attending. Though he hasn't joined a gang, he adopted a "gang member" persona and gradually grew into it as people responded to the image he created.[5]

While his parents have supported his education in words, in practice they have not been involved. Much of their indifference can be explained by their own lack of formal education. Civic's family has done well financially since their immigration and the parents have enjoyed spoiling their son with material goods, but these gifts, and his perception that his family is affluent, have only served to distract him from his schooling.

Civic's portrait also deepens our understanding of the role of family and ethnic identity in the successful adaptation of immigrant youth. Civic has remained close to his parents since immigration—unlike many of the other Chinese youth we have presented (as well as students in the study as a whole) whose immigration was followed by alienation from parents.[6] We see how family closeness is necessary but not itself enough to ensure that an immigrant child will adapt to American culture. Civic's identity remains staunchly Chinese, intensified by the ethnic basis of the fights he had at school. This deeply felt Chinese identity seems to deepen his rejection of anything "American."

In some ways it is ironic that while immigration has improved the family's life materially—the parents have experienced upward economic mobility and everyone seems to like it here—in terms of their child's education and schooling, immigration definitely was a change for the worse. In this sense, their experience is quite different from that of many other Chinese immigrant families. More typically, Chinese parents must contend with downward social mobility while their children thrive in school.

Myriam: Trauma and Resilience

Myriam is the perfect image of a young lady from the northern part of Haiti. She is a beautiful, dark-skinned girl, slim and very tall. At our first encounter, when she was thirteen years old, she was shy and hesitant but still very friendly. She seemed lonely and eager to talk, which is not surprising, considering that at that time she was living with only her father, who was in his eighties. Participating in the study is a form of socialization for her; aside from her visits to her ex-stepmother's house, she has no friends in her neighborhood. When we schedule our meetings, she often gives us a reminder call or calls to reschedule if she must, to make sure that our meetings take place. Her quiet smile appears before she answers our questions, and it is a brilliant smile because she has one of the Haitian marks of beauty—exquisite violet gums and beautiful white teeth.

Myriam's father is a Haitian army veteran, and her mother still lives in Haiti, with no immediate prospects for joining Myriam in the United States. Her parents have been divorced for several years. Myriam is the youngest child in the family; her brothers and sisters from other marriages are decades older and are married with their own families. Most of them were educated in Haiti.

Myriam's living situation has changed several times since she arrived in the United States. First she lived with her eighty-six-year-old biological father, but after two years she moved in with an aunt and uncle and their children. By the following year, she was back with her father, living in a one-bedroom apartment in a subsidized apartment complex for elderly and disabled people, a gloomy place for a teenage girl. The complex is in an area with a strong Haitian community, and her father knows some of the people in the building and the surrounding area—but for Myriam there are no peers nearby. The apartment is tiny: there is a bedroom, a living area that also serves as Myriam's bedroom, and a kitchenette next to the front door. Whenever we come to the house, her father takes a walk to allow Myriam some rare privacy during the interview.

When we first meet Myriam, she says she is happy living with her father despite the age difference and feels it is her duty to take care of him. Myriam misses her mother and is in frequent contact with her. She would like her mother to come to the United States one day, and she says that when she gets older, she will arrange it. Although her father stopped sending remittances after Myriam arrived, he tells her it is important to stay connected with her family in Haiti.

A Father She Had Never Known

Myriam has her own unique perspective on the picture of the girl with the books gazing over the farm fields, one that captures her own sense of displacement during the first year of the study:

> This girl just moved in this little village and got lost. She's asking these two farmers where to go and how to get home.

Indeed, Myriam's migration was very disruptive. The first family member to migrate to the United States was one of the father's daughters from another marriage, who later sent for her mother, who in turn enabled the father to emigrate from Haiti in the mid-1980s. He was the last of his family to enter the United States, and we can hypothesize that as an army official, he left Haiti for political reasons. He returned only once to Haiti—to visit Myriam, whom he had left when she was a toddler—and after that visit, he did not see her until she moved to the United States at age twelve, one year before we met her. Myriam was told that they were going to the United States because "We're going to have a better life. The schools are better, there are a lot more opportunities." Her father wanted all of his children to come to the United States because of the lack of security in Haiti.

Myriam recalls the separation from her mother and the awkward reunification with a father she did not know:

> "What happened when you said goodbye?"
> "I really couldn't say goodbye. Everyone was crying. I tried to say goodbye, but I couldn't."
> "How did you feel?"
> "I felt I was going to leave my mom alone and stuff like that. I am the only one that she has. My cousins, they used to come over all the time, but me and my mother, we were always together. I thought she was going to be alone."

"What was the worst thing about your leaving?"

"That I didn't know who I was going to live with, how my life was going to be. I knew of my father, I didn't know him."

"When you first got to your new home, what did you think?"

"I felt normal. I didn't feel anything. I missed my mom and I didn't know my dad. I see only my dad. First I didn't know that it was my dad. I thought we were just visiting someone before going to my dad's house. When my brother was leaving and left me there, I said, 'That's my dad?' I knew he was kind of old. I didn't know anything else."

"Do you remember some of the things you said to one another?"

"[He said] don't listen to no kids, all they do is drugs and call the police on their parents."

"Do you remember how you felt?"

"I was scared 'cause he used to put [this medication] in his eyes and they were always red. I had never lived close with old people like that before. I didn't do much; I just stayed in bed. I don't remember much."[7]

Myriam's father completed high school in Haiti and attended military school. He was in the army for thirty-six years, in the Duvalier era and afterward, and had subsequent administrative jobs. When he first came to the United States he worked in a restaurant, and now he is retired. He would like to continue working, but he says that employers will not hire someone who is so old.

Myriam's father likes the United States very much. Compared to Haiti, he says, the United States "is a lawful society. I like the sense of justice. It is fair if you abide by the laws. I can't live in a place where no one obeys the laws." When asked why he came to the United States, he replies: "At this point, I can only say that the main reason is because people respect you if you respect yourself. I can't live in chaos." He is proud that he is an American citizen. He would like all his children to remain in the United States because of the violence in Haiti. For Myriam, he wants better schooling. "School, I think, is like a mother or father. It allows you to eat, to have shelter, to put clothes on your back."

When we ask him what he wants for his children, he says: "For a man, someone who is a gentleman. For a woman—she has to be a lady—someone educated who carries herself well." He wants Myriam to work hard and take advantage of the opportunities that this country offers, because he thinks she is "brilliant" and could go far. "For girls, my first advice is: Even if a man is interested in you—ask yourself, are you ready? Are you finished with school? Can you take care of yourself? Those are the qualities people really like." Although her father believes that girls and boys should not date before age eighteen, he allows her to go to the movies with her friends. He says he does not let anything disturb Myriam's studies and wants her to concentrate on school and nothing else.

At first, Myriam says she wants to remain in the United States, although she misses her mother and the Haitian lifestyle tremendously. Now she wants to go back and forth to Haiti to see her mother and brother there. Before coming to the United States, she expected the United States to be a very rich country where people had easy access to work; today, she thinks that this is a myth. Regardless, she likes the schools here, except when she sees kids using drugs.

Myriam's initial statements were that she is happy living with her father and taking care of him, and the father said that he has a great relationship with his children. Our early view of this family however, turned out to be distorted—and we did not learn the full details until we became closer to Myriam. We had believed that although their family situation was unusual it was functional, and we certainly hadn't picked up on anything that prepared us for the dramatically different story that we heard during our fourth year of meeting with her, when she was sixteen years old. At that point, in the middle of discussing her reunification with her father, she dropped a shocker:

> At first, it was all right. The only problem that we had was that I just didn't know him. We didn't talk much, but it was fine up until I started to go to school. It was cold one day and I woke up late and I did not fix my bed, and he told me, "You mother of pig! You are not going to fix your bed?" and he started to hit me. I ran out and left for school, but I had left my school bag on the table. He called the police and they came to the school and I explained everything to them. After school I went home, and he did not open the door for me. He often does that, and when he does I wait outside until he opens, and when he does not open the door sometimes I go to my [ex-] stepmother who calls him and tell him that I am on my way home and to open the door for me. Well, that afternoon I knock and I knock, but he did not open the door. The police had told me at school that they would come by in the afternoon. While I was waiting outside the door they came, and I told them that he is not opening the door. The police knocked [on] the door and he opened it. When they were in, they fixed the bed for me and my father called his friend next door to translate for him, and he asked him to say

to the police that I hit him. He hit me, and I did not report it to the police! Anyhow, the police said that they did not believe him. He wanted the police to take me.

He kicked me out the same week, and I went to live with my [ex-] stepmother, who was living in a normal apartment at that time. She can't take me in now because she lives in a residence for old people, and they will not allow her to have anyone else in her house. After a few weeks had gone by, I heard that he was going have an eye surgery. I felt very sorry for him and I went back although I knew that he still did not trust me, but now he treats me worse. A lot [of] people think that it is always the kid who is at fault because she is young, but sometimes it is the parents who are at fault.[8]

The situation with her father, who by the end of the study is in his late eighties, has deteriorated so much that reconciliation does not seem to be an option.[9] An inspector visited their apartment, and upon seeing the conditions, asked her father through a translator whether he wished to obtain a two-bedroom apartment at the same rate that he was paying for the one-bedroom to assure better conditions for his daughter. He flatly refused and explained that he did not want Myriam in his apartment any longer. His attitude was so negative that the manager of the apartment complex has proposed allocating a one-bedroom apartment for Myriam and renting it to her for a low price.

One reason for their fights, according to Myriam, is that her father has never given her a key to their apartment. Often she is left to wait outside, and when her father does not arrive, she leaves either for the library or to join her friends. She has to spend most of her time with neighbors—Madame Ana and her family—who have helped her in times of crisis. This family has become a surrogate family for her, attending her school meetings and her graduation from middle school. Myriam no longer eats at home. She can buy food only because her ex-stepmother gives her money. Her father refuses to eat anything that she cooks for fear that she will poison him. He tells people she will kill him one day. Myriam says she cries all the time.

Myriam says that when her father evicted her from the apartment, he reported to her siblings and the police that she had hit him in the eyes, while she insists that she would never do such a thing. But there is some mystery surrounding the family situation. Despite Myriam's descriptions of his erratic and volatile behavior, when we interview him, he appears lucid, cooperative, and engaged, reflecting on the questions and giving detailed and insightful responses. He has his own litany of complaints about his daughter: "She gets home from school, she gets on the phone and is talking to a young man, from 5 P.M. on the phone till 11 P.M. I can't tell them to get off. I can't pull them off the phone. Talking to her doesn't work. You're supposed to be able to talk to your child. That hurts you. I can't hit her—any little scratch, and she can pull at it and make it worse and say I did it. So I can't hit her, and talking doesn't work. When she doesn't say 'Bon soir,' I still say 'Bon soir.' I still give her everything." He says that Myriam hits him. We, of course, cannot confirm the truth of such claims. Clearly, their relationship is highly dysfunctional and abusive.

We ask her when all this began, and it turns out that it has been going on all along:

> Actually, we never got along. 'Cause he doesn't understand me . . . He thinks because some other people made mistakes that I will make the same mistakes. Not everyone is the same. He is overprotective in a way like . . . He is just too overprotective. He thinks by calling me a bitch, a *millet* [a Kreyol word meaning mule], that would prevent me from doing bad things and that I would obey him. I did not know what [this word] meant. I had to wait until I had gone to my stepmother's house to ask her the meaning of *millet*. He called me a *millet* because I came back from church with my [ex-] stepmother. It was 10 P.M., and he asked me where I was and I told him. He does not want me to go to church during weekdays, but I do it in order to stay away from the house.[10]

We discuss the sisters and brothers who live in the same city. She says that none of them visit their father; they fear and resent him. She says her father had fourteen children with five different women. Myriam recounts stories that her half-brothers and half-sisters have told her over the years: that their father was abusive to the children and to his wives and partners, something that Myriam believes his military background provoked. She says he used to beat them, and that after each lash he would throw water on them. The wife would be beaten if she tried to stop him. They could not play outside; they would always be expected to have a book in their hands whether it was during the school year or a vacation. On the street, the wife could not talk or look at anyone, male or female, and no male family member could visit her. The children were always on the lookout when it was time for the father to come home from work: if he were to see them playing in the yard, he would beat them. One daughter who lives nearby never visits because he threw her out when she was thirteen. Another brother, who died recently, ran away after a beating from the father when he was twelve years old, went to live with his mother's family, and never returned. The father saw him for the first time as an adult when the son was dead in his coffin.

Myriam has some dependable social resources. During the first year after her arrival, she moved into a predominantly Haitian community, both in her school and in her neighborhood. After finishing middle school, she moved out of that sphere because her high school is in a Hispanic neighborhood, where she has made new friends and has new experiences. Her group of friends has grown to include Haitians, Hispanics, Cape Verdeans, and members of several other ethnic groups, with whom she had no contact prior to changing schools.

Myriam and her father were born and raised in the Baptist church and attend church weekly, though they go to different churches. Myriam tutors children at her church and has developed good relationships with the parents of her students. The church members take care of her, she says; they "support me by giving me money, respect, and encouragement." She is involved in other after-school activities such as dance and sports.

Myriam consistently reports having a good, supportive relationship with her ex-stepmother. Socially, she does not seem isolated, and, barring the father, her relationships with family members are strong. Yet she never stops longing for her mother:

> "Did you think much about your mother?"
> "Yeah, I miss her, and we talk about living together again. For her to come . . . I think that my life would be much better if I were living with my mother. She never used to curse me like [my father]."
> "Is there anything that you wish could have happened differently?"
> "I wish I did not have to separate from my mother. [I wish] I had not come. If I knew my father was like that, I would rather have stayed."[11]

Puzzling about Which Way to Go

Myriam attended three private schools in Port-au-Prince, the capital of Haiti, where the instruction was in French. When she first came to the

United States, she attended a local middle school where she was placed in a bilingual program. Later she was transferred to the mainstream program.

Myriam's attitudes toward school, teachers, and her peers fluctuate. She says that school is one of the things she likes most in the United States, although she has a lot of difficulties with math. She believes that success derives from a good education. At one point, however, when she is in eighth grade, she shares, "I wish that I was done with school entirely," "School is boring," and "Teachers are stupid."[12] Yet considering her loneliness at home, school for her satisfies social needs—if not academic aspirations—and her attitude toward school becomes more positive when she starts high school. She generally has good attendance, but she starts to miss many of her early classes: she has a long commute, and the school will not let students enter class late.

Myriam's report cards suggest she has always been a low-average student, and her academic engagement is lukewarm. Her father says she is doing well in school and brings home good grades, but perhaps he told us that to create the impression that he knows what is going on with his daughter academically. The only parts of school that truly capture her attention are extracurricular: the U.S. Army's Junior Reserve Officers' Training Corps (JROTC), the track team, and dance classes. Her eleventh-grade English teacher says, "Myriam started off strong in English class, but by the second half of the school year, there was a decline in her attendance and motivation. She is a terrific young lady but her interests have shifted to make school less of a priority. One area that she mentioned was taking up her time was her dance classes and performance."

Miriam's indecision in her personal and academic life seem to be captured in her narrative about the picture with the boy and the violin, created in the first year of the study:

> This boy used to do well at school. Then his parents bought him a violin because he was a good kid. Then he spent all his time playing the violin and stopped doing his schoolwork and failed. So he's confused now. He doesn't know if he wants to keep playing the violin or do his homework.

Myriam's English skills in the third year of the study are below the first percentile, and in the fifth year they barely increase to the first percentile. Her grades are consistently D's and C's, with an F every once in a while. These low grades may be less a function of her general abilities than of her weak English skills and the pressures of her difficult family situation.

Myriam has told us at different times that she wants to be a doctor, a computer engineer, or an optometrist. When she was in tenth grade, she surprised us by saying she was considering joining the army, a path several of her school friends are contemplating. She was the leader of the JROTC at her school and had won awards for her outstanding work with the group. Of JROTC, she said, "I really enjoy it because it teaches me leadership, self-responsibility, learning abilities, and self-esteem." The idea of military service intrigues her; it may be that the military promises a sense of control and strength. But she is not at all certain about this career path and needs some general counseling about her future. She tells us she has no one to talk to nor anyone to encourage her; the only person in whom she can confide is her ex-stepmother, whom she admires because she always has something positive to say to her. By the end of the study, however, when she is in eleventh grade, Myriam is considering obtaining a business degree in college or becoming a model—a distinct possibility given her height, beauty, and grace. In any case, she wants to find a job soon in order to purchase a car and to save money for her mother in Haiti.

Although Myriam doesn't think of herself as being popular in school, she does have many friends and develops an active social life. About her friends, she says: "When I am losing my strength, they encourage me . . . Most of them are really proud of me when I do good things." Although she has a few Haitian friends, most of her close friends are either Latino or white American.

Myriam's boyfriend in eleventh grade is nineteen years old, white, and a high school dropout who works as a carpenter. She says he motivates her to study and gives her good advice. But his race is creating tension in her community. She took him to her church one day and the entire church stared at him throughout the mass, she says. He was so embarrassed that they left the church together.

By the last year of our study, Myriam has begun to identify herself as a black American. She sees herself as being an American; she believes that one should adhere to the rules of the place where one is currently living. "Haitian people do not seem to understand that," she exclaims. "You can't be living here and using the rules of Haiti when you are no longer living there."

Both Myriam and her father believe that race is no great obstacle in this country. "[People's] race doesn't matter to me as long as I can be friends with them," Myriam says. Her father concurs: "It's not appearance; it is substance that really counts. People do not pay attention to color. They focus on capacity, and that is the truth." Unlike her father, Myriam does not believe that Haitian immigrants have the same chances as people born in the United States, but she believes that one can succeed here if one works very hard.

Absent Memories

Myriam is more Americanized than most of the other Haitian youth in our study. She wears contemporary teenage styles. She gels and flattens her hair into a ponytail, highlighting the features in her oval face. She is the only Haitian student we have talked to who considers herself a black American. That her boyfriend is a white American also suggests she is more Americanized than others. She has Haitian friends, but most of her friends are Latino or white. Her attitude about Haitians—that they don't understand they must adapt to the American system and live by American rules—further explains her chosen ethnic identification. She definitely does not reject Haitian culture, however.

Myriam's dysfunctional relationship with her father is taking a psychological toll, but she is resilient. Except for her father's unconfirmed claims that she is hitting him, we can connect no external behaviors to the trauma of her abusive home environment. She stays away from home as much as she can, spending time with friends and her boyfriend. This romance could be a positive influence in Myriam's life, counterbalancing her poor relationship with her father. Myriam's separation from her mother is also problematic and could have increasingly negative psychological effects over time. A realistic plan for reuniting with her mother has yet to be articulated, however. Myriam is getting through school, but at a level below her potential; we strongly suspect that she could be much more engaged if her family situation were different.

As with Civic, a theme of multiple losses emerges in Myriam's history: she leaves her mother to live with a stranger who is her father; she moves from home to home; she lives daily with pressure, loneliness, and possible abuse. In our conversations with Myriam, it is striking how often she does not remember things about the early parts of her move to the United States. Some of these experiences are likely too painful to remember.

León: Despite a Mother's Best Intentions

Like many California schools slapped together in the 1960s, Steeler High is a one-story, flat-roofed, rambling building of concrete and steel. Though large, the building is uncomfortably crowded, with nearly 1,800 students. The typical class size is around thirty students, the classrooms are stifling, and students often must drag chairs from other rooms to have a place to sit. The cafeteria is packed so tightly that students stand on benches in front of their lockers, using the tops of their lockers as lunch tables. There is a crush of bodies as the students move from class to class. Loud laughter and shouts punctuate the air. Hostile security guards who seem to like their power a little too much bustle about, shouting at students through megaphones or simply at the top of their lungs. Interactions between adults and students are more often corrective than connective. The halls are littered, grimy, and unwelcoming.

Students move about in highly gendered and racially segregated groups. Latinos dominate the mix in terms of numbers, if not status. More than 60 percent are Latino, the majority from Mexico; some have arrived within the last few months, while others are from families who have been living in the area for generations. The students who make up the high-social-status group in this school are black—and African Americans make up nearly 20 percent of the student population. They dress in the latest urban street fashions and are more likely to be found on the highly successful basket-ball team. The Asian student population—coming from the Philippines, China, and Vietnam—has grown by 16 percent in the last decade. More than half the students at Steeler are classified as English-language learners.

Most of the students are poor. Nearly 75 percent qualify for school lunch subsidies. Steeler High qualifies as a Title 1 school, entitling it to supple-mental federal funds for improving access to quality education. Retired faculty and graduate students from a local university donate their time to compensate for the school's disadvantages. Nonetheless, only 37 percent of the graduating students take the SAT, and, on average, those who do take it score dramatically below the national average: 130 points lower on the ver-bal SAT and 142 points below on the math. Few students meet the state minimum standards for achievement; on the high-stakes state assessment test called STAR given in 1999 (the second year of our study), only 10 percent of students scored at or above the 50th percentile on the reading test and only 18 percent did so on the math test.[13] Students hold low expectations for themselves and the teachers share that attitude.

The school reflects its run-down neighborhood context. Gang violence that starts in the streets all too often flows into the school. Fights break out weekly; what starts as rambunctious roughhousing can shift in a flash to something much more serious. Many students have easy access to weapons; consequently, lingering grudges can become very threatening. Students report feeling unsafe and tell tales of violent incidents at Steeler High or in its feeder middle schools—the shoot-out involving an escaped convict, the angry father who stabbed a teacher, a rape. In this toxic environment, engagement is the exception, not the norm.

This is the academic environment in which León finds himself. We first met him two years after he arrived in the United States from Mexico, when he was thirteen years old and enrolled in a sixth-grade ESL/bilingual program at Quentin Middle School, which is described in detail in Chapter 3. This middle school is a main feeder school for Steeler High and has an environment of danger and low achievement. When León entered Steeler High, he was not mainstreamed. Now in the eleventh grade, he is taking only English-language development, ESL language and literature, and sheltered math and science courses.

When we ask him how he thinks he is doing in school, León admits he is the same kind of student that he was in Mexico, "a bad student." He tells us: "I miss class a lot. My mom lets me be absent." When he first arrived in the United States he was more motivated than he had ever been, but his interest in school waned. He believes that he does his best, but he has low expectations for himself and thinks he is not all that smart. At the same time, he likes his school, and in spite of its tense atmosphere, has a generally positive attitude toward education and believes it is not hard to learn. This paradox—his enjoyment of school and learning, contrasted with his poor academic performance—is constant throughout the study. It seems that the circumstances of his life have obstructed a strong inner desire to study and learn.

León's grade point average has been low all through high school. His grades range from B through F, but the number of failing grades increase every year as his academic engagement withers. In eleventh grade, he has earned mostly F's (which, however, included several F pluses for passing one quarter out of the semester) and two D's, one in each of the two semesters.

León's teachers generally like him, but they all underscore his poor performance and attendance. His math teacher in eleventh grade tells us: "He is absent almost every day. However, when he is in class, he pays attention and completes assignments." This teacher rates León's behavior and punctuality as "good" but his motivation, effort, and attendance as "very poor." His English-language development teacher says that León "seems to be a student who is not interested in academics due to his low academic skill levels. He is a nice young man, but he seems more interested in socializing than attending classes. Sometimes his behavior is good, at other times it is poor. By poor I mean 'off task.'" She concludes: "Unfortunately, I am a new teacher and I have been unable to follow up on [his] lack of academic interest. Also he comes so rarely I have let him 'slip through the cracks.'" She rates his oral communication in English and his understanding of class material as "very good" and "good," respectively. Yet she rates his reading and writing in English as only "fair." Neither teacher sees León as having major behavior problems, which suggests that his difficulties stem from his lack of motivation and poor attendance.

It is not surprising that the teachers like him. León is warm and friendly, though at first a bit reserved. As we get to know him, we see that he likes to joke and is easy to talk to. He seems easygoing though somewhat distractible, and at times there are signs of tension and insecurity. León dresses like a "homeboy" in big, baggy clothes, big white sweatshirts, and baggy black jeans that are so long he can't avoid stepping on them. The huge sweatshirts are such an important element of his style that he wears one always, even when the California weather is hot. He has pierced ears and wears thin gold chains around his neck, while his teeth are somewhat crooked. He keeps his hair very short, black, spiky, and shiny, though in later years he dyes the ends bright red. He is very tall and thin, with dark eyes and a medium-brown complexion. In spite of his preference for a tough "homeboy" facade, León has a likable and polite demeanor.

A Mother's Efforts

León is originally from the city of Guadalajara, but he also lived for a time in Mexico City before emigrating. He arrived in the United States in the mid-1990s, when he was eleven years old, together with his mother and his sister, Ana, who is a year older than him. They joined an uncle who had been living in the United States for several years. The family's main reason for coming to the United States was economic. León's mother was barely making ends meet as a single mother in Mexico, and she heard that "here one could make a better living." León's father has not been a part of the family for a long time.

When we first walk into León's apartment for a home visit, we find Ana and a cousin's wife, who looks about seventeen years old, folding cardboard boxes and giggling together. We ask whether they are working on a school project, but it turns out that they are putting together a small cardboard dresser for the cousin's baby. The miniature make-it-yourself dresser has blue and white stripes like something out of *Alice in Wonderland,* and we feel like we have stumbled upon two girls playing dollhouse. The girls slip out to another room to chat and giggle away from our ears while the baby naps in the rocking chair in the living room. This is another one of those days that Ana is missing school with her mother's approval.

León's mother is a humble woman with a large heart. She looks exhausted from the long hours she puts in at the Mexican restaurant where she works. She tells us that her feet hurt, she is losing her eyesight, and she has little energy and loses her appetite. Yet she is babysitting a friend's child while we are there (and apologizes frequently for the distraction). She often watches this child on Mondays, her day off, without taking payment, because she knows the young mother is struggling; she sympathizes with her because she remembers herself having to leave her children with someone else so she could work. It breaks her heart to see the sad face of the child, who reminds her of her own babies crying when she had to leave them. The young mother tries to pay her, but she never takes the money.

The apartment is in a working-class northern California suburb, a neighborhood of predominantly African-American families. León says that his neighbors generally get along, except that there is always loud music playing at night. He feels safe going to school and on the way home. His mother has a very different perception; she feels uneasy. Because of her schedule, the children often stay home alone, and she doesn't want her neighbors to know that her children are there without her.

León's mother feels that life in the United States goes by very fast, especially for young people, who grow up faster than they do in Mexico. They want to become independent earlier and they lack respect. In her words, "I see kids who have no respect for their parents. They do not listen to them any more. They go out, stay out late. Thank God my kids haven't changed since we've been here, but I've seen it happen to others."

In general, she likes living in the United States now that she has found work. In Mexico, León's mother, who has a sixth-grade education, worked in a shoe factory. Now she works in a Mexican restaurant in a nearby city, where her brother and León also work. She says that money goes further here than in Mexico and she can better support her children.

She has no goals for herself in this country. At age forty-two, she is "too old for that," she says. She is here only to see her children grow up, get ahead, and get good jobs, which she thinks is impossible in Mexico. The schools here are better and have computers and other resources. "They are going to get more out of life here," she says. She doesn't plan on becoming a U.S. citizen because she thinks it is too hard and because she does not know English. She says that even if she had papers and became a citizen, "People here have a prosperous, progressive country. I don't feel American. Even if I became a citizen I would not feel American. My roots are in Mexico." She adds that it will be her children's decision whether to stay in this country when they are adults.

León says he likes that his nuclear family lives by itself. In Mexico, they lived with their grandmother. All the same, he misses his grandparents and would prefer to go back to Mexico "to be with family." León resents his mother's long hours and the fact that he and his sister see less of her now.

The family stays in touch with relatives in Mexico, but they phone them only rarely, every few months. León's mother sends money to her parents on special occasions such as Christmas and Mother's Day. Their social support in the United States is limited. The mother says they do not have friends, either Mexican or American. They do not get together with anyone regularly; this is also because she works so many hours, almost thirty days a month, and is completely exhausted on her few days off. The mother's brother lives nearby, but they are not close.

The mother and children have warm, sustaining relationships. To make up for her long absences, she is permissive when she is with them, rarely scolding or disciplining them. On Mondays, her only days off, she routinely allows Ana and León to stay home and spend the day with her. Being with them is important to her, even if it means that they miss school. Her circumstances are difficult and she cannot offer her children much academic support, but she makes a great effort to provide for them and to spend as much time with them as she can. León thinks highly of his mother and in the third year of the study, when he is fifteen years old, he tells us that she is the most important person in his life, someone who feels proud of him, treats him with respect, and helps him under any circumstance.[14]

According to his mother, their relationship hasn't changed since they came to the United States. If anything, they have become closer because it is just the three of them, and this closeness persists during the entire time we are in contact with the family. "We don't have many friends, I am the only person they have," she tells us in the first year of the study. Whatever disagreements they have—about going out, inviting friends over to see movies, coming home late—are resolved through discussion. She calls from work to make sure the children are home and have followed all her instructions. The mother says that when they get bad grades she gets upset and scolds them, but León tells us that "no pasa nada" (nothing happens). The children are alone at home after school. For a short time at the beginning of our study the mother had a boyfriend who was living with the family, but by the end of the study he is no longer there. "We are very united. [Previously] I had a partner. That's when they kind of got upset because they saw me with someone who is not their dad so [he and I] had problems and we separated. But since then, [the children and I] have been very close and they tell me their problems. Also, now that they see that I am alone and devoted to them, they feel more at ease and more comfortable."

Because of her long hours, limited education, and scanty knowledge of English, she cannot help her children with their schooling. She does not know whether they do all their homework because by the time she comes home from the restaurant, it is too late to check. "León and Ana have not been giving me their report cards," she tells us in the first year. "And I don't have time to go check on them at school. I did visit recently, though, because Ana's teacher told me that she was cutting classes and her grades were going down. So she now has to go to summer school." Their mother would like to be more involved at their school, but the most she has managed was attending a field trip when they were in middle school. She feels uncomfortable expressing her opinions to the teachers "because I don't know the right words to use, I don't know the language." She wants her children to do well and worries constantly about their well-being. Her main concern is that they spend too much time on their own while she is working. She tells them to "stay out of gangs and to do well in school."

Changes during the Following Years

> I guess she is looking around, watching how people work. She was coming back from school, I guess. I guess she thinks that . . . no, she's just studying so she won't have to work the way they are working out there. She feels lucky 'cause, I guess, she will study; I don't know. However, she wants to decide if she wants to study or if she wants to work.

This projected narrative at the end of the study (of a girl with books standing near a field where a worker toils) captures the way León seems torn between studying and working in the restaurant, where he is earning money, enjoying his social contacts, and feeling competent. Because he is absent so often, we find it hard to reach him in school to conduct our interview, so this time we decide to go to his job. The restaurant is in a fairly prosperous city neighborhood, about a fifteen-minute subway ride south of Steeler High. The restaurant is large, moderately expensive, and has a predominantly white clientele. During our visit, it is very busy. León, who waits tables about fifteen hours a week, doesn't get to wait on our table, but he sees us and gives us a look of recognition. We don't want to be intrusive and make him uncomfortable, so we just nod and continue with our conversation. León obviously likes working here. He is courteous and seems responsible, at ease waiting tables and talking to the clients.

We don't get to see much of him interacting with his coworkers, but in our few glimpses, he is friendly and seems comfortable with them. People of all ages work here, but most of them are young, between sixteen and twenty-five. Most, if not all, are Latinos, and there are equal numbers of men and women. It is quite possible that many, like León, are undocumented. We don't know whether León and his mother share the same schedule or whether working at the same place affects their relationship. Our most interesting observation from this visit is the contrast between his confidence at his job and his inadequacy in the classroom.

During his last year of high school, several changes occur in León's life. Ana's boyfriend has moved into in their small apartment. This development is something of a surprise: the mother expected that when her daughter turned eighteen, she would move out of the house—and in fact, the children used to tease their mother that in the United States, children leave home the minute they turn eighteen. And while the mother was initially opposed to Ana having a partner move in with her at such a young age, she now feels that his presence has not changed the family relationships; the boyfriend works all day and gets along well with León. León agrees that the boyfriend's presence has caused no problems. They are the same supportive and close family they have been since the beginning of our study.

The family has made some forward strides, though their socioeconomic status is much the same. Having all members of the family working has helped. Ana has a part-time job, her partner works full-time, and the mother and León continue to work in the Mexican restaurant. Their pooled income has allowed them to buy a small car, which they use to pick up their mother when she finishes work at 10 P.M. The mother says they are better off than they were in Mexico. "Here my kids study and I don't pay anything, no books, no anything," she says. "In Mexico, if one does not buy the books, one can't continue studying." Paradoxically, although her positive evaluation of their life is based on the children's schooling, the academic performance of both children has been weak. Ana barely graduated from high school, and León is struggling to graduate on time in his senior year.

At the end of his junior year, León had barely achieved eleventh-grade status. Because he was behind in earning credits for graduation and had often been absent, he was transferred to the nearby Continuation School for twelfth grade. This school focuses on students who are at risk of dropping out or who lack enough credits to graduate. It enrolls only seventy students, has three teachers and a counselor, and the students can make up their missing credits through an individualized program. León is doing better there than in his old high school: in the first quarter at Continuation School, he failed only one class. Yet his grades dropped sharply the next quarter and he failed five of his seven classes. He started missing school more as the year progressed, though not as often as when he attended

Steeler High. His teachers see his poor attendance as a problem and the principal says that León cares more about work than school, but they do not know how else to try to help him.

As before, León does not participate in any organizations or extracurricular activities. But the change to a smaller school has improved his social support system. The students all know each other, the staff, and the administration. During the last year of our study, when we explored his feelings about the school with a sentence-completion task, León said, "[The teachers] in the Continuation School are better. They check on you [whereas] Steeler High is a big school. They tell you what you need to graduate." León likes the individual attention. But the fact that his performance dropped again after his initial improvement suggests that he needs even more social and academic support, including possibly tutoring or a mentor.

León has bought a cell phone and enjoys having his own money to spend. The school principal tells us that for many students like León, earning money becomes their main focus and school takes second place. "When students first get a cell phone, they think they are millionaires!" she exclaims. This is especially common among the immigrant students, she says, and their parents seem to encourage such attitudes. León's mother tells us that when she saw that he was doing poorly at school she decided to take him out so that he could work, but her boss discouraged her. The lack of parental pressure for academic improvement, along with having an attractive job and money, has probably further sapped his motivation and focus.

Yet León maintains that he wants to attend college—"if I can." He recognizes the obstacles: his lack of fluency in English, his poor school record and study habits, and his lack of knowledge about getting into college. Money is another hurdle. Despite his abstract desire to go to college, León says that it is only somewhat likely that he will do so. Because of his bad grades, he is not even sure whether he will graduate from high school. In addition, he is worried about his undocumented status: At college, he says, "they ask for a lot of papers." He is well aware that these obstacles narrow his opportunities, a realization that probably further weakens his academic motivation.

León's mother says that the opportunities to get ahead in the United States are not the same for American-born citizens and Mexican immigrants because "we are not from here." She is mostly concerned that she and her children cannot get government help in getting job training, better jobs, or other services.

Being Mexicano

All of León's close friends are Mexican girls. Because he mostly socializes with girls, his peers call him names he doesn't like. When he was thirteen, he named two girls who were also in our study as his best friends; both are high achievers. Coming from a household headed by a single mother and having no close male figure in his life may have influenced his choice of friends.

León talks to his friends in both Spanish and English. Because the Continuation School has no separate English-language development programs for the English learners, all classes are conducted in English only, though Spanish is still frequently heard at the school. This emphasis on English has made León more comfortable speaking English with his friends. (At Steeler High, Spanish dominates as the informal language.) Yet his academic English lags considerably; he lacks the vocabulary and language sophistication needed to do well academically (as his grades show).

At work León uses mostly Spanish with his coworkers but English with customers. He listens to music in English, uses the computer to communicate mostly in English, and watches TV in both languages. At home, he frequently speaks in English with his sister but Spanish remains the dominant language for family conversations. Overall, León is comfortably bilingual.

With the exception of the two girls he was close to initially, most of León's friends share his attitudes about school. They think graduating from high school is important but that going to college is only somewhat important. León tells us that his friends think that getting good grades and doing well in school are only somewhat important or not important. He admits that his friends rarely help one another in school, that they ask him to cut school, and that they generally find school boring.

León reports conflicts between different ethnic and racial groups at his school. He dislikes when there are "fights with blacks," though it seems that he has not been involved in such a fight himself. He admits that these tensions generally do not cause him direct problems. Tellingly, he stated in eleventh grade that most U.S.-born Americans think that Mexicans are "dumb—just kidding. I guess nice people." In contrast, he says that Mexicans think U.S.-born Americans are "intelligent."

León identifies as a "Mexicano" and he is certainly rooted in his culture of origin. He misses the family he left behind in Mexico, especially his grandparents. For many years he longed to go back, and felt that his family was alone in its new home. More recently, however, he has grown accustomed to his new situation and speaks less often about returning. "We left Mexico when I was 10 and now I am 17," he says resignedly. "I guess here I'm used to it. And I haven't been back."

León's identity is based on his Mexican heritage but has a transcultural flavor. He feels comfortable speaking English and switching from one language to the other. This transcultural identity is pan-Latino: the social group he most closely identifies with in school and in his community is Latino—not just Mexican—and it consists of both immigrants and non-immigrants.

Failing to Break the Cycle of Disengagement

León, by his own admission, was never much of a student, and he sees his academic self as someone not very bright or capable. He has a well-meaning and loving mother, but she cannot guide him academically. She also is unable—or perhaps unwilling—to exert enough pressure to get him to perform the day-to-day behaviors necessary to do well in school, such as attending class and doing homework. León attends a dysfunctional middle school and high school in a city that ranks among the twenty-five most violent in the country. In contrast, he finds in the workplace a sense of competence, a place of predictability and routines, and the ability to help support his family.

In the abstract, León has a positive attitude about school, wants to do well, and talks about attending college. When he is in class he puts effort into doing the work, yet he is absent so much he cannot keep up. As discussed earlier, by the end of the fourth year of our study, León's disengagement and poor record led the administration to transfer him to a continuation school, a last hope for graduation.

While conversationally León is bilingual, his academic English is limited and his spotty attendance has probably stunted his acquisition of higher-level Spanish language skills as well. He has gained few, if any, critical thinking skills and no knowledge of college preparation, nor does he participate in the nonacademic aspects of school such as clubs and sports that might spur him to seriously consider continuing his education. León's lack of legal documentation has affected both his self-esteem and his academic motivation; he guesses, rightly, that lacking papers would make it difficult to get into college. He still talks about college, but his deeds—his worsening attendance and academic records—show that he is giving up. It is unlikely that he will advance academically beyond high school.

MANY low-achieving immigrant youth encounter serious obstacles upon arriving in the United States. They are most likely to be in schools and communities that do nothing to nurture an academic identity. Often there are family problems—illness, deep poverty, anomie, conflict, and lack of control. And many times one parent is coping with all the responsibilities of raising the children.

We are struck by the sense that many of these students enter the United States as weak students, with literacy gaps, interrupted schooling, and an absence of academic focus—and that these problems simply worsen in the new setting. In particular, given the pressing challenges of day-to-day survival, learning a new language to the level necessary to become academically competitive becomes not only an insurmountable obstacle, but also a source of deep frustration. In violent social contexts, not surprisingly, watching one's back becomes a more pressing and rewarding pursuit than gazing forward to a better academic future. As other pathways to success, such as the workplace, become much more alluring and attainable than school, these low-achieving immigrant students frequently let their optimistic resolutions to embrace educational opportunities in the new land fall away.

■ ■

CHAPTER 7

Portraits of Improvers

AN INITIAL PERIOD of transplant shock is part of every immigrant's journey. Before newly arrived immigrant youth can thrive, they must first become oriented to their new environment. As they acclimate to the new culture and begin to master the nuances of a new language, we might expect most immigrant students to improve academically and become more happily connected to their schools. Our study revealed a different story, however. To our surprise, academic improvement was the exception, not the rule.

Those students who did improve over time—only 11 percent of the students we studied—had a grade point average during the first year of the study that was not much better than that of our lowest performers: 2.32, or a C plus. With time, however, they made impressive gains—enough so that by the end of the study, they had managed to bring their average grades up to a solid B. What about these determined youngsters helped them to raise their grades?[1]

The improvers were fairly equally distributed across country-of-origin groups with one exception: Chinese students were nearly twice as likely to be found in this group. There was also a significant gender difference: Girls were 50 percent more likely to improve their grades over time.

Improvers were more likely to have working fathers than the declining and low-achieving students, and they were somewhat more likely to live in a two-parent home than either the low achievers or the precipitous decliners. Also, improvers attended schools with significantly fewer problems and reported less violence in schools than did the either the declining or low-achieving students. According to every other standard measure on our scales, however, we found very little difference between the improving students and their lower-achieving peers. (See Table 5.1.)

A qualitative analysis of the portraits, however, did uncover two interesting and distinctive patterns among the improvers. In some cases, the students had arrived in the United States after some sort of trauma—political turmoil in the country of origin, the death of a parent or caregiver, or neglect during a long separation. In such cases, it appeared that upon arrival, these students were simply unprepared to focus on their academic work— and it showed in their initial grades. Once significant healing had begun— and the students had become more acclimated to American culture—they had the emotional and cognitive resources they needed to concentrate on their schoolwork and improve their academic performance.

The other distinguishing pattern had to do with mentors. In nearly every case of a significant upward shift in performance, an advocate or mentor had entered the youngster's life, helping to change the course of his or her academic trajectory. A firm coach who demanded an improvement in behavior, a warm tutor who believed in the student, a counselor who clarified the route to college access—a caring person often made all the difference.

In the case of Rosette, we meet a young woman who lived through a period of extreme political and personal turmoil in Haiti, where political violence and assassinations were an everyday occurrence and schools were closed more often than they were open. Once she arrived at her new home, a caring and committed counselor patiently led her to a pathway of success. Initially slow to learn the ropes and alienated from her parents, Jane constructed a network of relations by involving herself in her church and spending long hours at the local Chinese community center. With Ramón, we see a determined mother who elicited the help of an advocate and eventually a caring tutor to thwart the perils of low teacher expectations.

Rosette: From Sorrow to Hope

Rosette's first memory is of violence. When we first met her at age twelve, soon after she arrived in the United States, she drew a picture of her mother being beaten. Her mother, she explained, is mentally ill; when she would leave the house in a state of hysteria, relatives would beat her and drag her home.

In 1986, the same year as Rosette's earliest memory, Jean-Claude "Baby Doc" Duvalier, the Haitian dictator, was overthrown after a brutal fifteen-year rule, leaving the country economically and socially traumatized. In 1991, Jean-Bertrand Aristide was elected in Haiti's first free democratic election. Rosette clearly remembers this event and the hope it evoked among the poor. Within seven months, however, Aristide was ousted. The military took over, and two months later the United Nations imposed an embargo. Over the next two years, Rosette witnessed events that are beyond comprehension. It was an era of torture, intimidation, disappearances, and exodus. "They beat and killed people," Rosette recalled. "I can't count how many of my uncles were killed in these political things." Children were also brutalized. Rosette recounted one such incident: "The situation was very bad in Haiti. When there were political problems, schools would close. When I was at my school in Haiti, they used to drop tear gas on the kids. I had to put a lemon to my nose and would run. The school would not let us leave school grounds because it was more dangerous on the streets." We asked her who used the tear gas. "People who are doing bad things," she responded. "Aristide was not in the country. At that time, those people wanted to destroy the country. It was so bad. I went to my aunt's home in the countryside to hide. I could not stay in the city. Every morning, there was a shooting."

Aristide returned to Haiti in 1994. Rosette was ten. Her childhood had been filled with the sounds of bullets, the sight of dead bodies, and a culture of fear. In Haiti, she never experienced an uninterrupted school year. Aristide was pressured to relinquish his power because his term was expiring. René Préval of the same political party gained power. The country continued to suffer massive trauma as Préval tried unsuccessfully to restore hope and a semblance of order.

Rosette remembers that time: "When Aristide was president, things were okay. Now that we have Préval, things are worse. When Préval leaves, I hope the country will be better. If I meet Aristide, I would tell him what to do so the country will change." We ask Rosette, "What would you tell Aristide?" She replies, "The first thing I would say is that he has to change the education system for children. Sometimes I walk on the streets—things I won't see here, I see in Haiti. Kids naked on the street. Kids lie dead on the ground. Children who are poor. This should not happen anywhere. We have a small country. Why do we destroy it? We won't have anything. People are killing each other."

During the mid-1990s, Haiti continued to suffer major hardships. Many waited for relatives to sponsor their visas while others took to small boats to flee across the dangerous Florida Straits. Rosette's paternal grandfather, who was already in the United States, applied on behalf of his children, and when Rosette was twelve, she and her father migrated to the United States.

While not all Haitian immigrant youth experience the level of violence to which Rosette was repeatedly exposed, certainly many were affected by cyclical school closings, routine chaos, and a general sense of insecurity. Many of the young people who lived through this era suffered to some degree from post-traumatic stress disorder, reporting anxiety, nightmares, and recurring memories of the horrible events they experienced.[2] Rosette's age cohort never knew Haiti under the Duvaliers; they were born either immediately before or after Baby Doc was ousted in 1986 and years past the 1971 death of his equally brutal father, the dictator François "Papa Doc" Duvalier. Their Haiti was filled with chants of revolution and cries for justice for the poor—a socialist revolution clamoring for basic rights gone awry. Curfews, embargos, coups d'états, and weak, inconsistent governments were the warp and weft of their childhoods. Perhaps because she survived this turmoil, Rosette is serious, mature, and precociously politically aware.[3]

The chaos in Haitian society was mirrored in Rosette's home. The story she tells about relatives beating her mother to subdue her and bring her home reflects their lack of understanding for the mentally ill. It is unclear exactly what role her mother played in Rosette's early life, but we know that when she was four, as her mother's condition worsened, her father became Rosette's primary caregiver. That is, Rosette's father took over her care even before the immigration because her mother was not available psychologically even when they were together. By the time she was fourteen and living in the United States, Rosette had no contact with her mother. Yet Rosette continually expresses a desire to take care of her mother and even to sponsor her to come to the United States. This may prove difficult because her paternal family dislikes her mother and suppresses any attempts to talk about her. Near the end of our study, we learn that her father had recently allowed Rosette to visit her mother in Haiti for the first time since her immigration. Before leaving, she contacted us and said, "This year my mother is not crazy and has a job at the airport." Rosette hopes against hope that her mother will continue to get better, and nurses her dream of helping her.

Testing the Limits

An attractive, brown-skinned young woman, Rosette is tall for her age. She was frail when she arrived in the United States, but she has gained weight. She recently had her hair straightened. Although she is naturally pretty, her pulled-back hair and neat clothes draw little attention to her features. She is pleasant and cooperative, but sadness is visible in her serious eyes.

During the first years of our study, Rosette abides by her father's insistence that she dress modestly. Because Rosette demonstrates her love for her father by doing everything he wants, she sticks to his dress code of simple, loose-fitting jeans and T-shirts. The issue of conservative dress is important to him. It represents his fear of losing control over his daughter and his desire that she maintain her innocence for as long as possible (he has also stated that he will not let her date until she is twenty-two). On one warm day when we meet with Rosette, she is wearing a heavy turtleneck that her father has insisted on.

Later on, however, once she starts working and is able to buy her own clothes, Rosette develops her own fashion sense, an integrated style that is neither "too Haitian" nor "too American hip-hop," but one that is far more modern than what her father likes. In addition, Rosette is known for her dancing skills and often performs traditional Haitian folk dances, which can be sexually provocative, with great joy, spontaneity, and graceful abandon. Rosette knows that with her clothes and dancing she is pushing her father's strict boundaries. "There are some things you are forced to do, and there are some things even when forced you will not do," she says with a touch of defiance.

Rosette still lives with her father, two aunts, and three cousins in a public housing development where many Haitians live. Two of her cousins are younger than she. Recently her grandfather joined the family, and now there are eight people in the one-bedroom apartment.

Overall, Rosette's father is disappointed with life in the United States, which is more difficult than he had expected. The rents are high, he says, and earning enough to meet basic costs takes a heavy toll: "You work more than you should, and this is dangerous for your health." He appreciates the greater respect people in the United States show each other, compared to how people behave in Haiti, except in one regard: he is unhappy with the lack of respect, control, and authority in American classrooms. His daughter's education was one of his primary reasons for migrating, he says, explaining, "Political reasons caused the school system [in Haiti] to go down."

In Haiti, Rosette's father went to high school and worked as a construction worker. Here he works as a dietary aide, though he is often out of work because of a heart condition. He is "very broke," he says, and the family needs assistance from relatives to survive. Rosette wants to do more to help her family, and sometimes she works. She puts particular emphasis on becoming successful so that she can help her mother in Haiti. Rosette's father, however, insists that school is a priority and discourages her from working. He does not want his only child to feel that money is more important than education.

At the beginning of the study, Rosette tells us that she wants to stay in the United States, go to college, and become a doctor. Rosette likes being in the United States: "In Haiti I got spanked more, and here I get spanked less," she says. She likes that teachers "speak with students and give them advice." Yet she feels the schools in Haiti are "better because there is more discipline in the classroom; here in the U.S., the kids have no respect for the teachers."

We meet Rosette's father also in the first year of the study and he tells us that he feels burdened by the responsibility of being a single parent in the United States and struggles to bring up Rosette with the right values:

Raising kids in Haiti, there are more eyes fixed on the child, like friends, family, everyone, but here, everyone has their personal affairs to handle. You are obligated if you are the father or if you are the mother. Especially that I'm alone with her, this is really different, because it would be better for me if I felt surrounded by all my family—more people to give attention to the child . . . The worry that a parent might have is if he doesn't give the child a good direction, and [then] if they want to bring the child's conduct in a good direction, it is too late for them. But if a parent always holds the child with their strength and courage in a straight line, they won't have any worries for when the child is growing up.

Her father claims he has a good relationship with Rosette. Both he and Rosette point to her obedience as evidence of their good relationship. But as the years pass, their relationship gets rockier. As she matures and develops, he becomes more critical and overprotective. While she says he can be supportive, she also complains that he is too strict. "Parents in Haiti really want the best for their kids," she reflects. "They don't want them to make the same mistakes. In the U.S., at 18 you're an adult, but for Haitians, even if you are 25 you are still like a kid. They can beat you at any age. Haitian parents don't care at all about kids having fun, just schoolwork."

Beyond his reluctance to accept that she is growing up, we sense the father might be particularly controlling because of his worry that Rosette might develop a mental illness like her mother's. Although she seems to want to please her father and obey him, she comes to feel they do not have a close relationship, and she tells him little about what goes on in her life. She seems to want his approval, but she feels he does not understand her.

When she is sixteen, we ask her:

"Do you think you can tell your father the truth about almost everything you do?"

"I just act the way I want to act, but sometimes I obey my dad or he would go crazy," she replies. "He won't accept if I want a boyfriend or close friends. I have a boyfriend no matter what, and it hurts me that I can't tell him. I just wish he would accept it. I hate having to lie . . . Sometimes I come home late and I have to lie. Yesterday, my boyfriend called home and said [to him], 'I'm her boyfriend. It's none of your business.' Father almost hit me. I had to say, 'He's just a kid playing around.'"

"What would happen if your father knew?"

"Kill me. Probably hate me for the rest of my life."

"Can you tell your father most everything that you think and feel?"

"I just don't picture myself talking to my dad about feelings."

Rosette has many aunts and uncles nearby, and she talks to them about problems at school, conflicts with peers, her boyfriend, the future. She is particularly fond of one aunt, whom she visits often, helping her to clean her house while sharing secrets, concerns, and ambitions. Still, Rosette reports feeling isolated. Her mother's absence leaves a gaping hole in her life;

she defines a good family as one in which "you stay with your mother and father and they never fight."

The family calls and writes to relatives in Haiti regularly, and keeps up with Haitian news. The father recently went back briefly to attend a funeral. While Rosette spoke to her relatives on the island once every three months or so when she first arrived, as the years pass, these contacts have dwindled.

Precarious Academic Improvement

Rosette attended parochial school in Haiti, where she was a good student. Most of Rosette's classes were in French, but Kreyol is her strongest language. When we first met Rosette at age twelve she had been in the United States for less than a year. She had been placed in a combined fifth- and sixth-grade Haitian bilingual class in middle school. One day, students in the bilingual humanities class listened to three Haitian songs and were assigned to write or draw what the song reminds them of. One song is Haitian hip-hop, one is Haitian roots music, and one is Haitian American roots music. The students wrote:

"The songs remind me of Haiti."

"It reminds me of carnival."

"It reminds me of drums."

"It reminds me of having fun in Haiti."

"I remember Haitian carnival. Have you gone? It is so much fun dancing in the streets for three days."

The music was infectious. Students danced in their chairs, even those who had said that their parents were strict Protestants who oppose dancing. Some asked the others to be quiet as they began to sing along. The students knew all of the songs and most of the lyrics, and many were familiar with traditional Haitian dances. They encouraged each other excitedly. Two girls who were struggling academically lighten up as they choreographed dance steps, singing along lustily.

After this classroom experience, four of the girls decided to teach themselves traditional dances and perform for the bilingual class. Even now, the dance group meets weekly in the basement cafeteria, where the walls are decorated with ceramic depictions of fish, seaweed, children of all races, and images of Toussaint L'Ouverture and Jean-Jacques Dessalines, the fathers of Haitian independence. Rows of tables connected to stools line the rest of the cafeteria. This week, a Haitian dancer is working with them. One of the girls explains, "We make dance and we go dance for kids." The other girls snicker at her broken English, but she continues, "We like dance." We encourage the girls to show us what they have learned. At first they are reluctant and keep making mistakes, but soon they get into the rhythm.

It is interesting in this context to see self-doubt in Rosette's narrative about the boy and the violin, from the first year of our study:

> The boy thought he knew how to play the violin after he took [a] few lessons, but his friends start making fun of him because he's not really good. The he went home very sad and thinking if he wants to quit playing the violin.

Indeed, in the second year of the study, Rosette's teachers began reporting that she is disruptive, disrespectful, and having academic difficulties, all of which we observe on several occasions. In fact, she first came to our attention because she was disobedient, failing her classes, and often in the school office. The school psychologist, along with the teachers, had begun wondering whether Rosette had a learning disability. The previous year, she had joined a peer leadership program for Haitian teens (Haitian Teens Confront AIDS—HTCA), but the leader was dissatisfied with Rosette's participation and asked that she not return the following year. Rosette was hugely disappointed. Over time, it becomes clear that Rosette is a vulnerable and wounded child longing for stability and a confidante.

Once Rosette started Reade High School, which is described in detail in Chapter 3, her attitude improved considerably. She became much more involved in her academic work and in extracurricular activities. Her teachers say she is attentive, asks questions, and makes a good effort. This newfound engagement in her schoolwork is bolstered by a Haitian school counselor who encourages Rosette's strengths. Rosette has started coming to school early for extra help, developing strong relationships with adults ("Some teachers I really love"), becoming a science mentor for younger girls, and becoming active in the Haitian Club. For the first time since migrating, Rosette makes the honor roll. Rosette's experience is dramatically different than that of many other participants in the study, whose success in a nurturing bilingual middle-school program splintered into failure once they reached the anonymity of high school. Rosette's middle-school experience was unhappy, but she has been lucky with her high school staff and experiences and is flourishing.

Despite this improvement, her father remains aloof, disapproving, and ever watchful. He never congratulates her, shows no pleasure in her accomplishments, and continues to discipline her for every minor infraction of his rules. Rosette is particularly sensitive to his opinions, and his unresponsiveness and lack of encouragement seem to have affected her well-being. Though her grades are improving, we notice that she seems depressed and has begun gaining weight. When she finally musters the courage to ask her father why he has never acknowledged her improved school performance, he explains that he is afraid to do so: he fears that praise may cause her to slack off. During this conversation, however, Rosette finally elicits his acknowledgment that he is pleased with her academic progress.

Rosette used to tell us about her interest in medicine, but in high school, she decides that she would rather study business in college. Rosette's father supports any career goal that Rosette chooses, but he wants her to go to a top-ranked university in the area. He wants his daughter to have "a great education and success in life." Rosette agrees. "I'll do anything to go to college," she says earnestly. "I don't see myself as finishing high school and just hanging there . . . A lot of people talk to me about it, and I always have it on my mind. I see a lot of people go to college, and I want to know what it's like." Nevertheless, Rosette has done no preparation for the SAT, though she will be a senior next year. She seems to be avoiding the SAT and, unconsciously, perhaps even college, which disappoints her counselors. They have talked to her many times in great detail about the steps necessary to go to college, but Rosette has been passive about acting on them. Perhaps she is concerned about her family's ability to pay for college. At one point her counselor worries that Rosette seems to be pulling herself out of the game to avoid disappointment.

Rosette's academic trajectory, though initially rocky, has improved significantly as she increased her effort and focus and received help from her attentive school counselor. Ironically, her relationships at home have become more strained as her school performance has improved. She seeks refuge in school from tension at home, where she feels "isolated within the family."

An Ethnic Haven

Rosette became president of the Haitian Club at Reade High School in ninth grade. She faced the challenge of organizing the club, setting up a board, and finding ways to satisfy students with different interests. Our research assistant spent some time helping her sort through her ideas and then attended the meetings throughout the year. Rosette not only organized the club but also managed to increase its membership. The members are primarily Haitian students who identify more with Haitian culture than with U.S. culture; two non-Haitians also joined because they enjoy the meetings, which are conducted in both Kreyol and English. Rosette and the other board members manage everything perfectly, with limited adult supervision. "I like the other kids in the club," Rosette confides. "We talk . . . They show me new things, we dance, we organize events, do fundraising by selling food. They teach me about cultural things." The Haitian Club's faculty advisers care about Rosette, and she cares about them, too, but she often behaves in ways they find inappropriate. For example, Rosette uses the Haitian Club as an excuse to miss classes, claiming that she is working on club-related matters when usually she is not.

Outside of school, Rosette has been involved in a church choir, and in the last year and a half, has attended weekly meetings and other activities of a youth group at her Roman Catholic Church—activities that win her father's approval.

Despite her involvement in these structured forms of socializing, Rosette has no best friend. Her father discourages friendships, which is not an uncommon practice in Haitian culture, because friends are seen as distracting and mostly bad influences. Additionally, her contacts are limited by the racial tension evident in her school. "[Students] don't get along," she says. "They lie about each other and put down the ones in other groups, especially the monolingual [English-speaking] kids . . . They make me feel like I should go back to my country. They make me feel like I don't belong here, but I know I'm here for a reason, to get an opportunity. It hurts me."

Work has been an important source of social contacts for Rosette. She has had several jobs in the past, though her father always pressures her to quit. Her current job is in a local pharmacy and she has been trying to increase her hours. With her earnings, she has been able to buy personal essentials.

The research assistant working with Rosette has become a crucial source of social support for her. When Rosette was graduating from middle school, she wanted to make sure that the research assistant was coming to her 3 P.M. graduation ceremony because no one from her family would be able to come at that hour. Rosette's father is grateful for the connection and shares his feelings and concerns about his daughter with the research assistant. He tells her about the challenges he faces regarding grades, curfew, and what he considers inappropriate behavior. Rosette at one point says she sees the research assistant as a mother figure, and later as "a big sister." Unfortunately, Rosette sometimes uses this relationship as a cover for going out; she at times claims to be with the research assistant when she is instead spending time with a boyfriend or with peers.

After eight years in the United States, Rosette maintains a strong Haitian identity and is not especially attracted to American culture. She still has some difficulty expressing herself in English and prefers to speak Kreyol. She has a thick accent and often stutters when speaking English. Her continued involvement in the Haitian Club and with Haitian folkloric dancing show how maintaining a Haitian identity matters to her. She wants to help rebuild Haiti, and on a more personal level, she sometimes uses her involvement with Haitian culture as an excuse to skip class or do other things that her father would oppose. That is, she is "using Haiti" as a way to assert herself.

Moving On Up

Rosette's young life is infused with graphic memories of violence, of living with fear and in hiding, of a traumatized and beaten mother. As a result, she has matured early and developed a strong social consciousness, analyzing the political situation in Haiti and discussing ways of helping children there. She misses her mother and is dedicated to helping her financially and eventually sponsoring her migration to the United States. Despite her traumatic childhood and an initial period of becoming oriented to U.S. culture, Rosette has found her academic footing and become an honor student.

We can account for this upward shift in a number of ways. As she adjusts to her new setting and develops the necessary language skills, Rosette creates the foundation for mastering academic work. As she regroups and focuses on school as a way to control the uncontrollable, to please a stern father, and to brighten her prospects, she mobilizes herself to achieve. She resourcefully engages her Haitian counselor, supportive teachers, and our research assistant to provide desperately needed emotional sustenance and guidance. And although it sometimes distracts her from schoolwork, Rosette's leadership in the Haitian Club provides her with a sense of purpose and ethnic pride along with an essential, cohesive network of supportive relationships.

Jane: Americanization, Chinese Style

Jane's family lives in a suburb outside a major Northeastern city. To get there by public transportation, we take the subway outbound to the last stop and transfer to a bus for an additional short ride. When we first visit on a warm Sunday afternoon, we have trouble finding their apartment, searching the neighborhood for their address and calling them twice for directions. After wandering for forty minutes, we finally hail a taxi, and even the taxi driver has to call from his cell phone to find his way. Finally, we find Jane's family in a government-subsided housing project hidden deep inside a large residential complex.

We are glad to have found the building, but our relief is short-lived. The building is old and neglected. As Jane buzzes us in, we enter a cramped, dingy hallway that halts at a gloomy staircase. Strips of old paint dangle from the ceiling. The sprinklers hang brokenly. Layers of graffiti cover the walls, and the only light glimmers from a single bulb hanging high overhead. Rap music throbs from the first-floor apartment. We rush up the stairs, anxious to find the apartment where Jane's family lives. Although our steps are light, the shabby building feels as though it could crumble under our feet.

Jane's family lives on the third floor. As we knock, Jane's mother greets us at once; she had been hovering near the door. Following common Chinese practice, we have bought oranges for the family. Jane's mother politely accepts them, later offering us oranges in a ritual of reciprocity. She ushers us into the tiny living room, where we find Jane and her younger brother, Darren. We feel immense relief. The orderly space is a haven from the seediness just steps away.

Daylight streams through the living-room windows, shining on freshly painted white walls. Two couches, one big and one small, rest against adjoining walls; a small tea table sits between them, piled neatly with Chinese newspapers. The TV is playing a Chinese soap opera. The kitchen opens off the living room, and the small apartment also has two small bedrooms. Darren and Jane share a room with two beds, the other bedroom is for their parents, and an uncle who lives with them sleeps on the living-room couch. Tammy, Jane's older sister, lives with their grandmother in Chinatown, which is closer to her high school, and only comes back for brief weekend visits.

By the time we complete our interviews with the children, it is almost 8 P.M. Jane's mother insists that we stay for dinner, promising that Jane and Darren will take us to the bus station afterward. At her repeated insistence, we politely accept. She cooks a delicious Chinese meal, and during dinner we talk with her in the kitchen while Jane and Darren eat in the living room, watching Chinese TV. We learn that Jane's mother finds her life here more difficult than it was in China emotionally, culturally, and psychologically. Her lack of English proficiency has made adjusting to the new culture very hard. To support the family, both of Jane's parents took low-paying jobs involving hard work and long hours—her father in a Chinese restaurant and her mother in a garment factory. She is making $650 a month on average. She earned more at the beginning, but as the economy slows, her boss has been cutting her hours each month. Like many immigrant parents, Jane's mother appreciates the opportunities for material fulfillment and educational attainment in the United States, saying that her only motivation for enduring this difficult new life has been the hope for a better future for her children.

Although they dislike the housing project, the parents and children generally feel safe in their neighborhood and understand that such a living situation is the best they can afford. At the end of the meal and interview, we say good night.

Together for the First Time

Jane came from a rural village in southern China, and even before her mother's migration in the early 1990s the family was dispersed. Jane was raised by her aunt, her father's elder sister, apparently because of her parents' job demands. Jane's mother immigrated first, and three years later, Jane, her father, younger brother, and older sister followed. Altogether, Jane and her mother lived apart for eight years; in the United States, the whole family lived together almost for the first time. These disruptions left deep marks, but the damage was masked in the early years of reunification by the young children's need for their parents' help. When we first met Jane's family, Jane was ten years old, and everyone seemed eager to believe that their relationships were good and strong. Jane described how she let her parents know that she loves them by helping her mother cook, wash dishes, and tidy up the house. She also helped with translations. On the surface, she fulfilled the cultural expectations of filial piety, a characteristic that she considers in a narrative she creates in the last year of our study. After viewing the picture of the girl with books near a farm, she relates:

> This girl grew up in a village. Everyone farms there. She does not want to be just a farmer. She wants to go to school. However, her parents (the two persons in the field) do not want her to go because she has to go outside the village in order to go to school and it is too far away [from home]. Her parents do not want her to go to school but rather they want her to be just a farmer. At the end, she will leave the village to attend school. Later she will do really well in school and will go home to pay a visit to her parents. When she leaves the village, her parents will feel very sad. However, when she returns home, they will feel very pleased because their child does so well in school. She feels sad when she leaves the village at the end because it's like something that her parents do not want her to do but still she has to do it. She feels sad because she does not listen to what her parents say.

Jane's mother thinks that because her children make few demands, they understand her worries. But slowly it becomes clear that from the beginning there have been gaps in communication, and they have widened with time. Jane's mother recalls that while the children were young, she made most of the decisions for them and would lecture them when they did anything wrong; as they grew more self-sufficient, they developed their own ways of thinking. Now, she says, "If I say 'no,' they will remain silent and will not do [whatever I do not approve] . . . They are still young. They do not know how to rebel yet. If they really have their own opinions when they grow older, I will ask about their opinions and will discuss with them."

Jane's mother recognizes that the communication between parents and children is faltering, but she sees the root of this problem as the children's need to speak English and Cantonese in their school's bilingual program, which has diminished their recall of Taisanese, the dialect spoken in their native region. She and her husband are dominant in Taisanese, and she does not seem to see that the children deliberately make little effort to use the parents' language. She explains: "My English is not good. For example, when we watch TV, I do not understand what people on TV are talking about so I usually ask my children. However, Jane and her younger brother do not know [well] how to translate English words into Chinese. Sometimes when I try to discipline them, they talk to me in English. They do not bother to speak Chinese to me, and I have no clue what they are talking about."

Jane speaks Taisanese, Mandarin, Cantonese, and English with varying degrees of fluency. Though the family comes from southern China, where Taisanese is spoken, the language of instruction throughout mainland China after the Cultural Revolution was Mandarin. When Jane and her siblings came to the United States, they were placed in a Chinese bilingual program, where the languages of instruction were Cantonese and English. Thus, Jane needed to learn Cantonese on the way to learning English. Because her network of friends uses Cantonese as a lingua franca, that has become her preferred language and she has allowed her Taisanese to atrophy, which makes it challenging to have complex conversations with her parents. We sense that the children use this language barrier as a strategy to avoid conflict, and perhaps even as a way to show how much or little they value maintaining a strong bond with their parents.

While her mother presents the communication problems as manageable and understandable, Jane confides that she tells her parents little about her life in school. If someone were to hurt her feelings, she would talk to her stuffed animal rather than her parents. When her parents yell at her, she either remains silent or retreats to her room, unafraid of their anger. "Maybe [they are] annoying," she says. "They yell at me day and night." Jane says her parents always fight, and we see these family tensions intensify over the five years of our study. "There are some things that my parents do not want me to do but I really want to do. Then we will quarrel with each other. After a fight, I will still do whatever I want. For example, one time I wanted to go out but my mother did not want me to. We got into a dispute. After that, I still went out. When I came home, we argued again. Then I went to my room until dinner was ready."

Jane is not only challenging her mother, she is also pointedly ignoring her—by speaking English, knowing that her mother does not understand the language, and by doing whatever she wants despite her mother's obvious disapproval. She wants to make her own decisions, like the rebellious farmers' daughter in her narrative. Her tone tells us that she alone decides what her parents will know about her, including where she is. She notes sarcastically: "[Someone at home] sometimes knows where I am, only if I tell them."

Initially, neither Jane nor her mother connected the tensions in their relationship to their lengthy separation. Later on, however, Jane begins to make the link. As we know, Jane never really lived with her parents even when she was in China. As far as she remembers, she had always lived with her aunt. Jane explains how she prefers to confide in people other than her parents:

> When I have something in mind, I do not tell them. When I was young, I told my aunt when something happened. However, after reuniting with my parents in the U.S., I cannot talk to my parents about everything. I feel closer to my aunt than my parents. I still talk to my aunt [in China] over the phone sometimes. For example, even when I had a boyfriend, I would tell my aunt but not my parents. My aunt would ask me about my boyfriend and I would tell her everything about him. I can't do the same thing with my parents . . . Maybe it is because they do not know me well. They do not know my habits and many other things about me. So, I am more likely to tell my friends or elder sister.

Jane believes that if she had always lived with her parents, they would "talk more, have more discussions and conversations." She also thinks that she might listen to and agree with her parents more if they had raised her when she was young. But as it is, she sees the rift as unbridgeable.

Jane is a year older than Darren, but they attend the same grade in the same school and share many classes. In one of our visits to their school, we ask them if their classmates know that they are brother and sister. "The whole world knows," Jane grumbles in Cantonese. She points out that next year will be different because Darren will be going to an exam high school while Jane will be staying in their current school. Darren says that being in the same class with his sister is "annoying." Nevertheless, Jane and Darren are generally close, depend on each other at home, and share many of their feelings. Jane also feels close to her older sister and shares her thoughts and problems with her.

The Supportive Role of the Chinese Community

Jane's family maintains contacts with friends and relatives in China through telephone calls, e-mail, and letters. Her mother has returned to China four times to visit family, and she has applied for her relatives to join her in the United States. Jane's father went back to China once to see his ailing mother. Jane's parents occasionally send remittances to family members. And of course, Jane keeps in touch with her aunt.

The family has friends and family in the United States, too. They see their relatives every day and meet with them at least once a week and on holidays in Chinatown for dim sum. They do not socialize with Americans.

Jane is well integrated into a peer network. She spends time with her friends outside school: hanging out downtown, playing games at the arcade, shopping for clothes, and dropping by her friends' homes. Her friends occasionally visit her house, too. Most of Jane's friends were born in the United States or came here when they were very young. When they get together, they usually speak Cantonese.

By the end of our study, when she is fifteen, Jane has started dating. Her older sister knows about this, but her parents do not. Jane says that if her parents knew that she had started dating, they would probably yell at her. Jane's mother has said that she would forbid her teenage daughters to start dating because she worried that dating might hurt their academic performance. "At least wait until college!" she says. "If they start dating in high school, I am afraid they may fail in school. I don't know what they can do if they do not graduate from college."

Jane has been involved with various community- and church-based extracurricular activities. At first, she went to the Chinatown Community Center with her brother after school. Even though the family was originally

Buddhist, in the United States they began attending services at a Christian church, and Jane participates in many of the activities there. "I can learn more about how Jesus saved the people in the world," she tells us. "I also see my friends and learn how to play Ping-Pong there. The songs sung in the church are very nice." Believing in God is an important part of her sense of self and she says that God plays the role of "helper" to her. "Sometimes when I encounter problems that I do no know how to deal with, I pray," she says. Some of her friends in the church are older people to whom she can go for support and guidance. By the end of the study, Jane had joined the Asian Community Center in Chinatown, where her older sister organized an after-school program that teaches teens not to fight, drink, or violate rules.

Jane says that she has experienced no discrimination in the United States. Encountering discrimination "depends on who you hang out with and where you go," she says, suggesting that she may have learned to sidestep problems by avoiding contact with non-Chinese. She says that her parents have never discussed racism with her or her siblings.

The majority of Jane's friends are Chinese and she speaks Cantonese with them. In addition, the only videos she watches are in Chinese. Although by the end of the study Jane calls herself an Asian American and says she feels "somewhat American and somewhat Chinese," she maintains a predominantly Chinese identity.

Finding Her Footing in School

Jane's narrative about the boy and the violin from the first year of the study is a tale of peer support and strong, if not perfectly consistent, determination:

> A long time ago, there was a boy who learned how to play violin. He did not play well. His teacher told him to go home to practice. He was upset. His good friend asked him to go out to play. He did not. He stayed home to practice the violin. One of his good friends taught him how to play violin, and gave him the instrument. The friend taught him how to play well . . . Finally, he played the violin.

Such qualities are apparent in Jane's own life at school. One day, after collecting test papers, we observed Jane and Darren's teacher reviewing math problems with the sixth-grade class. Jane, Darren, and three other students dominate the discussion, while the others remain silent until the teacher calls on them. Even then, the others are less enthusiastic than the more outspoken students. Next, the teacher shows the class a documentary film entitled *The Heart of the Dragon,* which depicts the harsh reality of Chinese peasants' living conditions. Chinese people believe they are descendants of the dragon, a mythical creature with superpowers and promises of prosperity. Focused on this symbol of China and the Chinese people, the film offers a story of a people's proud determination, and all of the students are riveted to the screen. Some, including Jane, are taking notes. Once, Jane turns around and asks us in Cantonese, "How do you say 'stove' in English?" Indeed, from the students' expressions, it is evident that some relate to the village scenes in a personal way. Some, including Darren, whisper about how strenuous the peasants' work is. After the class, we thank the teacher for allowing us to observe and tell her how much we liked the film. She smiles and in a soft voice explains that the film is a follow-up to a previous lesson about China. One can tell that she believes in and respects her students.

Jane finished second grade in a public school in China where the language of instruction was Mandarin; Jane also spoke Taisanese and had begun to learn Cantonese. Jane's mother told us that all three of her children were excellent students in China. After she arrived in the United States, Jane was placed in the bilingual program in an elementary school in Chinatown, where the principal, vice principal, and most of the students were Chinese. "I liked the school a lot because I had friends there who played with me, and the teachers cared about me," she says. When Jane went on to the local middle school, there were again many Chinese students, but there was no bilingual program. Though she has adapted and made friends, she is not fond of this school and is trying to transfer out. "It is very bad now," she says solemnly. "It is a nasty place. I don't like it because I feel that some teachers are very bad. They show favoritism. The lunch is very bad. I find it annoying to walk to the YMCA for gym on rainy and snowy days."

Jane has never talked to her parents about her plans and goals after high school, but she says that attending college is important to both her and her parents. At first she wanted to be a computer scientist and later a fashion designer. Her interest in academics fluctuates, however. (For example, when she performed a sentence-completion task in the fourth year of our study, she stated, "School is boring" and "My future will be boring.") With some self-reflection, she confides: "I don't put a lot of effort into my study. Sometimes I like to study and sometimes I don't. When I want to study, then I think about college. When I don't want to study, I feel like throwing away my books when I see them." She admits that she gets lazy about homework and that her study habits are sloppy: "When I have to study, I will turn on the television." Jane watches five to six hours of Cantonese soap operas daily. Still, she often spends a good hour and a half on assignments at night.

In general, Jane's teachers are positive about her behavior at school. They confirm that she completes all her homework assignments and has no behavioral problems. But her inconsistent engagement with her schoolwork is apparent in some of their comments. While her math teacher describes Jane as "a very good student" who "tries very hard and always tries to help other students," her ESL teacher says Jane "is normally very good in class. However, she is at times unfocused and can be distracted." Her math teacher writes: "Jane is well-behaved and cooperative. She is focused, prepared for class and enthusiastic about learning." But Jane's English teacher comments: "Jane is well-behaved and quiet—too quiet. I would like to see her participate more. She sometimes gets into little arguments with the boys."

We observe Jane chatting with her Chinese friends during class, disregarding her teachers. And when we ask her to tell us about something interesting that she is learning, thinking about, or doing, she replies, "Gossiping, talking with friends about boys and people that I like . . . also where to have fun, like going to downtown, Chinatown, the Arcade, and such."

In the first year of our study, the Jane we met was a friendly ten-year-old girl who was polite but quiet and having difficulty answering the questions we asked her regardless of the language in which she chose to respond. At that point she told us: "Sometimes the teachers praise me. I help my classmates to take care of their homework and explain the homework to them." But by the end of our study, she is more assertive and describes the many conflicts she has with other students and some teachers, even telling us about swearing at a white male teacher who had yelled at her and her friends. We ask:

> "How do you get along with your friends?"
> "Quite well . . . except for the few I have quarrels with. We yell at each other using foul language, intensively. Those who argue with me are all Chinese. There are two boys in my grade [seventh] and two girls from the eighth grade. The two boys often tease and talk negatively about us. At first I ignored them and reported it to the teachers. The teachers would yell at

them and talk to us a bit and that's it. It was not very helpful. So we just yelled back at them eventually. The other two eighth-grade girls, they just came to me and threw some foul language at me without any reason. So my friend would join me in yelling back at them."

Jane now attends a middle school where tensions and confrontations are common between peers, as well as between teachers and students. She has had to learn to fight back. But Jane is "[not happy with] my personality. I can get mad easily. When I get mad, I get into fights easily. I can become too mad to realize what I am actually doing at that moment. I hate my personality the most." And she worries that her behavior will be worse in high school: "I am in middle school now and I am already using vulgar language. I am afraid I will be used to the language and will get worse when I go to high school. I worry about my grades. When I am too involved in an argument or fight with someone in class, I participate less in class . . . maybe I will care more about my grades when I get to high school, but obviously I will not be the best [student in the class]."

Despite these difficulties, Jane's recent report cards show an improvement in her GPA, from a C average in third grade, to a B in fourth grade and B plus in fifth grade. Her grades in sixth grade are mostly A's with a few B's and show progress over the four marking periods. Most impressive is the improvement in her English skills over the years, which no doubt contributes significantly to the overall improvement in her grades. Of all the languages Jane knows, English is her strongest in terms of reading and writing. This is confirmed by her performance on standardized tests. The first time Jane was tested, she had been in the country for four years and was thirteen years old. Jane's verbal ability (English and Cantonese combined) was in the low-average ability range for her age (18th percentile), while her English-language proficiency score was merely in the second percentile.[4] On the Broad Math subtest of the Woodcock-Johnson, she scored in the average range. Two years later, the same standardized tests show that Jane's verbal ability had improved—her score for English and Cantonese combined was in the high average range of ability for her age (in the 87th percentile), while her English-language proficiency had increased to the 14th percentile. On the Woodcock Johnson achievement subtests, Jane scored very highly: 99th percentile on the Broad Reading subtest and 94th percentile on the Broad Math subtest.

Jane says she and her friends help one another with schoolwork. "Since the students from China are very good at math, when I have problems in math, I would ask them. They would help me," she says. "And when they don't understand English, I help them." When she gets a good grade, Jane says, her friends are proud and often congratulate her.

Jane's parents try to be involved in her education. They want all of their children to study hard so they can get good jobs and will not need to rely on hard labor for their economic survival. Jane is expected to achieve a B or better in her classes; if she didn't, her parents would scold her. They set rules about completing all homework assignments on time, but Jane doesn't always obey. When Jane has problems at school, one of her parents—usually her father—goes to talk with her teachers. Jane's parents realize that there are limits to how much they can help their children attain success in the United States: they do not have the "manpower and resources to help them," her father says. At home, there is no adult to help Jane with her schoolwork because her parents work long hours and neither knows English.

Jane's middle school holds its physical-education classes at the Chinatown YMCA gym because it lacks adequate on-site facilities. One day, we find Jane enthusiastically engaged in a basketball game. She sits down on a bench to catch her breath with her Chinese friends. She is wearing her shoulder-length black hair in two symmetrical braids. As usual, we find that she is easy to chat with and open to our questions. Jane has never hesitated to share her feelings, and today she volunteers that her best friends—three girls and one boy—are on the court. They are her best friends, she explains, "because we are all Taisanese." What is most noticeable about the physical-education class is how strongly degrees of assimilation, acculturation, and native culture and language maintenance influence the formation of social circles. Both Darren and Jane stay in the "Chinese circle." Their friends are Chinese immigrants who, like them, have maintained a strong Chinese cultural identity.

Learning the Ropes

Jane's academic challenges have gradually eased over time. This feisty young woman is bright and has strong mathematical skills. She has managed to acquire some fluency in four languages (though her effort and concentration waver). While she values education, like many of her American peers, she reports being bored with schoolwork. She is often distracted, talkative, and even rude in school. In short, she is in many ways an acculturated, typical American teenager.

Jane's fluctuating motivation is aggravated by tension with and alienation from her parents. Like several other Chinese families that we studied, Jane's family is experiencing an emotional distancing that has become more intense over time and in this case has been complicated by a long separation. Jane has had to learn to relate to her biological mother as her "mother" and to her aunt, who had been a maternal presence since she was an infant, as her "aunt." In addition, her father is involved in Jane's academic work, but seems somewhat remote—when we meet with the parents, it is the mother who dominates the conversations and thus we learn little about his role. In short, there is an emotional and relational vacuum within the family, and ultimately Jane completely rejects her parents' attempts to know what she is doing and what her plans are. The children casually switch into English to keep their parents in the dark about their plans and interests. The resistance to sharing a common language seems to be a symptom rather than a cause of the family's communication problems and lack of emotional closeness. The children use language as a weapon against their mother for the wounds wrought by the long immigration process.

This situation at home has perhaps taught Jane to be self-sufficient and more skillful at relying on others outside her family. Her friends, for example, provide her with critical emotional sustenance. But Jane also longs for adults to connect with her. Poignantly, during one research session, Jane turned to the research assistant and asked her to become her friend. She is also drawn to her ethnic church and to the neighborhood community center. This constructed network of relations, largely focused within the Chinese community, has eased her transition to her new homeland.

Ramón: Knowing the Right People

Ramón is a handsome young man with striking straight black hair, sensitive dark eyes, a rich cinnamon complexion, and high cheekbones that evoke the archetypical Mayan profile. He has a precociously serious demeanor and he tends to hang back, observing carefully. Even when he feels secure, he speaks softly. He has experienced much in his short life, and these experiences have left their mark on him.

Social Trauma

Ramón's father was a union activist in a town outside San Salvador. At a time of continuous political turmoil, before the signing of the 1992 peace accords between the government and the various insurgency groups under the leadership of the Farabundo Martí para la Liberación Nacional (or FMLN), union activists and political organizers were targets of paramilitary death squads.[5] Fearing for his life, Ramón's father fled to the United States, crossing the border illegally in Texas. He was captured and held in an Immigration and Naturalization Service (INS) detention center for six months until he was granted temporary refugee status. He then made his way to an East Coast metropolitan area noted for its universities and colleges, where his wife's brother and sisters and their families had settled a decade earlier. Once there, Ramón's father sought formal asylum. The volunteer translator who helped him became his advocate, finding him a pro bono attorney and a place to stay, as well as giving him job leads and tips about the cultural practices of his new land. After three years, he won asylum and immediately sent for his wife and two sons. At age nine, Ramón, his mother, and an older brother arrived in the United States in the late 1990s with temporary asylum status.

During the father's absence, Ramón's seventeen-year-old brother, Joaquin, had flirted with political activity, attending rallies and passing out protest leaflets with youthful zeal. At some point there was an assassination attempt on him, though the family never elaborates. And shortly before leaving El Salvador, Ramón and his mother were in a serious car crash. Fears for his father and brother and the terrifying accident left Ramón anxious and cautious, his mother says.

These traumas and the disorientation of migration have taken their toll on the mother as well. She seems to channel her sadness through her body. She complains of headaches, stomachaches, palpitations, and trouble concentrating, and says she often feels sad, apathetic, lethargic, and preoccupied. She cries easily and has flashbacks to frightening events. Ramón tells us that he feels healthy and rarely misses school, though at times he, too, is preoccupied with the past, feels tense, has trouble concentrating, lacks energy, feels sad, and has stomachaches.

The events of September 11, 2001, happened midway through our study, when Ramón was ten years old. The attacks on New York City and Washington, D.C., brought Ramón's fears to the surface. During an interview a month after the attacks, fireworks went off in the neighborhood. Ramón froze and then leaped into the researcher's arms. Trembling, he kept repeating *"tengo miedo; tengo miedo"* (I am afraid; I am afraid). It took him quite some time to calm down even when he realized that the explosions were fireworks, not something more ominous.

The family had been granted temporary protective status before the terrorist attacks, which authorized the father to work. But the family went into a documentation limbo as the INS morphed into Homeland Security after September 11, becoming a labyrinth of obscure bureaucratic forms and procedures. To complicate matters, the paperwork to process their green cards was delayed by a communication problem with their pro bono attorney. Because the attorney had volunteered his services, the family felt deeply indebted to him and ever reluctant to *"molestarlo"* (bother him). They had understood he would get in contact with them, while he had expected them to get in contact with him. A year and a half elapsed before they summoned the courage to get someone to call the lawyer on their behalf. Once the papers have been formally submitted, it takes three more years before the family is granted residency. The delays distress the mother, who tells us: "I want to become an American citizen if they give me the opportunity. I want to be legal and comply with the laws. I want to be legal." Ramón's mother laments that she could not visit her family in El Salvador during the protracted wait. Already anxious, she found this period of limbo deeply disorienting and unsettling.

Ramón's mother migrated in an effort to find both safety and educational opportunities for her children, and she believes that in moving to the United States she has come closer to achieving those ends: "My goal is to get ahead, principally for my children so they do something good for mankind." Still, she regrets the decline in the quality of her own life. In El Salvador, she had lived in a three-bedroom home and had a large garden. She had a rich network of friends and family. When she arrived, she found that her husband had arranged for them to live in a one-room third-floor walkup. The four family members share the space with one of the father's coworkers, whom the mother finds repugnant because of his coarse nature, vulgar language, and slovenliness. She complains about the harsh weather conditions, isolation, and feeling acutely self-conscious socially.

Despite their difficult living conditions, the family had no means to move at any point during the five years of the study. They were financially strapped because the father earns just over the minimum wage delivering baked goods to coffee houses, and the mother works part time as a janitor for a university at less than the living wage. While they often thought about moving to an adjacent town with more affordable housing, they chose to stay in their drafty one-room walk-up because the schools in this town were reputed to be significantly better and their neighborhood, an area predominantly populated by working-class second-generation Italian Americans and Irish Americans, was safe. There was also a large, well-equipped playground one building over from the apartment that gave Ramón a place to play safely with his friends, weather permitting.

Ramón's family has a strong network of support in their new home. The mother has a brother and two sisters who have settled nearby. One of Ramón's aunts lives in the same apartment building with her husband and a child to whom Ramón reports feeling close. These two families help each other with errands, exchange information, and trade childcare. The relationships with the other aunt and uncle are more problematic. The uncle hired Ramón's mother for a janitorial service he ran, but she reports that he underpaid her and was often verbally abusive. The other aunt, according to the mother, is a *chisimosa* (gossip) and often seems to be at the center of family dramas.

Despite her unhappiness, Ramón's mother finds an inner resourcefulness that, as we shall see, enables her to enlist the help she needs to fight for opportunities for her son. Starting with the translator, she built a network of adept mentors—some of them professors at the university where she cleaned buildings—who could guide her and advocate for her.

Dual Immersion

When Ramón first arrived, he remarked that his biggest surprise was that he "could not speak Spanish here." He simply had not realized that English was the language of the United States. Ramón learned English faster than many of our study participants, perhaps because he had more exposure to English-speaking environments than most. Nonetheless, he often spoke of his struggle to learn English. The first year of the study, he completed the sentence: "In five years from now . . ." with "I would like to able to speak English" and the sentence "I would like . . ." with "to be able to speak English well." He even finished the sentence "If only my family . . ." with "could speak English." Clearly the task of learning a new language seemed daunting. Shortly after arriving, he told the following story to accompany the image of the girl with books near a farm:

> The girl is going to school. Things are not going well at school because she doesn't speak English well. The teachers try to help her but it doesn't come easily. She tells her parents and they help her to read and the neighbors also helped.

Ramón embraces the goal of becoming bilingual. He tells us that he needs to learn English so he can "work and study here." He wants to continue using Spanish, too, "so that I can talk with my family." When asked which language is necessary to get ahead in the United States, he responds, "English and Spanish, because some people do not speak English and I could speak to them in Spanish, and if they could not speak in Spanish I could talk to them in English." Though he says "English is very important," he also considers it "very hard."

Through the family's volunteer translator, the mother secures an after-school babysitting job with a Latino family that has a son Ramón's age. The parents are concerned that their son is refusing to speak Spanish and love the idea of having their son "immersed" a few hours a day with a playmate and babysitter who can serve as informal Spanish tutors, an arrangement that begins within weeks of Ramón's arrival. Ironically, while this English-dominant playmate barely increases his use of Spanish, he succeeds in teaching Ramón and his mother survival English.

No one in Ramón's immediate family had finished high school. Ramón's mother had completed sixth grade in El Salvador, and his father and brother had finished eighth grade. After arriving in the United States, Ramón's brother Joaquin spent a year at a well-regarded local high school. But the school was ill-equipped to deal with a nineteen-year-old with an eighth-grade education and no English skills. After a year of frustration, and realizing that he was unlikely to meet the graduation requirements, Ramón's brother dropped out and took a job driving for the company where his father works. The father seems to feel that this was a sensible choice, but the mother is dismayed and determined that Ramón's fate would be different. She pours all her ambitions into supporting his academic success through her expanding network of sponsors and mentors. Overcoming her intense shyness, she asks everyone she thinks might have information about the local schools, including kindly professors at the university where she worked as a janitor. She wants to do everything she can to help Ramón realize his dream of becoming a doctor.

Ramón's mother learns that a dual-immersion language program would be best for her son. In dual-immersion programs, all subjects are taught 50 percent in English and 50 percent in another language—in Ramón's case, Spanish. Ideally, half the students in a Spanish-English dual-immersion program are native Spanish speakers and half are native English speakers. As mentioned earlier, there is mounting evidence that such programs, when carefully structured and competently staffed, can lead to the emergence of true balanced bilingualism: equal skills in both languages. But because of the high demand for spots in such programs, Ramón could not be placed in one until the second year of living in their new city.

In his first year, Ramón was placed in third grade in a neighborhood school with a reputation for low academic standards, mediocre teachers, and ethnic tensions, one of the lowest-performing schools in the city. Instead of a dual-immersion program, he was put in a transitional bilingual program, which offers general instruction in a student's first language and teaches English as a separate subject until the child is ready to move into an English-only classroom. During this year, a scandal with the principal erupted, shattering the school's fragile cohesion. The teachers' morale plummeted, and their attention was torn from the enterprise of teaching and learning. Tensions from this stormy climate trickled down to the students, and fights began to break out. Yet Ramón, despite having come from a village school and entering this alien tumult, earned high grades. In this setting, being a quiet and compliant child who makes no trouble and tries hard yielded him high B's.

The following year, in fourth grade, when he moved to the new dual-immersion school, everything changed. Suddenly, Ramón was exposed to a high-quality, demanding curriculum. His teachers were well qualified and held high expectations for their students. Many students, particularly the English-dominant children but also some of the native Spanish speakers, came from middle- to upper-middle-class families in which one or both parents were connected to the local universities as professors or graduate students. These parents want their children to learn two languages so that they will have a leg up in a rapidly globalizing world. Ramón was regularly exposed to strong peer and teacher language models; this rich academic English and Spanish environment served both to bolster his language learning and to foster his academic success.

As in many schools, however, the socially advantaged students commanded the bulk of teachers' positive attention and rose to the top of the class. In this context, Ramón had lower status than many of his peers. His parents have humble jobs and limited education. Ramón's dark skin and indigenous features, coupled with his reserved nature, render him nearly invisible. In our classroom observations, it seems that Ramón is barely on his teacher's radar screen. On one cold winter morning, our field notes reveal a pattern: "He sits leaning forward in his chair, with his head resting on his hand as he leans on his elbow for much of the class. He is alert and intently following the conversation. He does not raise his hand during the explanation of the homework (though he has done the work, unlike several of his peers). When the teacher asks about a book the students are reading, Ramón never volunteers an answer. When he finally, hesitantly raises his hand, the teacher ignores him." Clearly, the teachers hold low expectations for him, ignore him, and blame his academic difficulties on his lack of English. One teacher notes: "Ramón enjoys participating in small groups but he is hesitant to speak orally in large groups or whole class lessons due to his limited fluency in English."

Ramón's grades slump. His academic foundation was shaky, and he finds it hard to keep up with privileged middle-class children. Soon enough homework becomes a problem. The demands soar; the teachers tell us that many parents complain when they perceive their children get too little homework. But the middle-class students have academic supports at home—computers and Internet access, college-educated parents, and often, stay-at-home mothers willing and able to help with schoolwork. These students, with the active help of parents, turn in excellent homework and projects. Ramón, whose parents have little education and read and write haltingly in their native Spanish and not at all in English, cannot help him with a snowballing homework load. Ramón is on his own, and the quality of his work pales next to his peers'. His grades reflect his teachers' perceptions that he is doing poor work. Indeed, by the end of his third year in the United States and his second year in the dual-immersion program, his teachers recommend that he be held back for a year to "catch up." The teachers tell the mother that retention had "done wonders" for a child with a similar profile who had been retained the previous year.

Finding Someone to Help

This recommendation devastates Ramón and his mother. Disheartened, Ramón withdraws, and his mother fears that he will stop trying. She is torn between respecting the recommendations of school authorities and wanting the best for her son. She tells us that if the school gives up on her Ramón, he will give up on himself. She asks her mentors: What to do?

The mother has become adept at eliciting advice, support, and advocacy from those around her. She decides to seek the counsel of the asylum interpreter, community leaders, and the college-professor mother of the boy she babysat for. Finally, one of her friends accompanies her to a meeting with the principal and the teachers, acting as both interpreter and educational advocate. Against the advice of the school representatives, the mother refuses to let her son repeat a year. Going up against school authorities takes courage, but this wise though uneducated woman feels strongly that she knows what her son needs most. She insists that he be enrolled in an intensive summer-school program for academic enrichment. Her friend recommends finding someone in the community to provide daily after-school homework help, the kind of support routinely available to middle-class students from parents or paid tutors. The mother agrees that if these interventions fail to make a significant difference after a year, she will let Ramón be kept back the following year.

Both interventions prove transformational. Ramón makes excellent progress in summer school, and his teacher tells the principal that he is prepared for the next school year. The friend finds a bilingual graduate education student willing to volunteer an hour every day after school to help with math tutoring (an area of particular academic weakness for Ramón) and to oversee the completion of nightly homework. By the end of fifth grade, Ramón has pulled up his grades to steady B's with a sprinkling of A's, and he maintains this average into the following year, when our study comes to an end.

Ramón's story in this last year regarding the girl with books near a farm is revealing:

> The girl is sad because she does not want to have to work in the fields. She wants to go to school to learn a lot of things. She stays in the countryside because she wants to help her mother, and anyways her mother would not let her go. The good thing is that a professor comes to the country every week and teaches important things.

The theme of relationships providing help and orientation is a recurring one for Ramón. In response to the question "What do you think of when you think of a good family?" he responds: "One like mine. When you don't know something you can ask, and they will answer me." He tells us "[Teachers] treat students well, like when a student is feeling sad they help them. [Friends at school help me because] when there is something that I don't understand, they explain it and they help me." In response to the question "How do people in your after-school program help you or support you?" he responds, "When I didn't know how to do something, they taught me how to do it." All of his relationships—parents, teachers, peers, and community members—help him emotionally and tangibly.

Ramón is not passive, however. While his relationships serve an important supportive function, he recognizes that hard work is essential to attaining his educational goal of one day going to medical school. Hard work figures prominently in his imagination. He completes the sentence: "Good Salvadorian boys . . ." with these words: "work hard and get good grades." To go to college, he says, you "have to study a lot." He tells us that he most wants to be like his father when he grows up. When asked why, he responds: "because he works hard." To the sentence "In my future . . ." he responds, "I will work a lot," and to "Most Americans think Salvadorians are . . ." he replies "people that work hard." His story that year about the boy with the violin continues the theme:

> A boy feels sad because he want to learn how to play the instrument. The story ends when he gets into a music class and he works very hard and becomes very famous.

Package Deals

During the last year of the study, we ask Ramón, who is now twelve years old, whether, knowing what he now knows, he would still want to migrate the United States. Yes, he says: "Now we are all together. I go to a better school and I can learn more. I will be able to get a better job." He misses his faraway relatives and says his family has fewer friends than back in El Salvador, but the United States has come to feel like home to him.

Though Ramón is far from gregarious, he has developed close friendships both in and out of school. He has Latino friends from several countries and a close friendship with an American boy whose father is Latino. These friends help him whenever class material confuses him. Though he often speaks Spanish with his friends, he has made rapid progress in English, speaking with increasing ease with peers and adults alike. Like most youth his age, he listens to rap and R&B, on the radio and on his treasured CD player. He usually watches television in English, though he likes old comedies featuring Cantiflas, the great Mexican comedian. Five years into the study, he prefers speaking Spanish if given the option, but his English bears only the faintest trace of an accent. The dual-immersion school's goal to instill balanced bilingualism has borne fruit.

Ramón's relationship with his parents is warm and supportive. He admires his father, is clearly delighted to be living with him again, and identifies with his ethic of hard work. His mother is a rock of Gibraltar: fiercely protective, attentive, and able to overcome her natural shyness to advocate for Ramón in a crisis. Her "baby" has become the repository of her ambitions and dreams. While her own life continues to be a struggle—backbreaking work and many lonely hours—she has no doubt that the future is bright for Ramón. Ramón is blessed with a close family that provides a stable, loving environment. His mother maintains a strong voice of authority and is respected and loved by her Ramóncito, as she lovingly calls him, using the Spanish diminutive. He feels entirely comfortable having his parents make decisions for him. He clearly wants to please his parents, who sacrificed so much to give this young man the opportunity for a better tomorrow.

Ramón has made an impressive adjustment to his family's migration. At first he struggled, though it is easy to understand why. The trauma and personal loss of his father's sudden exile, his own traumatic car crash, and the assassination attempt on his older brother—such cumulative shocks would take a toll even on the most resilient adults, let alone a constitutionally shy boy who speaks English as a second language.

For children, school environments are critical. Ramón's first school resembled those that many of our students attend: it lacked resources and was burdened by a culture of low expectations, disrespect, and fear of violence. Though he received good grades, Ramón made little academic progress there.

Yet when Ramón transferred to a far superior school, he confronted new obstacles. In a much richer environment with privileged peers, he became all but invisible to his teachers—relegated, so to speak, to the back of the classroom by their subtle but repeated actions and inactions. His natural reserve worked against him. Though he was in a dual-immersion program, the teachers and principal seemed not to understand that it takes time to acquire written second-language skills. The teacher and principal blithely recommended retention without taking into account the emotional consequences of this decision.

The crisis of Ramón's potential retention propelled his mother to reach out to the mentors and friends she had acquired through her resourcefulness. The resulting summer enrichment program and a competent daily homework coach gave Ramón the academic scaffolding he needed until he gained his academic footing and began to flourish.

Ramón and his parents have created a robust social network that has sustained them through Ramón's difficulties in school—the mother has learned to develop and rely on a network of mentors, and Ramón has nurtured good friends who are happy to help him. These friends and confidantes also help heal the wounds caused by his personal losses and insecurities. Once a timid boy, Ramón has gained confidence as he learns that those around him are willing and able to help him when he needs it. When we see Ramón two years after the end of the study, he is taller and has a deep voice, but his radiant smile reminds us of the vulnerable child we met seven years earlier. He proudly volunteers that he had a "great year" in his new high school, where, with his tutor's help, he is building on the foundation he received in the dual-immersion program. We are confident that Ramón has learned that social supports make all the difference—a lesson we very much hope will guide him in sustaining his successful academic path.

To BORROW a metaphor from gardening, every migration includes a phase of "transplant shock." For the new arrivals to take root, the receiving soil and environment must be healthy and nourishing. But as every gardener knows, even in the best of circumstances, it also takes time for plants to flourish. When there are significant traumas prior to the transplant, the process is more delicate: it takes longer to adjust and old wounds are vulnerable to reopening in the event of even minor crises.

In order to become capable and happy in a new environment, immigrants need caring relationships. Children who have warm and supportive families have an obvious advantage. Moreover, families embedded within healthy communities are more likely to meet the needs of their children; think of Ramón's case, in which multiple advocates synchronized their energies to support him at a critical turning point. Also, cohesive communities often have better schools—most of our improving students attended schools that were less toxic than those available to the students who precipitously declined over time or those whose academic performance was consistently poor. As Jane's story demonstrates, in better schools peers are more likely to enjoy academics, and are more willing and able to help one another with schoolwork.

Teachers, mentors, and advocates played important roles in helping these students realize their potential, either by supporting and guiding them or by intervening to avert situations that would have derailed their progress. Watching Jane, we witness the power that comes from belonging to a protective church community and the positive influence of a well-staffed community center. In Rosette's story, an ever-watchful father, well-meaning though rigid, and a warm and caring counselor combine to help stabilize a young woman who had experienced emotional ruptures and social trauma.

For this small group of immigrant youth, time healed their serious emotional wounds, and a better-than-average constellation of social supports provided the nutrients that allowed them eventually to flourish. By the conclusion of this study, these youth had found their way in their new home.

CHAPTER 8

Portraits of High Achievers

GIVEN THE many obstacles immigrant youth must overcome—
ruptures in relationships, the challenge of mastering academic English
skills, and the toxic schools and neighborhoods many encounter—it is remarkable that so many of them manage to maintain consistently high
grades. Of our total sample of students, nearly a quarter sustained a steady
A-minus average throughout the five years of our study.[1]

We found that youth from all countries of origin were high achievers,
but a greater proportion were from China. Nearly half (47 percent) of the
Chinese youth in our sample maintained high grades across the course of
the study, whereas only 18 percent of Central Americans, 13 percent of Dominicans, 11 percent of Haitians, and 17 percent of Mexicans were in this
high-achieving group. A higher proportion of girls—27 percent in contrast
to 16 percent of boys—sustain this trajectory of very high achievement.
(See Table 5.1.)

As would be expected, high-achieving students were more likely than
their lower-performing peers to have strong English proficiency scores.[2]
They were also less likely to report problems of violence at their schools.
But their academic experiences tell only a part of the story: just as important, their families were stable and helpful. The high-achieving students,
who were more likely to live in intact families, were also much less likely to
report long separations from their parents and their reunifications seemed
to pose fewer, and less daunting, challenges.[3] Indeed, high achievers reported better family relationships and the fewest mental health issues. In
addition, their mothers had higher levels of education and their fathers

were significantly more likely to be working than were the fathers of any of the other groups of students. Consequently, high achievers had relational supports at home and at school that helped to mediate against the difficulties they encountered in their new contexts. With these supports, they were able to sustain their high initial optimism and motivation and were more likely to work hard on their studies.

In this chapter, we present in detail the experiences of five resilient immigrant youngsters who in many ways came to embody the qualities of highly engaged, high-achieving students. Each portrait is unique and represents a specific constellation of factors that lead to academic success. Joyce overcomes a number of obstacles—multiple separations, poverty, and struggles with a new language—but is such a conscientious and dedicated "perfect student" that she soon rises to the top of her class. Jean-Luc's tight-knit, religious family, deep respect for his cultural origins, better-than-average schools, and strong commitment to education sustain him in the pursuit of his lofty goals. Though Yadira juggles multiple identities and navigates a less-than-optimal initial school experience, she seizes the opportunity of a private school scholarship and flourishes in her new nurturing—and rigorous—school context. Rosa, graced with intelligence, beauty, charm, and determination, as well as with the support of a warm, closely bonded family and a supportive mentoring organization, becomes valedictorian of her impoverished school. Li has the good fortune of highly educated parents who know precisely how to guide him through the college pathway maze; their steady and firm guidance, combined with his extraordinary effort, drive, and engagement, gain him entry into the most competitive schools in the country. As we will see, these portraits capture tensions, contradictions, and paradoxes that are at the heart of even the most successful immigrant story.

Joyce: "A Miracle" against All Odds

Joyce tosses her long, jet-black hair, her eyes sparkling. With a charming smile and a friendly, sweet voice, she recounts her family's emigration from southern China to the United States: "My father came first. He came to the U.S. when I was very little. Then my mother came to the U.S. My mother gave birth to my brother in the U.S. At the beginning, I stayed with my maternal grandmother. When my grandmother went to Canada, I stayed with my uncle. Then my father, my mother, and my seven-year-old brother returned to China and came to the U.S. with me."

It is hard to keep track of the multiple journeys and separations that Joyce shares with us in a matter-of-fact way. Joyce was born out of wedlock eighteen years ago. Her father was a self-taught junior-college graduate who worked as a government official and teacher, and her mother was a seamstress. When Joyce was two, her father left her and her mother behind, and moved to the United States. His own mother, who had lived in the United States for many years, had applied for him and his siblings to come on a family reunion visa. He became a citizen when Joyce turned five, returned to China, married Joyce's mother, and brought his wife back to the United States, leaving Joyce in the care of her maternal grandmother because he wasn't sure he could get a visa for his child. Joyce stayed with her grandmother for two years until the grandmother herself immigrated to Canada, at which time Joyce was left with her uncle's family. Joyce's parents often sent her money, called her, and wrote to her, telling her that they cared about her and encouraging her to do well in school. Her mother visited her twice in China, bringing along her American-born baby son. But it was not until Joyce turned twelve that her parents and her younger brother all returned to China and brought her back with them to the United States. Finally, for the first time she could remember, Joyce was together with her whole family.

Though the family had maintained as much cohesion as possible during the many separations, there had been difficult moments. Joyce recalls her sadness when her mother first left her. Neither her mother nor her father— nor the grandmother who had brought her up—said farewell to her when they left China. Although Joyce knew exactly what day they were leaving, they never made formal goodbyes, reasoning that Joyce would cry if they did. They just left. Joyce holds back her tears as she tells this story. In this family, migration means never having to say goodbye.

In the United States, Joyce had to learn to live with her immediate family—her father, from whom she had been separated for ten years; her mother, whom she hadn't lived with since she was five; and her American-born younger brother, whom she had hardly met. Joyce describes her feelings when she first joined them: "I was not used to it at all. I had nothing to say to them. I felt strange." Joyce did not perceive the separations as abandonment, thanks to the parents' careful efforts to explain that their absence was temporary and necessary for the overall welfare of the family. And since arriving in the United States she has blossomed—having been reunited not only with her parents and grandmother, but also with nearly thirty relatives living in the area.

Before immigrating, Joyce's father, a one-time Chinese government official, owned a house given to him by the state. In the United States, he has worked as a cook in a Chinese restaurant for more than fifteen years, and his wife has picked up her old trade as a seamstress. Together, they make approximately twenty thousand dollars a year. We talk to him in the one-bedroom apartment the family shares in a bustling housing project in Chinatown. It is in the newest public housing complex in the Chinatown area—and is considered by many the best. Although the neighborhood is officially called Chinatown, it is not a segregated ethnic enclave but rather a crossroad for the mainstream society and the Chinese and Southeast Asian communities. Restaurants proffer Chinese, Vietnamese, Thai, Malaysian, Japanese, and Korean cuisine, attracting Asians and non-Asians alike. And familiar American chains such as Dunkin' Donuts and McDonald's, as well as medical centers and hospitals, compete for attention in the heart of the neighborhood.

Though Joyce's building is new, it is dark and gloomy. All the windows in the apartment face the same brick wall. The blinds are half closed, further dimming the already limited light. But the apartment's decor fights the shadows. Colorful wall calendars displaying Chinese landscapes and Chinese movie stars surround a pair of red, handwritten spring scrolls. The handwriting on the scrolls is childlike, with immature strokes and characters of uneven size. An entertainment center stands against the wall that separates the bedroom and the living room. One shelf displays a white porcelain Kwun Yin, the Chinese goddess of mercy. A vase of large yellow silk flowers adorns another. Around the television set are rows and rows of videos, all in Chinese. Joyce's brother's videogame console and DVDs sit nearby.

Joyce's father describes in a pragmatic way how life changed dramatically after immigration:

> America is powerful and affluent, but that's on the national level. On the personal level, America is not as good for us, the newcomers. Apart from the kitchen, there's no other place that we can find jobs. We have to work very

hard . . . I don't have other choices. When I was in China, I worked for the government. I was a secretary. Now, because I don't know English, I have to work in the kitchen. It's for survival. American life doesn't fit us. But I have come here, and I'm in my middle age; there's nothing much I can do. Besides, all my family members are in the United States now. All I want is to look forward to [the future], rather than looking at [my situation] now . . . All I can do is to work. I don't know English. There are many places that I can't go because I don't know the language . . . If I return to China, I can't get my old job again. [All I can do is to stay here], try to survive and to develop . . . [My goal] is to be a good parent. My children are successful; they can make some money to raise a family and to have their own career.

Despite the lengthy chronicle of separations, or perhaps because no one ever felt abandoned during those years apart, Joyce's mother holds a positive masculine image of her husband, which the child is attuned to and sustains. Joyce loves her parents and appreciates what they teach her. Since their reunion, the family atmosphere has been nurturing, harmonious, and compassionate; there are no signs of parental conflict. Joyce describes her family as "very warm." "I can express my love to my parents in everyday things," she says. "Be polite to them. I make rice while they're still at work. When they get home, they'll have rice ready for them. If I eat something, I'll ask them if they want some." An ethos of harmony and reciprocity underlies the rhythm of everyday life for this family.

Though during our five-year study Joyce generally lived up to the "good daughter" expectations at home, as she grew older she began to want more freedom, and some disagreements started to emerge. She now has a teenager's interest in fashion and jewelry—in fact, she spends almost the same amount of time dressing herself as she does studying—and her choice of clothing has started arguments. In particular, as she gains confidence in her performance at school, Joyce has become bolder in her style, wearing teenage jewelry such as beaded bracelets, silver bangles, colorful hair clips and four piercings in her ears—a radical transformation from the timid girl who arrived from China five years ago. Joyce is developing a taste for "pan-Asian" hip culture, rather than maintaining an exclusively Chinese or Chinese American identity.

Joyce's parents find these changes upsetting. "We want her to follow the Chinese tradition," her father complains. "She listens but not wholeheartedly." At one point her father was opposed to her frequently going out with friends, and while Joyce obeyed this rule without much protest during the first couple of years, she started to resist once she got to high school. Over time she began to mark her distance from her parents by such techniques as speaking English when she did not want them to understand what she was saying. The father's protectiveness flashed one day when we arrived to pick up Joyce for an interview. He had planned to leave the house with the son so that we could conduct the interview in the apartment, but having planned to bring Joyce back to our office, we had not brought a tape recorder. Grudgingly, he let Joyce go with us; we left our office telephone number so that he could reach Joyce if necessary.

Joyce explained her father's attitude, with slight sarcasm: "Chinese parents in the U.S. are very strict. Compared to Chinese parents, the American parents are less restrictive. They [Chinese parents] want you stay at home and read. You are not allowed to go anywhere. You are not allowed to go out, let alone going out at night. Going out with boys is even more strongly objected to by my parents. Sometimes I go out with friends and return at 5 P.M. They will say things, like 'Where have you been—it's so late?'"

With a Different Voice, New Mastery

During the first year of the study, we once sat next to Joyce during lunch in the cafeteria of her middle school. Joyce had arrived from China only a month earlier, and did not speak English. Miriam, a friendly white girl in Joyce's class, asked, "Are you here to teach Joyce English?"

We explained that we were there for research; someone else was to teach her English. Miriam persisted, insisting that we must teach Joyce English. "I want to say hi to Joyce, but she just looks at me."

"Maybe you can learn some Chinese and talk to her?"

Miriam liked the idea and asked how to say "Do you like school?" in Chinese. Joyce responded to her question with a definite "Yes"; both girls smiled, and Miriam seemed thrilled. Joyce said in Chinese that Miriam had been very friendly, while she, hindered by her lack of English, had been at a loss to respond.

In China, Joyce was a top student, a student leader who had won many prizes, including a third-place award in a national composition contest. Soon after she arrived in the United States, she enrolled in an urban middle school with a bilingual program. She knew no one. She knew no English. "I felt strange to be with them in the beginning," she recalls. Soon, though, she found that "teachers and schoolmates . . . they are very nice to me. Teachers treat everybody in the same way. If I don't know something, my classmates will teach me before I ask them." There were a few unpleasant incidents: "One day, some schoolmates [who were black] bullied me. I was in the restroom. I wanted to close the door. They kicked the door deliberately. My hand was caught in it and it hurt. I didn't tell the teacher. I don't know who they are. They hurt me, but forget it. It's okay as long as they don't do it again. They probably don't know who I am. They know I am new, and they know I'm Chinese."

Joyce also learned that completing her schoolwork took much more time now that she had to do it in English. In China, she could finish homework in half an hour and spend the rest of her time reading comic books, books about composition, and books about IQ tests, but now she needs three or four hours to finish her work. And like many of her Chinese peers in the United States, she cannot turn to her parents for help with her homework because they do not know English.

Yet Joyce's father, who had also been a teacher in China, does play an active role in Joyce's overall education, despite his limited English ability. His educational experience has had a strong impact on his philosophy of educating his children. Born into a poor family, he knew that his only way out of poverty was through education, but the chaos of the Cultural Revolution prevented him from getting as much schooling as he wanted. People around him were encouraged to attack intellectuals; to strive toward education was to resist the cultural current of the day. Joyce's father believed in the saying "Knowledge is wealth"; he kept studying on his own and eventually became a teacher. Looking back, he believes that if he had followed the current and behaved like the young people around him, he would have failed. From this experience, Joyce's father derived a principle that he encourages his children to adopt: be persistent and work hard. He tells them: "Put your heart into studying. Respect others. Don't be proud. Don't be self-satisfied . . . What counts is how much effort you have put in. The result doesn't matter." Joyce shares with us one of her father's favorite Chinese sayings: "Nobody knows you while you're studying hard for ten years; everyone knows you when you become famous overnight."

Thus Joyce's parents nurture a sense of the importance of education and provide her with moral support, even if they can't help her with homework. "My parents work all day long," Joyce says. "They don't have time to study. That's why they can't help me. But they support me with all their might. They encourage me to try my best, to get into a good college, get a good job after graduation." Her father does everything he can to help Joyce learn English. When Joyce first started attending school in the United States, he asked friends who knew some English to come over and help Joyce with her homework. He also bought English DVDs with Chinese subtitles, such as the Disney film *Mulan,* to help his daughter learn.

Joyce's sense of obligation is evident. "They always say that they are OK as long as I have tried my best," she says. "But I know that they want me at least to get into the honor roll. Even a B plus will make me feel guilty." Her parents have given her parallel and contradictory messages, and though acutely aware of this contradiction, she feels the pressure. On the one hand, her father says they teach her to "try your best. How you end up doesn't matter"; on the other, Joyce says, they bombard her with conversations about going to Harvard and getting a doctorate: "They talk about it all the time. That makes my head ache."

Joyce was unsure of herself in the first year. She thought of herself as a below-average student. But she adapted quickly, getting high grades, and six months after she first enrolled in an American school, Joyce was chosen to recite a poem in English with the school principal during the school's Chinese New Year celebration. Gradually, Joyce felt more comfortable at school. "The second half [semester] was better, since I've learned more English and get along better with teachers and classmates," she said. Joyce got nearly all A's at the end of her first year. With her new English "voice," she acquired a sense of confidence and mastery.

Social and psychological adaptation was still a struggle. We asked her during that first year what she would do if given a choice of staying in the United States or returning to China. She said she would prefer to go back: "If my mom, dad, and brother were in China, I would have stayed in China, since I know different places in China. I have many friends there. My grades were better in China. I know Chinese but I don't know English here." Like most immigrant students, her attitude would change as time went by.

During her first two years in the United States, Joyce was in the bilingual program. In her third year, she started attending some mainstream classes and believed that she was doing very well. She had ample reasons for her confidence. Her report cards consistently show A's and A pluses, with a B in art and a B plus in English reading during her first year. Her bilingual verbal testing conducted during the third year of our study illustrates her abilities, showing skills equal to those of a seventeen-year-old, although she was fourteen at the time. But as is true for so many immigrant students, Joyce found it frustratingly difficult to improve her English-language skills. Joyce's English ability was equivalent to that of a six-year-old. In testing conducted two years later, Joyce was almost sixteen and her bilingual ability that of a twenty-six-year-old, while her English ability had improved to that of a ten-year-old.[4]

Joyce's middle-school teachers thought highly of her and gave her the highest rating in all categories. Her language-arts teacher put two pluses after her checks of "very good" and "excellent."[5] Her science teacher said: "[Joyce] is a perfect student! She's a miracle! She is the best student that I ever had in my entire teacher career." Her language arts teacher raved: "She is the most attentive, conscientious student I've ever had. She comes to class well prepared, asks for help if needed and goes into great depth with her comprehension answers."

Sometimes, however, her teachers notice that Joyce can be a bit selfish. She does not particularly enjoy teamwork, and she is reluctant to help her peers. Although some of her teachers worry that Joyce may isolate herself because she is unenthusiastic about helping others, their fears seem unfounded. She has good relations with most classmates and many friends inside school—mostly Chinese, either born in China or in the United States—and outside school, mainly Asian girls she met in a summer program.

Joyce's middle school is in the inner city. Most of the students are African American or Chinese; few are white, and there are frequent reports of ethnic tension between black and Chinese students. Joyce says she feels safe at school despite the fights she has witnessed from time to time. "Sometimes students fight, but it doesn't hurt us," she says. "Most of the time it is blacks fighting with blacks. Some Chinese students fight too, but it's more playing than fighting. The Chinese students exchange words, but it is very rare . . . sometimes it's quite terrible on the [school] bus. People exchange words. Recently people threw things at each other. It's between black girls and Chinese boys. There aren't any whites on our bus."

During one of our meetings, Joyce describes her experience of "a little" discrimination:

> Mostly the blacks discriminate against the Chinese. They bully you because they assume you won't tell the teachers. Last time, on the bus, a girl deliberately put her feet up on my seat. I was very angry and I told her to go away. She didn't. She told her friends in the back. Show-off! She's, like, "Watch," and then she walked over and scolded me. I ignored her. Then she hit me. She hit me on my head. That night I told my father. The next day I told my teacher. Then the principal knew about it. Then one student was suspended. The rest apologized to me.

The "model minority" stereotype exerts its influence on the Chinese students in this middle school and is perpetuated by the school staff. For example, even though immigrant children who have been in the United States for less than three years are exempt from the statewide standardized tests, the administration asked the bilingual math teacher to send more Chinese students to take the math section of the test. One year, only three bilingual students were required to take the test, but the bilingual program sent eighteen Chinese students for the math portion, preparing them with special after-school tutoring sessions. By having more Chinese students take the math test, the school hoped to lift its overall school math scores. This practice to some extent perpetuates the stereotype that Chinese students' greatest strength is math. But at the same time, it boosts the Chinese students' self-esteem. Joyce is proud that she was one of the students chosen to pull up her school's overall achievement score.

Joyce continues to thrive, earning excellent grades as well as joining many after-school programs and clubs in and out of school. Adults like to help her. One after-school teacher devoted his own time to giving her piano lessons, and her summer camp counselor found her a tutor for computer skills at the Chinatown Youth Center.

One day, Joyce reaches us by telephone after she has been calling for several days. She tells us excitedly that she has passed the entrance exam for the city's elite high school and has been accepted to her dream school. We congratulate her, but we're a little worried: this transition can be difficult, particularly for students who are used to the nurturing environment of a bilingual program and the support of bilingual middle-school teachers.

It turns out that in the new high school, Joyce's early experience with change serves her well. After some initial difficulty, she begins to thrive. Sometimes she spends five hours a day on homework, and her excellent grades continue. Not surprisingly, because she knows well how to reach out to others, she soon finds a supportive adult in her new school, a Chinese teacher. Again, she joins after-school programs, including the Asian Club and a selective college-prep program at a local university.

Today, at the end of our study, Joyce is very different from the girl we first met five years ago. Dressed in a gray and black outfit of trendy black jeans, black leather shoes, and black coat, she exudes confidence. Transformed from the shy, timid girl she once was, she is comfortable with English and filled with hope. "My future will be very good," she says, adding, after a pause, "if I am willing to work hard."[6]

A Chronicle of an Identity Foretold

When Joyce was asked to create a story around the picture of the boy and the violin, she offered this narrative:

> This boy was from China. He just arrived in another country. Anyway, it was a strange country to him, like the U.S. or the United Kingdom. He used to play violin and he was very good at it. But after he came here, he had a lot of pressure from homework and studying, and he needed to adjust to other environments. That is why he didn't have time to learn to play the violin. In addition, because of his mood, he deserted the violin. But eventually, he became adjusted to the environment and overcame all difficulties. Therefore, he should succeed. He can adjust to the new environment, rekindle his interest in violin, and he can play it well. His feeling now should be helplessness; he experienced a lot of pressure. But after he has adjusted to the environment he will feel that actually the world is nice.

There is every reason for Joyce to be failing in school—multiple separations, poverty, a tough struggle with the new language, and the harassment she experienced at school—yet Joyce has been a top student since her arrival. Her teachers call her "a perfect student"—attentive, conscientious, and highly motivated. She has won awards for science and for composition. She participates in school activities, after-school programs, and college-prep summer camp. She was accepted to a competitive high school where she is getting all A's. Joyce has many good friends and a loving, happy family. Indeed, as one of her teachers exclaimed, Joyce is a "miracle."

Joyce's identity "floats" between being Chinese and being American. In some ways, particularly since she started high school, Joyce has become more Americanized—as we can see, for example, in her style of dress and in her attitude toward her parents' restrictions. When she first became a U.S. citizen, she considered herself both Chinese and American. Later, she switched back to identifying as Chinese, but she also claimed that the United States felt like home to her because her family is here: "I gradually felt that the U.S. is more like my home. I didn't feel that way when I first came here."

Clearly, though, she is not moving toward a solely American identity. She is exploring—in some ways, taking advantage of—her choices as a Chinese teenager growing up in the United States. She listens to pop music from the United States, Japan, Hong Kong, and Korea. She has become a fan of Korean pop culture. She speaks Chinese with her parents, and while she has friends from many ethnic backgrounds, her closest friends are Asian. Her style of dress is the typical blended one of Asian Americans—it is not exactly a Chinese or Hong Kong style, but it is not completely American, either. By blending aspects of Asian and American cultures, she is growing into a "global" teenager who feels free to choose from a wide array of styles.

While Joyce has changed before our eyes, her parents remain as they were when they first arrived. In some ways they have created, literally, a cultural barricade in their apartment, overloading it with Chinese artifacts. The space feels almost mummified: a frozen setting capturing the ethos of China as it was at the time of their departure. Joyce, who has become a butterfly flitting from culture to culture, is finding no place for herself in this isolated alcove.

Joyce's conflict with her parents may escalate as she gets older. For now, though, her mature behavior and reasoning, and her parents' cautious if ambivalent acceptance of her new cultural style, have kept their contrasting experiences with acculturation from generating serious conflict. Joyce's father does not entirely reject American culture; rather, the predictable Confucian pragmatist encourages her to have American friends so she can polish her English. Moreover, there is a certain congruence between the American discourse of self-betterment and her father's philosophy of life.

He uses many typical Chinese expressions, such as "stay firm," "be persistent," and "don't follow the stream," which, Joyce says, inspire her to study hard and stay focused. There is a key difference between the American model of success and the Confucian collectivistic discourse of betterment, however: Confucianism expects that the successful person will give back to the family. It would be interesting to see to what extent this postscript to Joyce's success story—the expectation of giving back—is preserved by immigrant Chinese youth as they acculturate to their new land.

Jean-Luc: Knowledge Is a Treasure

Jean-Luc attends a progressive, integrated middle school in his neighborhood. It is a school that is proud of its high student achievement and boasts that it has had the same principal for twenty-six years. It attracts middle-class parents who value the opportunity for involvement in school; parents often work in the classrooms and hallways as helpers and co-teachers. Most of the minority students, who make up about half of the student body, are from underprivileged Haitian families. Because of their work schedules and a cultural heritage of deep respect of and deference to school authorities, Haitian parents volunteer less than the others, and parental involvement seems to be greater in the mainstream program than in the bilingual classes.

The school is a small community, with 380 students and twenty-two teachers. The Haitian bilingual program includes approximately a quarter of the student population. More than a third of the students are in special-education programs, and 38 percent receive free or reduced-price lunches. The school has an unusual class structure, with each class consisting of two grades. This arrangement gives the younger students more time to adapt while the older students take on a mentoring role and establish a strong relationship with teachers.

The school is housed in a clean, richly decorated building. Haitian culture is represented everywhere in the building. There are wall panels dedicated to Haitian history, from slavery to independence. A colorful mural presides over the first floor, depicting Haitians' struggles for civil rights and for access to education. Another mural, on the third floor, dramatically depicts internal and external battles for freedom, using images of guns and tears and a portrait of the twice-elected president of Haiti, Jean-Bertrand

Aristide. The entire back wall of the cafeteria is an artistic representation of a popular Haitian folktale "The Magic Orange Tree." In the corridors around the cafeteria, students' ceramics hang on the walls, creating a multicultural scene of children from many races.

Despite these overt artistic expressions, the Haitian bilingual program itself is only ambivalently included in the school's vision. It is the only one of the bilingual programs that is not fully integrated with the other classes. While the "world language" Spanish program is integrated into the classrooms, the Haitian language program is not, since Haitian Kreyol is not considered a world language. Over time, we learn that the school is segregated in many other ways. For instance, the Haitian students in the bilingual program join other students only for gym and art. Jean-Luc, an attractive brown-skinned young man, was mainstreamed into the monolingual program after spending the first two years of our study in bilingual classes. Jean-Luc's teachers and his peers describe him as the smartest in the class. He is confident, articulate, and a joy to spend time with.

Worlds Apart: Transnationalism of the Heart

During the first year of our study, Jean-Luc had this to say about the picture of the girl with the books, gazing over the field:

> This young woman doesn't like to work hard on the field, so she decided to go to school and learn, but at the same time, she wants to help her parents and she feels bad that they have to work so hard for her.

During an interview at their home, Jean-Luc's parents are a delight to talk with, speaking with frankness, trust, and clarity. They also reveal the deep affection and connectedness they have for each other. Jean-Luc's mother responds to most of the questions, asking the father what he thinks, and he also chimes in. The father is a painter and a classical guitarist, and after the interview he plays classic Haitian tunes for us—"Choucon" and "Haiti Cherie"—as the mother sings along. This is a loving family—cohesive, respectful, and harmonious.

They tell us how Jean-Luc's father had to flee Haiti after an attempt on his life because of his active involvement in Haitian politics during the 1980s. As he put it, "We had to come because of the difficulties in Haiti. The present political problems [there] cause people not to look back." He feels lucky that he was able to escape and could rely on relatives in the United States to help him. Not surprisingly, he chose to settle in an area of the United States where many members of his family are living. He worked as a dishwasher, and it took him a decade to save the money necessary for his family to migrate and join him in the United States. During that time, he sent his family money monthly, wrote them letters regularly, and called home as often as he could. Jean-Luc, his two sisters, and his mother arrived in the United States in the late 1990s. His mother feels that they had no choice but to come for security reasons, and Jean-Luc adds that the family migrated because of "economic problems, since there are no jobs in Haiti."

Jean-Luc says that based on what he had heard from his father, he expected "the USA would be a big country with a lot of people." He adds, "I thought people had respect for each other." But he was taken aback by what he felt was a sense of insecurity and violence: "I don't like the violence, it's too much. It's even on television every day . . . [In the United States,] it's like you have a 'good bowl' [what we in the United States might call a "deck of cards"] and a 'bad bowl.' When it's good, you get help, can work, and go to a good school. When it's bad, there is violence and drugs." He is impressed that in the United States "everyone has the possibility to obtain education"; in Haiti, only the elite could count on going to school. And after spending some time in his new country, Jean-Luc has decided that what he truly enjoys about his new home are the school and libraries.

His mother also tells us that when coming to the United States, "what you expect is not what you find. You think you are able to accomplish things, but [being older] limits your possibilities . . . You have to work harder and are challenged with not having the papers you need. You are faced with discrimination and barriers. Even in jobs, because you are an immigrant you are discriminated against because you don't speak the way they want you to."

Jean-Luc's father continues to work as a dishwasher, and his mother is a nurse's aide in a nursing home. In Haiti, Jean-Luc's mother was a nurse and completed thirteen years of school. His father worked in a casino and completed ten years of school. While in Haiti, they may have been viewed as middle class; in the United States, however, they are more disadvantaged and live in subsidized housing.

Both of Jean-Luc's parents were born into the Catholic faith, but they decided to convert to the Seventh Day Adventist tradition. Even though this is one of the stricter Protestant sects, they are quite measured in their religious enthusiasm and have been able to protect their children from the fanaticism they have seen in some churches—revealing once again that the family gravitates to harmony and cohesiveness. Jean-Luc's mother explains that her conversion came during a crisis and after she had an insight and "found the answer in the Bible." Both parents turn to God when they have a problem. They attend church weekly and participate in church events regularly. Jean-Luc himself is not actively involved in organized church activities. He does not want to elaborate, but he explains that church is not a significant part of his world. His limited involvement in church has brought to his awareness some gender issues: "I think that I would have more pressure from society as a girl than as a boy. In my church, 99 percent of the leaders are male, and they will not allow females to do certain things." What is important is his relationship with God, and he separates spirituality from organized religion. "I feel safe because I pray a lot in the morning so I am not worried," he says. When listing the people who live in his household, the first person he lists is "Jesus," whom he feels is everywhere with him.[7]

Jean-Luc lives with both his parents and two sisters, one older and one younger, in a housing development near the school. His older sister recently started classes at a local university and stays in the dorms during the week, though she comes home every weekend. Although having the daughter living away during the week is an unusual decision for Haitian families, her parents explain that the family devoted much time to discussing this issue and came to the conclusion that living in the dorms would be best for their daughter's education.

Jean-Luc describes his neighborhood as "mixed." It includes several ethnic groups that, he believes, do not get along because "they don't communicate." Jean-Luc's mother also says that there is tension in the neighborhood: Her "Haitian neighbors are not neighbors. It's a dog-eat-dog world." In the Haiti of her memory, the neighborhood community was tighter and more family oriented. "I remember how Haitians were together. Despite the poverty, people shared. If they had a problem, they pulled together and helped each other out." The sense of community belonging and cohesiveness has been lost to migration.

Jean-Luc and his family have a strong bond and communicate well with each other. He describes his family as his "best friends." He is frustrated that his parents work long hours and they have little time to spend to-gether as a family. He admits that it was difficult to reunite with his father because of the lengthy separation. He did not know him well, but now, he explains, "I understand and am closer to my father." Interestingly, Jean-Luc's father reports that his son feels closer to his mother, even though the mother encourages the children to speak with both parents when they have problems.

We also hear Jean-Luc speak affectionately of his younger sister; he de-scribes joking with her and feeling close to her. They go to the same school, and he usually waits for her after classes so that they will ride the bus home together. As a matter of fact, the school's policy of pairing grades within the same classroom put Jean-Luc and his sister in the same classroom for a while, and they supported each other well in this setting.

The family's main source of social support is their church community. Jean-Luc's mother says she has few friends and believes that her Haitian neighbors are not interested in socializing, yet other Haitians in the United States have helped the family find jobs.

Thus Jean-Luc has strong support from his family, including his ex-tended family remaining in Haiti. He speaks in detail about one of his un-cles, whom he admires. "He learned a lot of things," Jean-Luc says. "He is a lawyer and does well." Since Jean-Luc is academically strong, he identi-fies his uncle as a supporter of his academic pursuits. Jean-Luc also sees his aunts, who live in Haiti, as actively involved in the family's decision-making, including decisions related to his academics. Over the years in multiple conversations and contexts, the relatives in Haiti come up often and with a sense of immediacy: they are quite present psychologically even if physically they are far away. This family practices a transnationalism of the heart that is sustaining—especially in moments of crisis and when dif-ficult choices need to be made. Jean-Luc's sister comments that her aunt is like a second mother to her and Jean-Luc and that they can always turn to her—even though she is back in Haiti.

Everything Is Easy

On one of our visits to the middle school, we see Jean-Luc walking alone down the main school hallway. He has grown taller and is quite handsome, with a traditional Haitian short hairstyle; he is wearing casual clothes that are not especially fashionable but are age appropriate. Jean-Luc rarely walks with friends or other students. Even at community events Jean-Luc is alone. He usually goes straight home after school. Occasionally he goes to the library to study, to read a book, or simply to browse.

Jean-Luc is friendly with everyone, yet he is a quiet, introspective young man who lacks close friends—a fact that does not bother him. His contacts at church and, above all, his relatives here and in Haiti are sufficient. The few friends he introduces to us are Haitian. They communicate in Creole, and he spends some time with them after school. "I am active in school, but I am calm and have few friends," he says. His understanding that friends can distract him from his studies becomes evident when he describes the pragmatic advice he would give to a cousin coming to the United States: "I will tell him to go to school and learn something, and don't waste time playing with other kids."

In Haiti, Jean-Luc attended an Adventist elementary school, one of the most prestigious religious schools in Port-au-Prince, where instruction was rigorous and mostly in French. His siblings also went to the school. They all read and write French fluently. "In Haiti, I was good," Jean-Luc says. "I was the smartest in the class." He feels that he obtained a good education at the school but also mentions that he received tremendous support from his mother. Discipline was tight at the school. "In Haiti, the kids don't waste time, they work very hard, and they listen to the teachers, but here kids do whatever they want," Jean-Luc says. "They don't listen."

Despite Jean-Luc's success at his Haitian school, his mother has some concerns about how the school affected her children. She fears that the ironclad teaching traditions may have stunted her children's autonomy. "In Haiti, students memorize without knowing," Jean-Luc's mother explains. "In the United States, students are able to study and understand . . . In Haiti, kids are forced to study everything. There are choices here, which I respect about the United States." She frequently returns to the importance of education—but her definition of education reaches into the domain of values: "A child should have the education of family values. With this support, you will do well in school. My father told me I couldn't leave you money, so knowledge will be your treasure. I teach my kids this."

When he arrived in the United States, Jean-Luc entered middle school, which he attended from the sixth grade to the eighth grade. For the first two years, he was placed in the bilingual program. In the third year, he was moved to the monolingual classrooms just as soon as his teacher felt that he was academically, socially, and behaviorally ready to be mainstreamed. One teacher did remark that Jean-Luc's English writing ability was initially only fair, yet he has always achieved excellent grades. Politeness and attentiveness go a long way in school. Later, Jean-Luc's teachers describe him as "great . . . a wonderfully motivated student, engaged, and hard working." His English teacher comments: "Jean-Luc is everything any teacher could wish for and more—eager, thirsty for knowledge, cooperative, hardworking." His literature teacher says, "Jean-Luc is an insightful and self-motivated young man. He actually volunteers to complete additional work. Last but not least, his sense of maturity far surpasses that of any student I have ever taught." The teachers are also impressed with his family's involvement in his work. Despite language barriers, his mother and father attend all parent meetings. The teachers have regular contact with the family, which is "very positive. They care a lot about Jean-Luc's academic progress and try to stay involved."

Throughout his three years at middle school and later at the high school, Jean-Luc has received honor grades. "I am a good student because I do all my homework and I respect teachers," he says. "You have to learn English. Once you learn English, in American schools everything is easy."

After completing eighth grade, Jean-Luc advanced to Reade High School, which is described in detail in Chapter 3. He is excited about his new school, yet he expresses some fear about being a freshman and sadness at leaving his old school. By the end of the study, however, he is well adjusted and happy at the high school. He remains confident about his intellectual abilities and academic achievements—after all, he is a highly engaged straight-A student. Now that he is in tenth grade, he has few problems with the material and finds some of the classes not as challenging ("boring" now enters his academic vocabulary). He wishes he could be placed in more Advanced Placement courses because everything is too easy for him. While his teachers characterize him as a model student, they sense that he is not challenged enough, which could eventually affect his motivation. One teacher sees Jean-Luc as having to put up with "really unmotivated students" in the class.

Jean-Luc's academic English, however, remains suboptimal. Even as late as his junior year in high school, Jean-Luc's English-language proficiency was probably limiting his academic advancement. His bilingual verbal ability, a combination of his English and Haitian Creole abilities, fell in the high average range for his age (84th percentile).[8] Yet his English-language proficiency, the overall measure of cognitive-academic proficiency in the English language, was in the 34th percentile for his age. This also seemed to have an effect on the results of the mathematics reasoning test, where he performed in the lowest 7 percent of his same-age peers who had the same Bilingual Verbal Abilities Test (BVAT) score.[9] One can only suspect how much more he would be advancing academically if his academic English were more fluent.

Another possible limitation to Jean-Luc's realization of his full potential comes from his lack of familiarity with the system for readying oneself for college. Despite his good grades, he doesn't know much about testing or college-preparation programs. He is slowly acquiring some information from his older sister and the counselors at Reade High School, but this information, it seems to us, is too basic and pro forma. He knows nothing about available summer pre-college programs or even the possibility of taking college-level courses at high school. He still does not know how important it is to volunteer and to develop a strong extracurricular portfolio, and his extracurricular activities remain very limited. Even though he is outstanding academically, he has not fully accessed the programs that other high-achieving students in his school have explored. We wonder if he would not have received a more ambitious preparation for college had he not been a newly arrived Haitian immigrant with working-class parents.[10]

Jean-Luc's professional goals have changed considerably through the years, but his commitment to attending college has always been firm. At one point, Jean-Luc said that after he graduates from college, he wants to be an inventor or a professional athlete. Since his father is a classical guitarist and a painter and Jean-Luc himself has considerable artistic talent, he feels that his parents would want him to become a professional musician or an artist. His mother only insists that she wants him to go to college, without specifying a particular profession. "I want my kids to have a better life than mine, and not worry about money, and have a good job." She herself dreams about going back to school one day and having a new career. For now, however, she lives her dreams through her children.

By the time Jean-Luc is in high school, his growing interest in technology is evident, and he says firmly that he would like to attend MIT. "I can get a scholarship because I work hard. I have a chance . . . I want to go to

MIT, I want to be an engineer . . . I want to go to college and study something that will help me, my family, my country." He secretly dreams of one day combining his artistic talents with his love for technology.

Blended Identity

Every year, the Haitian Club at Reade High School organizes a tribute to Martin Luther King Jr. The students read speeches, dance, play music, and sing songs devoted to Dr. King's legacy and the civil rights movement.[11] This is Jean-Luc's senior year at the high school, and we delight in seeing him take part in the tribute. Surprising those who know him as a serious but quiet student, Jean-Luc comes out to the podium and commands the audience's attention with a moving, thoughtful, and poetic speech that draws powerful parallels between the struggles of the civil right activists in the United States and the slaves' fight for liberation in his native Haiti—the world's first independent black Republic.

> Doctor King held on to that torch with one hand, pointing to the right direction with the other. His people and he were lynched, raped, humiliated, decapitated, and discriminated against. But there was something that drove them; there was something that kept them fighting. They kept their eyes on the prize; the prize of freedom. It wasn't long before what had happened in Haiti in 1804 became true in the wake of 1963, when all the colored [folks] declared their indisputable freedom, their indisputable liberation from discrimination.[12]

The audience rewards his performance with loud, enthusiastic applause.

Jean-Luc is quite aware of racism and its outcomes, and through this awareness of discrimination, he and his family find a connection to the United States. Cultural pride, family cohesion, and religious belief are important buffers for this well-integrated family. In the United States, Jean-Luc says, "discrimination is everywhere, you can't hide from it, and you can expect it from everybody." Jean-Luc blends an awareness of discrimination in the here and now and the historic Haitian struggle for freedom into a coherent narrative of self: he is a young Haitian immigrant of color now living in a country that famously defined the color line. The struggle continues, albeit in a new setting.

Jean-Luc's first impressions of the United States were quite different from his expectations. "Yes, it's very different. They don't really respect people, especially if you are black. I don't think the white people like blacks too much." Nonetheless, Jean-Luc believes Americans and Haitians have the same chance of getting ahead, "but Haitians have to work very hard." Painfully Jean-Luc shares with us, "Americans think Haitians are an inferior nation, and Haitians think that Americans are a threat."[13] In the school, "the principal mostly yells at Haitian students. There is one teacher that doesn't respect the Haitian students. Last week, a teacher came into the classroom and said, 'someone needs to take a shower.' It was in a Haitian classroom." Over the years he has learned that the media send unbalanced and misleading messages about whites and blacks in the United States: that white Americans "are all rich, they all have good jobs, working in businesses and they all live in the suburbs," while black Americans "are [presented] as very poor, they can't afford to live in a house, only in projects. They do hand labor, they talk dirty and are disrespectful. They are not educated."

Some of the social tensions and isolation that he feels in school are projected onto his narrative about the picture of the boy and the violin:

> This story is about a kid who is forced to play the violin by his parents. There is a course he is taking at his school. It is hard, but he has to pass the class. He is failing the class but he needs help from those who know how to play. At the end since he got no help from anyone, he gave up and failed the course.

Jean-Luc's mother is also aware of discrimination, and she is careful to discuss racial issues with her children to protect them from some of the problems they may face for their dark skin. Jean-Luc's parents are unusual in that they talk to their children in depth about discrimination. In a sense, the family's frank and direct talks give Jean-Luc a certain advantage over other immigrant children of color who are left to learn such lessons on their own. Additionally, this is a family where the parents work to preserve their Haitian language, culture, and traditions: "Our children must speak Haitian Kreyol and keep their culture and language. Haitians respect their culture and carry themselves well." Jean-Luc's father tells his children stories about his past and instills pride in their Haitian identity. Indeed, Jean-Luc seems most at ease when he is with his Haitian peers.

Almost There

Jean-Luc is a bright young man, mature and grounded in his beliefs and goals. He has a strong family foundation. It took his father ten determined years to arrange legal status for himself and his family, even though he came as a political refugee from Haiti. As we have seen in this book, immigrant youth can pay a significant penalty for the multiple family separations and reunifications typical of so many migrant journeys. In this case, the family was able to mitigate the potential negative consequences.

Part of this cohesive family's success has to do with how they respect their cultural heritage and incorporate it into their daily lives. They are an open and communicative family; they have instilled in their children the idea that as Haitian immigrants in a new country, they will need to work extra hard to have a chance. The parents talk to the children about racism, a topic that parents usually avoid, and they have lengthy conversations with the children on many other important subjects. The family also promotes a sense of realism. Realizing the possible consequences of discrimination, Jean-Luc has some "realistic pessimism"; in a constructive, rational way, he is grounded and aware of problems and limitations he is likely to encounter.

Toward the end of high school Jean-Luc grows more aware of the steps he must take to prepare for college. But to us this information seems to have been inadequate and poorly timed. In addition, Jean-Luc remains somewhat isolated from his peers. He could conceivably socialize with other high-achieving students in his school, but perhaps they are not welcoming. Considering that Jean-Luc is an inner-directed youth and has an independent mind, he might not fully feel this as an absence. His immediate and extended family all love him, he has a healthy sense of self, and he calmly knows his worth.

His teachers often compare Haitian students from the 1980s to the more recent immigrants. The stereotype is that Haitian students now are rude, poorly behaved, and low-skilled compared to previous Haitian immigrants. Jean-Luc always comes up as a positive exception. He is sensitive to this difference and it distresses him that other Haitian students are treated with less respect and are given fewer opportunities.

Many factors have contributed to Jean-Luc's stability and academic success. First and foremost is his cohesive family with its very adaptive system of open communication; second are the supports the family receives from the church. Third is his own character, maturity, and autonomy. Though other external support is limited, the family's strong bond has been instrumental in motivating all three siblings in their studies. In this poor, dignified, and happy immigrant family, all of the children have been honor students. The migration factors they have faced could be seen as negative—lengthy family separations and the toxicity of an environment saturated by discrimination and racism. Indeed, the family system has had to adapt from the collective culture of Haiti to the more individualistic culture of the United States. But they have found a way to fit this individualism within their own values and attitudes.

A year after our study was completed, we ran into Jean-Luc. We were saddened to learn then that he had not been accepted to the engineering program at MIT, which had been his goal. His high academic accomplishments did, however, earn him a scholarship to another very competitive engineering school, where his academic success should continue. He has a strong commitment to his education, a supportive family structure, and respect for his culture, all of which will sustain him on his journey toward his goals.

Yadira: "A Life-Changing Opportunity"

Yadira smiles radiantly as she confides, "It was always my dream to be with my mother." Her mother left the Dominican Republic to seek work, leaving young Yadira with her grandparents. Like millions of immigrants, Yadira's mother came to the United States wanting a better life and better schools for her children. During the four years that they were separated, Yadira's mother gave birth to two more children. When she was at last able to muster the resources, Yadira's mother brought over her own mother and Yadira for the long-awaited reunion.

Yadira came to the United States at age thirteen, and although she had pictured the United States as a beautiful and bountiful place, she had also heard that U.S. schools and neighborhoods could be dangerous. In movies and on television, she had seen vivid depictions of schools ruled by gangs. Family and neighbors in the Dominican Republic told her that children could do whatever they wanted and teachers couldn't stop them, perhaps because—in sharp contrast to mores in the Dominican Republic—teachers were forbidden to discipline students with corporal punishment. She had also heard that students carried guns. While this information worried her, none of it mattered because she and her mother were about to be reunited.

Although school was less enjoyable than she initially expected and the amount of homework seemed excessive, she was overjoyed to be in the United States and able to fully engage in her passion: playing sports, especially basketball, at which she excels. She relished the opportunity to play because in the Dominican Republic, girls are excluded from sports. She says she feels "special" because of her athletic abilities. Yadira is special in another way: she is a lesbian, and—unusual for any teenager, let alone a girl from an overwhelmingly Catholic culture—she has had very frank conversations with her family about her homosexuality.

Surprisingly, or perhaps reflecting a reality for many immigrants, coming out to her family has been easier than some of the other challenges she has faced. She has found learning the English language a particular burden: "In the beginning when I got here, I was punished for not doing English assignments—but I did not know—I had never heard English before. I really wanted to go back to the D.R. My uncle talked to me and asked me to think it through because I had fought a lot to get to this country and Mom had made a lot of effort. Then I said—well, I'll try to get accustomed. But it wasn't easy—I didn't have friends, I was going to be a 'bad girl.' But now I have friends and I am studying." Soon Yadira made friends and began to feel comfortable in her new school. And she was surprised and proud at the speed with which she learned English. The gangs she continues to encounter on the streets, however, still frighten her.

Her mother likes the prospects of life in the United States and enjoys seeing her children's educational progress. Paradoxically, though they live in a gang-ridden neighborhood, several times during our conversations she uses the word "tranquility" in describing her new reality in the United States. She believes that in the United States "everyone can be whatever they want to be," and that people can express many aspects of their identities, a theme that emanates from Yadira and the rest of her family as well. Her mother hopes that Yadira will stay in the United States permanently to study, work, and succeed. "I want my children to be independent. Yadira likes sports, goes to all the activities. I want them to be happy and to do what they like to do. I want them to be themselves. I also want my children to be affectionate, *cariñosos*, close, to take care of each other. In the Dominican Republic, people are very familial."

In Yadira's words, her mother is happy here "because everyone who is in the D.R. wants to come here, and now that she has her daughters and son here, she is happy—it was her dream, and she is happy."

Yadira's living situation is in constant flux. She lives with her mother and two younger siblings, a boy and a girl. At times her grandmother stays with them, and at times her Puerto Rican stepfather (the father of her two siblings) appears for brief periods. His presence is unpredictable and fleeting, and although from Yadira's stories it seems that he lives with them and supports them, the mother refuses to talk about him as a regular partner and refers to him as only her boyfriend. A topic that neither child nor mother likes to discuss is Yadira's biological father. Her mother claims that Yadira's father is dead; however, Yadira talks about her need to communicate with him and her sadness that he abandoned them.

The family has moved several times since Yadira arrived. First they lived in a neighborhood of mostly black Americans. Initially Yadira didn't feel unsafe, but her mother insisted she stay in the house, fearing shootings and fights in the streets. Soon enough, Yadira witnessed a brutal gang beating of a man and watched in panic the arrival of an ambulance, an incident that frightened her terribly and changed her mind about the neighborhood. As a result, the family moved to an uncle's house a few towns away, where Yadira shared a room with her mother, stepfather, and two half-siblings. The family relationships remained positive despite the cramped quarters, and Yadira describes how she enjoyed being together and doing things with her parents and siblings. The family has since moved again, this time into subsidized housing in yet another town. They found an apartment in a building for people with disabilities through the help of a social worker from the hospital where Yadira's brother receives treatment for a problem with his legs. The move was sudden, but both Yadira and her mother are pleased with the change. Her mother likes the neighborhood because it is tranquil and the community is helpful. Yadira, however, must travel about two hours both to and from the new private school in which she recently enrolled. Neither Yadira nor her mother complains about this change; rather, they celebrate its positive aspects.

Yadira's mother completed twelfth grade in the Dominican Republic. After graduation, she worked in a hair salon and drugstore. Lately, she has not worked because she needs to be at home caring full-time for her son, who has endured repeated leg surgeries. The family struggles financially and receives both subsidized housing and monetary support from the government. Their financial resources are limited; without such help, they would be mired in debt. Yet the family's stability is remarkable: despite the frequent moves from town to town, and the many adjustments that each move has entailed, the family has stayed close, loving, and communicative.

On Mothers and Daughters

When Yadira sees the picture of the girl with books overlooking the field, she chooses to tell this story:

> Maria lives in Ecuador, she's 18 years old, and she's finishing her high school year. She comes from a family of farmers. During her life she has learned how difficult it is to be poor. That's why she decided to finish high school. She wanted to be one of the best so she could go to college. The day has come and Maria is ready to leave her family and town behind to go to Venezuela to study in a university because she got a scholarship in poetry because she's really good at poetry. Even though Maria is sad to leave her family, she is also happy and excited for her future.

Yadira calls her family "wonderful"; trust is an important element of family life for her. She considers her mother a friend and appreciates her stepfather's involvement. She talks to her parents when there is a problem or a disagreement and shows her love by studying hard, helping with her half-siblings, doing household chores, and translating. Her closeness with her mother has intensified now that her mother is home during the day and is waiting there when Yadira returns from school. "[My mother] tells me I have to study more," Yadira says. "She always helps me with my homework the best she can since she does not know English."

Her mother always says, "God says, 'Help yourself that I'll help you,'" meaning that she expects Yadira to do her part. Her parents usually disapprove of teenagers going out alone or staying over at friends' homes for pajama parties. Her mother thinks the practice of letting girls date at a young age in the United States is wrong and that girls should wait until they are sixteen or even until after they have graduated from high school.

Yadira has stayed close to her relatives and friends in the Dominican Republic, calling them weekly. Her mother calls "back home" monthly or once every two months but has not visited the Dominican Republic since coming to the United States. Neighbors and friends from the Dominican Republic, whom they see at church on Sundays, are their sources of support in the United States. They also have American friends, but they don't see them socially. Yadira says she wants to be like her grandmother, who was a teacher in the Dominican Republic for thirty years and supported her five children. While Yadira feels loved by her grandparents, she wonders whether they would like all the ways in which she has changed in the past few years.

Yadira went to Monroe High School for two years, which is described in detail in Chapter 3. She then transferred to a much more stable private school in the eleventh grade. Soon after that, Yadira decided it was time to tell her mother that she is gay; this was a critical period in her relationship with her family. A sense that she was not being genuine with her mother motivated her decision to be open about her sexuality. She felt that she was living a double life. She knew that her mother worried when she went over to friends' houses because she thought Yadira might be seeing boys, and Yadira felt obligated to pretend that she liked boys, a deception that made her increasingly uncomfortable. She was encouraged by a male friend (who had been with her in both high schools) to be frank with her mother. He accompanied Yadira to her home, standing by as she told her mother the truth about herself. Coming from a strict Catholic background, the news shook Yadira's mother, who at first reacted strongly. She even stopped talking to Yadira for several weeks. She needed time to sort out her feelings and collect her thoughts. But Yadira's mother could not sit still for long. Soon she began seeking out information and guidance from multiple sources—a school counselor, trusted friends in the community, and a community-based group. She eventually went to Yadira and told her that she loved her very much and would always support her. This declaration of unconditional love meant the world to Yadira, allowing her to integrate her sense of being a dutiful "good" daughter and her emerging gay sexuality— fundamental aspects of her identity that she had previously kept separate. This climactic event also taught her how willing people are to offer her support, like the friend who stood with her during her deeply personal disclosure. Restoring her relationship with her mother has been crucial to her development.

Schools Matter

The stories that Yadira projected on the card illustrations through the years have substance and an evolving plot. They illustrate a defining concern with poverty and economic struggles. They also reflect her access to supports and her ability to accept help. During the first year of the study, for example, she interpreted the picture of the boy and the violin in this way:

> The boy is sad because he wants the violin and he can't have it because his parents make very little money. The boy asks God to grant him a wish and that was to get a violin as a present for his birthday. A teacher heard him, and the day of the boy's birthday the teacher gave him a violin as a gift because the boy was one of his best students.

In Yadira's narrative, the boy's wish for a violin is addressed to God, but ultimately a benevolent figure steps in to help: a "teacher heard him." Motivation, determination, the ability to elicit help, and success are themes that recur in all such stories she created during our study.

Yadira attended school in the Dominican Republic until the sixth grade. She recalls a much smaller school where the teachers hit the students. When she arrived in the United States, she was placed in sixth grade again, in a bilingual program at the local middle school where there were many other children from the Dominican Republic. After completing middle school, she transferred to Monroe High School, which is bursting with immigrant students from many countries and has a bilingual program that has helped many students. But this school, in addition to having fewer advantages than other schools in the area, has been significantly affected by violence: Yadira confided to us that students carried firearms and trafficked drugs under the teacher's nose. On her way home, Yadira felt particularly unsafe. Her concern about violence extended beyond the walls of her school and neighborhood, as she reflected: "I do not know what is going to happen to this world—*es muy peligroso* [it is very dangerous]."

Nevertheless, she said: "I like school very much because before I did not have friends to talk to and I did not know English. But now I do. Thanks to God—I never thought I would speak English, but now I do and I am very proud." While she learned English quickly, she still struggles to understand social contexts, like "understanding people, to know whether they were your friends, and what was the meaning of what they did."

Yadira was an excellent student in the Dominican Republic, and her strong engagement with academics continues in the United States. Her grades at Monroe High School are in the A and B range, and she describes herself as an above-average student—though she admits that she can be talkative in class. Her report cards attest to her high achievement and her improvement in grades over time, which become mostly A's with only a rare C in math. Her attendance has also improved each year, and now she rarely misses school. She was initially enrolled in the bilingual program and was gradually moved to English-speaking classes.

Yadira's teachers at Monroe High School speak highly of her abilities and performance, saying she has an excellent understanding of the material. They all consider her a very good student who pays attention in class, is motivated and works hard, asks questions, and has good relationships with teachers. Contact between teachers and Yadira's parents is mostly limited to notes sent home and back to school. Despite Yadira's own concerns about capturing social nuances, one teacher in particular says Yadira has "social know-how" and that her knowledge of "how to use social supports" will take her far. Clearly this teacher has confidence in her. She wrote: "Yadira is very cooperative and her overall behavior is good. She is well motivated and goal-oriented." Yadira appreciates her teachers' support and generally is open to asking for help. But sometimes, she says, teachers snap at her for asking a question. They put her on the spot by saying "I already answered that," and her peers laugh.

Yadira impressed her English teacher, who reported: "Yadira is a bright, enthusiastic, lively and engaged member of her English class. She is always interested in learning and her high level of participation reveals a hardworking and insightful student. She is exceptionally positive, even during stressful times, and she consistently challenges herself. She is an absolute joy to teach!" Her math teacher found Yadira attentive and earnest but believed she felt uncomfortable about asking questions and was considerably anxious. This difference reflects Yadira's attitude toward the two subjects: math is harder for her than English.

The last year of Yadira's involvement in the study marked a crucial turning point in her academic path. When we called her to set up a meeting, she exclaimed: "I have so many things to tell you! My life has changed so much!" When we see her, Yadira tells us that one of her teachers initiated a conversation with her mother, proposing to transfer Yadira to a prestigious private school. The teacher believed that her current high school was not the best place for Yadira and could serve neither her academic nor her emotional needs. Yadira's confusion about her sexual identity had led her to wonder whether something was "wrong." But she felt comfortable approaching this teacher, who assured her that such feelings are to be expected, that it is normal to feel uncertain at times. These conversations were helpful, and Yadira, with the teacher's continued support, sat for an exam and received a scholarship to the private school.

Yadira's move to the new school turned out to be life-changing. She now has access to excellent supports: superb teachers, caring counselors, and understanding peers. Her social horizons have expanded, and she has a girlfriend. She feels she has a different perspective on school and has become "smarter about things." She says she has read more books in one year at her new school than she did the whole time she attended her old school. She has discovered a new love, poetry, which is "a door opened for me." Although the adjustment was hard, especially in math because she has to study more than ever, it has been worth it. The classes are small, and the teachers know her well and care for her. The supports at the new school are, she says radiantly: *"fenomenal!"*

Yadira works much harder now and the fruits of her labor are sweet. She received one of the most prestigious and competitive English awards the school gives. Although she has consistently earned A's in English, surpassing many students who have spoken English all their lives, she was not expecting the honor. In fact, Yadira says, the day of the awards she told her mother that she did not want to go to the ceremony because there would be nothing for her. But the school made a special effort to ensure she would be present by calling her mother ahead of time to let her know that Yadira had won. Mother and daughter attended the ceremony, and both were proud of her accomplishments. "That was one of the happiest days of my life," Yadira later confided.

Yadira feels that her new school is tremendously supportive. She mentions that the school even gave her a laptop computer so she could complete her homework on the train during her long commute to and from school. And one day she could hardly wait to share some amazing news: the school, she said, had promised that if she continued to excel, it would do everything in its power to take care of her "documentation problem." Yadira currently lacks legal residence in the United States, but a number of school administrators, recognizing her abilities and tremendous potential, want to support her entry into college. (Without documentation, it is nearly impossible for a student to wade through the welter of paperwork required for college admission, especially if the student needs financial aid.) While it is possible that some of the well-connected members of the school administration might have the power to help Yadira legalize her status, the school might be creating a hope that could later collapse if the legal procedure does not materialize. In any case, Yadira has real hope that her legal status will not block her path to college, easing a fear that for many other undocumented students has had devastating consequences: when they learn their prospects are nil, they lose their enthusiasm for working hard at school.

Early in the study Yadira informed us that she really wants to play professional basketball but has also considered studying business administration. She later shifts her interests from business and sports to psychology and adds plans to attend graduate school. What remains constant throughout these changing plans and ideas are her unshaken optimism and drive. She has no doubt that she will get into college. It's her priority, and she puts higher education ahead of having a family of her own. Yadira is very grounded and has a clear idea of what she needs to win a college acceptance: good grades, strong SAT scores, meaningful recommendation letters, participation in extracurricular activities, volunteer work, and excellence in sports. She remains acutely aware that her undocumented status is a major obstacle, but she hopes that the help that her school has offered will materialize. She confidently states, "My future is promising." Yadira's self-confidence in school and sports is key to her resilience. Her belief in her abilities, her mother's support, and the extensive resources of her private school have led her to surmount the challenges that have come her way, including the complicated process of clarifying her sexual identity.

A Rainbow of Colors and Identities

Yadira's close friends are mostly African American and Dominican, and she speaks English with all of them. She and her friends share similar tastes in food—"we love pizza"—and in music ("merengue"). She feels supported by her friends; however, the support of her family seems more consistent and important to her. Her mother comes first.

As a darker-skinned Dominican, Yadira experienced the racial and ethnic tensions that dominated the social landscape in Monroe High School. She was especially sensitive to the tensions between Puerto Ricans and Dominicans: her Dominican friends grew angry if she mingled with Puerto

Ricans, and she cringed when her Puerto Rican friends sneered at Dominicans. She said that white students were racist and that Dominicans, especially darker-skinned Dominicans, detested whites. As she moved to the
new private school, these tensions eased.

One aspect of sports that particularly attracts Yadira is the diversity
of the students whom she plays with and against. She finds a sense of belonging and camaraderie in sports, where students of different ethnicities,
races, and nationalities all come together. She feels her teammates are a
major source of support. They love and help each other. But she also mentions some racial distinctions related to sports at her school: for example,
African-American students tend to play basketball, a mixed group plays
volleyball, a lot of Dominicans and some African-American students play
softball, and whites generally do not become involved in sports.

In her new high school, Yadira is involved in other activities besides
sports. "We are working with this club right now for Latino people 'cause
all the ethnic groups at the school had their groups, so we tried to start a
Spanish club," Yadira says. "We had a presentation against violence, we do
field trips, we are going to go hiking . . . I'm excited . . . I love it because I
think it is interesting to try to make something work out for Latinos in the
school. We don't have many opportunities so I want to help to create some
. . . On top of that, it is inspirational. Because if you are doing well and nobody acknowledges it, well, 'I'm not going to do nothing 'cause nobody
cares.' But if you know that someone is looking up to you, you are going to
keep doing good."

At Monroe High School, Yadira was close to the Spanish counselor, who
calls Yadira a "treasure," and to her ESL teacher, who even asked the head
of the ESL program to let Yadira stay in her class to receive extra help
for the state standardized tests. It was this teacher who saw that Yadira
had a potential that the high school simply could not meet; it was she
who helped Yadira apply for a scholarship to the private school. This ESL
teacher was also intimately informed about Yadira's personal situation,
particularly her struggle with her sexual identity and her mother's Catholic
values, a knowledge that reflects Yadira's trust in her. Not surprisingly,
Yadira admires this ESL teacher: "I want to be like her when I grow up.
Well not exactly like her, 'cause I'm my own person, but I would like to
have the same way of seeing things. She is, like, so happy about life."

At the new high school, Yadira has also found support. The teachers and a counselor have helped her significantly. School personnel stood behind her when she disclosed her homosexuality; in particular, the school counselor guided Yadira and talked to her mother about this sensitive family issue. Yadira also speaks of another teacher who has a gay brother; the teacher talked with her many times and made her feel better as she was undergoing important changes in her persona. As mentioned earlier, Yadira has a girlfriend at school, whose picture she gives to us in loving trust.

When Yadira went public about being gay, her friends gathered in the school cafeteria, welcoming her and telling her that they loved her and were proud of her. Yadira had dreaded the idea of "coming out" in her old high school for fear of harassment and even violence. Had she come out there, she says, "They would have stoned me." Yadira is well aware that students in some schools are intolerant and can't deal with ambiguity in sexual identity for either adults or youth, rejecting any periods of confusion. Had Yadira remained in her previous high school, the issue of her sexual identity could have crushed her progress, as it did for one former classmate. Yadira values her lesbian identity and continually searches for information on lesbian support groups and feminist rights.

As one of the few students of color in her new school, Yadira also confronts the complexities of racial and ethnic identities and loyalties. She identifies herself as Dominican, *"cien por ciento"* (100 percent). Her friends are of diverse ethnicities, but when she plays sports, she feels that students see her as "the black girl." This identification makes her uncomfortable because it does not feel genuine; she is dark but she is *"pura Dominicana."* She is proud of her Dominican identity and feels that other people from her country of origin are "great, happy, and smart." She believes Americans, however, think Dominicans are "lazy and stupid," while Dominicans think "Americans are racist."[14] She insists that she has not felt discrimination in her new school but that outside of school it is another matter:

> "Oh, yes, but not in school. We were in the train station, and we got in the train. We were a group of girls; we were going home. And there was this lady, we were, like, talking, loud, hyper or whatever. And she was 'Oh, I don't know why I got on this train. So many Spanish girls here.' And she stood up from her seat, and she looked at us like she was going to hit us. I was like, 'Please, let's be quiet 'cause we don't want any trouble.' And she was [like],

'Oh, you guys don't be quiet, I just want to get out of this train. This is not my day. I hate Spanish kids.' Oh my God, that shocked me. This was last year [in 9th grade], and I still remember."

"How did you feel afterward?"

"That was the first time I felt really discriminated. It wasn't just about that, but she was so loud, other people could hear. And they were, like . . . I don't like people to feel sorry for me. I don't like that at all, and they were all looking at us, and they looked at us as if nothing had happened. But, if we Spanish people were doing that to white people, they wouldn't look like that but maybe call the police. But they didn't mind. Everybody that was there— the majority was white . . . they were laughing. So I never took that train again. I was so shocked that I never took the train again."

Yadira's identity formation has been a complex and sometimes painful process as she has tried to reconcile where she fits sexually and ethnically. But overall, she has achieved a sense of stability, clarity, and confidence: she is a proud, dark, *lesbiana Dominicana* going places.

An Upward Spiral

In spite of the multiple risk factors that could have conspired to work against her, Yadira has thrived as an immigrant. She excels academically, and her college future seems secure, if only her legal status can be resolved. A key factor in her progress has been the bond with her mother, who places a high value on education and is focused on assuring her children's success in school. Yadira's mother keeps a close watch on her but allows enough flexibility so that Yadira can adapt to new environments.

Yadira's own love for studying, inner strength, and endless optimism are also crucial. These attributes endear her to adults and attract their willing support. Without the help of adults such as the Spanish counselor and the ESL teacher at her previous school, Yadira might still be engaged and posi- tive but lack the opportunities and tangible supports she has encountered by switching schools. Her story demonstrates the life-changing influence that adults can have if they take a child under their wing and the child is willing to trust them. It also shows the importance of a positive attitude. People like Yadira, and so feel moved to extend themselves for her.

Yadira's process of clarifying her sexual identity could have been a sig- nificant risk factor had she remained in the homophobic environment of her first high school; fortunately, her new school has accepted her warmly.

Indeed, Yadira's strong academic and athletic identity, and her network of good friends, have anchored her in disorienting times. That her mother overcame the struggle with her own cultural values and fully accepted her daughter as a lesbian has been another key to Yadira's positive development.

Yadira's mother is a resourceful immigrant. She understands that there are "games" to be figured out in this new country, and she has successfully navigated the system. She wants Yadira to change the history of the family by becoming the first to attend college. The family has taken the American paradigm—"you can become anything you want"—and has broken it into realistic, concrete, and pragmatic steps. Unlike other less successful immigrants, who often engage in delusional magical thinking about their future success, Yadira is grounded and realistic about her future. She understands that hard work, luck, and above all, relationships are the key to ensuring success—even as she is aware of the Damocles's sword of legal status hanging over her head.

Parts of Yadira's story read like a fairy tale—a poor, dark-skinned, illegal immigrant receiving an elite private school education—while other parts illustrate the difficulties of her daily life: constant economic worries, a sick sibling who has undergone multiple surgeries, a single mother navigating life in a foreign land. One could expect a pattern of spiraling decline, with accumulating challenges and loss of resources. For Yadira, however, each triumph lays the groundwork for the next phase, and success in one domain or situation propels positive developments in another. For example, her academic standing enabled her to get a scholarship; then the students at her new school accepted her sexual orientation and the administrators proposed to help legalize her immigrant status. For many undocumented youth, being illegal (which is usually an impediment to receiving financial aid for college) saps their determination to achieve. Yadira, however, has reason to hope that this obstacle may be overcome.

One day late in the study, Yadira relates in detail the plot of a book, *The Giver,* that her favorite teacher had recommended. "It is about a Utopia that they try to create," she explains. The Giver is the only one in the community who possesses a full awareness of the world; the others cannot experience emotions and see the world in black and white. The Giver shows the others "all the emotions, all the memories, all the colors, to feel love, to feel desire." Like the Giver, Yadira knows the emotions and colors of a complex identity; unlike others in her situation, she has experienced sadness and struggle but also success, joy, and most importantly, acceptance.

Rosa: ¡Si, Se Puede!

"Si, se puede" translates to "Yes, it can be done," and was the rallying cry of César Chavez, the famous union organizer for immigrant agricultural workers in the United States. For our study participant Rosa, it captures perfectly the determined spirit of the successful immigrant student.

Carrying flowers, posters, and balloons, a happy throng converges at the entrance of the Steeler High School auditorium. Parents, grandparents, sisters, brothers, aunts and uncles, and friends are gathered to celebrate the accomplishments of 402 students, mostly ethnic minorities, who are graduating from high school. As the band plays, the theater fills up, and soon the graduating students file in.

On the stage, seats are reserved for the administration and a select group of five honor students. Rosa, the valedictorian, stands tall and proud among the honorees, her dark vivacious eyes, smooth olive skin, and long jet-black hair gleaming. She delivers the graduation speech in a flawless English, with poise, precision, and wit, enthusiastically encouraging the other students to take the challenge to succeed and make themselves, their families, and their countries proud. The shy and disoriented immigrant child we first met five years earlier—who would venture into the world of English only hesitantly and cautiously, has become a self-possessed, precociously mature young woman on her way to major in engineering at a world-renowned research university with a full four-year scholarship. For some youth, immigration is utopia realized.

After the other graduation speeches, the honor students' names are read. In many urban schools with large minority populations, most of the honor awards go to Asian students, but on this occasion more than half of the awards go to Latino students. In this profoundly disadvantaged high school, in a city that has been rated one of the twenty least safe in the country, a handful of students are realizing their potential despite the huge obstacles in their way.

Rosa is an unusually gifted student who combines perseverance with intelligence, self-confidence, and charm. She is lucky to have a strong family—united, loving, and ambitious—and teachers and counselors who guide and inspire her. She has resourcefully garnered additional support from groups like Upward Bound and Alma Latina, which provided academic assistance, guidance, and information about college entry and financial aid. Rosa's journey demonstrates how supportive networks of relations—familial and communal—can align to help a determined and resourceful young woman achieve her dream.

In the Land of Make-Believe

When Rosa was twelve, her parents gathered their six children in their home in Guadalajara (a city with a hundred-year history of immigration to the United States) to announce a family trip to Disneyland. This was the indirect and ultimately uncomplicated way in which the parents initiated the immigration process for their children. None of the recurring doubts or conflicting emotions that generally accompany such decisions afflicted this family. Leaving home, relatives, and friends failed to spur the usual emotional tidal waves; the trip was framed as a simple family outing to "the land of make-believe." Though the journey started with a fantasy, neither Rosa nor her brothers and sisters seem to resent what others might call a deception. The parents explain that they moved to seek "a better, more tranquil, and more economically secure life" for their family. While the fantasy of the "land of make believe" and a current of optimism have entered the family lore and keep the dreams aloft, the family's expectations and orientation are well grounded in the circumstances of the real world they now face. Rosa's mother grapples with questions about gains and losses, and the whole family levelheadedly takes on the complex challenges they have faced since arriving in the United States.

Before immigration, the parents' impressions of this country came from relatives and from a previous trip north of the border. Soon after their arrival, Rosa's mother recalibrated her expectations: "I already knew that life here would be boring and monotonous." Despite this view, she says that her life is better: "Maybe I have become accustomed, and things have gone well for us. Thank God, since we arrived my husband has had work, and one year after we arrived we could buy a house." The mother's biggest regret is that her children are growing up away from their extended family members, whom she misses very much. Over time we learn that everyone in Rosa's family shares these sentiments; nonetheless, they are willing to endure these losses to give the children "the chance to become bilingual (and) to guarantee they will go to the university." In Mexico, the mother says with a sigh, university admission is difficult and sometimes takes years to accomplish.

Prior to her arrival in the United States, Rosa's knowledge about her future homeland came from movies and television, which she feels glamorized it significantly. "Houses are not as large and beautiful" as she had expected, and she did not "expect to find drugs and gangs in school." But she was pleasantly surprised by the ethnic diversity of her school and the multiple languages spoken by her peers, which endlessly fascinate her. She likes shopping in the mall with her cousins and finds it oppressive to be cooped up in her house because her neighborhood is gang infested and prone to outbreaks of violence. She dislikes the discrimination she perceives both in school and in the community, and is frustrated because she still cannot communicate in English as fluently and effortlessly as she would like. The hardest thing about immigration was leaving her friends, teachers, and school, but given the choice of staying or going back, she "would stay. I have made new friends and adapted to school and life in general."

Today Rosa is a beautiful, poised, and intelligent young woman. In conversation she is respectful and thoughtful, and her responses are often insightful and philosophical. This is not to say she is always easygoing—flashes of temper followed by a warm laugh add to her charm. She complains mildly about having to help with younger siblings, and swears half-jokingly that she will never marry.

All in the Family

Rosa lives with her parents and five of her six siblings in a small, tidy house in a mostly Latino community that is also home to some black families. Well-maintained flowerpots adorn the porch; the garden facing the busy street is well cared for. In the living room, drawings and ceramics done by the children are displayed with pride. Rosa is the second eldest of the six children; she has a brother a year older and a sister a year younger, both in their late teens, and there are a preteen brother and a little brother and sister as well. On many of our visits, tempting aromas emanated from the kitchen along with the happy sounds of mother and children cooking together. Relatives come and go in this house, sometimes just passing by and visiting for a meal, other times spending a few nights. These visits and other family events, which often center around food, allow Rosa to maintain a strong connection with her extended family, but these occasions have become fewer as the family's stay in the United States has lengthened.

During the last year of the study, when we visit the family, we see that they have rearranged the living room. They removed a wall that had separated the kitchen from the living room, making the space larger and lighter and creating room for a large sitting area and a desk with a brand new computer. If these changes mean little in themselves, they point toward a sense of confidence in the moderate accumulation of financial security. The computer station—an investment in the children's education and a tool to connect to the outside world—has replaced the dining-room table, which on our first visit was the center of activity and the hub of family gatherings. Symbolically and practically, education is now at the very center of this family's life.

Rosa's mother and four of her six children are seated in the living room, conversing with ease and warmth. As we chat with the family, the younger children ask to use the computer, and soon Rosa and her older brother leave for the Upward Bound program to which they both belong and have greatly benefited from. Now that Rosa is graduating, she will surrender her place in Upward Bound to her next-youngest sibling, who has waited eagerly to join. This low-income minority program, organized by the local university, prohibits more than two siblings from belonging at the same time.

Rosa's family entered the United States with greater status and more resources than many Mexican migrants. Rosa's mother completed the eleventh grade in Mexico. A vivacious and obviously intelligent woman, she was employed for a while as a secretary but eventually the family was able to invest its savings in buying a pharmacy—a business she operated until migration. Today, she works as a janitor. For her, migration has been a huge loss in status. During an early conversation, we learn that Rosa's mother works from 5 P.M. to 2 A.M. so that she can be with the children during the day, when she also tries to take a nap. On most days, the children have cleaned the kitchen and tidied the living room by the time she awakens from her rest. Rosa's mother is proud that Rosa is doing well academically but worries that she seems so pressured by all the deadlines she must meet before graduation. In addition, while they are proud of Rosa's achievements, they are a bit overwhelmed by the college offers, applications, invitations, and scholarships she has received.

Rosa's father reached the thirteenth grade (equivalent to the first year in university) while in Mexico, where he later worked in commerce. Today, he also works as a janitor at the nearby university and recently took on a second job to supplement the family's income. Rosa and her siblings have pleaded with him to stay home—"We tell him we need our Papi more than clothes and outings," she says. Her father suffers from back problems that forced him to be on disability for a period of time, and they fear that he is exhausting himself.

The family is Catholic and attends Mass every Sunday. Their religiosity is part of the parents' larger moral project of raising their children. They hold to the belief that they must raise children who are *bien educados*. Unlike the meaning of an educated person in the United States, which implies diplomas and tangible skills, in this family *ser educado* also refers to leading a moral, well-mannered, and good life.

During the last year of the study, we ask Rosa,

> "In Mexico, how would most people describe a good girl?"
>
> "That she should be uncomplicated, and like the nursery rhyme says, 'she should know how to sew, how to embroider' . . . and also be studious and religious."
>
> "How important is it for you to meet these expectations?"
>
> "Very important . . . and I come pretty close."

Rosa shares with us that her most important source of social support comes from her family, both immediate and extended. Asked about her social networks, she presents a long list of people who talk with her about her future and encourage her, and says she feels responsible to this large group. Unlike many immigrant children, her entire immediate family came to the United States intact, preserving its strong cohesion. They stay connected with their extended family, both in the United States and in Mexico. The family radiates a sense of confidence that they can rely on one another. Rosa willingly seeks help from others and is happy to offer it as well. She is close to her parents and freely asks their advice. For her, a "good family" is one that is "united, in communion with one another, where parents understand their children, and the children do their best to please the parents." Her parents, she confides, "want the best for me, they protect me, and watch that nothing bad happens to me"; she has "the best of mothers" and "the best of fathers," although she wishes "that they gave me more freedom and let me have more friends." She shows her love for them by "doing chores, telling them I love them, and getting good grades." Rosa's older brother and cousin are strong role models, and she admires them for their determination to excel and the encouragement they offer her. In turn, she feels she must be a role model for her younger siblings, although she can become annoyed if she feels they overwhelm her.

For her *quinceañera* (fifteenth birthday), a rite of passage celebrated for Mexican girls, Rosa was given the opportunity to go back to Mexico for a visit. While in many immigrant families being sent back to the country of origin is a correctional strategy used to punish bad behavior, in Rosa's case the visit was framed as a reward for her achievement in school. While there, she reconnected with relatives with whom she had been close before leaving Guadalajara. These renewed bonds have strengthened her desire to maintain a positive and proud identity as a high-achieving *Mexicana*.

Thriving in a Toxic School

Rosa attended school in Guadalajara until the sixth grade and fondly remembers her teachers and fellow students there. She describes that school as more demanding in terms of homework and behavior and more attractive than the neighborhood middle school where she entered seventh grade in the United States. From there Rosa went on to Steeler High School, one of the poorest and most troubled high schools in the city, one where racial tension, gangs, and violence regularly disrupt the school day. The police patrol daily. Metal detectors flank the entrance. Rosa has had teachers who are burned out and sometimes disparaging; one told Rosa's class that the students are "animals," an insult that she found incomprehensible. Yet during our visits to this school, we have also met dedicated educators who are trying to reverse its deplorable reputation. In addition, the school offers services to help students reach their goals, though the students have to seek them out.

By all measures, Rosa is an outstanding student, persevering and focused. Like many of the other high-achieving students in our study, Rosa is well grounded, aware of the challenges she faces, and not at all prone to the magical thinking about easy success that seduces so many immigrant students who are otherwise struggling. As she humbly notes: "I'm a good student. I study for my exams and turn in my homework on time. That is all. You have to work hard." She is nearly a straight-A student, having only received two B's during her entire high school career. She earned her A's in challenging college-preparatory courses such as Latin, chemistry, algebra II, and various Advanced Placement courses. Yet Rosa continues to struggle on standardized English-language proficiency measures. After four years in the country, her standard English score was in the eighth percentile rank, increasing to the 34th percentile two years later.[15] Rosa struggles with her written assignments and she finds standardized tests especially challenging. Her determination is evident as she reflects, "Most [other students] think that the people that don't know English lack possibilities. It is up to us to show them that we can learn as well as the others."

This determination and self-direction are vividly illustrated by her success in organizing an advanced physics course at her high school after finding out that she needed the credits to be accepted at the college she had chosen. Together with another Latino student, Rosa contacted a nearby university and arranged to have an instructor sent to the high school to teach the physics course. Rosa and her friend negotiated two hours a week of free tutoring and weekly trips to the university's laboratories for additional lab work.

We visit Rosa during her calculus II course. The atmosphere of the classroom is both productive and focused, yet relaxed. The ten girls and four boys work together in small groups to solve complicated problems, periodically getting up to consult reference books or to ask assistance from the teacher. Rosa is actively engaged, surrounded by a close-knit group of girls who have been together in the most advanced classes offered at the school: calculus, Latin, and college physics. They form part of a select group of stellar students that is largely self-reliant and self-directed. Their conversations are lively as they exchange cooking recipes, decode math formulas, work on complicated physics problems, and brainstorm about their futures. This is a "sorority" bound by both heart and intellect.

Rosa's teachers in eleventh grade gave her glowing reports. Her chemistry teacher exclaimed: "Excellent! Rosa is a hard worker, who contributes in class and helps others," giving her high marks all around. Her counselor said simply, "We need more like her."

Rosa is a firecracker—active, alert, and busy. She is a teacher's aide for one of the Spanish teachers. She attends tutoring sessions run by one local college and participates in two after-school college-pathway support groups (Alma Latina and Upward Bound), where she spends approximately six hours a week and has become a group leader and counselor. Over time, the director of the Upward Bound program, which is sponsored by a local university, has become her mentor, tutor, and friend. Somehow, Rosa finds time to work sixteen hours a week in the mall bakery, volunteer at a convalescent home, and tutor other children. Unlike many of our study participants, Rosa has plentiful sources of information about how to move on to college. The Upward Bound tutors, her counselor, and her teachers all take a special interest in her. Her older brother, whom she admires, is a college student who has figured out a path to college acceptance and guides Rosa along it. She wants to become an architect or engineer, and her parents wholly support her goals. She is optimistic, completing the sentence "My future will be . . ." with the word "brilliant!"[16]

Rosa has many friends in school, drawn mostly from the Latino population, in particular students from El Salvador and Mexico; some are recent immigrants, and others have lived in the United States all their lives. Although they can communicate in English, they often choose to speak in Spanish. During recess and lunchtime, they congregate in areas they consider "theirs" and rarely mingle with the rest of the students. After five years in the study, Rosa has expanded her circle of friends to include Asians, whites, and African Americans. Though friendly with them, she confides that she can't count on them regarding school matters because she is much more intensely engaged in her academic work than most of her peers. Now a senior and in the fifth year of our study, she sees the picture of the girl with the books looking over a farm and says:

> This is the story of two good friends, Rosalinda and Ana. Rosalinda liked parties and dancing. Ana liked school and family. When they grew up, Rosalinda fell in love with a handsome man and left home without finishing her studies. Ana was sad. She could no longer share as much with her friend because she was so busy working, plowing and doing heavy chores.
> Rosalinda got pregnant, had children and her life did not change. Ana graduated from the university and now works in computers—no longer doing strenuous work.

In this narrative, two life paths are contrasted, and a choice has to be made. One involves relying on a man for support, the other is centered on hard work, independence, and education. The girl who took the path of immediate gratification came to a dead end, while the one who focused on hard work ended up with a better life.

Rosa is well liked by her peers and was elected "Queen of the Snow Ball." At the Snow Ball, the entire high school votes for princesses, from among whom the queen is elected. The school has celebrated this event for many years and, in spite of its gendered implications, it showers great prestige on its winners. The Snow Queens from each city high school compete for the final title. In her practical way, Rosa says the competition was fun but also a lesson in the value of preparation. For the citywide competition, she reflects with both maturity and meta-cognitive awareness, she did not prepare extensively or polish her speech enough. Other contestants, she added, had better answers for the judges, and one of the other girls won the final title. "I should have prepared better," she concludes.

Rosa is proud in a matter-of-fact way about her Mexican identity, though she moves confidently between spheres that require a Latina or a mainstream persona. Though Rosa is reticent about her experiences of prejudice and discrimination, she is skeptical about Americans' perceptions of Mexicans. "They think we are ignorant," she says—an awareness that only intensifies her desire to succeed. She defines a successful person as one who "applies herself or himself in his studies, stays away from drugs, worries about her family, and remembers her roots." That this personal code guides her life is evident in nearly all our conversations and exchanges with Rosa over the years.

In Rosa's worldview, success comes only with effort and considerable determination. When in the first year of our study she was asked to explain the picture of the boy with the violin, she offered this narrative:

> The story is of a boy that had a hard exam in school, and he failed because he did not want to study at all. His parents got very angry. He went back to the teacher for a new opportunity. This time he studied very hard and passed the exam.

Rosa's response to this image reveals some concerns with adequacy that must have been on her mind at that point (soon after her own migration to the United States). With the guidance and pressure of her parents, the help of her teachers, and her own hard work, she, like the boy in her imagined story, eventually achieved resounding success.

Rosa's family arrived in the United States in search of a fantasy but found a reality that, while challenging, has been worth the sacrifice, family members say. A large family with six children, they made the journey intact. Although they live in a dangerous city and have experienced some downward social mobility, subsisting on two janitorial salaries, her parents stay positive by focusing on their children's futures. The parents accept their losses. They acknowledge that they have not learned the English language beyond the level needed for "getting by." They long for their extended family in Mexico and suffer from a sense of cultural dislocation. Nonetheless, they view their sacrifices as worthwhile given the opportunities they have afforded their children.

Gradual cultural changes in Rosa's family occur over the years of our study: less and less time is spent preparing dinner as a family, less time is spent with the children at night, a new computer sits proudly in the living room, an SUV is parked in the driveway, and eventually the two older children scatter to different universities. The children are busier than ever, always studying or doing homework with their tutors. The family has weathered these transformations without relinquishing its Mexican identity and family closeness, values dear to them. This pattern of migration assumes sacrifices from the parents as well as a compensatory sense of obligation and responsibility from the children. Rosa's dreams for the future are, in part, relationally defined: "I want to graduate from college. I wish that my parents would work less, that there is less violence, less corruption, and no discrimination. I want to help them in the future."

In the years since her migration, Rosa has metamorphosed from a shy and disoriented newcomer to a confident freshman engineering major at a research university known the world over for its Nobel Prize winners in multiple disciplines; from a timid middle-school student whose ability to speak English was frustratingly limited to a highly accomplished mathematician. Rosa has been intent on succeeding, and over time she has developed a strong work ethic with extensive leadership and organization skills. She rarely accepts defeat or takes no for an answer. She has excelled in a school that can easily be described as one of the most toxic and chaotic in the nation.

Rosa's story is one of a balanced life, filled with like-minded friends, family, work, volunteering, and high standards of academic work. She remains positive about her future, motivated and supported by mentors and tutoring programs that have shown her the way. The family's bonds have been preserved, in sharp contrast to the experience of many other new-comer families, in which alienation of the children from the parents is a sad byproduct of the cultural dislocations all migrants experience. In Rosa's case, immigration has not only been a positive experience but also has elements of poetic justice: Rosa is now majoring in engineering at the same university where her father works as a janitor.

Li: Good Fortune and Hard Work

Li, a tall, thin seventeen-year-old with short hair; sincere, attentive eyes; and an air of serious purpose, is now a senior at a highly coveted high school. In the school newspaper office, where Li is editor, talking is difficult. Twenty-five students rush for deadlines, shouting their opinions about the next issue over the hum of fifteen computers. Dressed in the collegiate-style garb that most boys at his school favor—loose khakis, polo shirt, sneakers—Li is carrying a new trophy, the "Coach Award" for excellence. As he sets it down, a student tosses a manuscript in front of Li and asks him to edit it; without looking, Li puts it aside and returns to focus on our conversation despite the distractions. He seems almost contemplative, pausing slightly before each response, choosing his words carefully, and only occasionally smiling. He moves smoothly between Mandarin and English, demonstrating his mastery of both languages. He speaks accent-less English and a refined Chinese that reflects his privileged urban origins. Since the start of the study, Li has come across as serious, bright, curious, ambitious, and armed with the self-confidence needed for success in this country. Now, five years later—and eight years after his immigration into the United States—he is living up to his parents' and teachers' high expectations.

Li's family immigrated to the United States from China, where his mother managed the technology wing of a state enterprise and his father was a professor. Both of Li's parents have doctoral degrees; together, they earn more than $80,000 a year, far more than other families in our sample. Li's father had hoped that his immigration would advance his career, but while he teaches at a prestigious university, he confides that the family's social status is lower here than it was in China—over the years he has come to feel that as a Chinese immigrant he is mostly "invisible."

The family lives in a large suburban house in a middle-class neighborhood with a negligible crime rate. Most of their neighbors are white Americans; only about 5 percent are Asian. Li's family feels safe and has never witnessed violence in the community.

Like many Chinese couples who started families during the era of the Chinese government's single-child policy, Li's parents have no other children. Indeed, Li is the focus of his parents' considerable hopes and ambitions. When we first met the family, shortly after migrating, both Li and his parents reported that they were happy with their relationship. Their energies were focused on one another, and they shared the goal of high accomplishment for each family member. The parents felt that Li communicated readily with them, sharing most of his concerns and troubles. Likewise, Li said that his parents were his role models and that he wanted to be like them. He admired their good jobs and financial stability and, above all, "their moral characters," which he saw as the most important thing he could take from them. "I wish they could become younger, because I want to stay with them as long as possible," he said in the first year of the study. At that point, he wanted to spend more time with his parents: "I want them to learn swimming so that they can swim with me. I want them to take care of themselves more, not only think of me."

Over time, however, a sense of estrangement emerged. Now, at the end of the study, the father says sorrowfully, Li avoids his parents. They ask him daily about school, and he responds tersely. Everything the parents discuss with Li seems to become a point of contention, from what to have for dinner to where to go for summer vacation. "If I would say rice [for dinner]," his father explains, "he would say dumplings, and, if I would say dumplings, he would say rice. It's like this adolescent psychology that I do not understand. So, in the end, we just stop discussing things. Whenever there is a choice, he would disagree with you." His father sees the influence of American parent-adolescent relationships, but he feels confused and helpless at the threshold of the world his son has entered—one where the brand names and clothing styles are organized in a incomprehensible status system, where no one is allowed to touch Li's things, and where Li feels no need to explain his thoughts, feelings, or decisions. "Now he does not want to communicate with us—[not about] many important or deep things, the values, how should a person live his life, et cetera. He doesn't want to talk to us. I think with friends he probably talks about [these issues]. He used to be little and that was fine, but now there is just not much that we can discuss, even like things and people in school, he does not want to talk and we do not know." Li, however, attaches little importance to his changed relationship with his parents. He takes for granted that there will always be cultural frictions between them. His actions now seem to be influenced by the behaviors of his American peers, although he says that ultimately he prefers the Chinese rules and follows his parents' logic.

Li has a tight-knit extended family and is particularly close to his four grandparents. Of their most recent visit, he admits: "When they left, I cried." His paternal and maternal grandparents make him feel loved and accepted, and he visits them in China and they visit him in the United States. The family keeps up with relatives and friends back in China through letters, phone calls, and weekly e-mails. They also see his uncle's family and the friends they have made in the United States, getting together with them for long weekends or parties every other month, more often during the summer and holidays. And unlike many other immigrant families, Li's parents socialize with American colleagues at least a couple of times a year.

Always at the Top

Li's school is one of the oldest and most highly respected public high schools in the United States, with a program that would be the envy of many a suburban school district. Entry is based on a competitive exam and students' grade-point averages. Founded in the seventeenth century, the school has a college matriculation rate of 99 percent and a dropout rate of only 0.2 percent. The school fosters partnerships with museums, universities, hospitals, and businesses. It offers alumni mentoring programs—its Alumni Hall of Fame features world-famous writers and musicians and five signers of the Declaration of Independence—after-school tutoring, and a Saturday "success school" for additional tutoring. In front of the entrance stands a classical statue that represents the "goodness of knowledge," flanked by long, colorful posters that say "Welcome Parents" in English and "Welcome" in Chinese, French, Spanish, and seven other languages.

The school occupies a spacious four-story building. On a typical day, students stroll through the halls in twos and threes. Many Asian students walk with white or black students, suggesting that the school is well integrated. Occasional fights between students from this school and students from other schools have received media attention, but violence, drugs, and weapons are rarely an issue here.

Calls to honor and a respect for order are evident everywhere. On nearly every wall, the "Honor Code Pledge" is posted: "I pledge to uphold the school values of honor and integrity. I will not lie, cheat, plagiarize, or steal. I know that if I violate this honor code, I will be disciplined according to school policy." The instruction seems traditional: in every classroom, often crowded with thirty or more students, the teacher stands at the front, sometimes at a podium, and the students sit at desks, row upon row. In most classrooms, teachers lecture or students sit quietly, working alone. Other students complain of constant stress in this high-pressure academic environment, but Li praises the school and seems to handle its demands effortlessly (though he mentions one stellar student who committed suicide earlier in the year). He lauds the opportunities for internships and jobs in interesting places. He likes the new addition with its large, light-filled rooms. The English and math departments are good, he says in his precise manner, "but science is a bit weaker . . . the scientific equipment and books are really decrepit, and some of the teachers, . . . they feel maybe too passionate about something, so they can't take any criticism."

He sees other weaknesses. He thinks the school's reputation for high scores on state tests rests on past glories and that some of its extracurricular activities are underfunded.

The school's size is another problem. It has 2,400 students, and when he first arrived, Li says, he felt disconnected. "Teachers and administrators are somewhat distant to the students," he says. "It's a huge school, so they really do not give younger students any special attention. They give most of their attention to seniors, especially in the earlier part of the year, at their busiest time for college applications . . . I rarely see an administrator talk to a younger student as they do to an older student." Li has found that he does best when he relies on himself. During his senior year he told us: "The teachers don't like to answer questions, so I read the books one more time to try to solve the problems. I asked them several times but I found that was not helpful, so I stopped asking them. Every time they would say, 'I only have 15 minutes, I have to go soon.' So they don't want to answer any questions at all."

Li has always been an excellent student. In China, where he completed the equivalent of elementary school, he was named class monitor and chosen to carry the national flag at school ceremonies, an honor he recalls with fond pride and sees as an emblem of his Chinese identity. Li has been the top student in his class since he arrived in the United States, including at his current high school. In fact, he has earned virtually all A's for the past four semesters. Because of the school's high standards, his father says proudly, "less than ten out of three thousand students there are receiving such good grades in the whole school every semester." Li's strong grades are even more impressive given that he is taking a demanding college-track course load. Math is his strongest subject, but he finds that "English is the most challenging and most rewarding because it feels very good to write a good essay."

Destined to Be a Doctor?

Both of Li's parents have been deeply involved in his education. This was particularly true during the first years after his arrival. Li's father stresses the importance of parents' obtaining information on exams, schools, and other topics related to their children's education. He notes that America offers many opportunities and resources that are hidden from the public; as a result, many Chinese immigrant parents are unaware of what is available. He networks actively, looks up information, solicits it from friends, and organizes Chinese immigrant parents' groups to share information on the American school system and Chinese students' performance in it.

Li's father also takes an active role in Li's day-to-day academic work. He motivates his son and secures for him a wide range of resources and services rather than working with him on specific assignments or homework. When Li was in middle school, however, he did intervene directly, removing Li from a bilingual program. He felt that the program was teaching superficially in Chinese and impeding Li's speedy acquisition of English. In general, however, Li's father feels that the schools block parents from having a direct influence:

> Although [this high school] is a very good school, for its teaching method it
> is somewhat like a Chinese one, they actually don't encourage communica-
> tion between teachers and parents. The communication must go through a
> liaison. The teachers rush out of school as soon as the classes are over. There
> are parent-teacher meetings, but they don't answer your questions . . . Par-

ents are in one class for five minutes. Then move to another class . . . So I believe that it mainly depends on individual students themselves to do well at school . . . I think it is appropriate for me to express my concerns to the teachers, but I don't do that very often. There are two reasons for this: First, my child is doing very well in school; second, I feel that it won't make any difference if I express my concerns. So I just give up. Expressing concerns to the school might be useful. But I never think of trying to do so. They have their own ways of teaching, and it's been like this for many years. They won't listen to what you want to say at all.

When Li first came to the United States, his father bought him books and other materials on English, math, and Western culture. His mother has long helped him with math and science, giving him problems to solve that are more difficult than those assigned at school. Both parents keep a close eye on Li's studies, spending at least an hour with him daily. When Li gets a less-than-satisfactory grade—meaning below an A—his parents sit down with him, try to figure out the reason, and then help him. For example, his father identified science vocabulary as one of Li's weaknesses. While Li knew many concepts in Chinese, his father felt he had not learned them in English, and so he subscribed to the Discovery Channel and took Li to the library and borrowed many science books for him to read.

Overall, Li appreciates his parents' involvement in his education. His self-confidence is high, but he also knows that his parents will step in if needed, which makes his perception that teachers are unwilling to give extra help easier to bear: "I don't need help. If I needed help, my Mom can help me in science and my Dad can help me in math and history." He likes that his parents push him to work hard and manage his time effectively: "They always push me. Although I don't like it at the moment, it's good for my future." And yet he does feel pressured by their expectations: "They want me to have all A's all the time." He says he cannot afford to get a B; a B would kill his chances of getting into a great college. During the first year of the study, when we asked him to tell a story about the picture of the boy with the violin, this dynamic emerges:

> The child's parents wanted him to learn violin. He was very happy in the beginning and wanted to learn. So he participated in violin class at his school. He practiced and practiced then he hurt his hands. His parents still wanted him to practice. He couldn't bear it anymore. He was very angry in the pic-

ture because he wanted to stop but his parents didn't think so. He thought about it, realizing that it could be helpful for him if he learned the violin. He then continued to practice.

Going to college is now the chief goal for both Li and his parents. There has never been a moment's doubt that university is his destiny. Li's list of choices consists of elite Ivy League schools and highly prestigious technology institutes. Midway through the study, he was quite certain that he wanted to become an ophthalmologist. In his senior year, however, his interests have shifted, and other fields—especially politics and economics—now intrigue him. His father sees this change as evidence of his friends' influence. Now Li says that he is fascinated by "the stability effect of real estate on American economics, especially after the terrorist act [of September 11, 2001]. People are relocating to find new jobs, and this exchange of housing is positive to the market, not only sales, but also agents, contractors, architects. Everyone benefits." Li shifts among his newly emerging interests—social science, business, journalism—and what his parents see as his irrevocable path: natural science and eventually medical school. "My mother says, 'You have to be a doctor, doctor, doctor.' She always tries to get around the issue and would say 'I'm not forcing you to be a doctor, but other professions aren't as secure' or, 'you won't be ashamed if you're not a doctor, but you won't make as much money.'" To satisfy both himself and his parents, he plans to pursue a double major in biology and management, a compromise that leaves both doors open. Taking on this double task will require considerable extra work.

Li's extraordinary motivation translates into a high level of behavioral engagement: he sticks to the tasks he's expected to complete, both within and outside of school. A member of the National Honor Society, he spends about three hours every day on homework. His teachers think highly of him. His biology teacher says Li has a "very positive attitude and behavior—doing very well." His teachers say he does an "excellent" job of understanding class material, as well as reading and speaking in English. He identifies his guidance counselor as an important adult in his life; this counselor has explained the steps Li must follow to win acceptance at a competitive college.

When we gave Li the Bilingual Verbal Abilities Test (BVAT) after he had been in this country for six years, his verbal ability (English and Chinese combined) was in the 99th percentile. When compared with native English speakers at his age level, even his English-language proficiency was considered far superior.[17] Li is one of the few students in our study who is as proficient in English as in his native language and for whom English is not a barrier to academic pursuits.

As a result of Li's persistence and determination, he was accepted to both of his top-choice colleges. He has chosen to attend a top technology institute that he considers "more serious"; he learned that 57 percent of the students in the freshman chemistry class at this institution failed last year, while at the Ivy League school where his father teaches, 90 percent of the students graduate with honors. His college acceptances have not alleviated the pressure, however. Everyone in the freshman class of his selected school, according to Li, received virtually perfect scores on the math SAT; therefore, another test awaits, which will further rank those students according to their mathematical proficiency. He admits that choosing which college to attend was a struggle, but he allows himself to take pleasure in the fact that he could reject the Ivy League university that his high school peers most often select as their top choice. As a sort of compromise, after he is done with his undergraduate degree, Li plans on attending either the business school or the medical school at the Ivy League university where his father teaches.

Pragmatically Choosing Activities and Relationships

Unlike many immigrant students who stick to their old ways of studying in the United States—a narrow focus on academics, with little thought for other activities—in high school Li pays close attention to his engagement in extracurricular pursuits. Shortly after migrating, Li noted that in the United States "it is not enough to only rely on the school . . . [M]agazines for gifted talented students . . . tell you what books to read, how to choose a college and how to prepare . . . [It is important to be] involved in not only many, but different kinds of extracurricular activities—volunteering job, sport team, music, student government, and something like premed and writing for the newspaper."

Li's engagement with school certainly extends beyond his coursework. His list of extracurricular activities is almost exhausting to hear, and he sees all of them as directly related to his successful college application. He

represented the state at the Math Olympics, was captain of the school ten-
nis team, played basketball, played violin in the school string ensemble,
volunteered at the Red Cross, held summer internships in the governor's
office, worked as an editor on the school newspaper, and tutored other students after school. In one discussion when he was a junior, he explained
how he fits everything in his day:

> "Li, what is something that you are currently learning or thinking about
> that you find really interesting?"
>
> "I'm working right now at the dental school. We are trying to find the
> gene responsible for a [facial disease]. It causes excessive viral tissue to grow
> where your normal healthy bone cells should be, so your face ends ups look-
> ing a little bit weird."
>
> "How long have you been doing this?"
>
> "I started last year and I continued this summer. During the summer I
> worked 40 hours a week."
>
> "What about weekends—how do you spend your weekend?"
>
> "Saturday morning, I practice tennis or I have a tournament somewhere.
> And then in the afternoon, when my parents go shopping, I finish up on
> whatever schoolwork is left over and do some SAT prep by myself. And then
> I might go to the movies with my friends. On Sunday I sleep late. In the
> morning I read the papers online and in the afternoon I watch some sports
> on TV."
>
> "Do you like [playing tennis]?"
>
> "[I do]. I get good exercise. It keeps me healthy, and it gives me a good
> chance to practice my leadership skills with some of the younger players,
> and then the older players can give me advice on how to play and how to
> deal with college."

Unlike many immigrant students from China who mainly have Chinese
friends, Li has a thoroughly mixed group of companions, both girls and
boys and from a variety of ethnic backgrounds. Like Li's approach to extracurricular activities, this is a strategic decision: Li considers it important
for his future to have friends from different ethnic backgrounds, to develop
an "outgoing character," and to get along with everyone. Li's friends are
among the school's top students. Some have already graduated and now attend Ivy League schools. Not surprisingly, these friendships can be somewhat competitive: "When I get a good grade, my friends get jealous, but
then they get over it," Li says. When friends are discussed in more depth,
however, Li cannot name anyone from school with whom he feels really

close, and he frequently stresses his self-reliance. He rarely shares problems or concerns: "I don't tell my problems to anyone because I can solve them myself. Most of my problems are about balancing the schedule between school, work and play." He says he does not trust people with his secrets because "they talk too much to each other." While he is popular in school and has many acquaintances, intimate peer friendships seem to be missing from his life.

Pressure remains a constant over the years. During the last year of the study, when we ask "How would your life be different if you were a girl?" he answers that he would have less pressure. Rather than meaning pressure from parents, Li means social pressure from other boys. "[If I were a girl,] I wouldn't feel as many pressures from other people from the same gender. Boys are more likely to single out and make fun of those who do not fit the perception of 'coolness.' Say there is a school dance. It is socially acceptable for a girl to go by herself. However, if a boy went alone, other boys would call him gay. It happens everywhere."

At the start of the study, Li found it challenging to be on good terms with everyone at school because he felt some people were arrogant and looked down on China. "I think the American bombing of the Chinese embassy in Belgrade was intentional," he said then. "I'm angry when I listen to this kind of news. They don't know the truth. This affects my relationship with my American classmates since they are too busy to talk about this in school. It's only at home that I talk about it. My parents don't feel as strongly as I do about the issues. I can be mad in my heart, but can't show it outside. Otherwise you can't make friends with Americans."

During the last year of the study, Li notes that Chinese people face discrimination throughout the United States: "Chinese have fewer opportunities than Americans. Chinese have to try harder, because there are only a few positions available to Chinese." But Li also believes that Chinese people have "a lot more opportunities" in the United States than do the non-Chinese, because "the Chinese families are more forceful in their child's getting ahead—the strong backbone motivation." When we ask what he would tell others about discrimination, Li said, "Ignore it, because you're probably better than whoever discriminates against you."

Li retains a strong ethnic Chinese identity even after living in the United States for almost a decade and despite his many friends from different ethnic backgrounds—with whom he speaks mostly English, but sometimes also Spanish. It is much more important for him to celebrate Chinese holidays than American ones. He puts a high value on meeting the Chinese standards for being a good son—even, paradoxically, as his father reports that Li has become increasingly distant from his parents. Early on, he framed his drive for success around the ultimate purpose of returning to China, which he saw as having a brighter future than the United States: "I want to go to college in America and then go back to China. American universities are better than those in China. America as a country is deteriorating—too much crime, the government officials don't care about the people. They are only concerned with their positions. On the contrary, China is getting better and better. It's safer there. Its technology is also developing." He also said: "China will develop faster in the future, for example by 2050. China will have all the technologies like here. I think China will be better then the U.S. There is a 50 percent chance for me to go back to live in China in the next 10 to 20 years." He contrasted the active economic growth of China with the poverty, "garbage," crime, and stagnation in his view of the United States.

More recently, Li's attitudes have shifted, and currently he feels that the United States is more like home for him because he has spent more time here, he is now a citizen, and his English has improved. Li's larger world—TV, radio, magazines—exists almost exclusively in English, although he continues to speak Mandarin "80 percent" of the time at home with his parents. The hardest thing about living in America now, Li says, is "listening to Americans saying bad things about the Chinese government." His parents, Li notes, have contributed to his strong Chinese identity through the language and culture they share with him, but independently he has developed an interest in Chinese politics. Li's advice to someone coming from China would be: "Life is faster here. People may seem rude, but that is the way they are. Do not be intimidated, try new things, but retain your traditional values, because values are more fragile than any superficial goods."

A Convergence of Good Fortune and Hard Work

Li is the archetype of the "model minority": the über-achieving, highly motivated Chinese student so typical of the American portrayal of Asian immigrants. His highly educated, highly skilled parents support his every academic need, presenting a coherent belief system about the importance of education, which Li readily makes his own. Li's is a journey through the intense pressures that drive ambitious newly arrived immigrant youth to succeed in American schools. His obvious intelligence, internalized drive to succeed, hard work, and ability to forge useful relationships converge to help him realize his ambitions.

Often ignored in this utopian view of Chinese immigrants' adaptation is escalating alienation within the family, which affects Chinese families more than those from other countries. Li's father is deeply saddened by his declining ability to communicate with Li, and he struggles to articulate his sense of the loss of intimacy and rapport with his son. As is typical of Chinese families with an only child, Li is the center of his parents' lives and ambitions, particularly because they feel that they have made sacrifices in their professional careers to offer better opportunities for their son. It pains Li's parents not to be able to talk to Li as before and to see him drift away from the family. We are reminded of the old Chinese adage "be careful what you wish for." Immigrant parents will their ambition to their children, whose very success ironically removes them from the intimacy of the family.

For Li, however, being his parents' child is only one aspect of his busy persona, which now includes preparing for college and new horizons. He appears more concerned about his relations with his peers at school, managing his complex after-school activities, and his decision about which school to attend than with his parents' sadness about losing their close relationship with him.

For all of Li's admirable accomplishments, there is, as in every immigrant story, an inescapable element of loss. This poignancy is captured metaphorically in a short narrative that Li tells in the fifth year of the study about the picture of the boy and the violin:

> James' parents are both world-renowned musicians. Even though he has no natural talent himself, they coerced him into playing the violin. Today his instructor gave him a very difficult piece to play and he failed miserably doing so. Now he is contemplating his future, staring deep into the bridge of the violin asking it [for] hard answers it cannot produce. Later, he approaches his parents to have a family discussion about this. Although reluc-

tant, they come to the conclusion that it's best for James to concentrate on what he feels he can do well rather than something that his parents want him to.

This vignette reveals themes that have come to characterize Li's social world and his academic ambitions since arriving in the United States. In this story, as in his real life, the parental figures are world-renowned professionals who are highly demanding and expect their son to excel. Li describes "James" as being in a contemplative mood, reflecting about his future and unable to find the answers he longs for. The boy has the strength of will to initiate a family discussion about the pressure of his parents' demands. The way the tension is resolved in this narrative task illuminates themes central to understanding Li's adaptation to the new country and what he wants from his own parents: the parents in the vignette come to see that James needs to do "what he feels he can do well instead of something his parents want him to do."

For Li, finding the answers in his real life is a double task. Li not only does what his parents wish, but also explores his own evolving interests. It's a common dilemma of growing up American in a Chinese family: conflicting expectations from his parents and peers about his future, as well as the tug of his own disparate desires. His parents assume that he will study natural sciences and become a medical doctor. High school has exposed him to other fields and his interests have changed, but he mixes his latest ideas with the original plan, integrating old and new. He negotiates over his father's dream that Li attend the university where the father teaches by planning to attend graduate school there. He bolsters his argument for attending the technological institute by deploying the family's narrative of hard work and excellence, showing them that the school he chose is even more demanding and has a higher failure rate than his father's university. He honors his mother's dream that he become a "doctor, doctor, doctor" by planning a double major, sticking with premed biology while pursuing his nascent interest in business and social science. Although it requires a phenomenal effort, Li searches for compromise and integration, attempting to satisfy both his parents and himself.

Li follows a path so strictly oriented to Ivy League success that any diversion is unthinkable. He has internalized his parents' achievement motivation—his actions manifest this drive unwaveringly—yet ambivalence and internal conflict emerge in Li's picture-based narratives, such as this one he wrote in the fifth year of our study (while contemplating the picture of the girl gazing over a field with an armful of books):

> There were two sisters growing up together. When it was their teenage years, one decided to go to college, and the other decided to work on a farm. This sister had to wear a school uniform and study all day long. The other sister wore beautiful clothes, rode on the horse, went to different places, and made money by working on the farm. This sister (in uniform) envied the other sister very much. However, she felt that studying was more useful and she could contribute to the world. So she continued to study.

On one level, Li is paradigmatically "compelled to excel" and unfaltering in his dedication to attaining exceptional educational success.[18] On another level, however, swirling currents of desire and curiosity buffet him. He lives with the pull of his tenacious academic drive and yet he hankers for spontaneity, for the freedom to let the current take him to unforeseen landings.

Li has had at his disposal optimal resources for academic success—highly educated and successful parents who know the university system well and ample economic resources that have given him access to educational opportunities that are unavailable to families that are less well off. These resources, coupled with Li's intelligence, flexibility, and drive for success, place him at a considerable advantage over other immigrant youth. While others see studying as the only way out of their life circumstances, Li internalizes his parents' expectations, makes them his own, and surrounds himself with other high-achieving peers who are pursuing the same goals. A pragmatic, driven attitude, a willingness to work hard toward a clear goal, and knowledge about how to employ the system have helped Li achieve his extraordinary success.

Li has worked hard to prepare for a bright future: in describing the "steps of going to college," Li's list is exhaustive: "hard classes, good grades, good SAT, sports team, music, publication, volunteer, awards, funny essay, recommendations, and internship. I have done all of these." Indeed he has.

IN THESE portraits of high-achieving students, four factors emerge as critical to academic success—family resources; social supports outside of the home; school contexts; and the child's disposition (which here means the ability to work hard, to remain optimistic yet realistic, and to recruit the support of others, including peers, friends, teachers, and counselors). Significantly, the feature that seems to drive the disposition of every single high-achieving portrait in our research is the youngster's willingness and ability to work long hours. But the four features often work together to help the immigrant child: for example, Rosa's beauty, intelligence, and hard-working nature are irresistible to the counselor at the after-school program who not only takes her under her wing but also connects her to influential, helpful people at the university. Joyce, too, reports how adults at the nearby after-school center "love" to help her.

The family system is immensely important. As we witness in Li's portrait, he works very long hours but is sustained in part because both his father and mother invest considerable resources—including time and money—to insure a stellar academic journey. When the parental authority voice remains relevant and legitimate, there is often a cohesive ethos of mutuality, harmony, and reciprocity that nurtures success—often because the student wants to give something back to the parents in return for their tremendous sacrifices.

Yet in nearly all of the portraits the families slowly drift apart. This distancing often starts with small conflicts over peers, curfews, style of dress, and the like. But it eventually escalates as the youth begin to forge their own paths. This process happens to all families, immigrant and nonimmigrant alike. After all, one of the fundamental functions of the human family is to transfer the skills, competencies, values, and sensibilities to the next generation so that the children can eventually carry on autonomously and independently in new households. To succeed, parents everywhere must, paradoxically, make themselves irrelevant so their children can carry on without them.

Immigration only accentuates this general human predicament. That is, immigrants must be careful what they wish for. The more they impose their own frustrated ambitions on their children, the more likely it is that that the children, as they succeed, will become foreigners in their own home. When this happens, the easy intimacy and warmth of the inward-looking immigrant family that sticks together to survive in a new land is lost as the children become ever more comfortable in the idioms of the new society. For Li, his enviable academic success comes at a cost: Li's father no longer recognizes this successful young man. Li has become a stranger—an immigrant—in his own family.

If families are paramount, the portraits suggest that school contexts also matter. Yadira thrives in her new private school. It offered safety when she needed it most, as well as a rich array of academic opportunities, caring adults, like-minded peers, and even a possibility of becoming a legal immigrant. In the case of Jean-Luc we are left to wonder how much further this bright, serious, hard-working young man would have gone if he had received more attention and guidance in high school—including timely information about college admissions policies. With proper guidance, he may have been able to enter the school of his dreams rather than settling on the college he eventually enrolled in.

Religiosity is a recurring theme in the social lives of many immigrant youth. Jean-Luc's family is deeply religious and draws important support from their church. Jean-Luc shared with us how he prays every morning and how it makes him feel centered the rest of his day. Immigrants are overwhelmingly people of faith, and when they are challenged personally—such as when they need to adapt quickly to the new American culture—they often draw important emotional and tangible support from their religious beliefs.

Perhaps this is the best place to address an elephant in the room: the case of Chinese immigrant exceptionalism. After all, more than half of all high achievers in this study are Chinese immigrant students. What is going on? A variety of factors contribute to this pattern. A greater proportion of Chinese students arrive with more resources than students from the other groups. Their parents tend to have, overall, higher levels of education upon entry and are more likely to have better jobs and incomes once they settle in the United States. Chinese newcomers are less likely to endure lengthy and complicated family separations during the migration process, are less likely to have undocumented status, and are less likely to attend the most troubled schools. They more often attend integrated schools where they come in contact with American children from mainstream households—which can act as powerful linguistic models. Chinese immigrants, via the model minority cultural complex, are expected by teachers to excel in school. Put differently, Chinese students have to prove that they are *not* good students.

In addition, Chinese immigrants enter the United States from a culture that, for about three thousand years, has more or less worshipped education for its own sake and as the most powerful means for improving one's social status. Consequently, Chinese immigrant youth understand the culture of testing—testing was the main route to enter highly coveted jobs in the Chinese state hierarchy. Chinese parents arrive in the United States with an understanding that all schools are not equal, that admission to college is essentially a game that needs to be skillfully and strategically played. More acculturated Chinese-origin immigrants and second-generation Chinese who have high levels of educational capital become powerful brokers who impart to new arrivals, often with Talmudic dedication and in minute detail, the skills and cultural savoir faire needed to succeed in school. Lastly, Chinese immigrants, especially girls, spend more hours doing homework and more consistently turn their work in on time than do immigrants from other countries. Given these advantages, it is hardly surprising that Chinese-origin youth do better academically than other groups.

No man is an island—and immigrants in particular need to create social connections to replace those they have left behind. Some immigrant youth make positive social connections that are enormously beneficial. After-school programs such as the Upward Bound and Alma Latina programs discussed earlier—programs that are rigorous, academically engaging, and help newcomers make friends with both like-minded youth and influential adults—can be life-transforming. For immigrant youth, supportive mentors found through such programs, or through school or family connections, can be powerful cultural brokers, showing them the ropes of the new culture at a time of identity confusion, multiple options, and significant transitions.

■ ■

Immigration Policy Dilemmas

IMMIGRATION CYCLES in and out of public focus, generating ambivalence in the best of times, hysteria in the worst. Sometimes immigration stands starkly in the glare of public attention; sometimes the public eye is elsewhere and interest in the topic subsides, leaving the contradictions of U.S. policy and the problems of immigrants themselves languishing in the shadows. At times when other matters obscure the topic, Americans—when they think about immigration at all—feel a hazy warmth toward immigrants, celebrating their past contributions to our country. During these periods, discussions about immigration reflect its private and familial dimensions: the great sacrifices, travails, and triumphs of our ancestors, how they braved seemingly insurmountable odds in their epic journey to the United States, and other misty-eyed family legends loosely based on historic facts. Never mind the terrible discrimination that waves of new arrivals from Ireland, Eastern Europe, and the Mediterranean faced; never mind how hard it was for them to learn English and how many never found good jobs; never mind how long it took the dominant white Anglo-Saxon Protestants to accept them as worthy, loyal, and equal U.S. citizens. Immigrants are loved but only looking backward: since the end of the nineteenth century, Americans have celebrated immigrants' proud achievements after the fact while remaining deeply anxious about migration in the here and now.

In mid-2006, exactly twenty years after the last major overhaul of U.S. immigration policy (the U.S. Immigration Reform and Control Act of

1986), the quiescent public discourse of immigration began rumbling, eventually erupting into a full debate. Talk of immigration saturated the airwaves: popular television commentators and countless radio talk-show hosts hyperventilated about "broken borders" and the "illegal-alien invasion," which some called the "Mexican reconquista." By the end of May 2006, millions of people—especially undocumented immigrants and significant numbers of children of immigrants—had taken to the streets of major U.S. cities, saying "enough" to the immigrant bashing and daring to clamor for the right to stay in the United States.

But the harsh spotlight on border controls has blinded us to the broader picture. Heretofore, we have simply failed to consider what is at stake, in the long term, with the current wave of immigration. We have neglected to consider that children of immigrants make up the largest-growing segment of the child population of the United States, now constituting 20 percent of our nation's youth and projected by the year 2040 to make up a third of young Americans. Immigrant-origin youth are literally our future. Therefore, we need to develop a much more ambitious approach to immigration policy: one that directly addresses immigrant-origin youth, that is relevant to the realities of the twenty-first century, and that is fair, workable, and humane.

In particular, our current approach to immigration fails to consider how best to incorporate the children of newly arrived immigrants (whether or not they have documentation status) into American society. We have no national policies for helping young immigrants who arrive during the middle and high school years.[1] Our new, expanded federal education standards seem blind to the existence of newcomer youth. Nowhere is this ignorance more painfully obvious than in the mandated testing of No Child Left Behind (NCLB). The data show that newly arrived immigrant youngsters cannot possibly cope with complex tests in English after just one year in their new country. In fact, even after seven years in the United States many still struggle to develop their English-language skills, simply because the task is so difficult—native English speakers would experience the same hardship if placed in a new language setting. To date, we have no strategy to ease the transition of immigrant youth to college or to the labor market. Instead, we seem to rely on an unreasonable faith that once young immigrants cross the border, the logic of the market will work magically to transform them into proud, loyal, and productive citizens. Or perhaps if we ignore them, they will simply fade away. This current "non-policy" fails young immigrants and their families; it also robs the United States economy of some of its most promising future contributors.

Our anemic approach to incorporating immigrants' enthusiasm and talents into American society has been fostered by a national historical obliviousness that has been warped by a collective fantasy. It is the product of distortions of our experience and facile comparisons between immigration now and the mythic immigration of yesteryear. Our laissez-faire nonpolicy rests on one of the foundational myths of our citizenry: "My immigrant great-grandparents pulled themselves up by their bootstraps, so the new immigrants can, too—if they want to." But this sink-or-swim approach ignores the fact that many immigrants in the days of Ellis Island sank at a great cost to themselves, their families, and our society.

Just over one hundred years ago, the U.S. public response to large-scale immigration from Ireland, Eastern Europe, and the Mediterranean was also nearly apoplectic. Would-be immigrants who were European Jews, Catholic Irish, or Italian were especially suspect on cultural, religious, and security grounds. There were endless debates as to whether Jews and Catholics could ever succeed in a predominantly Anglo-Saxon Protestant America. A hundred years ago, a large swath of the U.S. citizenry was near panic that these immigrants were bringing their anarchistic battles to U.S. soil. Newspapers and magazines were filled with draconian predictions of the inassimilable nature of the "human garbage" that was coming to our shores.[2] The passage of time has demonstrated the barrenness of these dire predictions: today, five justices on the U.S. Supreme Court are Catholic and two are Jewish.[3]

Thus neither the cultural nor the security anxieties of the post–September 11th era are new or unique. As the French remind us, the more things change, the more they remain the same. The earlier debates are recycled today, structurally intact, with new anxieties aroused by and focused on large-scale Hispanic immigration. For example, in a widely quoted (if empirically underwhelming) treatise, Samuel Huntington articulates deep reservations and considerable anxiety about the cultural wisdom of continued large-scale immigration from Mexico to the United States. Yet a cool-headed examination of the data might offer some therapeutic relief from contagious migration anxiety. Mexican immigrants today behave much like their predecessors—they are deeply family oriented; they want their children to learn English; they are most often people of faith; they want better jobs; and, in growing numbers, across generations they marry members of other ethnic groups.[4]

When immigration comes into sharp political focus, the public mood is charged, if not openly xenophobic. People and pundits indulge in fearful hand-wringing about its economic and cultural consequences, its effect on native citizens, and above all in the age of global terrorism, the urgent need to have a semblance of control over our international borders. While we wax sentimental about past immigration, we worry about its present state and future consequences—even if both sets of feelings tend to be misplaced.

What is instructive about the current cycle of discussion about immigration is how it repeats the elemental structures of an anti-immigrant sentiment that is as old and as American as immigration itself. It also reveals how the nation's policies have become surreally disconnected from the realities of immigration in the fields, streets, offices, factories, and above all, schools of the United States. The street protests of mid-2006 came as Congress finally undertook a major new immigration bill. In its original form, the bill would have criminalized and deported millions of undocumented immigrants and harshly penalized anyone aiding them. The bill was in equal parts mean-spirited, naïve, and unworkable. What would turning approximately 12 million undocumented immigrants into felons accomplish, other than overwhelming the criminal justice system? What, exactly, would be its social and economic consequences? Could the United States implement a massive deportation campaign? Many undocumented migrants have relatives who are U.S. citizens; would we be willing to break up millions of families?

The bill that President George W. Bush eventually signed into law failed to systematically address immigration reform. Nothing in the new bill addressed the fate of undocumented immigrants already in the United States or the need for more visas and possibly a new guest worker program. Congress settled for approving (but not allocating money for) the first seven hundred miles of what was to be a futuristic fence along the country's border with Mexico, our second-largest trading partner. The bill considered only the nation's southern border, although nearly half of the undocumented immigrants (who have overstayed their visas) entered the country elsewhere. Moreover, nowhere is there any discussion of how we might help the children of immigrants become integrated and well-functioning members of our society.[5]

If in the short term such policy initiatives are ineffectual, in the long view, many of them are irrelevant to the modern realities of migration. The United States today has no coherent policy to rationally and humanely control movement across its international borders or to smooth the transition of immigrant adults and their children into their new society once they are here. The results of recent border-control initiatives are equivocal at best. In recent years we have been spending more than ever to beef up controls and security at our international borders yet the United States now has the largest number of undocumented immigrants in its history— a clear indictment of the failed immigration policies currently in place.

Perhaps even more importantly, today's ever-more-complex global economy necessitates a more sophisticated approach. A century ago, powerful political frameworks—most famously, the well-greased city political machines like Tammany Hall in New York—eased the integration of immigrants by offering basic supports: jobs, housing, medical care. In contrast, once today's immigrants cross the border or disembark at JFK, LAX, or O'Hare international airports, they are largely left on their own. Our data suggest that while some immigrant youth find their path and thrive in their new country, too many lose their way.

Today's realities reveal the limitations of simplistic historical comparisons. One hundred years ago, the nascent "Fordist" industrial expansion meant that even if 70 to 80 percent of all new immigrants from Italy, Ireland, and Eastern Europe had minimal formal education, they could, over time and across generations, leverage the mobility of the shop floor to achieve a middle-class standard of living. By contrast, if 70 to 80 percent of today's Asian, Caribbean, and Latin American immigrants dropped out of high school, most would succumb to permanent poverty.

The difference is that today's globally linked economies and societies are unforgiving of those without the higher-order cognitive and meta-cognitive skills, cultural sophistication, and ability to manage complexities that are typically imparted in high school and college. Americans understand this: record numbers, well over a quarter, of U.S. citizens now have at least a bachelor's degree.[6] Yet too many immigrant youngsters, like other poor youth and youth of color, get a mediocre high school education; they are abandoned outside the gates of the pathway that leads to college and later to meaningful, stable, and well-paid work.

Very few of the schools described in this book had clearly thought through—let alone implemented—strategies to ease immigrant students' path to college and the knowledge-intensive economies of the global era. Yet policies matter. Countries like Canada and New Zealand that better co-ordinate their migration objectives with realistic language and educational-integration policies tend to generate better high school grades among their immigrant youngsters.[7] Urban schools in the United States—especially in cities that are being transformed by large-scale immigration—ought to be the front lines of an ambitious new incorporation agenda. Instead, we found them at best wanting and at worst, toxic. The lack of imagination displayed at the front lines of integration is short-sighted—no, incompre-hensible—considering what is at stake for the future of our economy and society.

Several alternative futures lie before us. We can agree with Samuel Hun-tington in one respect: there is nothing preordained about integration. It is the product of specific policies and experiences, and the more we cultivate human development in terms of wellness and education, the better the long-term chances that today's newest Americans will be ready to give back to their new society. But we differ from Huntington in recognizing that the more we cultivate our immigrant youth—however and from wherever they arrive, and whatever their numbers—to grow up to be engaged and productive citizens, the more able they will be able to contribute fully in a twenty-first-century environment. To achieve this vision, we need a new agenda based on evidence and reason, not on romantic nostalgia or dysto-pian fear-mongering.

Failure to change could bring us closer to the scenario now unfolding in Western Europe. There is little doubt that five decades of neglect and am-bivalence regarding its immigration policies have led to Europe's greatest postwar failure: its inability to incorporate a large number of immigrants who are increasingly segregated, disenfranchised, and disadvantaged in the new labor market. Most ominously, throughout Western Europe, the marginalized children of immigrants seem to be turning into a permanent underclass, one that is strikingly over-represented in the penal system.[8] In recent years Western Europe has also proven to be a fertile breeding ground for fundamentalist terrorism. The children of immigrants, almost by definition, have much greater expectations than their immigrant parents. Frustrated in their ambitions, without a place in the cultural narrative of the nation, locked out of adequate education and the most desirable jobs, too many of Western Europe's second-generation immigrants are nursing their wounds with the false balm of long-distance nationalism and militant nihilism.[9] The terrorist bombings and plots in London (July 2005 and August 2006), the furious street riots in France (October and November 2005), the Madrid train bombings (March 2004), and the murder of the controversial Dutch filmmaker Theo van Gogh (November 2004)—all of these incidents involved immigrants and the children of immigrants in Europe, prompting many to worry that such tragedies might happen here.

Except for the elements of militant religious fundamentalism, what is happening in Europe today echoes the emergence of marginalized gangs that nearly always accompanied failed immigration policies in the United States. Successive waves of Italian, Irish, and Eastern European immigrants, among others, responded to marginality and discrimination by forming their own social spaces, in large part in the underground economy and society. An angry, alienated, disenfranchised second generation exacts a huge societal price, threatening to undermine the contributions and achievements of the first-generation immigrants.

A brighter future depends on the implementation of an ambitious new agenda for immigrant incorporation. Rather than rest with the lazy assumption that border controls are a substantive immigration policy, we must finally focus our attention on what happens after immigrants and their children cross the border. We need to go well beyond the general principle of family reunification—the philosophical bedrock of U.S. immigration policy—and enact coherent policies to ensure that the energy immigrant families bring to their new home is well harnessed. How do we minimize lengthy family separations by facilitating faster reunification and a saner process toward citizenship? How do we best support immigrant families as they finally reunite in their new home? How do we build on the momentum and optimism that motivate immigrants to search for a better tomorrow? How do we make sure that the children of immigrants have a good shot at becoming productive, engaged, and thoughtful citizens in the global societies of the twenty-first century?

Evidence suggests that we are wasting enormous amounts of talent and energy. The data presented in Chapter 1 show that only 24 percent of immigrant youth thrive in our schools while over half see their grades decline the longer they are in the country. Many of the schools that are potential gateways to incorporation for immigrant children and youth are nothing but toxic sinkholes. A disconcerting proportion of newly arrived immigrant youngsters, despite their initial high hopes, are disengaging, giving up, and failing. What are the costs—personal and societal—when an immigrant youth who could end up at Princeton winds up in jail? Many who today oppose immigration pointedly ask about the costs of educating immigrant youths. An even more pressing question is: What are the long-term personal, familial, and societal costs of undereducating, or failing to educate, our immigrant youngsters?

So what should we do?

Engaging and Relevant Schools. Strikingly, many of the schools that newly arrived immigrant students encounter are ugly, hostile, and dangerous. All too often, immigrant children enter schools that have for generations failed to prepare poor and native-born minority students; these failing schools are even less able to serve newcomers in transplant shock who must learn a new language and social ethos, as well as acquire the skills needed to navigate the electronic cultures of the digital age.

Paradoxically, many families migrate to seek a better education for their children, only to find their children mired in the worst schools in the United States—schools that are racially, linguistically, and economically segregated. The day-to-day routines in these schools are mind-numbing. Deep divisions cut every which way—between the races; between immigrants and the native-born; between more acculturated immigrants and more recent arrivals; between students in bilingual programs and those in mainstream programs; between administrators and teachers; between teachers and parents; between teachers and students. Anomie and isolation prevail. Most disturbing, violence and a culture of fear pervade too many of these schools. Students devote much of their energy to managing their fear and staying safe, and so have little left over for learning academics. In such schools, no student—immigrant or otherwise—is well served. Like our portrait subjects Léon and Mauricio, many immigrant youngsters with considerable potential become completely derailed by the toxic schools they attend.

Ample evidence shows that a school's climate drives its students' academic experience. Strong and compassionate leadership, engaging teachers, and involved counselors and other staff can set a tone of respect, high expectations, and tolerance. In such contexts, engagement and learning will surely take place. In today's high-stakes economy, schooling matters more than ever. One hundred years ago, immigrant youth could drop out before completing high school without much penalty, but today the costs of so doing are far higher: the average high-school dropout will earn $19,169 per year compared to $51,554 for the average college graduate (and $78,095 for the average individual with an advanced degree).[10] Today's globalized world requires the capacity to think analytically and creatively within and across disciplines. It requires the ability to work with people from diverse backgrounds. It requires both a historical and global perspective. And it requires a new model of schooling.[11] In the predigital economy, students needed to be grounded in reading, 'riting, and 'rithmetic. The new economy, as the Gates Foundation has cogently suggested, and as we mentioned in Chapter 3, requires an educational system that provides *rigor* in challenging classes, *relevance* to engaging topics that "relate clearly to [students'] lives in today's rapidly changing world," and *relationships* with adults "who know them, look out for them, and push them to achieve."[12]

Our data suggest that recently arrived immigrants whose schools provided meaningful, nurturing relationships and stimulating classes were much more likely to sustain their motivation than those students in weaker schools—who tended to drift intellectually and lack supportive relationships with teachers and peers. Rosa succeeded not only because of her great drive, but also because a number of adults, spotting her as a winner in a dysfunctional school, invested heavily in her success. Students who received the cognitive stimulation and social supports they needed performed much better. Li was highly stimulated by his multiple activities, as well as by his school—which demanded high standards and was rigorous and intellectually invigorating. Our nation's priority must be to develop more schools that provide engaging academic climates, not only for our immigrant students, but for all of our nation's children. We need schools that maintain high standards and expectations for all students. We need our children to learn *how* to learn so they may become the lifelong learners they need to be to do well in our new economy. Settling for dysfunctional warehouses that nurture little but anomie and a sense of grievance will generate tremendous social costs in lost human potential and will likely continue to feed our voracious penal system, the repository of growing numbers of disenfranchised boys and young men.[13]

Realistic Language Policies. Nowhere is our unrealistic thinking about immigration more self-defeating than in its approach to language. In a globalized economy, multilingualism ought to be seen as an asset, not a divisive threat. Yet we are doing everything we can to suffocate the languages that immigrants bring with them. We neither support the use of languages other than English nor use them intelligently as tools to help immigrant students learn English. Over and over in the course of our study, we heard the accusatory questions: Why are *they* speaking Spanish (or Chinese or Creole)? Why are *they* not learning English faster? We want our immigrants to forget their languages and to learn English overnight, and we want our schools to make them do it on the cheap. Yet the intense emotions around immigration and language have at their source the flawed historical analogy alluded to earlier: "My great-grand-parents came from Italy [or Eastern Europe, or Central Europe] and they made it without any special programs. Why do we need special language programs for immigrants *now?*" Hindsight serves us poorly. In the previous century, there were many German and other bilingual schools. To the question, "why don't the new immigrants want to learn English like my grandparents did?"—we must reply that in fact, in many neighborhoods a century ago business was conducted, newspapers written, and plays performed in German, Yiddish, or Italian, and the first generation never really mastered English as we may imagine they did.

The United States, which has been aptly termed a "cemetery for languages," has always been immensely ambivalent about multilingualism.[14] It is true that Germans, Italians, Poles, Russians, Japanese, and countless others brought their languages with them to the United States—and within two or three generations, there is ample evidence that these languages of origin all but disappear. In a global society, however, compulsive monolingualism is dangerously anachronistic. Powerful economic, social, diplomatic, and security needs argue for cultivating multilingualism. The United States has always celebrated the bilingualism of the elites; at Harvard and other prestigious colleges, we always had plenty of eager undergraduates drop by to practice their Spanish and French on us. It is time to view immigrant bilingualism and its accompanying linguistic diversity as a cultural resource to be nourished. The United States is simply too vibrant a society—and English is too universal a language now—for us to be threatened by the phony bogeyman of linguistic balkanization. English reigns supreme today, here and all over the world, as the lingua franca of business, science, diplomacy, and pop culture. It is high time for us to shed our neurotic ambivalence and to nurture immigrant bilingualism. We should make normative multilingualism an educational objective for all youth growing up in the global era, immigrant and native alike.

And immigrants want to learn English. Ramon, for example, was driven to learn English, but faced tremendous difficulty acquiring academic-level fluency—only after he was placed in an appropriate dual-immersion program with systematic mentoring and extra tutoring after school did he begin to show significant progress. In three decades of basic research in this field, we have never met an immigrant parent who told us he did not want his children to learn English. On the contrary, immigrant families view English as the yellow brick road to better jobs and a better life in the United States. But our data show that learning the academic English required to interact creatively and meaningfully in today's knowledge-intensive global economy takes more time than our impatient policy-makers (many of whom have never mastered another language to a high level of fluency) would like.[15] Immigrant youth will fool you with their chameleon-like ability to pick up enough English to discuss with ease the latest international soccer tournament, cool video game, or fashion frenzy. Yet when we sat with them and systematically tested their verbal abilities in more complex domains, a sobering pattern emerged. The vast majority of the immigrant students in our study, who had all been in the United States for more than five years, were testing well behind their native born peers in academic English. Even high-performing, highly motivated students like Lotus and Henry found themselves floundering once they began taking courses with native-born students in more competitive mainstream programs.

Current proposals that force newly arrived immigrant students to take high-stakes testing in the regime of No Child Left Behind after just one year in the United States would have very negative results. Our data suggest that the vast majority of immigrant children cannot possibly be expected to master the complex intricacies of academic English in one year of study, particularly in the highly dysfunctional schools where huge numbers of newly arrived immigrant students are concentrated. Subjecting newly arrived immigrant youth to the annual testing regimes required under No Child Left Behind (NCLB) would push more youngsters toward premature disengagement from school. Such testing might well become more of a punishment than an objective assessment of timely progress. We witnessed too many immigrant youth like Andrés check themselves out of the schooling game as a result of their multiple failures in mandatory high-stakes testing.

During our five-year studies of immigrant students and their schools, it became painfully obvious that U.S. language policies are literally all over the map. Each state, each district—each school—seems to have its own set of priorities, rules, and predilections. Sometimes even teachers in the various bilingual and ESL programs serving immigrant students *in the same school* could not succinctly explain to us the basic structure and logic of their own school's program. The students themselves could not readily tell us whether they were in a bilingual program, ESL program, or pull-out program. The only programs that seemed to have some general coherence were the dual-immersion programs.

Also alarming is the nearly universal sense of alienation within schools between the academic programs for native speakers and those for immigrant students. In many schools, the separation and segregation between the immigrant English-language learners and their native-born peers was total. We found few meaningful exchanges and friendships between newly arrived immigrant youngsters and native-born students. The result is innumerable missed opportunities: immigrant youngsters have little exposure to the linguistic modeling their U.S.-born peers could provide, and U.S. students miss out on acquiring knowledge about the world beyond our borders. Our data show that those few immigrant youngsters who had even one native English-speaking friend were able to learn English much more quickly and completely. For example, we saw Ramon's rapid improvement in English skills and academic performance when he was placed in a dual-immersion program that systematically exposed him to both English- and Spanish-speaking peers. Comfort and fluency in English were strengthened by his close friendship with an English-speaking classmate.

In short, we need schools to support directly immigrant students' enthusiasm for learning English, avoid premature high-stakes testing that can demean newcomer children and derail their academic progress, and nurture school cultures where immigrant and native students are well integrated and can share the richness of their varied backgrounds, perspectives, and native languages.

Embracing Hyphenated Identities. One hundred years ago, few Irish immigrants—and even fewer Central or Eastern Europeans Jews—yearned for the old country; in those days, assimilation meant a sharp break with the old world. Many of today's immigrants, however, experience the kind of "transnationalism of the heart" described in Chapter 2. Mauricio, like many Dominicans, enjoys visiting the country of his birth and maintaining regular contact with loved ones back home. Andrés longs to return "home" to see again his beloved grandparents. Myriam dreams of bringing her troubled mother to the United States to reunite the fragmented family. Rosette has ambitious plans to one day work to help rebuild the Haiti of her childhood. Jane remains very involved in the local Chinese community even as she works to become an American.

Advances in transportation and especially in communication technologies, unimaginable to the Ellis Island generations, help immigrant youngsters stay close to the relatives and friends they left behind; in some cases frequent visits also sustain their connections to their homelands. But these dual cultural loyalties should not alarm Americans. The data presented in this book, and in our online supplement, demonstrate that even though immigrant youth may remain culturally identified with their country of origin, they put down their roots in U.S. society. Just as important, those roots are not fed by the mainstream of yesteryear, the white Anglo-Saxon Protestant ethos that served as the point of reference to earlier waves of immigrants. That referent, like so much else, has been swallowed by globalization—a change that has a positive side. In the diverse new "face" of America, immigrant children recognize opportunities to contribute to a dynamic and powerful nation that interacts with colleagues and friends around the world.

The forces of a multicultural global youth culture exert a powerful force on today's youngsters. For the immigrant youth we studied, this meant that as they entered the U.S. experience, they learned to balance their lives in the unstable hyphen between their home cultures and this increasingly globalized youth culture. These sensibilities carry more weight with immigrant youth today than anything most Americans would identify as an artifact of white Anglo-Saxon Protestantism. (One seemingly American strain of culture did make a significant impression on our study participants, however. Even as most immigrants described in this book remained socially distant from their African American peers, the linguistic, musical, and fashion sensibilities developed and nurtured by African American urban youth often dominated their cultural landscape.)

Because of global migration, children and youth growing up today are likely to work and network, love and live with people from different national, linguistic, religious, and racial backgrounds—an experience once limited to cities but now found in suburbs and small towns across the land. From the moment they set foot in the United States, immigrant youth must adapt to competing cultural models and social practices that include complicated relationships among race, ethnicity, and inequality. For them, transcultural communication, understanding, empathy, and collaboration are no longer abstract ideals; they are part of day-to-day life. And to the extent that immigrants succeed in accommodating and contributing to these multiple cultures, they have much to teach their native-born peers.[16]

The call for immigrants to give up their languages, to leave their cultures behind, and to acculturate in fast-forward has unanticipated consequences. Such abrupt personal and social transformations undermine the cohesion and inherent authority of the immigrant family and community. Jane's refusal to speak her family's native language, for example, has created a huge rift between them. Even as they build bridges to their new society, immigrant youth need to be able to continue bonding with, talking to, and respecting their parents. If they reject their cultures of origin, they risk becoming alienated from their communities, families, and ultimately, themselves.

For generations, the magnetic pull to Americanize has drawn immigrants to internalize a sense of being American. Irish-Americans, Italian-Americans, Polish-Americans—all may have a fondness for their ethnic roots, but they are to the core Americanized in their identities and loyalties. Problems occur when a person's internalized sense of belonging ("I am an American") is met by exclusionary attitudes and practices in the host society ("You are not one of us—you are Muslim, or Caribbean, or Chinese")—even when his or her family has lived in the new country for several generations. The inevitable consequences of this exclusion are alienation, anomie, dislocation, and social strife. We need to recognize that in today's global economy and marketplace of ideas, the ability to encompass cultural differences and diversity can be an edge—economically, diplomatically, and strategically. When intelligently managed, diversity and difference can strengthen the cultural fabric of the nation.[17]

Building Mentoring and Community Supports. A domain ripe for creative policy work that could help immigrant families enormously is community supports and mentorship. Our data show that immigrant children and youth rarely have access to supportive after-school programs, mentoring opportunities, and community-based organizations. Lotus confided in us that there was no adult in school she really trusted. Henry shared that there were no adults at school he could turn for support. At best, we found a lone counselor, a committed teacher, or a responsible staff member who took the initiative to connect an immigrant youth with a community program that helped the youngster live a fuller life. Yet the evidence suggests that such programs, when carefully planned and well staffed, can help all children and may play an especially important role in the lives of disoriented new arrivals in need of direction.

Many immigrant youngsters crave mentors to help them in areas where their parents and other relatives really cannot—a fact brought home to us by the intensity of some students' attachment to members of our research team. Mentors can act as cultural guides to help newcomers find their way during the turmoil of adolescence in a new country. Caring adults can illuminate the college-admissions pathway that native-born middle-class parents find daunting and immigrant families find incomprehensible. The importance of caring teachers, counselors, and mentors was evident in the portraits of Marieli, Rosette, Yadira, Joyce, and Ramon.

We learned through our study that girls were much more likely than boys to receive the support of mentors. Since immigrant boys often encounter serious difficulties in their journey to the new land, mentorship opportunities should be designed with immigrant boys' specific needs in mind. Boys need strong role models who can show them by deed what they can achieve in the new land. Had Civic, Henry, Andrés, or Mauricio had warm, charismatic, and accomplished male mentors, they would have been at far less risk of losing their way. None of these boys, and in fact almost none of our newcomer participants, were linked to community resources or mentoring organizations. There are wonderful organizational models developed for refugees—programs like these could also serve well newly arrived immigrant youth.[18]

Behind nearly every successful immigrant youth journey we found a mentor—from the church, the athletic team, or from the local community center. The case of Ramon exemplifies what a difference mentors can make at critical turning points in the lives of immigrant youth. Yadira's public school counselor nurtured and guided her while she struggled to apply to a more rigorous and demanding private school. In Joyce's case, we found several adults in school helping her in a multiplicity of ways. But in too many cases we encountered during our fieldwork, mentorship relationships started by chance encounters. We need a coordinated effort to link every immigrant youngster who wants a mentor with a wise elder ready to help.

Addressing Undocumented Immigrant Youth. A final domain where our policies are out of touch with reality is undocumented immigration. Today there are an estimated 1.8 million children and youth living in the United States as undocumented immigrants. In addition, approximately 3.1 million youth are U.S. citizens living in households headed by unauthorized immigrants.[19]

While we never asked any of our informants directly about their documented status over the years, we came to know well many who did not have papers. These youth and their families were like other immigrant families in basic ways. Many, like the mother of Marieli, waited patiently for years for her visa to be approved so they could be reunited. Frustrated by the seemingly interminable waiting lists—over five years, which demonstrates another way our immigration policies are out of touch—she finally ventured to send for her daughter without the required papers.

Some youngsters came to pay dearly for their parents' decision to bring them here without papers. As they were approaching high school graduation, some immigrant students were stunned to discover that they could not qualify for financial aid for college. Yadira kept an optimistic attitude, seemingly against the odds, that somehow she would eventually beat the system and find a way to regularize her status; it helped immeasurably that the authorities at her school took it upon themselves to assist her in this process. Others, like Marieli, began to disengage from high school, knowing that there would be no realistic way for them to pursue a college education. Some of these students, like Léon, made a premature transition to the labor market.

What are we to do with the millions of immigrant youth growing up in families without papers? Should they be punished for the "sins" of their parents, who brought them here without the proper documents? Are we willing to pay the price of having nearly two million children and youth living in the shadows, sentenced to managing life as undocumented immigrants? Will these youngsters go back to their countries of origin? And if so, how can they be expected to manage when much of their education—both formal and informal—has taken place in the United States, and has rendered them outsiders in their parental homeland? This premise of concern about immigrant children's future prospects in their native lands was the claim of the proponents of Proposition 187, the 1994 California ballot initiative that would have, among other things, prevented undocumented immigrant youth from enrolling in primary and secondary schools. But the preponderance of evidence suggests that the vast majority of these immigrant youth will indeed remain in the United States, growing ever-deeper roots in our society even if they remain outside the law. Are we willing to pay the social costs of driving these youth deep into a world of illegality? The answer must be no. We need the political courage to face the reality that millions of youth are growing up in our country as undocumented immigrants and find the formula to regularize their status. Building a wall at the border will do nothing to address this problem. These youth are already in the United States and will remain here. Our challenge is to make sure that they will one day be able to better themselves and contribute to their new society.

The stunningly high proportion of newcomer students, both legal and undocumented, who endure long separations from their parents is an issue of serious concern. Not only do the separations extract a high emotional cost for both parents and children, but they also often result in complicated and conflictual periods of adjustment when the family is finally reunited. Our case studies show just how distressing these multiple separations can be for immigrant families. During the entire five years of our study, Myriam remained separated from her mother in Haiti. Jean-Luc was separated from his father for ten years before joining him. Andrés was re-united with his mother after being separated for six years. Marieli, whose father was killed before migration, was separated from her mother for seven years—and upon reunification remained resentful of her mother for having left her behind and for having had a new baby in the United States.

IMMIGRATION—with or without the rosy glow of nostalgia—is central to the history and culture of the United States. And in the globalized world of the twenty-first century, it remains central to our future. Any effort to address immigration that fails to fully consider just how much our com-petitive edge rests on attracting and nurturing immigrant talent will cost us dearly. Every year, the United States receives "high-quality" human cap-ital, worth an estimated $50 billon a year.[20] This human capital comes to us in the skills of Ghanaian physicians, Jamaican and Philippine nurses and childcare workers, Indian computer programmers, Argentine scientists, Bulgarian artists, Mexican Hollywood stars, and Dominican baseball play-ers—to name just a few examples—who choose to build their lives in our land. In the measured words of former Federal Reserve Bank chairman Alan Greenspan, "Under the conditions that we now confront, we should be very carefully focused on the contribution which skilled people from abroad, as well as unskilled people from abroad, can contribute to this country, as they have for generation after generation." Are we prepared to leverage this human potential by nurturing the children of these immi-grants? Or would we rather pay the significant price of letting this human resource go to waste?

In the next generation, the United States—like Europe—will likely en-counter more, not less, migration. As nearly 80 million baby boomers re-tire over the next decades and as the white European-origin population of the United States maintains low fertility rates, the United States will face complex choices. In the words of President George W. Bush: "The retire-ment of the baby-boom generation will put unprecedented strains on the federal government. By 2030, spending for Social Security, Medicare, and Medicaid alone will be almost 60 percent of the entire federal budget. And that will present future Congresses with impossible choices—staggering tax increases, immense deficits, or deep cuts in every category of spend-ing." By 2030, the United States, like many Western European countries to-day, will likely be forced to turn to immigrants to deal with its "impossible choices." Immigrant workers may once again be summoned—this time to take care of retired citizens, pay into the Social Security system, and help the country maintain its economic vitality.

The United States of America—like Canada, Australia, and New Zealand—is one of a handful of advanced democracies in the world that can claim immigration as both history and destiny. The quasi-sacred narrative of our nation's birth and growth—our own creation myth—has migration at its core and at every turn in the tale: the original settlement by Native Americans beginning some twenty thousand years ago; the arrival of the English, Spanish, and Dutch settlers five centuries ago; the involuntary migration of millions of Africans; the great transatlantic exodus between the end of the Napoleonic wars and the First World War. The current wave of new immigration from Latin America, the Caribbean, and Asia is but the latest chapter in our epic.

All the hopes that the United States has always represented for political freedom, prosperity, and a future that is better than the past continue to be at the heart of each and every immigrant journey. And this is not a one-way street—our society has become ambivalently addicted to the labors of these hopeful newcomers. But immigrants are not simply disembodied arms summoned to the country for their labor—immigrants are human beings and they come with their families or form families once they arrive. Immigrant-origin youth come with big dreams and their initial boundless energies and optimism offer a great, if untapped, national resource. Sensibly and compassionately embracing this wave of our youngest new arrivals will allow them to constructively unleash their great potential to the benefit of all Americans.

Notes

All technical notes and interview protocols, as well as narrative and sentence completion coding, are available in an online supplement at steinhardt.nyu.edu/immigration/archive.html, which can also be accessed via www.hup.harvard.edu/catalog/suamov.html. The supplement is organized to match the sequence of chapters found in this book.

Introduction

1. U.S. Census Bureau 2006.
2. Landale and Oropesa 1995.
3. Rong and Preissle 1998.
4. Capps et al. 2004; Portes 1996; C. Suárez-Orozco 2000; Szalacha et al. 2003; Orfield and Yun 1999; García-Coll and Magnuson 1997; C. Suárez-Orozco and M. Suárez-Orozco 1995; Olsen 1977.
5. Passel 2006.
6. Hernández and Charney 1998.
7. Capps et al. 2004.
8. Suro and Passel 2003, p. 5.
9. New York Department of Education 2007.
10. Los Angeles Unified School District 2007.
11. For more information on country-of-origin sending contexts, see the online supplement, Introduction, note 1.
12. For more information on the recruitment procedures, see ibid., note 2.
13. Ibid., note 3.
14. Ibid., note 4.
15. For more information on the attrition rate, see ibid., note 5.
16. Ibid., note 6.
17. Ibid., note 7.
18. Ibid., note 8.

19. Ibid., note 9.
20. Please refer to Table I.1 for details.
21. U.S. Census Bureau 2006.
22. Hook 2006.
23. See the online supplement, Introduction, note 10.
24. Ibid., note 11 and Table 2.
25. See Table 3 in the online supplement for the top two occupational niches.
26. See Table 4 in the online supplement for employment rate details by group.
27. See ibid. for details.
28. Capps et al. 2004. See also the online supplement, Introduction, note 12.
29. Please see Table 2 in the online supplement for details.
30. See the online supplement, Introduction, note 13.
31. See Table I.1, for details.
32. Branch 1999; Bronfenbrenner 1988; Doucette-Gates, Brooks-Gunn, and Chase-Lansdale 1998; Hughes, Seidman, and Edwards 1993; Sue and Sue 1987.
33. Knight and Hill 1993.
34. See Campbell and Stanley 1963; and Gillespie 1991.
35. Cooper et al. 1998.
36. See the online supplement, Introduction, note 14.
37. Professor Min Zhou in the Department of Sociology at UCLA was a consultant for our Chinese sample. We consulted with Dr. Paul Farmer of the Harvard Medical School and the Department of Anthropology on the particular issues facing Haitians. We also consulted with Carol Berrote-Joseph regarding linguistic challenges faced by Haitians and Lilian Bobea on Dominican culture and migration to the United States.
38. Spradley 1980.
39. See the online supplement, Introduction, note 15.
40. McLoyd and Steinberg 1998; C. Suárez-Orozco and M. Suárez-Orozco 1995.
41. These scales are described in more detail in Chapter 1. Also please refer to the online supplement for interview protocols as well as subscale descriptions and items.
42. See the online supplement, Introduction, note 16.
43. Ibid., note 17.
44. Murray 1943; online supplement, Introduction, note 18.
45. Bellak 1986; Lindzey 1961.
46. DeVos 1973; C. Suárez-Orozco, M. Suárez-Orozco, and Todorova 2005; see also the online supplement, Introduction, note 19.
47. See Introduction, note 20, in the online supplement.
48. M. Suárez-Orozco 1989; C. Suárez-Orozco and M. Suárez-Orozco 1995.
49. See the online supplement, Introduction, note 21.
50. Ibid., note 22.

51. Ibid., note 23.

52. C. Suárez-Orozco and M. Suárez-Orozco 1995.

53. For the sample teacher-behavior checklist, see the online supplement.

54. For a sample teacher interview, see the online supplement.

55. Muñoz-Sandoval et al. 1998.

56. See the online supplement, Introduction, note 24.

57. Ibid., note 25.

58. Ibid., note 26.

59. Ibid., note 27.

60. Ibid., note 28.

61. Lawrence-Lightfoot and Hoffmann-Davis 1997.

62. Miller, Hengst, and Wang 2003; Yin 2002.

63. Stake 1994.

64. See the online supplement, Introduction, note 29.

65. Ibid., note 30.

66. Kluckhohn 1949.

1. Academic Engagement and Performance

1. All names of students and schools used throughout this book have been changed to protect the identities of our participants.

2. See the online supplement, Chapter 1, note 1.

3. C. Suárez-Orozco and M. Suárez-Orozco 1995.

4. Vigil 2002.

5. Eccles, Midgley, and Adler 1984; Eccles, Wigfield, and Schiefele 1998; Eccles and Midgley 1992; C. Suárez-Orozco, M. Suárez-Orozco, and Doucet 2003.

6. Ibid.; Fredricks, Blumenfeld, and Paris 2004.

7. Hernández and Charney 1998; Portes and Rumbaut 2001.

8. Steinberg, Brown, and Dornbusch 1996.

9. Grades were a primary outcome measure used in this study. Report cards were gathered for each participant during each year of the study, and an academic grade-point average was calculated by averaging the grades for math, science, language arts, and social studies courses.

10. See the online supplement, Chapter 1, note 4.

11. Ibid., note 5.

12. Eccles and Roeser 2003.

13. See the online supplement, Chapter 1, note 6.

14. Ibid., note 7.

15. Astone and McLanahan 1991; Boyce Rodgers and Rose 2001; Kim 2004; Pong, Dronkers, and Hampden-Thompson 2003.

16. Aufseeser, Jekielek, and Brown 2006; Portes and Rumbaut 2001.

17. See the online supplement, Chapter 1, Table A.
18. Bourdieu and Passeron 1977; Jencks 1972; Madaus and Clarke 1998; Sirin and Rogers-Sirin 2005; White 1982.
19. C. Suárez-Orozco and M. Suárez-Orozco 2001.
20. See the online supplement, Chapter 1, Table A.
21. Ibid.
22. Connell 2000; Kleinfeld 1998; Spring 1994; U.S. Department of Education 1995; C. Suárez-Orozco and Qin 2006; Brandon 1991; García-Coll, Szalacha, and Palacios 2005; Portes and Rumbaut 2001; Rong and Brown 2001; C. Suárez-Orozco and Qin-Hilliard 2004; Way and Chu 2004.
23. Brandon 1991; Dunn 1988; Gibson 1988; Lee 2001; López 2003; Portes and Rumbaut 2001; Qin 2003; C. Suárez-Orozco and Qin-Hilliard 2004; Waters 1996.
24. Stanton-Salazar 2001; Qin 2003; see also C. Suárez-Orozco and Qin 2006.
25. López 2003; C. Suárez-Orozco and Qin 2006.
26. Kenny-Benson et al. 2006.
27. López 2003; C. Suárez-Orozco and Qin 2006.
28. Crul and Doomernik 2003; DeVos 1980; López 2003; Ferguson 2000.
29. Adams 1994; Gibson 1988; Waters 1996. See also C. Suárez-Orozco and Qin 2006.
30. Gibson 1988; M. Suárez-Orozco 1998; Waters 1996. See also C. Suárez-Orozco and Qin 2006.
31. Connell 2000. See also C. Suárez-Orozco and Qin 2006.
32. C. Suárez-Orozco and Qin 2006.
33. Fuligini and Pederson 2002.
34. Olsen 1997; Sarroub 2001; Valenzuela 1999; Waters 1996.
35. See the online supplement, Chapter 1, Table A.
36. Ibid., note 3.
37. C. Suárez-Orozco and M. Suárez-Orozco 2001.
38. Elmore, Abelmann, and Fuhrman 1996.
39. Hulpia and Valcke 2004; Slotnik and Gratz 1999. See Chapter 3 for greater detail about the role of these factors in student performance.
40. Waters 1999.
41. Wilson 1997; Massey and Denton 1993; Orfield and Yun 1999; Orfield and Lee 2006; García-Coll and Magnuson 1997; Mehan et al. 1996; Willis 1977.
42. Bryk and Schneider 2003; Currie et al. 2000; McLaughlin and Talbert 1993; Samdal et al. 1998.
43. Elliott, Hamburg, and Williams 1998, 3–28.
44. Garbarino and Dubrow 1997; O'Donnell, Schwab-Stone, and Muyeed 2002.
45. See the online supplement, Chapter 1, note 8.
46. Ibid., Table A. Note that this finding is consistent with that described in Portes and Rumbaut 2001.
47. See the online supplement, Chapter 1, Table A.

48. Ibid., note 9; Muñoz-Sandoval et al. 1998.

49. Portes and Rumbaut 2001.

50. Ruiz-de-Valasco, Fix, and Clewell 2001.

51. Collier 1992; Cummins 1991; Klesmer 1994.

52. See the online supplement, Chapter 1, Table A.

53. Ibid.

54. Fredricks, Blumenfeld, and Paris 2004; Greenwood, Horton, and Utley 2002; National Research Council 2004; Steinberg, Brown, and Dornbusch 1996.

55. Rumberger 2004.

56. See the online supplement, Chapter 1, note 10.

57. Ibid., Table A.

58. Cauce, Felner, and Primavera 1982; Dubow 1991; Levitt, Guacci-Franco, and Levitt 1994; Wentzel 1999.

59. Portes and Rumbaut 2001; Zhou and Bankston 1998.

60. Cobb 1976; Sarason, Sarason, and Pierce 1990; Wills 1985.

61. Fredricks, Blumenfeld, and Paris 2004.

62. Stanton-Salazar 2001.

63. Gibson, Gándara, and Koyama 2004; Hill and Madhere 1996.

64. Berndt 1999; Ogbu and Herbert, 1998; Steinberg, Brown, and Dornbusch 1996.

65. Hamilton and Darling 1996; Lynch and Cicchetti 1997; Pianta 1999; Roeser and Eccles 1998; Roffman, C. Suárez-Orozco, and Rhodes 2003.

66. Rhodes 2002.

67. Ibid.

68. Hamre and Pianta 2001; Pianta 1999; Goodenow 1993; Jenkins 1997; Midgley, Feldlaufer, and Eccles 1989; Roeser and Eccles 1998; Reddy, Rhodes, and Mulhall 2003; Ryan, Stiller, and Lynch 1994.

69. See the online supplement, Chapter 1, note 11.

70. Ibid., note 12.

71. Ibid., note 13.

72. Ibid., note 14.

73. Currie et al. 2004; Hernández and Charney 1998; Suárez-Orozco, Todorova, and Qin 2006.

74. Karatzias et al. 2002.

75. Samdal et al. 1998.

76. Bankston and Zhou 2002.

77. C. Suárez-Orozco and Qin 2006; online supplement, Chapter 1, note 15.

78. Ibid.

79. Portes and Rumbaut 2001.

80. Schunk 1991.

81. See the online supplement, Chapter 1, Table A.

82. Kao and Tienda 1995.

83. Fuligini 1997.

84. C. Suárez-Orozco and M. Suárez-Orozco 1995.

85. See the online supplement, Chapter 1, note 17.

86. Ibid., Table A.

87. Ibid.

88. Ibid.

89. See the online supplement, Chapter 1, note 18.

90. Baker 1999; Rumberger 2004; Wang, Haertel, and Wahlberg 1994.

91. Bryk and Schneider 2003; Stanton-Salazar 2004.

92. Fredricks, Blumenfeld, and Paris 2004; Greenwood, Horton, and Utley 2002; Marks 2000; Steinberg, Brown, and Dornbusch 1996.

93. See the online supplement, Chapter 1, note 19.

94. Ibid., Table A.

95. Ibid., note 20.

96. Ibid., note 21.

97. Ibid., note 22.

98. Ibid., Table A.

99. Ibid., note 23.

100. See Boston 2003; Brookhart 1994; ibid., note 24.

101. See the online supplement, Chapter 1, note 25.

102. Ibid., note 26.

103. Ibid., note 27.

104. Ibid., note 28.

105. Ibid., note 29.

106. Ibid., Table A.

2. Networks of Relationships

1. M. Suárez-Orozco 2005; Borjas 1994; Massey, Durand, and Malone 2002; Piore 1971.

2. C. Suárez-Orozco 2004b.

3. Waldinger 1997.

4. M. Suárez-Orozco 2005.

5. Heller and Swindle 1983.

6. Falicov 1980 and 1998; C. Suárez-Orozco and M. Suárez-Orozco 2001.

7. Portions of this section were first reported in C. Suárez-Orozco, Todorova, and Louie 2002; Glick Schiller 1992; Basch and Blanc-Szanton 1992.

8. Hondagneu-Sotelo 1994.

9. Ibid; Hill 2004.

10. Arnold 1991; Simpao 1999.

11. Winnicott 1958.

12. Western 1989.

13. Ainsworth 1989; Bowlby 1973.

14. Ainsworth 1989.

15. Ibid.

16. Boss 1991; Doka 1989; Feshbach and Feshbach 2001; Hepworth, Ryder, and Dreyer 1984; Neimeyer 2001; Payne, Horn, and Relf 1999; Shapiro 1994.

17. Goldstein, Wampler, and Wise 1997; Payne, Horn, and Relf 1999.

18. Boss 1991.

19. Doka 1989.

20. Shapiro 1994; Silverman 2000.

21. Shapiro 1994.

22. Ibid.

23. Silverman 2000.

24. Ibid.

25. Soto 1987; Bagley 1972; Burke 1980; Gordon 1964; Sewell-Coker, Hamilton-Collins, and Fein 1985; Waters 1999; Gordon 1996.

26. Burke 1980; Gordon 1964; Sewell-Coker, Hamilton-Collins, and Fein 1985; Soto 1987; Waters 1999.

27. Soto 1987.

28. Bagley 1972; Burke 1980; Gordon 1964; Sewell-Cocker, Hamilton-Collins, and Fein 1985.

29. Bowlby 1973.

30. Arnold 1991; Sciarra 1999.

31. Forman 1993; Burke 1980; Wilkes 1992; Rutter 1971; Hohn 1996; Burke 1980; Wilkes 1992.

32. See the online supplement, Chapter 2, note 1.

33. Ibid., note 2.

34. Ibid., note 3.

35. Ibid., note 4.

36. Partida 1996.

37. Arnold 1991; Chestham 1972.

38. Ibid.

39. Glasgow and Gouse-Shees 1995.

40. All quotations have been translated from the respondent's native language.

41. Perez-Foster 2001.

42. Simpao 1999.

43. Boti and Bautista 1999.

44. Arnold 1991; Falicov 1998; Falicov 2002.

45. Falicov 2002.

46. Shapiro 1994.

47. Clarke-Stewart et al. 2000; Falicov 1998; Hohn 1996; Lyons-Ruth 1996; Shapiro 1994; Weissbourd 1996.

48. Boothby 1992; Perez-Foster 2001.

49. Falicov 2002; Arnold 1991; Burke 1980.

50. Glasgow and Gouse-Shees 1995.

51. Robertson and Robertson 1971.

52. See the online supplement, Chapter 2, note 5.

53. Levitt 2001.

54. Holmes and Rahe 1967; Downs, Driskill, and Wuthnow 1990.

55. C. Suárez-Orozco and M. Suárez-Orozco 2001.

56. See the online supplement, Chapter 2, note 6.

57. Hurrelmann et al. 1988; Paulson, Marchant, and Rothlisberg 1998.

58. See the online supplement, Chapter 2, note 7.

59. Ibid., note 8.

60. Ibid., notes 9 and 10.

61. C. Suárez-Orozco and M. Suárez-Orozco 1995.

62. Valenzuela 1999; Faulstich-Orellana 2001.

63. Faulstich-Orellana 2003.

64. Portions of this section were adapted from C. Suárez-Orozco, Pimentel, and Martin in press.

65. Fuligini and Pederson 2002.

66. These items were adapted from a scale developed by Fuligini (1997).

67. Zhou and Li 2004; V. S. Louie 2004.

68. Gibson, Gándara, and Koyama 2004; Stanton-Salazar 2004.

69. Portions of this section were adapted from C. Suárez-Orozco, Pimentel, and Martin in press.

70. Stanton-Salazar 2004.

71. Erickson 1982; Gibson, Gándara, and Koyama 2004; McDermott 1977; Raley 2004.

72. Gibson, Gándara, and Koyama 2004.

73. See the online supplement, Chapter 2, note 11.

74. Ibid., note 12.

75. Berry et al. 2006; Bornstein and Cote 2006.

76. Gordon 1964.

77. Ferguson 2001.

78. See the online supplement, Chapter 2, note 13.

79. Ogbu and Herbert 1998; C. Suárez-Orozco and M. Suárez-Orozco 1995.

80. Rhodes 2002.

81. Roffman, C. Suárez-Orozco, and Rhodes 2003.

82. Rhodes 2002.

83. Ibid.
84. Noam 2004; Roffman, C. Suárez-Orozco, and Rhodes 2003.
85. Zhou and Li 2004.
86. Noam 2004.

3. Less-Than-Optimal Schools

1. Edwards 2006.
2. C. Suárez-Orozco and Qin-Hilliard 2004; Gardner 2004.
3. C. Suárez-Orozco and M. Suárez-Orozco 2001.
4. Gates Foundation 2006.
5. Marks and Printy 2003; Poston, Stone, and Muther 1992; Weiss 2005.
6. C. Suárez-Orozco and M. Suárez-Orozco 2001, 133.
7. Orfield and Lee 2006.
8. Ibid., 4.
9. Capps 2001.
10. Ibid.
11. Luthar 1999.
12. Elliott, Hamburg, and Williams 1998.
13. Johnson, Arumi, and Ott 2006, 3.
14. See the online supplement, Chapter 3, note 1.
15. Ibid., note 2.
16. Ibid., note 3; Elmore, Abelmann, and Fuhrman 1996.
17. Hulpia and Valcke 2004; Slotnik and Gratz 1999; Gregory, Nygreen, and Morgan 2006.
18. Robertson 2001.
19. Orfield and Lee 2006.
20. Ibid; Noguera 2002; Noguera 2003.
21. Noguera and Wing 2006.
22. See the online supplement, Chapter 3, note 4.
23. Ibid., note 5.
24. Ibid., note 6.
25. Ibid., note 7.
26. Ibid., note 8.
27. All names of people and schools in these ethnographies are pseudonyms.
28. The most dangerous cities are listed online at www.governmentguide.com/community_and_home/morganmostdangerouscities.adp (accessed July 6, 2006).
29. See the online supplement, Chapter 3, note 9.
30. The state currently requires students with "limited English proficiency" (LEP) but who have been enrolled in U.S. schools for more than three years to take the test.
31. Tatum 1997.
32. Described in Chapter 2.

33. See the online supplement, Chapter 3, note 10.
34. C. Suárez-Orozco and M. Suárez-Orozco 1995; ibid., note 11.
35. Weinstein 2002.
36. Ibid., 290.
37. C. Suárez-Orozco 2000.
38. See the online supplement, Chapter 3, note 12.
39. Ibid., note 13.
40. C. Suárez-Orozco and Qin-Hilliard 2004.
41. Note that data presented in the following section first appeared in ibid.
42. See the online supplement, Chapter 3, notes 14 and 15.
43. Ibid., note 16.
44. Ibid., note 17.
45. Ibid., note 18.
46. Horn, Flores, and Orfield 2006.
47. Bernstein et al. 2006.
48. Two legislative measures have been proposed to address this problem: The 2003 "DREAM Act," S. 1545 and "Student Adjustment Act," H.R. 1684 (formerly H.R. 1918), though the fate of these bills is far from certain.
49. U.S. Census 2006.
50. Ruiz-de-Velasco, Fix, and Clewell 2001.
51. Delpit 1995.

4. The Challenge of Learning English

1. See C. Suárez-Orozco and M. Suárez-Orozco 2001, chapter 2.
2. Huntington 2004, xvi. See Alba and Nee 1997 for alternative perspectives grounded in data rather than rhetoric.
3. Cohen 2006.
4. Portes and Hao 1998.
5. Tremblay and Gardner 1995. Indeed, August and Hakuta (2005) have documented that in English as a Second Language environments, the drive to learn English is very strong among nearly all of the students. See also Zucker 1985.
6. See the online supplement, Chapter 4, note 1.
7. Ibid., note 2.
8. Ibid., note 3.
9. Ibid., note 4.
10. Ibid., note 5.
11. Butler and Hakuta 2005.
12. Grosjean 1999.
13. Peal and Lambert 1962; quotation cited in Butler and Hakuta 2005, 114.
14. Fishman 1977; Valdés and Figueroa, 1994.

15. Ibid.

16. Cummins 1991; Bee et al. 1982.

17. Cummins (1991) bases his estimate of five to seven years on an idealistic, well-funded Canadian immersion context, while Collier (1992) reports that ten years is a more realistic time frame. Previous literacy in native language, quality of language instruction, opportunities to use and develop the language, as well as other factors work together to facilitate or impede second-language development.

18. See the online supplement, Chapter 4, note 6.

19. Muñoz-Sandoval et al. 1998.

20. See the online supplement, Chapter 4, notes 7 and 8.

21. Ibid., note 9.

22. Ibid., note 10.

23. Ibid., note 11.

24. Ibid., note 12.

25. Ibid., note 13.

26. Ibid., note 14.

27. Cummins 1991.

28. Entwisle and Anstone 1994; Gass and Selinker 2001; Páez 2001.

29. Heath 1983; Schieffelin and Ochs 1986.

30. August and Shanahan 2006; Butler and Hakuta 2005.

31. Ibid.

32. Preadolescents also seem to have a greater capacity to "replicate intonational patterns." See Gass and Selinker 2001, 336.

33. See the online supplement, Chapter 4, notes 15 and 16.

34. Gass and Selinker 2001.

35. Ibid.

36. Skehan 1989.

37. Gass and Selinker 2001.

38. Brehm and Self 1989; Gardner 1985.

39. Gass and Selinker 2001.

40. Ibid.

41. August and Hakuta 2005; Fishman 1977.

42. Gass and Selinker 2001, 333.

43. August and Hakuta 1997.

44. Lindholm-Leary 2001; Thomas and Collier 2002.

45. Louie 2003; Thomas and Collier 2002; see also the online supplement, Chapter 4, note 17.

46. Online supplement, Chapter 4, note 18.

47. C. Suárez-Orozco and M. Suárez-Orozco 2001; Thomas and Collier 2002.

48. Thomas and Collier 2002.

49. The experiences of our participants were not atypical. In a longitudinal study of

students attending New York City public schools, many students, in particular Spanish- and Kreyol-speaking students, received inconsistent language services over the years. The performance of students who received inconsistent second-language instruction was considerably lower than that of students who received either consistent bilingual or consistent ESL instruction (Tobias personal communication).

50. Note that Massachusetts passed the Unz initiative in 2002, the year the data collection phase of our study was completed.

51. This was particularly the case following the passage of Proposition 227 in California in 1997.

52. See the online supplement, Chapter 4, note 19.

53. STAR in California and MCAS in Massachusetts; ibid., note 20.

54. Orfield and Yun 1999; Valdés 1998; Olsen 1997.

55. Faltis 1999; Ruiz-de-Valasco, Fix, and Clewell 2001.

5. Portraits of Declining Achievers

1. This group represents 24.7 percent of the entire sample (see Chapter 1).

2. This group represents 27.8 percent of the entire sample (see Chapter 1).

3. Please refer to Table 5.1, which pertains to all the portrait chapters.

4. All reported differences were tested for significance. For categorical variables we report percentage and establish significance with chi square; for continuous data we report least square means and establish significance with ANOVA (analysis of variance); significance levels: * <.05; ** <.01; * <.001. See Table 5.1.

5. Eccles and Roeser 2003.

6. More than a quarter (26.4 percent) of the precipitous decliners reported having long separations from parents followed by complicated reunifications. They were also nearly twice as likely as students in other academic trajectory groups to characterize as a "serious problem" the statement "You were separated from your parents for some time and it has taken a while to get used to one another."

7. Since there were ethical dilemmas in asking questions about documentation, we did not systematically gather these data. During meetings with many of our students, however, their families would in many cases let us know when they were struggling with issues of documentation. For example, they would tell us that what they disliked most about immigration was the "crossing" or they would tell us that an obstacle for getting ahead was their lack of documentation. Our analyses of the case studies revealed that students whom we knew were undocumented were disproportionably found among the precipitous decliners and our lowest achievers.

8. Ainslie 1998.

9. Based on the Bilingual Verbal Abilities Test (BVAT).

10. Using the Psychosomatic Symptom Scale, we can see that her score was very low, only 8.0, when we administered the scale in the beginning of the study, but jumped to 29.0 by the end of the study (the mean for the sample is 18.8). The score is not, however, excessively high; the maximum score for the sample was 48.0.

11. This term is even broader in scope than "moral education" and encompasses all teachings in how to become an intelligent, sensible, and traditional human being.

12. Henry scored at the 88th percentile on the combined score and at the eighth percentile for English proficiency on the Bilingual Verbal Abilities Test.

13. On the Broad Reading subtest he scored in the third percentile, while on the Broad Math subtest he scored in the 94th percentile. These scores are based on the Woodcock Johnson Test of Achievement subtests.

14. Based on the Sentence Completion Task.

15. In the Sentence Completion Task at the fourth year of the study.

16. In the TAT task at the first year of the study.

17. During an additional "separations interview" we conducted in the fourth year of the study, we focused on issues surrounding family separations.

18. Vigil 2002.

19. Ogbu 1978.

20. Majors and Gordon 1994.

21. Thirty-one percent of the students are eligible for the reduced-price lunch program.

22. Based on the Bilingual Verbal Abilities Test.

23. Golan 1981; Schlossberg 1984.

6. Portraits of Low Achievers

1. Please refer to Table 5.1.

2. Based on the Sentence Completion Task.

3. Ibid.

4. Ibid.

5. C. Suárez-Orozco 2000.

6. Qin 2006.

7. From a "separations interview" conducted during the fourth year of the study.

8. Myriam states that she missed several days of school in order to take care of her father after the eye surgery. This lengthy quotation is from ibid.

9. Our research team communicated with the counselor in Myriam's about this home situation, and they, as well as the police, were aware of what was going on.

10. From a "separations interview" conducted during the fourth year of the study.

11. Ibid.

12. Based on the Sentence Completion Task.

13. According to the district school report, in authors' possession.

14. According to the Networks of Social Relations Questionnaire.

7. Portraits of Improvers

1. Please refer to Table 5.1.

2. Desir 2005.

3. Rosette's score on the Psychosomatic Symptom Scale was high compared to the average for the sample (the mean was 18.8 in Year 5 of the study). Her score was 33 in Year 1 and 40 in Year 5.

4. Based on the Bilingual Verbal Abilities Test.

5. See the online supplement for details.

8. Portraits of High Achievers

1. Of our sample, 22.5 percent demonstrated a high achieving academic trajectory (as defined in Chapter 1), maintaining an A-minus average over the five years of the study (Year 1: 3.47; Year 2: 3.63; Year 3: 3.61; Year 4: 3.50; and Year 5: 3.46).

2. Please refer to Table 5.1.

3. Of the high achievers, 57.8 percent reported not having been separated from their nuclear family during immigration. This is a significantly lower rate of separation than for all the other groups and much less than the total sample rate of separation, which was 85 percent. Further, only 2 percent of the high achievers reported that a long separation followed by a complicated reunification posed a serious problem in their family. They were by far least likely to call a "serious problem" the statement "You were separated from your parents for some time and it has taken a while to get used to one another."

4. Based on the Bilingual Verbal Abilities Test.

5. Based on the behavior checklists administered to teachers.

6. From the Sentence Completion Task.

7. Based on the Network of Relations.

8. Based on the Bilingual Verbal Abilities Test.

9. Woodcock-Johnson Psycho-educational Battery, Revised.

10. Desir 2005.

11. This observation was made by the research assistant one year after the official completion of our study.

12. Desir 2005.

13. Based on the Sentence Completion Task.

14. Ibid.

15. Based on the Bilingual Verbal Abilities Test.

16. Based on the Sentence Completion Task.

17. He scored in the 93rd percentile on the Broad Reading subscale and in the 99th percentile on the Broad Math subscale of the Woodcock Johnson Test of Achievement-R.

18. Louie 2004.

Conclusion

1. Ruiz-de-Valasco, Fix, and Clewell 2001.

2. Simon and Alexander 1993; C. Suárez-Orozco and M. Suárez-Orozco 2001.

3. See Religious Affiliation of the U.S. Supreme Court, www.adherents.com/adh_sc.html (accessed December 3, 2006).

4. Alba and Nee 1997; Glendon 2006.

5. At the time this book went to press, yet another immigration reform proposal was being discussed. No doubt the debate will continue for years to come.

6. American Community Survey 2006, U.S. Census Bureau; see www.census.gov/acs/www (accessed May 17, 2007).

7. OECD 2005.

8. Wacquant 1999.

9. On being locked out of adequate education, see PISA 2003; C. Suárez-Orozco 2004a.

10. Edwards 2006.

11. M. Suárez-Orozco and Qin-Hilliard 2004; Gardner 2004; Sussmuth 2005.

12. Gates Foundation 2006.

13. Kennedy 2001.

14. Lieberson 1981.

15. Levy and Murnane 2007.

16. Sommer 2002.

17. C. Suárez-Orozco 2004a.

18. Examples of refugee resettlement organizations that have a long history of serving newcomers well include: the International Rescue Committee; Migration and Refugee Services, U.S. Conference of Catholic Bishops; the Hebrew Immigrant Aid Society; and the Lutheran Immigration and Refugee Service. These organizations have over the years developed many effective practices to facilitate the integration of newcomers, nearly half of whom are children.

19. Pew Hispanic Center 2006.

20. Mandel 2006.

References

Abel, T. 1973. *Psychological Testing in Cultural Contexts.* New Haven, Conn.: Yale University Press.

Adams, D. 1994. Predicting the Academic Achievement of Puerto Rican and Mexican-American Ninth-Grade Students. *Urban Review* 261:1–14.

Ainslie, R. 1998. Cultural Mourning, Immigration, and Engagement: Vignettes from the Mexican Experience. In M. M. Suárez-Orozco, ed., *Crossings: Mexican Immigration in Interdisciplinary Perspectives.* Cambridge: David Rockefeller Center for Latin American Studies and Harvard University Press.

Ainsworth, M. D. S. 1989. Attachments beyond Infancy. *American Psychologist* 444:709–716.

Alba, R., and N. Nee. 1997. Rethinking Assimilation Theory for a New Era of Immigration. *International Migration Review* 31: 826–874.

Arnold, E. 1991. Issues of Reunification of Migrant West Indian Children in the United Kingdom. In J. L. Roopnarine and J. Brown, eds., *Caribbean Families: Diversity among Ethnic Groups,* pp. 243–258. Greenwich, Conn.: Ablex.

Astone, N. M., and S. S. McLanahan. 1991. Family Structure, Parental Practices, and High School Completion. *American Sociological Review* 563:309–320.

Aufseeser, D., S. Jekielek, and B. Brown. 2006. The Family Environment and Adolescent Well-Being: Exposure to Positive and Negative Family Influences. nahic.ucsf.edu/index.php/nahic/article/the_family_environment_adolescent_well_being (accessed June 23, 2006).

August, D., and K. Hakuta. 2005. Bilingualism and Second-Language Learning. In M. M. Suárez-Orozco, C. Suárez-Orozco, and D. B. Qin, eds., *The New Immigration: An Interdisciplinary Reader,* pp. 233–248. New York: Brunner-Routledge.

———, eds. 1997. *Improving Schooling for Language-Minority Children: A Research Agenda.* Washington, D.C.: National Academy Press.

August, D., and T. Shanahan. 2006. *Developing Literacy in Second-Language Learners: Report of the National Literacy Panel on Language-Minority Children and Youth.* Mahwah, N.J.: Lawrence Erlbaum.

Bagley, C. 1972. Deviant Behavior in English and West Indian School Children. *Research in Education* 8:47–55.

Baker, J. A. 1999. Teacher-Student Interaction in Urban At-Risk Classrooms: Differential Behavior, Relationship Quality, and Student Satisfaction with School. *Elementary School Journal* 1001:57–70.

Bankston, C., and M. Zhou. 2002. Being Well vs. Doing Well: Self-Esteem and School Performance among Immigrant and Nonimmigrant Racial and Ethnic Groups. *International Migration Review* 362:389–415.

Barry, T., and D. Preusch. 1986. *The Central American Fact Book.* New York: Grove Press.

Bee, H. L., K. E. Barnard, S. J. Eyres, C. A. Gray, M. A. Hammond, and A. L. Spietz. 1982. Predictions of IQ and Language Skill from Perinatal Status, Child Performance, Family Characteristics, and Mother-Infant Interaction. *Child Development* 53:1134–1156.

Bellak, L. 1986. *The Thematic Apperception Test, the Children's Apperception Test, and the Senior Apperception Technique in Clinical Use,* 4th ed. New York: Grune and Stratton.

Berndt, T. J. 1999. Friends' Influence on Students' Adjustment to School. *Educational Psychologist* 341:15–28.

Bernstein, L., M. Cannon, H. Kim, S. McDonald, and M. Moremen. 2006. Bowling for Undocumented Immigrants: Policy Issues in Immigration, Education, Employment, Social Services and Legal License EADU 8110. www.arches.uga.edu/~melissa7/doc/Policy_20Paper.doc (accessed July 20, 2006).

Berry, J. W., J. S. Phinney, D. L. Sam, and P. Vedder, eds. 2006. *Immigrant Youth in Cultural Transition: Acculturation, Identity, and Adaptation across National Contexts.* Mahwah, N.J.: Lawrence Erlbaum.

Boothby, N. 1992. Displaced Children: Psychological Theory and Practice from the Field. *Journal of Refugee Studies* 52:106–122.

Borjas, G. J. 1994. The Economics of Immigrants. *Journal of Economic Literature* 32:1667–1717.

Bornstein, M. H., and L. R. Cote, eds. 2006. *Acculturation and Parent-Child Relationships: Measurement and Development.* Mahwah, N.J.: Lawrence Erlbaum.

Boss, P. 1991. Ambiguous Loss. In M. M. F. Walsh, ed., *Living beyond Loss: Death in the Family,* pp. 164–175. New York: W. W. Norton.

Boston, C. 2003. *High School Report Cards: ERIC Digest.* Education Resources Information Center (ERIC), www.eric.ed.gov (accessed May 21, 2007).

Boti, M., and F. Bautista. 1999. *When Strangers Meet.* Montreal: National Film Board of Canada. Film.

Bourdieu, P., and J. Passeron. 1977. *Reproduction in Education, Society and Culture*. Beverly Hills, Calif.: Sage.

Bowlby, J. 1973. *Separation, Anxiety and Anger*. New York: Basic Books.

Boyce Rodgers, K., and H. A. Rose. 2001. Personal, Family, and School Factors Related to Adolescent Academic Performance: A Comparison by Family Structure. *Marriage and Family Review* 334:47–61.

Branch, C. W. 1999. Race and Human Development. In *Racial and Ethnic Identity in School Practices: Aspects of Human Development*, pp. 7–28. Mahwah, N.J.: Lawrence Erlbaum.

Brandon, P. 1991. Gender Differences in Young Asian Americans' Educational Attainment. *Sex Roles* 251/252:45–61.

Brehm, J., and E. Self. 1989. The Intensity of Motivation. *Annual Review of Psychology* 40:109–131.

Bronfenbrenner, U. 1988. Foreword. In R. Pence, ed., *Ecological Research with Children and Families: Concepts to Methodology*, pp. ix–xix. New York: Teachers College Press.

Brookhart, S. M. 1994. Teachers' Grading: Practice and Theory. *Applied Measurement in Education* 74:279–301.

Bryk, A., and B. Schneider. 2003. Trust in Schools: A Core Resource for School Reform. *Educational Leadership* 60(6): 40–44.

Bureau of the Census. 2000. *Current Population Reports*. Washington, D.C.: U.S. Census Bureau.

Burke, A. W. 1980. Family Stress and Precipitation of Psychiatric Disorder: A Comparative Study among Immigrant West Indian and Native British Patients in Birmingham. *International Journal of Social Psychiatry* 261:35–40.

Butler, Y. G., and K. Hakuta. 2005. Bilingualism and Second Language Acquisition. In T. K. Bhatia and W. C. Ritchie, eds., *The Handbook of Bilingualism*, pp. 114–144. London: Blackwell.

Campbell, D. T., and J. C. Stanley. 1963. *Experimental and Quasi-Experimental Designs for Research*. Chicago: Rand-McNally College Publishing.

Capps, R. 2001. *Hardship among Children of Immigrants: Findings from the 1999 National Survey of America's Families*. Washington, D.C.: Urban Institute.

Capps, R., M. Fix, J. Ost, J. Reardon-Anderson, and J. S. Passel. 2004. *The Health and Well-Being of Young Children of Immigrants*. Washington, D.C.: Urban Institute.

Cauce, A. M., R. D. Felner, and J. Primavera. 1982. Social Support in High-Risk Adolescents: Structural Components and Adaptive Impact. *American Journal of Community Psychology* 104:417–428.

Central Intelligence Agency. 2006. *The World Factbook*. www.cia.gov/cia/publications/factbook/index.html (accessed January 7, 2006).

Chestham, J. 1972. *Social Work with Immigrants*. London: Routledge and Kegan Publishing.

Clarke-Stewart, K. A., K. McCartney, D. L. Vandell, M. T. Owen, and C. Booth. 2000. Effects of Parental Separation and Divorce on Very Young Children. *Journal of Family Psychology* 142:304–326.

Coatsworth, J. H. 1994. *Central America and the United States since 1945: The Clients and the Colossus.* New York: Twayne International History Series.

Cobb, S. 1976. Social Support as a Moderator of Life Stress. *Psychosomatic Medicine* 385:300–314.

Cohen, N. 2006. So English Is Taking Over the Globe: So What? *New York Times,* August 6.

Collier, V. P. 1992. A Synthesis of Studies Examining Long-Term Language-Minority Student Data on Academic Achievement. *Bilingual Research Journal* 161/162:187–212.

Connell, R. W. 2000. *The Men and the Boys.* Berkeley: University of California Press.

Cooper, C. R., J. F. Jackson, M. Azmitia, and E. M. López. 1998. Multiple Selves, Multiple Worlds: Three Useful Strategies for Research with Ethnic Minority Youth on Identity, Relationship and Opportunity Structures. In V. McCloyd and L. Steinberg, eds., *Studying Minority Adolescents: Conceptual, Methodological, and Theoretical Issues,* pp. 111–125. Mahwah, N.J.: Lawrence Erlbaum.

Crul, M., and J. Doomernik. 2003. The Turkish and Moroccan Second Generation in the Netherlands: Divergent Trends between and Polarization within the Two Groups. *International Migration Review* 374:1039–1064.

Cummins, J. 1991. Language Development and Academic Learning. In L. M. Malavé and G. Duquette, eds., *Language, Culture, and Cognition,* pp. 161–175. Clevedon, Eng.: Multilingual Matters.

Currie, C., K. Hurrelmann, W. Settertobulte, R. Smith, and J. Todd. 2000. Health and Health Behaviour among Young People. *WHO Policy Series: Health Policy for Children and Adolescents,* no. 1. Copenhagen: World Health Organization Regional Office for Europe.

Currie, C., C. Roberts, A. Morgan, R. Smith, W. Settertobulte, O. Samdal, and V. Barnekow Rasmussen, eds. 2004. Young People's Health in Context: International Report from the HBSC 2001/2002 Survey. *WHO Policy Series: Health Policy for Children and Adolescents,* no. 4. Copenhagen: World Health Organization Regional Office for Europe.

Delpit, L. 1995. *Other People's Children: Cultural Conflict in the Classroom.* New York: New Press.

Derogatis, L. R. (1977). The SCL-90 Manual I: Scoring, Administration and Procedures for the SCL-90. Baltimore: Johns Hopkins University School of Medicine.

Desir, C. 2005. Lot Blo Do: Across Waters; Haitian Students Search for Identity in United States Schools. Ph.D. diss., Harvard Graduate School of Education.

DeVos, G. 1973. *Socialization for Achievement: Essays on the Cultural Psychology of the Japanese.* Berkeley: University of California Press.

———. 1980. Ethnic Adaptation and Minority Status. *Journal of Cross-Cultural Psychology* 111:101–125.

Doka, K. J. 1989. *Disenfranchised Grief: Recognizing Hidden Sorrow.* New York: Lexington Books.

Doucette-Gates, A., J. Brooks-Gunn, and L. P. Chase-Lansdale. 1998. The Role of Bias and Equivalence in the Study of Race, Class, and Ethnicity. In V. C. McLoyd, ed., *Studying Minority Adolescents: Conceptual, Methodological, and Theoretical Issues,* pp. 211–236. Mahwah, N.J.: Lawrence Erlbaum.

Downs, C. W., G. Driskill, and D. Wuthnow. 1990. A Review of Instrumentation on Stress. *Management Communication Quarterly* 41:100–126.

Duany, J. 2002. Los países: Transnational Migration from the Dominican Republic to the United States. migration.ucdavis.edu/ceme/more.php?id=19_0_6_0 (accessed March 14, 2006).

Dubow, E. F. 1991. A Two-Year Longitudinal Study of Stressful Life Events, Social Support, and Social Problem-Solving Skills: Contributions to Children's Behavioral and Academic Adjustment. *Child Development* 62(3): 583–599.

Dunn, J. 1988. The Shortage of Black Male Students in the College Classroom: Consequences and Causes. *Western Journal of Black Studies* 122:73–76.

Dussel, E. 1998. Recent Structural Changes in Mexico's Economy: Preliminary Analyses of Some Sources of Mexican Migration to the United States. In M. Suárez-Orozco, ed., *Crossings: Mexican Immigration in Interdisciplinary Perspectives.* Cambridge: David Rockefeller Center for Latin American Studies and Harvard University Press.

Eccles, J. S., and C. Midgley. 1992. The Development of Achievement Task Values: A Theoretical Analysis. *Developmental Review* 12:265–310.

Eccles, J. S., C. Midgley, and T. Adler. 1984. Grade-Related Changes in the School Environment: Effects of Achievement Motivation. In J. G. Nicholls, ed., *The Development of Achievement Motivation,* pp. 283–331. Greenwich, Conn.: JAI Press.

Eccles, J. S., and R. W. Roeser. 2003. Schools as Developmental Contexts. In G. R. Adams and M. D. Berzonsky, eds., *Blackwell Handbook of Adolescence,* pp. 129–148. London: Blackwell.

Eccles, J. S., A. Wigfield, and U. Schiefele. 1998. Motivation to Succeed. In W. Damon and N. Eisenberg, eds., *Handbook of Child Psychology,* 5th ed., vol. 3, pp. 1017–1095. New York: John Wiley and Sons.

Edwards, V., ed. 2006. Diplomas Count: An Essential Guide to Graduation and Policy Rates. Special issue, *Education Week* 25(41).

Elliott, D. S., B. A. Hamburg, and K. R. Williams, eds. 1998. *Violence in American Schools.* New York: Cambridge University Press.

Elmore, R., C. H. Abelmann, and S. H. Fuhrman. 1996. The New Accountability in State Education Reform: From Process to Performance. In H. F. Ladd, ed., *Holding Schools Accountable: Performance-Based Reform in Education.* Washington, D.C.: Brookings Institution.

Entwisle, D. R., and N. M. Anstone. 1994. Some Practical Guidelines for Measuring Youth's Race/Ethnicity and Socioeconomic Status. *Child Development* 65(6): 1521–1540.

Erickson, F. 1982. Taught Cognitive Competence and Its Immediate Environments: A Neglected Topic in the Anthropology of Education. *Anthropology and Education Quarterly* 13(2): 149–180.

Falicov, C. J. 1980. Cultural Variations in the Family Life Cycle: The Mexican American Family. In M. McGoldrick, ed., *The Family Life Cycle: A Framework for Family Therapy.* New York: Gardner Press.

———. 1998. *Latino Families in Therapy: A Guide to Multicultural Practices.* New York: Guilford Press.

———. 2002. The Family Migration Experience: Loss and Resilience. In M. Suárez-Orozco and M. Paez, eds., *Latinos: Remaking America.* Berkeley: University of California Press.

Faltis, C. J. 1999. Creating a New History. In C. J. Faltis and P. M. Wolfe, eds., *So Much to Say: Adolescents, Bilingualism, and ESL in Secondary Schools,* pp. 1–9. New York: Teachers' College Press.

Farmer, P. 2003. *Pathologies of Power.* Berkeley: University of California Press.

Faulstich-Orellana, M. 2001. The Work Kids Do: Mexican and Central American Immigrant Children's Contribution to Households and Schools in California. *Harvard Educational Review* 71(3): 366–389.

———. 2003. Responsibilities of Children in Latino Immigrant Homes. In C. Suárez-Orozco and I. Todorova, eds., *Understanding the Social Worlds of Immigrant Youth: New Directions for Youth Development,* vol. 100. New York: Jossey-Bass.

Ferguson, A. A. 2000. *Bad Boys: Public Schools in the Making of Black Masculinity.* Ann Arbor: University of Michigan Press.

Ferguson, R. F. 2001. Cultivating New Routines that Foster High Achievement for All Students: How Researchers and Practitioners Can Collaborate to Reduce the Minority Achievement Gap. *ERS Spectrum* 19(4): 34–41.

Feshbach, J., and S. Feshbach. 2001. *Psychology of Separation and Loss.* San Francisco: Jossey-Bass.

Fishman, J. 1977. Language and Ethnicity. In H. Giles, ed., *Language, Ethnicity and Intergroup Relations.* London: Academic Press.

Forman, G. 1993. Women without Their Children: Immigrant Women in the U.S. *Development* 4:51–55.

Fredricks, J. A., P. C. Blumenfeld, and A. H. Paris. 2004. School Engagement: Potential of the Concept, State of the Evidence. *Review of Educational Research* 74(1): 54–109.

Fuligini, A. 1997. The Academic Achievement of Adolescents from Immigrant Families: The Roles of Family Background, Attitudes, and Behavior. *Child Development* 69(2): 351–363.

Fuligini, A., and S. Pederson. 2002. Family Obligation and the Transition to Young Adulthood. *Developmental Psychology* 38(5): 856–868.

Garbarino, J., and N. Dubrow. 1997. *Children in Danger: Coping with the Community Consequences of Violence.* San Francisco: Jossey-Bass.

García-Coll, C., and K. Magnuson. 1997. The Psychological Experience of Immigration: A Developmental Perspective. In A. Booth, A. C. Crouter, and N. Landale, eds., *Immigration and the Family*, pp. 91–132. Mahwah, N.J.: Lawrence Erlbaum.

García-Coll, C., L. Szalacha, and N. Palacios. 2005. Children of Dominican, Portugese, and Cambodian Immigrant Families: Academic Pathways during Middle Childhood. In C. Cooper, C. García-Coll, T. Bartko, H. Davis, and C. Chatman, eds., *Developmental Pathways through Middle Childhood: Rethinking Contexts and Diversity as Resources.* Mahwah, N.J.: Lawrence Erlbaum.

Gardner, H. 2004. How Education Changes: Considerations of History, Science, and Values. In M. Suárez-Orozco and D. B. Qin-Hilliard, eds., *Globalization: Culture and Education in the New Millennium*, pp. 235–258. Berkeley: University of California Press.

Gardner, R. C. 1985. *Social Psychology and Second Language Learning: The Role of Attitudes and Motivation.* London: Edward Arnold.

Gass, S. M., and L. Selinker. 2001. *Second Language Acquisition: An Introductory Text.* 2d ed. Mahwah, N.J.: Lawrence Erlbaum.

Gates Foundation. 2006. The 3Rs Solution. www.gatesfoundation.org/Education/RelatedInfo/3Rs_Solution.htm (accessed August 1, 2006).

Gibson, M. A. 1988. *Accommodation without Assimilation: Sikh Immigrants in an American High School.* Ithaca, N.Y.: Cornell University Press.

Gibson, M. A., P. Gándara, and J. P. Koyama. 2004. *School Connections: U.S. Mexican Youth, Peers, and School Adjustment.* New York: Teacher's College Press.

Gillespie, R. 1991. *Manufacturing Knowledge: A History of the Hawthorne Experiments.* Cambridge, Eng.: Cambridge University Press.

Glasgow, G. F., and J. Gouse-Shees. 1995. Themes of Rejection and Abandonment in Group Work with Caribbean Adolescents. *Social Work with Groups* 4:3–27.

Glendon, M. A. 2006. Principled Immigration. *First Things* (June/July): 23–26.

Glick Schiller, N., L. Basch, and C. Blanc-Szanton. 1992. Transnationalism: A New Analytic Framework for Understanding Migration. In N. G. Schiller, L. Basch, and C. Blanc-Szanton, eds., *Towards a Transnational Perspective on Migration: Race, Class, Ethnicity, and Nationalism Reconsidered*, pp. 1–24. New York: New York Academy of Science.

Golan, N. 1981. *Passing through Transitions: A Guide for Practitioners.* New York: Free Press.

Goldstein, R. D., N. S. Wampler, and P. H. Wise. 1997. War Experiences and Distress Symptoms of Bosnian Children. *Pediatrics* 100(5): 873–878.

Gonzalez, S., F. Bean, A. Latapi, and S. I. E. Weintraub. 1998. U.S. Immigration Policies and Trends: The Growing Importance of Migration from Mexico. In M. Suárez-

Orozco, ed., *Crossings: Mexican Immigration in Interdisciplinary Perspectives*. Cambridge: David Rockefeller Center for Latin American Studies and Harvard University Press.

Goodenow, C. 1993. Classroom Belonging among Early Adolescent Students: Relationships to Motivation and Achievement. *Journal of Early Adolescence* 13(1): 21–43.

Gordon, M. M. 1964. *Assimilation in American life: The Role of Race, Religion, and National Origins*. Oxford, Eng.: Oxford University Press.

Gordon, S. W. 1996. "I go to 'Tanties": The Economic Significance of Child-Shifting in the Antigua, West Indies. In C. Barrow, ed., *Families in the Caribbean: Themes and Perspectives*. London: Oxford University Press.

Green, G., J. Rhodes, A. Heitler-Hirsch, and C. Suárez-Orozco. Under review. Engaging Relations: The Influence of Supportive School-Based Relationships on the Academic Engagement of Latino Immigrant Students.

Greenwood, C. R., B. T. Horton, and C. A. Utley. 2002. Academic Engagement: Current Perspectives in Research and Practice. *School Psychology Review* 31(3): 328–349.

Gregory, A., K. Nygreen, and D. Moran. 2006. The Discipline Gap and the Normalization of Failure. In P. Noguera and J. Y. Wing, eds., *Unfinished Business: Closing the Racial Achievement Gap in Our Schools*, pp. 121–150. San Francisco: Jossey-Bass.

Grosjean, F. 1999. Individual Bilingualism. In B. Spolsky, ed., *Concise Encyclopedia of Educational Linguistics*, pp. 284–290. London: Elsevier.

Hamilton, S. F., and N. Darling. 1996. Mentors in Adolescents' Lives. In K. Hurrelmann and S. F. Hamilton, eds., *Social Problems and Social Contexts in Adolescence: Perspectives across Boundaries*, pp. 199–215. New York: Aldine D. Gruyter.

Hamre, B. K., and R. C. Pianta. 2001. Early Teacher-Child Relationships and the Trajectory of Children's School Outcomes through Eighth Grade. *Child Development* 72(2):625–638.

Hassini, M. 1997. *L'école: Une chance pour les filles de parents Maghrebins*. Paris: L'Harmattan.

Haveman, R., and B. Wolfe. 1995. The Determinants of Children's Attainments: A Review of Methods and Findings. *Journal of Economic Literature* 23:1829–1878.

Haw, K. 1998. *Educating Muslim Girls: Shifting Discourses*. Philadelphia: Open University Press.

Heath, S. B. 1983. *Ways with Words: Language, Life, and Work in Communities and Classrooms*. New York: Cambridge University Press.

Heller, K., and R. W. Swindle. 1983. Social Networks, Perceived Social Support, and Coping with Stress. In R. D. Felner, ed., *Preventative Psychology: Theory, Research, and Practice in Community Intervention*. New York: Penguin.

Hepworth, J., R. G. Ryder, and A. S. Dreyer. 1984. The Effects of Parental Loss on the Formation of Intimate Relationships. *Journal of Marital and Family Therapy* 10:73–82.

Hernández, D., and E. Charney. 1998. *From Generation to Generation: The Health and*

Well-Being of Children of Immigrant Families. Washington D.C.: National Academy Press.

Hill, H. M., and S. Madhere. 1996. Exposure to Community Violence and African American Children: A Multidimensional Model of Risks and Resources. *Journal of Community Psychology* 24:26–43.

Hill, L. 2004. Connections between U.S. Female Migration and Family Formation and Dissolution. *Migraciones Internacionales* 2(3): 60.

Hohn, G. E. 1996. The Effects of Family Functioning on the Psychological and Social Adjustment of Jamaican Immigrant Children. Ph.D. diss., Columbia University.

Holmes, T., and R. Rahe. 1967. The Social Readjustment Rating Scale. *Journal of Psychosomatic Research* 11:213–218.

Hondagneu-Sotelo, P. 1994. *Gendered Transitions: Mexican Experiences of Immigration.* Berkeley: University of California Press.

Hook, J. 2006. Poverty Grows among Children of Immigrants in the U.S. www .migrationinformation.org/USFocus/display.cfm?ID=188 (accessed March 15, 2006).

Horn, C. L., S. M. Flores, and G. Orfield, eds. 2006. *Latino Educational Opportunity: New Directions for Community Colleges.* New York: Jossey-Bass.

Hughes, D., E. Seidman, and D. Edwards. 1993. Cultural Phenomena and the Research Enterprise: Toward a Culturally Anchored Methodology. *American Journal of Community Psychology* 21(6): 1–170.

Hulpia, H., and M. Valcke. 2004. The Use of Performance Indicators in a School Improvement Policy: The Theoretical and Empirical Context. *Evaluation and Research in Education* 18(1–2): 102–119.

Huntington, S. 2004. *Who Are We? The Challenge to America's National Identity.* New York: Simon and Schuster.

Hurrelmann, K., U. Engel, B. Holler, and E. Nordlohne. 1988. Failure in School, Family Conflicts, and Psychosomatic Disorders in Adolescence. *Journal of Adolescence* 11:237–249.

Jencks, C. 1972. *Inequality: A Reassessment of the Effect of Family and Schooling in America.* New York: Harper.

Jenkins, P. H. 1997. School Delinquency and the School Social Bond. *Journal of Research in Crime and Delinquency* 34(3): 337–367.

Johnson, J., A. M. Arumi, and A. Ott. 2006. How Black and Hispanic Families Rate Their Schools. *Reality Check 2006.* www.publicagenda.org/research/pdfs/rc0602 .pdf (accessed July 7, 2006).

Kao, G., and M. Tienda. 1995. Optimism and Achievement: The Educational Performance of Immigrant Youth. *Social Science Quarterly* 76(1): 1–19.

Karatzias, A., K. G. Power, J. Flemming, and F. Lennan. 2002. The Role of Demographics, Personality Variables, and School Stress on Predicting School Satisfaction/Dissatisfaction: Review of the Literature and Research Findings. *Educational Psychology* 22(1): 33–50.

Kennedy, R. 2001. Racial Trends in the Administration of Criminal Justice. In N. J. Smelser, W. J. Wilson, and F. Mitchell, eds., *America Becoming: Racial Trends and Their Consequences* vol. 2, pp. 1–20. Washington, D.C.: National Academy Press.

Kenny-Benson, G. A., E. M. Pomerantz, A. M. Ryan, and H. Patrick. 2006. Sex Differences in Math Performance: The Role of Children's Approach to Schoolwork. *Developmental Psychology* 42(1): 11–26.

Kim, H. J. 2004. Family Resources and Children's Academic Performance. *Children and Youth Services Review* 26(6): 529–536.

Kleinfeld, J. 1998. *The Myth that Schools Shortchange Girls: Social Science in the Service of Deception.* Washington, D.C.: Women's Freedom Network.

Klesmer, H. 1994. Assessment and Teacher Perceptions of ESL Student Achievement. *English Quarterly* 26(3): 8–11.

Kluckhohn, C. 1949. *Mirror for Man: The Relation of Anthropology to Modern Life.* New York: Whitssley House.

Knight, G. P., and N. E. Hill. 1993. Measurement Equivalence in Research Involving Minority Adolescents. In V. C. McLoyd and L. Steinberg, eds., *Studying Minority Adolescents: Conceptual, Methodological, and Theoretical Issues,* pp. 183–210. Mahwah, N.J.: Lawrence Erlbaum.

LaFeber, W. 1984. *Inevitable Revolutions: The United States in Central America.* New York: W. W. Norton.

Landale, N. S., and R. S. Oropesa. 1995. *Immigrant Children and the Children of Immigrants: Inter- and Intra-Ethnic Group Differences in the United States.* Population Research Group (PRG) Research Paper 95–2. East Lansing: Michigan State University.

Lawrence-Lightfoot, S., and J. Hoffmann-Davis. 1997. *The Art and Science of Portraiture.* San Francisco: Jossey-Bass.

Lee, S. J. 2001. Exploring and Transforming the Landscape of Gender and Sexuality: Hmong American Teenaged Girls. *Race, Gender and Class* 81:35–46.

Levitt, M. J., N. Guacci-Franco, and J. L. Levitt. 1994. Social Support and Achievement in Childhood and Early Adolescence: A Multicultural Study. *Journal of Applied Developmental Psychology* 15:207–222.

Levitt, P. 2001. *The Transnational Villagers.* Berkeley: University of California Press.

Levy, R., and R. J. Murnane. 2007. How Computerized Work and Globalization Shape Human Skill Demands. In *Learning in the Global Era,* ed. M. M. Suárez-Orozco. Berkeley: University of California Press.

Lieberson, L. 1981. *Language Diversity and Language Contact: Essays by Stanley Lieberson.* Stanford, Calif.: Stanford University Press.

Lindholm-Leary, K. J. 2001. *Dual Language Education.* Clevedon, Eng.: Multilingual Matters.

Lindzey, G. 1961. *Projective Techniques and Cross-Cultural Research.* New York: Appleton-Century-Crofts.

Loo, C. M. 1998. *Chinese America: Mental Health and Quality of Life in the Inner City.* Thousand Oaks, Calif.: Sage.

López, N. 2003. *Hopeful Girls, Troubled Boys: Race and Gender Disparity in Urban Education.* New York: Routledge.

Los Angeles Unified School District. 2007. School Enrollments. search.lausd.k12.ca.us/cgi-bin/fccgi.exe?w3exec=enroll0 (accessed May 17, 2007).

Louie, J. 2003. Media in the Lives of Immigrant Youth. In C. Suárez-Orozco and I. Todorova, eds., *Understanding the Social Worlds of Immigrant Youth: New Directions for Youth Development,* vol. 100. New York: Jossey-Bass.

Louie, V. S. 2004. *Compelled to Excel: Immigration, Education, and Opportunity among Chinese Americans.* Stanford, Calif.: Stanford University Press.

Luthar, S. 1999. *Poverty and Children's Adjustment.* Thousand Oaks, Calif.: Sage.

Lynch, M., and D. Cicchetti. 1997. Children's Relationships with Adults and Peers: An Examination of Elementary and Junior High School Students. *Journal of School Psychology* 35:81–99.

Lyons-Ruth, K. 1996. Attachment Relationships among Children with Aggressive Behavior Problems: The Role of Disorganized Early Attachment Patterns. *Journal of Consulting Clinical Psychology* 64(1): 64–73.

Madaus, G., and M. Clarke. 1998. *The Adverse Impact of High Stakes Testing on Minority Students: Evidence from One Hundred Years of Test Data.* Paper presented at the High Stakes K–12 Testing Conference, New York.

Mahler, S. 1995. *American Dreaming: Immigrant Life on the Margins.* Princeton, N.J.: Princeton University Press.

Majors, R. G., and J. U. Gordon, 1994. *The American Black Male: His Present Status and His Future.* N.p.: Burnham, Inc.

Mandel, M. 2006. Why the Economy Is a Lot Stronger than You Think. *Business Week,* February 3, pp. 62–70.

Marks, H. M. 2000. Student Engagement in Instructional Activity: Patterns in the Elementary, Middle, and High School Years. *American Educational Research Journal* 37(1): 153–184.

Marks, H. M., and S. M. Printy. 2003. Principal Leadership and School Performance: An Integration of Transformational and Instructional Leadership. *Educational Administration Quarterly* 39(3): 370–397.

Massey, D., and N. Denton. 1993. *American Apartheid.* Cambridge: Harvard University Press.

Massey, D., J. Durand, and N. J. Malone. 2002. *Beyond Smoke and Mirrors: Mexican Immigration in an Era of Economic Integration.* New York: Russell Sage Foundation.

McDermott, R. P. 1977. Social Relations as Contexts for Learning in School. *Harvard Educational Review* 47(2): 198–313.

McLaughlin, M. W., and J. E. Talbert. 1993. *Contexts that Matter for Teaching and Learning.* Stanford, Calif.: Center for Research on the Context of Teaching, Stanford University School of Education.

McLoyd, V., and L. Steinberg, eds. 1998. *Studying Minority Adolescents: Conceptual, Methodological, and Theoretical Issues.* Mahwah, N.J.: Lawrence Erlbaum.

Mehan, H., I. Villanueva, L. Hubbard, and A. Lintz. 1996. *Constructing School Success: The Consequences of Untracking Low Achieving Students.* New York: Cambridge University Press.

Midgley, C., H. Feldlaufer, and J. S. Eccles. 1989. Student/Teacher Relations and Attitudes toward Mathematics before and after the Transition to Junior High School. *Child Development* 1(60): 981–992.

Miller, P., J. Hengst, and S. Wang. 2003. Ethnographic Methods: Applications from Developmental Cultural Psychology. In P. Camic, J. Rhodes, and L. Yardley, eds., *Qualitative Research in Psychology.* Washington, D.C.: American Psychological Association.

Muhr, T. 1991. ATLAS.ti—A Prototype for the Support of Text Interpretation. *Qualitative Sociology* 14(4): 349–371.

———. 1997. ATLAS.ti: The Knowledge Workbench—Short User's Manual. Berlin: Scientific Software Development.

Muñoz-Sandoval, A. F., J. Cummins, C. G. Alvarado, and M. L. Ruef. 1998. *Bilingual Verbal Ability Tests: Comprehensive Manual.* Itasca, Ill.: Riverside Publishing.

Murray, H. 1943. *The Thematic Apperception Test.* Cambridge: Harvard University Press.

Nagin, D., and R. E. Tremblay. 1999. Trajectories of Boys' Physical Regression, Opposition, and Hyperactivity on the Path to Physical Violent and Non-Violent Juvenile Delinquency. *Child Development* 70(5): 1181–1196.

National Research Council. 2004. *Engaging Schools: Fostering High School Students' Motivation to Learn.* Washington, D.C.: National Academies Press.

Neimeyer, R., ed. 2001. *Meaning Reconstruction and the Experience of Loss.* Washington, D.C.: American Psychological Association.

New York Department of Education. 2007. State Education Department List of Bilingual/ESL Network Information. www.emsc.nysed.gov/biling/info.shtml (accessed May 17, 2007).

Noam, G., ed. 2004. *After-School Worlds: Creating a New Social Space for Development and Learning,* vol. 101. New York: Jossey-Bass.

Noguera, P. 2002. Beyond Size: The Challenge of High School Reform. *Educational Leadership* 59:60–63.

———. 2003. *City Schools and the American Dream: Reclaiming the Promise of Public Education.* New York: Teacher's College Press.

Noguera, P., and J. Y. Wing, eds. 2006. *Unfinished Business: Closing the Racial Achievement Gap in Our Schools.* New York: Jossey-Bass.

O'Donnell, D. A., M. E. Schwab-Stone, and A. Z. Muyeed. 2002. Multidimensional Resilience in Urban Children Exposed to Community Violence. *Child Development* 73(4): 1265–1282.

OECD. 2005. *The Definition and Selection of Key Competencies: Executive Summary.* Paris: Organization for Economic Cooperation and Development.

Ogbu, J. U. 1978. *Minority Education and Caste: The American System in Cross-Cultural Perspective.* New York: Academic Press.

Ogbu, J. U., and S. Herbert. 1998. Voluntary and Involuntary Minorities: A Cultural-Ecological Theory of School Performance with Some Implications for Education. *Anthropology and Education Quarterly* 29:155–188.

Olsen, L. 1997. *Made in America: Immigrant Students in Our Public Schools.* New York: New Press.

Orfield, G., and C. Lee. 2006. *Racial Transformation and the Changing Nature of Segregation.* Cambridge: Civil Rights Project at Harvard University.

Orfield, G., and J. T. Yun. 1999. *Resegregation in American Schools.* Cambridge: Civil Rights Project at Harvard University.

Páez, M. 2001. Language and the Immigrant Child: Predicting English Language Proficiency for Chinese, Dominican, and Haitian Students. Ph.D. diss., Harvard University.

Partida, J. 1996. The Effects of Immigration on Children in the Mexican-American Community. *Child and Adolescent Social Work Journal* 13:241–254.

Passel, J. S. 2006. *Size and Characteristics of the Unauthorized Migrant Populations in the U.S.* Washington, D.C.: Pew Hispanic Center.

Paulson, S. E., G. J. Marchant, and B. A. Rothlisberg. 1998. Early Adolescents' Perceptions of Patterns of Parenting, Teaching, and School Atmosphere: Implications for Achievement. *Journal of Adolescence* 18:5–26.

Payne, S., S. Horn, and M. Relf. 1999. *Loss and Bereavement.* Philadelphia: Open University Press.

Peal, E., and W. E. Lambert. 1962. The Relationship of Bilingualism to Intelligence. *Psychological Monographs,* 1–23.

Perez-Foster, R. 2001. When Immigration Is Trauma: Guidelines for the Individual and Family Clinician. *American Journal of Orthopsychiatry* 71(2): 153–170.

Pew Hispanic Center. 2006. *Size and Characteristics of the Unauthorized Migrant Population in the U.S.: Estimates Based on the March 2005 Current Population Survey.*

Pianta, R. C. 1999. *Enhancing Relationships between Children and Teachers.* Washington, D.C.: American Psychological Association.

Piore, M. J. 1971. *Birds of Passage: Migrant Labor and Industrial Societies.* New York: Cambridge University Press.

PISA. 2003. *Where Immigrant Students Succeed—A Comparative Review of Performance and Engagement.* Paris: OECD Programme for International Student Assessment (PISA).

Pong, S. L., J. Dronkers, and G. Hampden-Thompson. 2003. Family Policies and Children's School Achievement in Single- versus Two-Parent Families. *Journal of Marriage and Family* 65(3): 681–699.

Portes, A. 1996. Children of Immigrants: Segmented Assimilation and Its Determinants. In A. Portes, ed., *The Economic Sociology of Immigration: Essays on Networks, Ethnicity, and Entrepreneurship.* New York: Russell Sage Foundation.

Portes, A., and L. Hao. 1998. *E Pluribus Unum:* Bilingualism and Loss of Language in the Second Generation. *Sociology of Education* 71(4): 269–294.

Portes, A., and R. G. Rumbaut. 2001. *Legacies: The Story of the Second Generation.* Berkeley: University of California Press.

Poston, W. K., Jr., M. P. Stone, and C. T. Muther. 1992. *Making Schools Work: Practical Management of Support Operations.* Newbury Park, Calif.: Corwin Press.

Qin, D. B. 2003. "Gendered Expectations and Gendered Experiences: Immigrant Students' Adaptation in Schools." *New Directions for Youth Development* 100: 91–110.

———. 2006. Our Child Doesn't Talk to Us Anymore: Alienation in Immigrant Chinese Families. *Anthropology and Education Quarterly* 37: 162–179.

Raissiguier, C. 1994. *Becoming Women, Becoming Workers: Identity Formation in a French Vocational School.* New York: State University of New York Press.

Raley, J. D. 2004. "Like Family You Know?" Schools and the Achievement of Peer Relations. In M. A. Gibson, P. Gándara, and J. P. Koyama, eds., *School Connections: U.S. Mexican Youth, Peers, and School Achievement,* pp. 150–172. New York: Teachers College Press.

Reddy, R., J. Rhodes, and P. Mulhall. 2003. The Influence of Teacher Support on Student Adjustment in the Middle School Years: A Latent Growth Curve Study. *Development and Psychopathology* 15:119–138.

Rhodes, J. E. 2002. *Stand by Me: The Risks and Rewards of Youth Mentoring Relationships.* Cambridge: Harvard University Press.

Robertson, J., and J. Robertson. 1971. Young Children in Brief Separation. *Psychoanalytic Study of the Child* 26:264–313.

Robertson, S. 2001. *The Great Size Debate.* Scottsdale, Ariz.: Council of Educational Facility Planners.

Rodriguez, G. 1996. *The Emerging Latino Middle Class.* Malibu, Calif.: Pepperdine University School of Public Policy.

Roeser, R. W., and J. S. Eccles. 1998. Adolescents' Perception of Middle School: Relation to Longitudinal Changes in Academic and Psychological Adjustment. *Journal of Research on Adolescence* 8(1): 123–158.

Roffman, J., C. Suárez-Orozco, and J. Rhodes. 2003. Facilitating Positive Development in Immigrant Youth: The Role of Mentors and Community Organizations. In D. Perkins, L. M. Borden, J. G. Keith, and F. A. Villaruel, eds., *Positive Youth Development: Creating a Positive Tomorrow.* Brockton, Mass.: Klewer Press.

Rong, X. L., and F. Brown. 2001. The Effects of Immigrant Generation and Ethnicity on Educational Attainment among Young African and Caribbean Blacks in the United States. *Harvard Educational Review* 71(3): 536–565.

Rong, X. L., and J. Preissle. 1998. *Educating Immigrant Students: What We Need to Know to Meet the Challenges.* Thousand Oaks, Calif.: Corwin Press.

Ruiz-de-Valasco, J., M. Fix, and B. C. Clewell. 2001. *Overlooked and Underserved: Immigrant Students in U.S. Secondary Schools.* Washington, D.C.: Urban Institute.

Rumberger, R. 2004. Why Students Drop Out of School. In G. Orfield, ed., *Dropouts in America: Confronting the Graduation Rate Crisis.* Cambridge: Harvard Education Press.

Rutter, M. 1971. Parent-Child Separation: Psychological Effects on the Children. *Child Psychology and Psychiatry* 12:233–260.

Ryan, R., S. P. Stiller, and J. H. Lynch. 1994. Representations of Relationships to Teachers, Parents, and Friends as Predictors of Academic Motivation. *Journal of Early Adolescence* 14:226–249.

Samdal, O., D. Nutbeam, B. Wold, and L. Kannas. 1998. Achieving Health and Educational Goals through Schools: A Study of the Importance of School Climate and the Student's Satisfaction with School. *Health Education Research* 13(3): 383–397.

Sarason, I. G., B. R. Sarason, and G. R. Pierce. 1990. Social Support: The Search for Theory. *Journal of Social and Clinical Psychology* 9:133–147.

Sarroub, L. K. 2001. The Sojourner Experience of Yemeni American High School Students: An Ethnographic Portrait. *Harvard Educational Review* 71(3): 390–415.

Schieffelin, B., and E. Ochs. 1886. Language Socialization. *Annual Review of Anthropology* 15:163–191.

Schlesinger, S., and S. Kinzer, eds. 1999. *Bitter Fruit: The Story of the American Coup in Guatemala.* Cambridge: David Rockefeller Center Series on Latin American Studies.

Schlossberg, N. K. 1984. *Counseling Adults in Transition: Linking Practice with Theory.* New York: Springer.

Schunk, D. H. 1991. Self-Efficacy and Academic Motivation. *Educational Psychologist* 26:207–231.

Sciarra, D. T. 1999. Intra-Familial Separations in the Immigrant Family: Implications for Cross-Cultural Counseling. *Journal of Multicultural Counseling and Development* 27(18): 30–41.

Sewell-Coker, B., J. Hamilton-Collins, and E. Fein. 1985. West Indian Immigrants. *Social Casework* 60:563–568.

Shapiro, E. R. 1994. *Grief as a Family Process: A Developmental Approach to Clinical Practice.* New York: Guilford Press.

Shweder, R. 1991. *Thinking through Cultures: Expeditions in Cultural Psychology.* Cambridge: Harvard University Press.

Silverman, P. R. 2000. *Never Too Young to Know.* New York: Oxford University Press.

Simon, R. J., and S. H. Alexander. 1993. *The Ambivalent Welcome: Print Media, Public Opinion, and Immigration.* Westport, Conn.: Praeger.

Simpao, E. B. 1999. Parent-Child Separation and Family Cohesion amongst Immigrants: Impact on Object Relations, Intimacy, and Story Themes. Ph.D. diss., Long Island University.

Sirin, S. R., and L. Rogers-Sirin. 2005. Components of School Engagement among African American Adolescents. *Applied Developmental Science* 9(10): 5–13.

Skehan, P. 1989. *Individual Differences in Second-Language Learning.* London: Edward Arnold.

Skidmore, T. E., and P. H. Smith. 2001. *Modern Latin America,* 5th. ed. Oxford, Eng.: Oxford University Press.

Slotnik, W. J., and D. B. Gratz. 1999. Guiding Improvement. *Thrust for Educational Leadership* 28(3): 10–12.

Sommer, D. 2002. American Projections. In M. Suárez-Orozco, ed., *Latinos: Remaking America.* Berkeley: University of California Press.

Soto, I. M. 1987. West Indian Child Fostering: Its Role in Migrant Exchanges. In C. Sutton and E. Chaney, eds., *Caribbean Life in New York City: Sociocultural Dimensions,* pp. 131–149. New York: Center for Migration Studies.

Spindler, G., L. Spindler, and M. Suárez-Orozco. 1994. *The Making of Psychological Anthropology,* vol. 2. Fort Worth, Tex.: Harcourt Brace.

Spradley, J. P. 1980. *Participant Observation.* Orlando, Fla.: Harcourt-Brace-Jovanovich.

Spring, J. 1994. *American Education.* New York: McGraw-Hill.

Stake, R. 1994. Case Studies. In N. Denzin and Y. Lincoln, eds., *Handbook of Qualitative Research.* Thousand Oaks, Calif.: Sage.

Stanton-Salazar, R. D. 2001. *Manufacturing Hope and Despair: The School and Kin Support Networks of U.S.-Mexican Youth.* New York: Teachers College Press.

———. 2004. Social Capital among Working-Class Minority Students. In M. A. Gibson, P. Gándara, and J. P. Koyma, eds., *School Connections: U.S. Mexican Youth, Peers, and School Achievement.* New York: Teachers College Press.

Steinberg, S., B. B. Brown, and S. M. Dornbusch. 1996. *Beyond the Classroom.* New York: Simon and Schuster.

Stephenson, W. 1953. *The Study of Behavior: Q Technique and Its Methodology.* Chicago: University of Chicago Press.

———. 1982. Q Methodology, Interbehavioral Psychology, and Quantum Theory. *The Psychological Record,* 32, 235–248.

Strauss, A., and J. Corbin. 1990. *Basics of Qualitative Research: Grounded Theory Procedures and Techniques.* Newbury Park, Calif.: Sage.

Suárez-Orozco, C. 2000. Identities under Siege: Immigration Stress and Social Mirroring among the Children of Immigrants. In A. Robben and M. Suárez-Orozco, eds., *Cultures under Siege: Social Violence and Trauma.* Cambridge, Eng.: Cambridge University Press.

———. 2004a. Formulating Identity in a Globalized World. In M. Suárez-Orozco and D. B. Qin-Hilliard, eds., *Globalization: Culture and Education in the New Millennium,* pp. 173–202. Berkeley: University of California Press and the Ross Institute.

—————. 2004b. Reflections on Research of the Immigrant Experience, working paper series 04/05–2, no. 04/05–2. Cambridge: David Rockefeller Center for Latin American Studies.

Suárez-Orozco, C., A. Pimentel, and M. Martin. In press. The Significance of Relationships: Academic Engagement and Achievement among Newcomer Immigrant Youth. In J. Holdoway and R. Alba, eds., *Immigration and Education*. New York: Teachers College Press.

Suárez-Orozco, C., and D. B. Qin. 2006. Gendered Perspectives in Psychology: Immigrant Origin Youth. *International Migration Review* 40(1): 165–198.

Suárez-Orozco, C., and D. B. Qin-Hilliard. 2004. The Cultural Psychology of Academic Engagement: Immigrant Boys' Experiences in U.S. Schools. In N. Way and J. Chu, eds., *Adolescent Boys in Context*, pp. 295–316. New York: New York University Press.

Suárez-Orozco, C., and M. Suárez-Orozco. 1995. *Transformations: Immigration, Family Life, and Achievement Motivation among Latino Adolescents*. Stanford Calif.: Stanford University Press.

—————. 2001. *Children of Immigration*. Cambridge: Harvard University Press.

Suárez-Orozco, C., M. Suárez-Orozco, and F. Doucet. 2003. The Academic Engagement and Achievement of Latino Youth. In J. Banks and C. McGee-Banks, eds., *Handbook of Research on Multicultural Education*, 2d ed. San Francisco: Jossey-Bass.

Suárez-Orozco, C., M. Suárez-Orozco, and I. Todorova. 2005. Wandering Souls: Adolescent Immigrant Interpersonal Concerns. In D. G. DeVos and E. DeVos, eds., *Narrative Analysis Cross-Culturally: The Self as Revealed in the Thematic Apperception Test*. Boulder, Colo.: Rowman and Littlefield.

Suárez-Orozco, C., I. Todorova, and J. Louie. 2002. Making Up for Lost Time: The Experience of Separation and Reunification among Immigrant Families. *Family Process* 41(4): 625–643.

Suárez-Orozco, C., I. Todorova, and D. B. Qin. 2006. The Well-Being of Immigrant Adolescents: A Longitudinal Perspective on Risk and Protective Factors. In F. A. Villaruel and T. Luster, eds., *The Crisis in Youth Mental Health: Critical Issues and Effective Program*, vol. 2, pp. 53–84. Westport, Conn.: Praeger.

Suárez-Orozco, M. 1989. *Central American Refugees and U.S. High Schools: A Psychosocial Study of Motivation and Achievement*. Stanford, Calif.: Stanford University Press.

—————. 1994. Remaking Psychological Anthropology. In G. Spindler, L. Spindler, and M. Suárez-Orozco, eds., *The Making of Psychological Anthropology*, vol. 2, pp. 8–59. Fort Worth, Tex.: Harcourt Brace.

—————. 1998. *Crossings: Mexican Immigration in Interdisciplinary Perspectives*. Cambridge: David Rockefeller Center for Latin American Studies and Harvard University Press.

———. 2005. Everything You Ever Wanted to Know about Immigration But Were Afraid to Ask. In B. Epps, K. Valens, and B. Johnson González, eds., *Passing Lines: Sexuality and Immigration.* Cambridge: Harvard University Press and David Rockefeller Center for Latin American Studies.

Suárez-Orozco, M., and M. Paez. 2002. *Latinos: Remaking America.* Berkeley: University of California Press.

Suárez-Orozco, M., and D. B. Qin-Hilliard. 2004. *Globalization: Culture and Education in the New Millennium.* Berkeley: University of California Press.

Sue, D., and S. Sue. 1987. Cultural Factors in the Clinical Assessment of Asian Americans. *Journal of Consulting and Clinical Psychology* 55:479–487.

Suro, R., and J. S. Passel. 2003. *The Rise of the Second Generation: Changing Patterns in Hispanic Population Growth.* Washington, D.C.: Pew Hispanic Center.

Sussmuth, R. 2005. Globalization and Learning: Keynote Address. Paper presented at the First International Conference on Globalization and Learning, Stockholm, March 17.

Szalacha, L. A., S. Erkut, C. García-Coll, J. P. Fields, O. Alarcón, and I. Ceder. 2003. Perceived Discrimination and Resilience. In S. S. Luthar, ed., *Resilience and Vulnerability: Adaptation in the Context of Childhood Adversities,* pp. 414–435. Cambridge, Eng.: Cambridge University Press.

Tatum, B. 1997. *"Why Are All the Black Kids Sitting Together in the Cafeteria?" and Other Conversations about Race.* New York: Basic Books.

Thomas, W., and V. Collier. 2002. *A National Study of School Effectiveness for Language Minority Students' Long-Term Academic Achievement.* Berkeley: Center for Research on Education, Diversity and Excellence, University of California.

Tremblay, P., and R. Gardner. 1995. Expanding the Motivation Construct in Language Learning. *Modern Language Journal* 1(79): 505–518.

U.S. Census Bureau. 2006. *The 2005 American Community Survey.* Washington, D.C.: U.S. Government Printing Office.

U.S. Department of Education. 1994. *Research Report: What Do Student Grades Mean? Differences across Schools.* Washington, D.C.: U.S. Department of Education, Office of Research.

———. 1995. *Conditions of Education, 1995.* Washington, D.C.: National Center for Educational Statistics.

Valdés, G. 1998. The World Outside and Inside Schools: Language and Immigrant Children. *Educational Researcher* 27(6): 9.

Valdés, G., and R. A. Figueroa. 1994. *Bilingualism and Testing: A Special Case of Bias.* Norwood, N.J.: Ablex.

Valenzuela, A. 1999. Gender Roles and Settlement Activities among Children and Their Immigrant Families. *American Behavioral Scientist* 42(4): 720–742.

Vane, J. R. 1981. The Thematic Apperception Test: A Review. *Clinical Psychology Review* 1:319–336.

Vélez-Ibañez, C. 1996. *Border Visions: Mexican Cultures of the Southwest United States.* Phoenix: University of Arizona Press.

Vigil, D. 2002. *A Rainbow of Gangs: Street Cultures in the Mega-City.* Austin: University of Texas Press.

Wacquant, L. 1999. "Suitable Enemies": Foreigners and Immigrants in the Prisons of Europe. *Punishment and Society* 1(2).

Waldinger, R. 1997. *Social Capital or Social Closure? Immigrant Networks in the Labor Market.* Paper presented to the Conference on Immigration and the Socio-Cultural Remaking of the North American Space, David Rockefeller Center for Latin American Studies, Cambridge, April 11–12.

Wang, M. C., G. D. Haertel, and H. J. Wahlberg. 1994. What Influences Learning? A Content Analysis of Review Literature. *Journal of Educational Research* 84:30–43.

Waters, M. 1996. The Intersection of Gender, Race, and Ethnicity Development of Caribbean American Teens. In B. J. Leadbeater and N. Way, eds., *Urban Girls: Resisting Stereotypes, Creating Identities.* New York: New York University Press.

———. 1999. *Black Identities: West Indian Dreams and American Realities.* Cambridge: Harvard University Press.

Way, N., and J. Chu. 2004. *Adolescent Boys in Context.* New York: New York University Press.

Weinstein, R. S. 2002. *Reaching Higher: The Power of Expectations in Schooling.* Cambridge: Harvard University Press.

Weiss, S. 2005. *District and School Leadership: The Progress of Education Reform,* vol. 6, no. 2. Denver: Education Commission of the State.

Weissbourd, R. 1996. *The Vulnerable Child.* Reading, Mass.: Perseus.

Wentzel, K. R. 1999. Social Influences and School Adjustment: Commentary. *Educational Psychologist* 34(1): 59–69.

Western, D. 1989. Are "Primitive" Object Relations Really Preoedipal? *American Journal of Orthopsychiatry* 59:331–345.

White, K. 1982. The Relationship between Socioeconomic Status and Academic Achievement. *Psychological Bulletin* 91:461–481.

Wilkes, J. R. 1992. Children in Limbo: Working for the Best Outcome When Children Are Taken into Care. *Canada's Mental Health* 40:2–5.

Wilkie, J. W., E. Alemán, and J. G. Ortega, eds. 2000. *Statistical Abstract of Latin America,* vol. 36. Los Angeles: UCLA Latin American Center Publications.

Willingham, W. W., J. M. Pollack, and C. Lewis. 2002. Grades and Test Scores: Accounting for Observed Differences. *Journal of Educational Measurement* 39(1): 1–37.

Willis, P. 1977. *Learning to Labour: How Working Class Kids Get Working Class Jobs.* Farnborough, Eng.: Saxon House.

Wills, T. A. 1985. Supportive Functions of Interpersonal Relationships. In S. L. S. S. Cohen, ed., *Social Support and Health,* pp. 61–82. Orlando, Fla.: Academic Press.

Wilson, W. 1997. *When Work Disappears: The World of the New Urban Poor.* New York: Vintage.

Winnicott, D. W. 1958. *Through Pediatrics to Psycho-Analysis.* London: Hogarth.

Womack, J. 1983. *Trouble in Our Backyard: Central America and the United States in the Eighties.* New York: Pantheon.

Woodcock, R. W., K. S. McGrew, and N. Mather. 2001. *Woodcock-Johnson III Tests of Achievement.* Itasca, Ill.: Riverside.

Yin, R. 2002. *Case Study Research: Design and Method.* Thousand Oaks, Calif.: Sage.

Zhou, M., and C. I. Bankston. 1998. *Growing Up American: How Vietnamese Children Adapt to Life in the United States.* New York: Russell Sage Foundation.

Zhou, M., and X. Y. Li. 2004. Ethnic Language Schools and the Development of Supplementary Education in the Immigrant Chinese Community in the United States. In C. Suárez-Orozco and I. Todorova, eds., *Understanding the Social Worlds of Immigrant Youth: New Directions for Youth Development,* vol. 100. New York: Jossey-Bass.

Zuker, R. 1985. *Social Psychology and Second Language Learning: The Role of Attitudes and Motivation.* London: Edward Arnold.

Acknowledgments

THIS BOOK reports the findings of the Longitudinal Immigrant Student Adaptation Study (LISA), which we conducted during our tenure as co-directors of the Harvard Immigration Projects. The findings released here have been in the making for ten years and are a product of a community of scholars—including the principal investigators, Carola and Marcelo Suárez-Orozco, postdoctoral fellows, graduate students, research assistants, consultants, and administrative staff. It gives us great pleasure to acknowledge the many individuals, foundations, and institutions that have made this work possible.

In designing this study we chose to make it a mentoring and research training project. Rather than following a strictly work-for-pay model, where the research assistants (RAs) exclusively acted as employees, we provided extensive training and ongoing support. This way, we thought, we would not only improve the quality of our data, but also explicitly mentor a new generation of scholars undertaking interdisciplinary cross-cultural research. We offered our graduate students the opportunity to incorporate their own ideas and, in some cases, encouraged them to use the project for their own data-gathering needs. To date, we have had a dozen dissertations and qualifying papers emerge from the study.

The RAs of the project came from a variety of origins, including the countries represented in this study. The nature of the study required that the majority of the RAs be bilingual and bicultural. Their bicultural sensibilities facilitated the recruitment of participants, allowed them to act as cultural interpreters in contextualizing emerging findings, and contributed to the long-term commitment of students and their parents to our study. Indeed, a common language among RAs, students, and parents facilitated the gathering of the data, enhanced the quality of the data, and was fundamental for maintaining the rapport necessary to minimize attrition in a longitudinal study. The RAs' bilingual skills were also crucial as we developed culturally appropriate data-collection strategies and translated and fine-tuned our research protocols.

We were extraordinarily lucky to have worked with a dynamic and dedicated team of RAs during the study. It is our pleasure to thank them for their individual and collective efforts on behalf of the LISA study. Their dedication to the students who participated in this study gave voice to the oft-ignored concerns of newly arrived immigrant youth.

Because California leads the way in the new immigration, we thought it essential to develop a site on the West Coast. Through the recommendation of George DeVos, emeritus professor of the Anthropology Department at University of California, Berkeley, we came to know Curtis Vaughn, who took on the responsibility of West Coast Project Director for the LISA study. He helped to recruit, train, and supervise a stellar team of Berkeley-based graduate students including Laura Alamillo, Marco Bravo, Carmina Brittan, Sonya Cotero, Dafney Dabach, Claudia Flores-Somera, Celeste Gutíerrez, Teresa Huerta, Sarah Hughes, Monica López, Laura López-Sanders, Julia Macias, Marcela Nazzari, Brecca Rodriguez-Griswold, Leah Rosenbloom, Regina Segura-Khagram, Lilia Soto, and Lorena Soto. In addition to our weekly meetings with director Vaughn, we had the pleasure of monthly meetings with this dedicated and insightful group of researchers. The California portion of the LISA study was headquartered at the Berkeley campus of the University of California. We are grateful to Professor Stanley Brandes, then the chair of the Anthropology Department, for generously offering us facilities at Kroeber Hall to conduct our meetings.

Our Chinese team consisted of Cantonese-, Mandarin-, and Taisanese-speaking graduate assistants. Working under the supervision of senior RAs Yu-Mui Wan and Desiree Qin, they did an extraordinary job of capturing the complexity of the new Chinese immigration to the United States with a focus on the student and family perspective. The Chinese team members also included QunWei Ai, Jennifer Chen, Iris Hui, Michele Kan, Vincent Leung, Yih-Shiuan Liang, Josephine Louie, Zuwei Shi, Peichi Tung, and Silvia Yuan.

The Dominican study team consisted of a diverse, multinational, multiethnic group of RAs with at least one thing in common—they all were passionately devoted to the Dominican youth and families they came to know over the course of their research. Esther Adames, then a Harvard graduate student and now a principal in a largely Latino school in Atlanta, deployed her dense networks within the Dominican community in the greater Boston area to recruit RAs and to facilitate our entry into the Dominican community. This vivacious and energetic team included Consuelo Aceves, Jeanette Adames, Rosa Armendariz, Lillian Bobea, Silvia Covelli, Yohanni Cuevas, Mariela Paez, Claudia Pineda, Blanca Quiroz, Eliane Rubenstein-Avila, Griselda Santiago, Nora Thompson, Elizabeth Vazquez, Claire White, and Rebecca Zichlin.

Alix Cantave, the director for Haitian studies at the University of Massachusetts Boston, played a pivotal role in providing entree into the Haitian community by facilitating the recruitment of both participants and RAs. Alix's cheerful can-do attitude, extensive networks in the community, and thoughtful insights made him a critical asset during the first years of the study. Charlene Desir, a bilingual counselor and Harvard doctoral student with a deep commitment to Haitian youth, quickly took on the role of lead RA role for this team. She was joined by Sophia Cantave, Alexandra Celestin, Valerie Chanlot, Mathylde Frontus, Darlene Jeanniton, Blondel Joseph, and Regine Ostine.

Of course, data gathering is but an initial step in a lengthy and complex research enterprise such as this one. The masterful statistical insights of Professor Terrence Tivnan of the Harvard Graduate School of Education proved crucial for the development of statistical instruments as well as to our initial analyses of emerging data. Josephine Louie took the principal role in organizing, cleaning, maintaining, and indexing the data as well as running descriptive analyses. Professor Michael Milburn of the University of Massachusetts Boston was very helpful in developing initial quantitative analyses. After we moved from Harvard to New York University, we came to rely on the extraordinary quantitative analytic talents of Juliana Pakes. Her dedication, insightfulness, and magisterial command of our data set were essential for the presentation of our findings. Also while at NYU, we were delighted to work with three outstanding graduate students—Avary Carhill, Francisco (Frank) Gaytán, and Margary Martin— who worked closely with us as we developed various aspects of the quantitative analyses. Avary took a tenacious and meticulous approach to the conceptualizing, analysis, and interpretation of the language data. Frank unflappably ran analysis after analysis of the network of family and relational data, quietly and precisely offering new insights. Margary culled school-district websites and developed the descriptive data set of key indicators of school quality. We also want to thank Professors Lawrence Aber, Erin O'Connor, Kathy McCartney, and Jean Rhodes for the astute analytic insights they offered to us during the writing of this book.

Several postdoctoral scholars worked with us during various phases of the study, adding immeasurably to the richness of our understanding. Irina Todorova worked with us for the duration of the data-gathering phase of the project (and beyond) as our senior qualitative analyst in charge of the projective data, field notes, and case studies. Fabienne Doucet joined us for three years, co-heading the Haitian research team and developing a comparative parallel study of second-generation Haitian origin youth. Diana Larisgottia developed and conducted focus-group interviews with a subset of Spanish-speaking students. As part of her post-doctoral experience, Vivian Louie, now on the Harvard faculty, met with our research team and provided insightful comments about the emerging findings in our Chinese group. Allyson Pimentel joined us at NYU to examine the data on discrimination as well as the role of relationships in student engagement. Desiree Qin, after serving as the senior RA on our Chinese team at Harvard and completing her dissertation with us, joined us at NYU for an additional postdoctoral year, during which she further developed her nuanced interpretation of the gendered patterns of academic performance and mental health.

Several individuals played crucial administrative roles in the organization of this large, bicoastal enterprise. Gretchen O'Connor, always with good humor and seemingly effortlessly, kept our budget and finances in pristine shape. Robin Haratunian and Kimberly McDuffie kept the endless stream of incoming interviews, field notes, report cards, and other data well organized. In addition, various students worked in our offices organizing materials and databases, coding, and running analyses. They include Rebecca Borr, Linda Caswell, Quentin Dixon, Soo Hong, Norma Jiménez, Kwang Kim, and Carrie Parker. Steve Song took on the enormous task of organizing the data set for its move to NYU.

We also had the privilege of being able to recruit a willing and generous community of consultants and colleagues. Each brought to the project his or her unique scholarly expertise in one or more of the topics. These consultants joined us at Harvard, taking time out of their busy schedules to listen to our emerging plans and to provide guest lectures and meetings with our community of RAs. Professors KaiMing Cheng, George DeVos, Paul Farmer, John Ogbu, Alejandro Portes, George Spindler, Mary Waters, and Min Zhou provided wise counsel and shared their wisdom with our enthralled research team.

Longitudinal, interdisciplinary, and cross-cultural research is not only logistically challenging and conceptually demanding, but also extremely expensive. We are delighted to express our gratitude to the Cultural Anthropology Division of the National Science Foundation (with special thanks to then program officer Stuart Plattner) for its original grant to the project. In addition, we received two separate grants from the W. T. Grant Foundation (special thanks to President Robert Granger and Vice-President Ed Seidman) as well as two additional grants from the Spencer Foundation (thank you to then-president Patrica A. Graham). We are also most grateful to the Ross Institute of New York (and especially to founder Courtney Sale Ross) for generously hosting our sabbatical at the breathtakingly beautiful East End campus of the Ross School. This serene surrounding provided just the milieu for our complete immersion into this rich and complex data set as we drafted various iterations of this book.

This project was made possible by the hospitality of seven school districts in the states of California and Massachusetts. These districts generously provided access to approximately a hundred schools. It takes courage to open one's doors to inquisitive strangers knowing that they will encounter not only the good intentions and energetic efforts of dedicated teachers and staff, but also many of the intractable problems that poor schools too often face. We offer our insights in good faith in the hope of bettering schools' abilities to serve their newcomer immigrant students. We particularly thank the principals, other administrators, teachers, counselors, and staff involved in this project. To protect confidentiality, we identify no district, school, or individual by name. We hope that this collective thank you to all of those working tirelessly on behalf of immigrant youth will suffice.

We are most indebted to the immigrant families and their children who allowed us into their lives during a difficult time of transition. Your trust, transparency, and insights are not only the intellectual foundation of this book but also its very heart and soul. The moving stories you share resonate deeply with us as fellow immigrants. We trust and hope that we have done justice to the lessons you have taught us.

We would like to thank Elizabeth Knoll, senior editor at Harvard University Press, for her confidence in this project. After working with us on an earlier volume, she reached out during the early phases of the study, keeping in touch over the years with both encouraging words and wise counsel. We are deeply grateful to Barbara Sevin, who read and edited multiple versions of the student portraits as well as other sections of this book. She provided a savvy editorial eye and kept us honest by sweeping "academese" from our prose. Julie Carlson did a masterful job editing our words. As a result of their work, we hope, this book is not only rigorous in its social science, but also accessible to a wider readership.

Over the years our own children, Marisa and Lucas, have had to learn to co-exist with their multiple adopted academic siblings—our graduate students and our study participants. They have demonstrated endless patience and great generosity in sharing their parents during countless meetings and conversations about protocols, occasional crises, emerging findings, and the writing of this book. ¡Un millón de gracias hijos!

Index

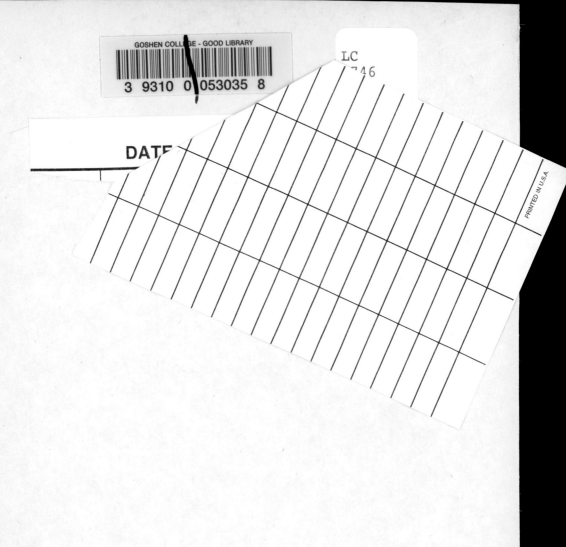